Iosif Volotskii
and Eastern Christianity

Iosif Volotskii and Eastern Christianity

Essays Across Seventeen Centuries

Edited by David Goldfrank,
Valeria Nollan, and Jennifer Spock

Washington, DC

Copyright © 2017 by David Goldfrank
New Academia Publishing, 2017

All rights reserved. No part of this book may be reproduced or transmitted in any form or by any means, electronic or mechanical, including photocopying, recording, or by any information storage and retrieval system.

Printed in the United States of America

Library of Congress Control Number: 2017936071
ISBN 978-0-9981477-3-4 paperback (alk. paper)

4401-A Connecticut Ave., NW #236 - Washington DC 20008
info@newacademia.com - www.newacademia.com

Contents

List of Illustrations	vii
Preface, *Donald Ostrowski*	xii
Acknowledgements	xv
Introduction – Iosif Volotskii: A Half Millennium Retrospective, *David Goldfrank*	1
I ANTECEDENTS	31
Introduction, *Christopher D.L. Johnson*	33
1 The World as Cenobium: Greek Patristic Foundations of the Contemplation of Nature in Eastern Christianity, *Rev. Joshua Lollar*	39
2 "No one can doubt that the Father is greater": Constantius II and the Council of Sirmium," *Edward Mason*	65
3 The Deacon Dioscorus and Justinian's Indecision, *Joshua Powell*	87
4 Pious Forgeries: The Simultaneous Use and Critique of Spurious Texts in the *Disputatio cum Pyrrho*, *Ryan W. Strickler*	105
II IOSIF AND RUSSIA	127
Introduction – *David Goldfrank*	129
5 What Was New about Commemoration in the Iosifo-Volokolamskii Monastery? A Reassessment, *Ludwig Steindorff*	137
6 Iosif Volotskii's Disputational Technique (*Ars Disputandi*), *David Goldfrank*	153

7 The Debate with Iosif (*Prenie s Iosifom Volotskim*), A Fictive Disputation, *Donald Ostrowski* — 183

8 Deacon Feodor Ivanov as a Follower of Iosif Volotskii or The *Enlightener* and Feodor's Screed "About the Wolf and Predator Nikon," *Kevin M. Kain* — 213

9 Old Believers and Icons, *Evgeny Grishin* — 239

III ORTHODOXY AND MODERNITY — 263

Introduction - *Valeria Z. Nollan* — 265

10 The Defense of Human Dignity in Nineteenth-Century Russian Thought, *Randall A. Poole* — 271

11 Russian Foreign Policy and the Change of Dynasty in Greece (1862-1864), *Lucien J. Frary* — 307

12 Eastern Christianity as 'Survival' and 'Oriental Other' in the *Lectures* of Arthur Penrhyn Stanley, *Christopher D. L. Johnson* — 333

13 How the Orthodox Philokalic Tradition Came to Modern (Literary) America, *Rev. John McGuckin* — 349

14 The Russian Orthodox Church in Italy Today: A Kaleidoscope Clarifying Itself, *Valeria Z. Nollan* — 371

Contributors — 391

List of Illustrations

1 (p1) – From Iosif's 16th c. Grave Icon.
Source: See note 119 to the Introduction.

2 (p4) – Iosif's skull.
Source: See note 119 to the Introduction.

3-4 (p14) – Evfimii Turkov's sketches of Iosifov Monastery and its major structures (1581/2).
Source: See the "Nekropol'"essay in note 14 to the Introduction.

5 (p15) – Diagram of the imagined original Iosifov iconostasis.
Source: See note 110 to the Introduction.

6 (p17) – Forensic Reconstruction of Iosif's Face.
Source: See note 119 to the Introduction.

7 (p39) – Coptic Icon of Macarius the Great.
https://orthodoxwiki.org/ File:AbbaMacariusTheGreat.jpg

8 (p54) – (11th-12th c.) Chios Nea Moni mosaic of Anthony the Great.
Photo by Svetlana Tomeković: see https://ica.princeton.edu/tomekovic/display.php?country=Greece&site=28&view=site&page=2&image=35

9 (p55) – Chios Nea Moni mosaic of Maximus the Confessor.
http://s93.photobucket.com/user/afkimel/media/Saints/maxim-nea-moni-chios-s11.jpg.html
or: https://pemptousia.com/2015/01/saint-maximus-the-confessor/

10 (p65) – Bust of Emperor Constantius II.
Museum of Archeology, University of Pennsylvania; photo by Mary Harrsch: https://plus.google.com/+mharrsch

11 (p79) – Modern Orthodox icon by Aidan Hart of the First Ecumenical Council (I Nicea, 325).
http://www.orthodoxartsjournal.org/designing-icons-pt-7-architectural-and-natural-settings-in-icons/

12 (p80) – Sistine Chapel late 1590s painting the First Ecumenical Council.
https://en.wikipedia.org/wiki/File:Nicea.jpg

13 (p87) – Emperor Justinian I, Bishop Maximian of Ravenna, and court officials: choir mosaics of San Vitale Basilica in Ravenna.
https://en.wikipedia.org/wiki/File:Meister_von_San_Vitale_in_Ravenna_003.jpg

14 (p105) – 14th-c. illustrated Bulgarian translation of the Chronicle of Constantine Manasses depiction of the severing of the tongue and right hand of Maximus the Confessor in 662.
https://pemptousia.com/2015/01/saint-maximus-the-confessor/

15 (p118) – The Bulgarian 'Manasses' depiction of the Sixth Ecumenical Council (681).
https://www.newworldencyclopedia.org/entry/Third_Council_of_Constantinople

16 (p137) – Iosifov Monastery 1581/2 *Obikhodik* (Table Customary) page with the Arsenii and mother "Marfa" (Maria) Golenin "middle" size commemorative feast.
Source: See Steindorff's Speisenbuch in note 20 to Chapter 5.

17 (p147) – Iosifov Monastery Uspenskii Sobor diagram with excavation shafts of 16th c. elite burials.
Source: See Chernov's essay in note 14 to the Introduction.

18 (p153) – Late 1560s-1570s (*Litsevoi letopisnyi svod*) Illustrated Chronicle depiction of Iosif composing *Prosvetitel'*.
http://www.runivers.ru/bookreader/book481263/#page/139/mode/1up

19 (p160) – Illustrated Chronicle depiction of 1490 Moscow synod accusations.
http://www.runivers.ru/bookreader/book481263/#page/136/mode/1up

20 (p175) – Illustrated Chronicle depiction of the 1490 Synod affirming the Trinity Doctrine.
http://www.runivers.ru/bookreader/book481263/#page/138/mode/1up

21 (p183) – Pskov-Pecherskii (Caves) Monastery (in 2002). From li-user homaaaxel: http://community.livejournal.com/monastyri_mira/80915.html, CC BY 1.0, https://commons.wikimedia.org/w/index.php?curid=3601779

22 (p203) – The imagined dispute between Ibd Rushd (Averroes, 1126-98) and Porphyry (234-301) in c. 1350 Manfredus de Monte Imperiali's medical *Liber de herbis et plantis* (Book of Herbs and Plants).
https://en.wikipedia.org/wiki/File:AverroesAndPorphyry.JPG

23 (p213) – Patriarch Nikon in his Resurrection "New Jerusalem" Monastery.
https://en.wikipedia.org/wiki/File:Portrait_of_Patriarx_Nikon.jpg

24 (p218) – 19th-early 20th c. Old Believer depiction of Patriarch Nikon's alleged conversing with the Devil.
From Oleg Tarasov, *Icon and Devotion* (2002 English edition), 147: original in the Library of the Academy of Sciences, St. Petersburg.

25 (p221) – 19th-early 20th c. Old Believer depiction of Patriarch Nikon's actual destruction of icons.
From Oleg Tarasov, *Icon and Devotion* (2002 English edition), 195: original in the Library of the Academy of Sciences, St. Petersburg.

26 (p239) – 18th c. Old Believer (Vyg Community) small copper triptych of the Deesis.
From *Neizvestnaia Rossiia: k 300-letiiu Vygovskoi staroobriadskoi pustiny: katalog vystavki* (GIM 1994), p. 41: original in the State Historical Museum, Moscow.

27 (p244) – 18th c. Old Believer small copper triptych with the Tikhvin Bogomater, the Vernicle, and Sts. Sergii Radonezhskii and Varlaam Khutynskii.
From *Neizvestnaia Rossiia: k 300-letiiu Vygovskoi staroobriadskoi pustiny: katalog vystavki* (GIM 1994), p. 41: originals in the State Historical Museum, Moscow.

28 (p254) – Cross Cover of the small Deesis triptych.
From *Neizvestnaia Rossiia: k 300-letiiu Vygovskoi staroobriadskoi pustiny: katalog vystavki* (GIM 1994), p. 41: originals in the State Historical Museum, Moscow.

29 (p271) – Aleksandr Radishchev (1749-1802), unknown Artist.
https://en.wikipedia.org/wiki/Alexander_Radishchev#/media/File:Radishchev_color.jpg

30 (p271) – Ivan Kramskoi 1905 painting of Vladimir Soloviev
https://upload.wikimedia.org/wikipedia/commons/d/d5/Vladimir-Solovyov.jpg

31 (p277) – Ivan Kireevskii.
http://origins.osu.edu/sites/origins.osu.edu/files/Article_Ivan_Kireevskii.jpg

32 (p286) – 1905, portrait by Leonid Pasternak of Boris Chicherin
(thanks to Wikipedia user Shakko).
https://en.wikipedia.org/wiki/Boris_Chicherin#/media/File:B.N._Chicherin_by_L.Pasternak_(1905,_GIM).jpg

33 (p307) – King Othon (Otto) of Greece riding with his consort Amalia of Oldenberg, 1853.
https://commons.wikimedia.org/wiki/Template:LIFE#Copyright

34 (p312) – King Othon.
Anne S.K. Brown Military Collection, Brown University Library

35 (p314) – Aleksandr Ozerov, Russian "Minister" in Athens (1857-1861):
https://ru.wikipedia.org/wiki/Озеров_Александр_Петрович

36 (p333) – Rev. Arthur Penhryn Stanley, 1872 *Vanity Fair* caricature.
https://en.wikipedia.org/wiki/Arthur_Stanley_(priest)#/media/File:Stanley_in_Vanity_Fair.jpg

37 (p335) – Stanley, *The Eastern Church* Title Page
(orig., 1861, Georgetown University 1869 ed. Library Copy).

38 (p338) – Stanley's Floor Diagram of Moscow's Uspenskii Sobor.
(orig., 1861, Georgetown University 1869 ed. Library Copy).

39 (p349) – J.D. Salinger's Franny contemplating, from Masha Deykeute's 2010 literary blog.
https://bluedragonfly10.wordpress.com/2010/01/17/franny-and-zooey/

40 (p. 354) – Paisii Velichkovskii, first *Dobrotolubie* printing (1793).
See note 9 to Chapter 13.

41 (p364) – J.D. Salinger's Franny's head: 2013 book cover redesign by Ambrosia Shapiro.
http://cargocollective.com/ambrosia/Book-Cover-Redesign-Franny-and-Zooey.

42 (p369) – St. Catherine's Russian Orthodox Church in Rome, overlooking the Vatican and St. Peter's Basilica (official photo).
https://oca.org/news/headline-news/metropolitan-tikhon-welcomed-at-romes-russian-orthodox-church

Preface

Donald Ostrowski

The Association for the Study of Eastern Christian History and Culture (ASEC) developed out of a conference that Nickolaus Lupinin and I organized at Harvard University in March 2002. The conference gathered together some 30 scholars engaged in research on the Russian and Ukrainian Orthodox churches. One of the participants, Andrei Pliguzov, remarked on the need for a professional, academic organization to promote research and scholarship on the history and culture of Eastern Christianity. That summer Nick and I followed up on Andrei's suggestion by gathering a small group of scholars involved in Eastern Church studies in or near Cambridge, Massachusetts, (including Olga Strakhov, Hugh Olmsted, and Russell Martin) for several meetings to put together a founding document of such an organization. That document was presented at the annual business meeting of the Early Slavic Studies Association (ESSA) in November 2002 in Pittsburgh, Pennsylvania, and was given approval by the ESSA.

In September 2003, Paul Bushkovitch and Laura Engelstein organized a follow-up conference at Yale University to the Harvard conference of 2002. At that conference ASEC was formally founded. Nick served as the first president of the organization and I served as secretary from 2003 to 2006. ASEC was incorporated in July 2005 and has affiliate status with the Association for Slavic, Eastern European, and Eurasian Studies (ASEEES).

ASEC has held biennial conferences since 2005. The first four conferences were held in Columbus, Ohio, under the auspices of Ohio State University's Center for Slavic and East European Studies, Department of Slavic and East European Languages and Literatures, and the Hilandar Research Library. Most of those conferences have led to the publication of a select number of papers in a special volume. Thus far, three volumes of publications have resulted from these conferences. The October 2005 conference resulted in the publication of *Culture and Identity in Eastern Christian History: Papers of the First Biennial Conference of the Association for the Study of Eastern Christian History and Culture*, edited by Russell E. Martin and Jennifer D. Spock with the assistance of M. A. Johnson, vol. 1 of "Eastern Christian Studies," *Ohio Slavic Papers*, vol. 9 (2009). The October 2007 conference resulted in the publication of *Centers and Peripheries in the Christian East: Papers from the Second Biennial Conference of the Association for the Study of Eastern Christian History and Culture*, edited by Eugene Clay, Russell Martin, and Barbara Skinner, *Russian History*, vol. 40 (2013). In the meantime, select papers from the two conferences that started it all (the one at Harvard in March 2002, the other at Yale in September 2003) has been published by Ohio State University's Center for Slavic and East European Studies, Department of Slavic and East European Languages and Literatures, and the Hilandar Research Library as *The Tapestry of Russian Christianity: Studies in History and Culture*, edited by Nickolas Lupinin, Donald Ostrowski, and Jennifer B. Spock as vol. 2 of "Eastern Christian Studies" (= vol. 10 of Ohio Slavic Papers), 2016. And there are plans to publish select papers from the 6th biennial conference held in 2015.

The March 2013 ASEC conference resulted in the publication of the present volume. This collection of articles complements an ambitious project in Russia to commemorate Iosif Volotskii and his monastery with conferences and conference volumes. Two of those volumes have already been published. In 2008 appeared *Prepodobnyi Iosif Volotskiii ego obitel'. Vol. 1: Materialy nauchno-prakticheskoi konferentsii posviashchennoi 520-letiiu osviashcheniia pervogo monastyrskogo kamennogo khrama – Uspenskogo sobora – i 80-letiiu so dnia rozhdeniia Mitropolita Volokolamskogo i Iur'evskogo Pitirima*, which included 34 papers from a conference held in 2006. In 2013 appeared *Prepodobnyi Iosif Volotskii i ego obitel'. Vol. 2: Materialy nauchno-prakticheskoi konferentsii posviashchenno i 530-letiiu osnovaniia Iosifo-Volotskogo monastyria i 20-letiiu vozrozhdeniia v nem monasheskoi zhizni*, which included 30 papers from a conference held in 2009.

A third from a 2015 conference marking the 500th anniversary of Iosif's death awaits publication. Whereas those conferences and publications were strictly Iosif and Iosifov Monastery focused, the accomplishment of the present volume and its progenitor conference is to place Iosif, his writing, and his heritage within a broader historical, cultural, and theological context. ASEC is delighted that our contributors include some specialists in Byzantine and Russian religion, history, and thought at the initial stages of their careers as well as mid-level and senior scholars.

Acknowledgments

A product of the Fifth Biennial Conference of the Association for the Study of East Christian Culture and History (ASEC), held at Georgetown University on March 8-9, 2013, this volume owes its very existence to all who made the meeting possible, starting with the ASEC members and officers; also the Eastern Kentucky University Department of History; Georgetown University's Medieval Studies Program, Center for Eurasian, Russia and East European Studies, Department of History, and Department of Theology; and The Ohio State University's Resource Center for Medieval Slavic Studies. Among those behind the scenes who helped to make the conference a success were Predrag Matejic and M. A. "Pasha" Johnson of the Hilander Research Library at Ohio State, Sandra Strachan-Vieira of Medieval Studies and the Institute of Medieval Philosophy at Georgetown, recent Georgetown Ph.D. Daniel Scarborough, who is presently on the History Faculty of Nazarbaev University in Kazakhstan, and Carol Dockham, a Georgetown Ph.D. candidate, who tragically died in September 2016, as we were finishing the last edits to this volume. The editors are likewise grateful to Father Patrick Viscuso for some initial editorial help with the first set of essays; to Archimandrite Sergei, Locum Tenens (*Namestnik*) of the Iosif-Volotskii Stauropigial Male Monastery, for permissions to reproduce pictures from the *Prepodobnyi Iosif Volotskii i ego obitel'* volumes; to Aidan Hart, Mary Harrsch, "li-user homeaaxel," "Wikipedia user Shakko," Masha Deykeute, Ambrosia Shapiro, and the Brown University Library for permission to reproduce photos; to Carole Sargent of Georgetown Office of Scholarly Publications, President's Office, Woodstock Library, and Geladrin Center's Michael Mattason; and to New Academia founder and publisher Anna Lawton for their encouragement and support.

Introduction: Iosif Volotskii
A Half Millennium Retrospective

David Goldfrank

1 – From Iosif's 16th c. Grave Icon

September 9, 2015, marked the 500th anniversary of the passing of one of the most commanding and remarkable figures in Russian history, Iosif Volotskii. It was in his honor that our Association for the Study of Eastern Christian History and Culture held its biennial conference in March 2013, where the first drafts of this volume's essays were presented. Steeped in traditions and sacred writings, Iosif would probably have approved of the subject matter of our first section that looks at early Eastern Church history. And as a passionate and engaged activist, he likely would have been curious about our middle section devoted to him and how some of his interests played out in early modern Russia in places where religion remained paramount, though our unavoidable secular approach would have left him cold. How he or any other zealous late medieval abbot, teacher, and father confessor would have related to the issues of our third section on our modern, technologically explosive era is impossible to fathom, except, probably to remind us, as he did his monks, of such timeless wisdom as "it is a great calamity where laws and canons do not dwell."[1] So who is the man whom we are honoring with this volume?

Iosif was a monastery founder, the initiator of his era's greatest 'start-up,' who not only left his mark on almost every important aspect of the church life of his day, but even influenced the powerful Muscovite monarchy's 'scenarios of power.' His monumental *Book Against the Heretics* (known later as *Prosvetitel'* {*Enlightener*}) evinced a unique combination of rhetoric, logic, apologetics, dogmatics, homiletics, invective polemic, sacred history, and strictures for rulers and ruled. This work elucidated, fortified, and protected Muscovy's brand of Orthodoxy and helped to educate Russian churchmen and form their mentalities well into the seventeenth century.[2] His testamentary monastic Rule articulated Muscovite cenobitic principles, foregrounding communal prayer, meals, and labor, as well as the positions of the superior, council elders, and specific officers,[3] while his related *synodicon* likewise furthered the rationalization and standardization of the lucrative and mission-supporting commemoration practices of Russia's abbeys.[4] And his well-administered monastery itself, with its networks of personnel connected also to his abbey of tonsure, Pafnutiev-Borovskii, nurtured and matriculated a cohort of writers and prelates, including two major collective-project organizers, Metropolitans Daniil (r. 1522-1539, earlier hegumen of Iosifov, 1515-1522) and Makarii (r. 1542-1563, earlier Archbishop of Novgorod, 1526-1542, and also, perhaps, Iosif's great-great nephew).[5] This cohort collectively dominated the Muscovite Church and culture into the 1560s, their disciples' and followers' continuing to be of capital importance through the Time of Troubles of the early seventeenth century.[6]

What can we say with certainty about Iosif himself in the light of scanty reliable sources? Dating his birth to 12 November 1439 or 1440,[7] we can pretty well trust the reports of the (maybe 1518) "Little Annal (*letopischik*) of Iosif" and other such straightforward evidence to sketch a biography. He was a monk from February 1460 in Pafnutiev (Rozhdestvo Bogoroditsy) Monastery in Borovsk, then served briefly as hegumen there, from 1477 to 1479,[8] and founded the Volokolamsk Monastery in June, 1479, near his family's ancestral lands under the protection of his territorial prince, Boris (d. 1494).[9] The text indicates that Iosif himself initiated his *synodicon* (commemoration book) in 1479, when he founded his monastery.[10] The abbey's land records and the "Little Annal" trace the growth of the cloister and erection of two major masonry edifices in Iosif's lifetime, the masonry Uspenskii Sobor (Cathedral of the Dormition) during 1484 to 1486, and the refectory in 1506.[11] The monastery's donation book adds the commencement of the octagonal Hodigitria Church at the base of bell tower in 1511 to 1512,[12] and allows a ca. 1490 dating of the initial Uspenskii Sobor burial enclosure.[13] Archeology then permits us to specify some of the dimensions and building materials of these structures.[14]

We learn from the document itself of Iosif's serving as father confessor for and of his presence at the preparation of the will of Boris's younger son, Ivan of Ruza, who in 1503 testated his appanage (*udel*) not to his older brother, Fëdor of Volok, but to their uncle Ivan III (r. 1462-1505).[15] Extant epistles and *Prosvetitel'* reveal Iosif's crucial political-literary involvement in the suppression of the "Jewish reasoning Novgorod Heretics" in 1504 and 1505.[16] The testament of the monastery as a corporate entity supplies 1507 as the date for the transfer from subordination to his local prince Fëdor over to Grand Prince Vasilii III (r. 1505-1533).[17] Other extant epistles contain the quarrel over this transfer with Fëdor and with Iosif's diocesan archbishop, Serapion of Novgorod (r. 1505-1509),[18] and they provide some intriguing information about the rival Vozmitskii Cloister in the town of Volokolamsk itself.[19]

Dating Iosif's two major compositions is much more difficult, since they both appear as works in progress, composed over time in several recensions. The oldest recorded date—on the donation inscription of a codex containing complete brief versions of both his Rule and *Prosvetitel'*—is 1513/1514 (7022). But the earliest known death date of one of its major copyists (Nil Sorskii) is 1508, and then internal evidence and extant working manuscripts from the monastery's library send us back earlier in time.[20] The Iosifov Monastery

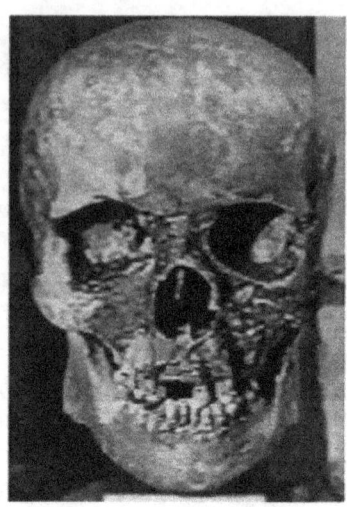

2 – Thanks to the work of archeologists and forensic medicine experts in 2001-2002, scholars are certain they have Iosif's well preserved skull.

"Little Annal" has Iosif dying 9 September 1515 at the age of 75 or, more likely, 76,[21] but physical weakening may have led to Daniil's *de facto* succession as early as 1511 or 1512.[22]

Allowing us some further glimpses into the founder's life is the apparently later copying from what may have been Iosif's personal archive by two of his more powerful trainees from the 1510s and 1520s, Nifont Kormilitsyn (hegumen of Iosifov, 1522-1544, archimandrite of Moscow's Novospasskii, 1543-1554, and bishop of Sarai (Krutitsy, 1554-1561) and Feodosii (hegumen of Novgorod's Khutynskii Monastery, 1531-1542, and Archbishop of Novgorod, 1542-1551), as well as by the latter's disciple Evfimii Turkov (hegumen of Iosifov Monastery, 1575-1587), and Iosifov trainee, Vassian Koshka (hegumen of Vozmitskii. ca. 1554-1568).[23] Iosif claimed that he quit as successor hegumen of Pafnutiev and left due to Grand Prince Ivan III's court officials' appropriating the monastery's dependents.[24] Several of his later letters to clerics and laymen indicate his readiness to lower a hellfire-homiletic boom in defense of his establishment, as he insisted not only on the propriety of tonsuring someone else's bondsman, but also on the cloister's right to have runaway monks returned.[25] Other sets of epistles show how he argued the church's deadly case against dissidence and his own case against Serapion.[26]

Autobiographical references in his "Response to the Censorious and Brief Account of the Holy Fathers of the Monasteries of Rus'" (*Slovo* 10 of his testamentary Rule), recount some of the influential elders whom he claims to have encountered in his early career— Hegumen Savva (d. 1467, not the founder) of Tver's Savvin Monastery, his long-time anchorite brother Varsonofii, (Prince) Efrosin (Teprinskii) of Tver's Savvateev Monastery, founder-hegumen Makarii of Kaliazin (d. 1483), and Spiridon of Troitsa-Sergiev (hegumen, 1467-1474), besides, of course, Iosif's own mentor, founder-hegumen Pafnutii of Borovsk (1394-1477).[27] And in this Rule Iosif likewise indicates that he settled at first at the site of his monastery with like-minded comrades.[28] This is amplified by Iosif's most factual *vita*, composed in 1546 by his last personal cell-servant and entomber, Bishop Savva Chernyi of Krutitsa (r. 1544-1554).[29] The most famous of Iosif's original comrades was Kassian Bosoi ("Barefoot"), who lived into his early 90s, and whom Vasilii III venerated.[30]

Disciples and admirers recounted Iosif's life in four separate guises—another sign of his impact. Slightly earlier than Savva's Life of Iosif stands his nephew-writer Dosifei Torporkov's comparatively late "Funerary Oration" and related *Volokolamsk Patericon* (both maybe 1545-1546),[31] and a bit later came an 'anonymous,' more literarily flourishing, anonymous "Life," written by the 1550s, maybe by the South Slav Lev Filolog.[32] There is no reason for us not to recast in real-life terms, and thereby more or less trust, the following hagiographic data: the story of the great-grandfather Sania's immigration from "Lithuania" (likely from today's Belarus); Iosif's early literacy-education at the local Volokolamsk Vozdvizhenskii monastery;[33] his prodigious liturgical memory ("learned all the divine writings by heart"); his informed and calculated selection, on the advice of Savva of Tver, to take the tonsure at Pafnutiev; the 13 February 1460 date of that tonsure noted earlier from the "Little Annal;" Iosif's laboring both in the bakery and as *ustavshchik* (in charge of the liturgies); his personal care for his disabled and soon tonsured father; and his simultaneous rise to a leading position among Pafnutii's monks to be a logical choice, on the basis of manifest abilities, for the succession.

Regarding Iosif's devotional mentality, one might speculate on the exemplary effect on Iosif of the raising of Pafnutiev's masonry church "painted by the elder, Mitrofan, [*and*] Dionisii, the most skilled masters" in 1467/1468, according to the "Little Annal of Pafnutii,"[34] since in 1486 Dionisii headed the team of iconographers that included Iosif's nephews or junior cousins, Vassian and Dosifei Toporkov and painted the monastery's masonry Uspenskii Sobor.[35] We can also note a Iosifov manuscript inscription of a heavily hesychastic codex as "Iosif's old miscellany," which also contains the pseudo-Hippolytus "Discourse on Revelation,"[36] signaling both a desire to understand if not master stillness (hesychasm) and a typical concern about end times for a person of his era. He also owned, and partially or fully copied, two gospels, a psalter, liturgical works, and collections of the rhetorically and theologically useful sermons of Gregory Nazianzus, as well as the ascetic favorite, *Ladder* of John Climacus, which Iosif partially or fully copied as registered in the 1591 Iosifov inventory.[37] But when Savva tells us that as a youth Iosif acted after services totally as a devout monk would, in constant prayer in his cell, one has to recognize in this depiction a hagiographic trope concerning a saint's youth.[38] For Iosif's behavior, as well his writings, shows him eagerly founding and building up a cenobium, where the stillness stood as only one option, along with reading or handcrafts, for the monks' individual cell time, while their participation in collective liturgies, meals, and whatever labor or service the superior assigns or approves was mandatory.[39]

Savva's Life of Iosif makes the witting or unwitting mistake of conflating the non-lethal 1490 and lethal 1504 synods against the "Novgorod Heretics" under the presiding secular presence of the future Vasilii III (not his father, the reigning Ivan III),[40] but Savva at least, correctly in my opinion, limits the recounting of Iosif's public quarrels to those conflicts for which we have his credible paper trail: over the alleged "heretics" and their suppression and over his imbroglios with Prince Fëdor and Archbishop Serapion.[41] The anonymous "Life," however, adduces two more interesting episodes, one that can be corroborated by other reliable sources, and one that cannot. Accordingly, Iosif blessed two disciples, Nil Polev and Dionisii Zvenigorodskii, to travel to Nil Sorskii's hermitage to study stillness,[42] which they actually did. Polev served as one of Sorskii's literary executors,[43] and both disciples contributed to Iosifov's becoming, so far as we can ascertain, the single richest repository of Sorskii's writings, more so than either his Sora hermitage or its patron abbey, Kirillo-Beloozerskii,[44] while Sorskii himself participated in the copying of the earliest extant complete copy of *Prosvetitel'*.[45]

The second episode would have Iosif attending a Moscow synod in 1503 that considered the propriety of monastic landholding.[46] Here the paper trail leads us not only to codices no earlier than the 1550s and 1560s, but also to contradictory writings that conform completely to the issues that clearly raged at that time, better so, if not completely, than to those of 1503, as Donald Ostrowski and the late Andrei Pliguzov have demonstrated.[47] Iosif's own defense of monastic property (or one written as if by him, but surviving only in post-1518 versions) is connected to Prince Fëdor's specific attacks on Iosif's monastery, not to any threats of secularization by Ivan III or to any writing by Nil Sorskii or his followers.[48] But very knowledgeable and respected contemporary scholars differ completely on this matter, with some such as G.M. Prokhorov, R.G. Skrynnikov, N.V. Sinitsyna, and A.I. Alekseev, adhering to the older paradigm that accepted the notion of a fundamental rift between Nil Sorskii and Iosif,[49] rather than compatible outlooks with complementary differences in monastic pedagogy, as do this writer and some current Russian churchmen.[50] And for a commemorative volume, it is necessary to underscore the open nature of this issue and in fact concede that to date, the Ostrowski-Pliguzov position concerning the monastic lands issue has not caught on in Russia, though some specialists, like Elena Romanenko, occupy a middle ground. Accordingly, she allows that the issue of monastic land was raised at the synod in 1503, but that Nil only gave his "personal opinion," while, as with the Nil-specialist Fairy von Lilienfeld's later judgment, there was no fundamental rift with Iosif.[51]

The all-important question of the nature of these "Novgorod Heretics," as Iosif, and before him, Archbishop Gennadii of Novgorod (1486-1503), termed them—sometimes with "Jewish-reasoning" attached[52]— is even more complex to disentangle. For here the issue of Iosif's honesty, or maybe the degree of his exaggeration and dishonesty, in depicting their views and actions, is at stake. By means of meticulous analysis of extant manuscripts in the 1950s, the late Ia. S. Lur´e sketched a credible progression and escalation of related accusations and name-calling, starting with Gennadii's epistles, then several of Iosif's, followed by his "Account of the Recent Heresy of the Novgorod Heretics" introducing the Brief *Prosvetitel'*, and finally his later Extended *Prosvetitel'* discourses—all of this indicating a lack of trustworthiness on his part and pointing to the utility for the accusers, rather than credibility regarding the accused, of the "Judaism" charges.[53] Andrei Pliguzov challenged and tried to modify some of Lur'e's textual schemata, but not his characterization of these dissidents simply as "Novgorod" and also, due to location, "Moscow" heretics.[54] And Anatolii Grigorenko, profiting from, among others, Jana Howlett's attempt to decipher the inconsistencies of Gennadii's epistles[55]—our earliest sources for these dissidents—hypothesized that the real issue in Novgorod centered on objections to the liturgy and communion, while Metropolitan Zosima's real offence was to downplay the efficacy of services for the dead.[56] Among current specialists honoring Iosif and his legacy, N.N. Lisovoi stated flatly:[57]

> ... the term *zhidovstvo* used by Iosif does not have in view either Judaism as a religion, or Jewishness as a ethno-religious or cultural community, nor the historians' and archeologists' fabricated Judaeo-Christianity of the Early Church, but means a specific type of *deviation*.

On the other hand, simultaneously with Lur'e and down to the present, Slavicist adepts in Hebrew, most notably, Moshe Taube, linked the translations from Hebrew into East Slavic in the latter 15th and early 16th centuries to these dissidents. He has pointed out the similarities of the brief chain "Poem on the Soul," recorded by the influential diplomat-*d'iak* and accused heresiarch, Fëdor Kuritsyn, under the name "Laodicean Epistle," to analogous Hebrew compositions and thus has shown that it may represent such a translation or adaptation.[58] And in successive publications A. I. Alekseev has challenged Lur'e's paradigm and argued that in every case the *Prosvetitel'* version is the source of what Lur'e envisioned as its source in an epistle or separate *slovo* (discourse).[59] Alekseev has likewise contended that in the light of the translations of medieval Roman Catholic anti-Jewish treatises which Archbishop Gennadii commissioned, the burden of proof over whether contemporary Judaism and Jews were in some way central to these dissidents lies with the detractors of the common sobriquet "Judaizers," not with the proponents.[60] And among current specialists honoring Iosif, A.V. Shcherbakov, without worrying how Judaic the alleged heresy was, but following Iosif in seeing it as the rejection of all Christian dogmas and hence a capital danger, argues:

> The feat of the destroyers of the heresy of the "Judaizers," Archbishop Gennadii and Saint Iosif Volotskii, registered by grace in the assembly of the saints, is immortal. We, living in the 21st c., are indebted to these strugglers for their having smashed the plot of the "Judaizers" to conquer Holy Rus' from within by means of penetrating the sphere of the highest authority ....[61]

Perhaps all of these views about the dissidents contain elements of historical truth, insofar as some Slavic Judaica was available in Russia and stimulated a modicum of fresh thinking about philosophical, theological, calendrical, and governmental matters, and also revealed to certain discerning minds the intellectual limitations of even the most well-read among the Russian clergy. But at the same time, the accused heretics themselves left no traces of their having been genuine Judaizers in any meaningful sense of the term, that is, using the Old Testament to dispute central doctrines and practices of Eastern Orthodoxy. They rather would have been more open-minded and bold critics of the Orthodox leadership of the day, and so, in Gennadii's and Iosif's eyes, required suppression *à tout prix*. Whatever the case here, one fact stands out: Iosif was a masterful pedagogue-polemicist and defender of Orthodoxy as he understood it.[62]

When we attempt to characterize Iosif's legacy to Russia and its Church, we are perforce at times speaking collectively of him and his closest comrades and collaborators, which is how he for the most part he presented himself. With *Prosvetitel'* he divides the world into the correctly believing and worshiping Orthodox, who achieve eternal salvation if they live properly, and everyone else, headed by "Satan's army" of heretics, who aim to bring down the Orthodox faith,[63] just as his army of demons strives to lead monks and other practitioners of pious living astray:⁶⁴ hence Thomas S. Seebohm's characterization of Iosif's theology as "monastic."⁶⁵ Not at all Manichaean, Iosif depicts the real world as a fine place to be fully enjoyed within the confines of piety,⁶⁶ and he displays full optimism in the saving power of saints' intercessions and of commemorative prayers for the dead.⁶⁷ Implicitly, Russia, as the only remaining sovereign Orthodox realm, is the ideal country in which to dwell, but its rulers must remain steadfast in the faith and vigilant against heresy, less the realm perish as other Orthodox realms have fallen.⁶⁸ So the Orthodox should be ever watchful and employ every trick in the book to expose such dissidents.⁶⁹ The church canons may prescribe receiving the genuinely penitent back into the fold, but untrustworthy and deceitful heretics must be either executed or confined for life.⁷⁰

For almost a century and a half specialists have been trying to figure out how to characterize Iosif's legacy in the realm of monarchical thinking, since his writings promoted non-obedience and even resistance to a brutal and blaspheming "tsar," who is really a "tyrant" (*muchitel'*), yet at the same time not only assumed the divine establishment of rulers' authority to punish or be clement,⁷¹ but also repeated early Byzantine strictures vaunting the "tsar's" authority as "like unto God."⁷² Some modern scholars have found the differences between these two positions to be explainable chiefly as utterances occasioned by Iosif's original opposition to Ivan III's protection of some dissidents in contrast to the late-life need of Vasilii III's backing against Fëdor and Serapion and for a continued hard line against dissidence.⁷³ Other specialists have considered these positions to be essentially reconcilable,⁷⁴ which is substantiated elsewhere in Iosif's compositions⁷⁵ and by the corpus of writings and compilations produced or commissioned by Dosifei Toporkov, Metropolitans Daniil and Makarii, and Archbishop Feodosii. Regarding crowned authority, these works contained homiletics prescribing Orthodox piety and the promotion and protection of it and also historical accounts idealizing harmony between prince and prelate,⁷⁶ while not neglecting historic tyrants to be opposed.⁷⁷ Iosif for his part, while normally lauding pious and saintly churchmen, also called for and explicitly praised opposition to the alleged heretic Metropolitan Zosima.⁷⁸ But later, if Savva's Life is to be believed, Iosif quite realistically urged Vasilii III's brother Iurii (then suspected of disloyalty and contemplating flight), to submit completely to the sovereign and trust in his clemency.[79] So the litmus test for everything in Iosif's legacy was strict Orthodoxy, "according to the Divine Writings," as he so often stated.[80] And it was thus no accident that in the seventeenth century, first Patriarch Nikon, then an Old Believer opponent of Nikon's reforms, and finally a polemicist against the Old Belief, each of whom considered himself nothing but Orthodox, revered and borrowed freely from Iosif.[81]

Iosif's reputation and legacy, however, certainly did not enjoy smooth sailing within the modernization process of his native land and church. More so than Nil Sorskii, Iosif was his generation's most productive writing teacher, and his authority and influence were seemingly unmatched, so long as two generations of his disciples and their allies dominated the Russian Church into the 1560s. In the 1550s his authority was mobilized authentically in the interest of both Church reform and suppression of dissidence,[82] and inauthentically, perhaps, though not at all betraying his values, in defense of ecclesiastical property.[83] His authority in dogmatics, however, ceded somewhat, especially after the 1580s, to the persecuted, yet productive, immigrant, Italian-educated Maksim Grek (Michael Trivolis fl. in Russia, 1517-1556), whose overall erudition and literary sophistication foreshadowed the gradual westernization of Russian intellects in the seventeenth century, and whose overall manuscript copies of his works outnumbered Nil's and Iosif's combined.[84] Iosif's Rule, however, served as the most authoritative model in Muscovy, even for a female cloister, in the sixteenth century,[85] as well as for Patriarch Nikon in the seventeenth century.[86] But after Peter the Great's (r. 1682-1725) secularization policies and the advent of Enlightenment thinking to Russia, the monastic resurgence initiated by Paisii Velichkovskii's revival of hesychasm, which was as friendly to cenobiticism as Iosif and his disciples had been to Nil Sorskii's hesychasm, the latter's spiritual writings were placed on recommended reading lists, but Iosif's were not.[87]

Iosif's seeming demise as an authoritative monastic father was paralleled by much more respect for Nil or Maksim than for Iosif in nineteenth-century scholarship, as he was seen as too formal, ritualistic, uncritical, authoritarian, and fanatic for the type of Orthodoxy that many educated people of the day wished to promote.[88] This occurred in part due to the discovery and initial publication of the mid-sixteenth century depiction of enmity between Nil and Iosif.[89] Nevertheless, in the model "Regulations" (*Pravila*) prepared by Church authorities as late as 1910, one can sense Iosif's practical, Studite-inspired organizational principles.[90] Most of Iosif's key works, it should be noted, had been published, albeit uncritically, by the end of the 1860s. Later, two incomplete manuscript catalogues were published: one in 1882 by Hieromonk (*Ieromonakh*) Iosif of the 236 codices that were transferred to the Moscow Seminary library in 1859, and then to the present Russian State Library in the 1930s; and another in 1891—that which P.M. Stroev in 1817 made of 690 codices (there had been 1150 in 1573, 707 in 1778).[91] A catalogue of the 435 Iosifov codices transferred to the Eparchial Library at Moscow's Vysokopetrovskii Monastery in 1863, and then to the State Historical Museum in 1921, was issued only in 1991.[92]

Twentieth-century Russian scholarship in emigration certainly recognized Iosif's pastoral talents, preaching of social peace, dedication to charity, and other services to society that accompanied his brutal intolerance of heresy. Kologrivov and Fedotov, for example, characterized Iosif's authoritative and stern caring as a type of late medieval Russian sanctity original to his mentor Pafnutii.[93] We know Pafnutii, however, mostly from the hagiographic portrait painted by Iosif's brother Vassian (hegumen of Simonov, 1502-1505; archbishop of Rostov, 1505-1515), plus a few additional comments by Iosif himself and Dosifei Toporkov.[94] Meanwhile, Iosif enjoyed an interesting fate at the hands of different Soviet scholars, one of whom presented him as a spokesman for Russia's "Church Militant" of his time,[95] and another of whom treated the entire monastic colonization movement as that of peasant-exploiting ecclesiastic "signiors" (*feodaly*).[96] But the best of these scholars not only accomplished splendid codicological and textological work on Iosif's manuscript convoys and a good deal of critical publication of his works and monastery's records, but also produced fine history, highlighting his role and accomplishments.[97]

Thomas Seebohm took the analysis of our subject's work to a new plane with his rather neglected in-depth study, issued in 1977, of the thought of Nil, Gennadii, and Iosif, following which it would be difficult dismiss Iosif's capabilities as a theologian, writing pedagogue, and disputer. Seebohm used the translated patristics, Western scholasticsm, and Hussitism as points of reference, and examined closely as well the translated "Arabic-Hebrew" works that circulated in Western Rus' around 1500 in order to create a very rich monograph. Swimming against the standard tide in religious scholarship, pointing, rather, to the role of the different positions and basic interests along with the similar foundations of all three Russians, and emphasizing Iosif's profound sense of the complex and many-sided human-God relationship evident in Scripture, liturgies, and monasticism, Seebohm flatly rejected any characterizing of Iosif's spirituality as "external formalism."[98] In a curious fashion, the slightly earlier, simultaneous codicological and orthographic work of Boris Kloss and Gelian Prokhorov, proving that Nil had copied forty per cent of the earliest extant complete manuscript of *Prosvetitel'* (brief redaction),[99] proved to be a cogent counter, with Nil's prestige as the clincher, to the modern dismissal of consideration of Iosif as an Orthodox authority to be taken seriously on his own terms. The best example of this transformation of attitudes toward Iosif may be the call by the late Fairy von Lilienfeld, author of the first profoundly patristics-based study of Nil's thought, for a thorough study of Iosif, whom she considered to have been Russia's "first genuine theologian in the contemporary meaning of the word."[100]

Meanwhile the Russia's Orthodox revival, commencing in the late Soviet period, and continuing with gusto as these pages are being written, has led to a many-sided analysis of Iosif and his legacy, with archeological and other material-culture investigations and an even richer appreciation of the various sides of religious culture that the 1970s and 1980s witnessed in Russia. Examination of the soil and masonry structures indicates a forest or man-made fire at the site of Iosifov's original, wooden Uspenskii Sobor and point to the 1422 Sergiev Monastery Troitsa Sobor as the model for the dimensions of Iosif's masonry rebuild in 1484-1486.[101] The design of Iosifov's ultimately Italian-influenced octagonal church falls midway between those of the Moscow kremlin's Ivan Velikii (John Climacus, not Ivan III) Bell Tower (1505-1508) and Suzdal's (female) Pokrov Monastery Church of the Venerable Wood of the Venerable

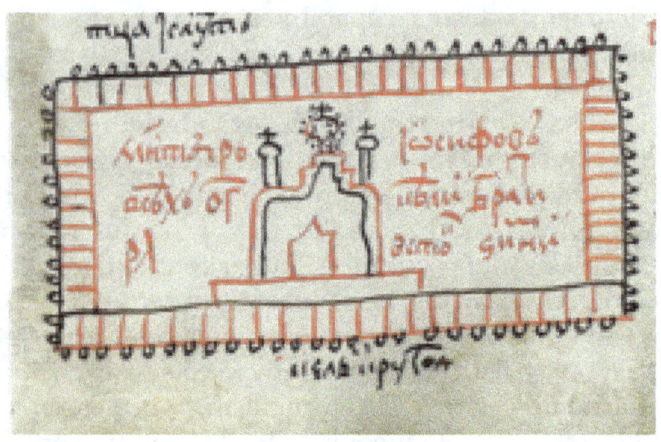

3-4 – The 1581/2 *Obikodhnik* (Customary) of Iosifov *igumen* Evfimii Turkov (r. 1575-1587) contains these simplified sketches by him first of the monastery and with its cells and the Uspenskii Sobor (Dormition Cathedral) accompanying the feast of the Dormition (15 August), and then of the Trapeza with its Theophany (*Bogoiavlenie*) church (or maybe the octagonal bell tower) accompanying the feast for that holiday (6 January).

Cross (1520s-1530s),[102] while the decorative aspects evince similarities with the early 1500s Moscow churches, the local Volokolamsk Church of the Resurrection, and the Suzdal-Pokrov octagonal church.[103] Earlier studies indicated the Iosifov refectory was similar in design and size to its contemporaries, such as that of Andronnikov Monastery in Moscow.[104] And comparisons of shrouds point to a connection between the ateliers of the wives of both Boris (d. 1494) and his son Fëdor of Volokolamsk (d. 1515) to Iosifov's iconography and book production.[105]

As for the significance of Iosif's dedications of his major edifices, M.S. Serebriankova has proposed that the selection of *uspenie Bogoroditsy* (Dormition of the Theotokos) for the sobor and *bogoiavlenie* (Theophany) for the refectory church symbolized respectively the monk's potential "ascent to heaven" and "spiritual transfiguration, divinization" on earth.[106] In contrast, Hegumen-became-Archimandrite Sergii Voronkov claimed that Iosif's honoring the Theotokos as the "receptacle of the godhead" in *Prosvetitel'* is the key for why he chose to dedicate his monastery to her.[107] Affirming the earlier scholarship of Viktoriia A. Meniailo, Archimandrite Sergii has argued from the monastery inventories that Iosif's seven-meter high iconostasis placed a Rublev-type Old Testament Trinity icon to the viewer's right of the church's *tsarskie vraty* ('royal doors'—between

5 – Diagram of the imagined original Iosifov iconostasis.

the congregation and the sanctuary), where we normally see an icon of Christ; that this iconostasis contained Russia's first-known waist-high icons; and that Iosif's deesis tier included on the flanks, outside the normal seven icons,[108] two great martyrs and two pillar saints. Accordingly, the latter were linked to Iosif's recommending continuous praying,[109] and the entire complex interpreted as representing hesychastic and eschatological divinization of the monk,[110] to which I would adduce that for Iosif, the monastic's *ascesis* is his or her form of sacrificial witness or martyrdom for his faith, as Iosif adapts from Ephesians:

> And likewise our Lord Jesus Christ, the eternal King, as *he also gave, some to be apostles, others prophets, others evangelizers, others pastors and teachers,* martyrs and confessors, monks and ascetics *to the perfection of the saints in the work of the creation of the body of Christ* ... .[111]

Is Iosif's legacy part of this revival? I would think so. A 1994 modern Russian translation of *Prosvetitel'* sold out a 30,000 print run,[112] and conferences devoted to Iosif and the monastery held in 2006 and 2009 have led to two massive volumes, somewhat devotional-adulatory, but largely scholarly, exploring all sorts of issues, many of which have already been addressed and cited in the foregoing paragraphs.[113] In addition, we might note that one specialist interpreted Iosif's Rule as evincing a compromise between the regulated, cenobitic "Studite *typicon* (*ustav*)" and likewise disciplined, but more individualistic "Jerusalim" or "Sabbaite" "*typicon*".[114] Another suggested a progression in the Iosifov Monastery-generated depictions of saintly types from Pafnutii's eschatological concerns, to Iosif's anti-heretical emphasis, to his successors' concentration on *ascesis*.[115] Still another researcher made a daring stab at breaking down Iosif's use of symbols according to scriptural and patristic types.[116] And since Iosif's sources and his use of them have yet fully to be identified and sorted out, much work in that domain, as well as other aspects of analyzing Iosif's work, remains to be done. This could be helped, as another scholar indicates, by the publication of two of the four unpublished Kazan Seminary "*kandidat* compositions" from 1858 to 1917 now housed in the Tatarstan National Archive.[117] Among the most important recent research into Iosif's theology, however, stand the perceptive, penetrating, and thorough works of the Hungarian scholar Ágnes Kriza, which analyze his defense and doctrines of icon veneration within the context of not only his Byzantine iconophile sources, but also liturgical passages, hesychasm and Orthodox, as opposed to Catholic, teachings concerning the nature of the Son.[118]

But for me and maybe also some of our readers, perhaps the most intriguing is work done with Iosif's physical remains, showing him not as having the stylized long, thin nose and hands so typical of iconography of ascetics. Rather, he appears to have been muscular and about 116.4 cm. or 5'4" at death, and hence, likely a robust, solid 5'6" in his prime (a good size for the period), capable of the physical labor and lengthy, attentive chanting he demanded of others and himself. So our versatile, charismatic, reforming, theologically-inclined, pedagogue-abbot and saint of the Russian Church maybe would have looked in his forties, if shaved and sheared (which he would not have been as an adult monk) and without his cowl (which he sometimes was), calm and energetically contemplating (which he probably often was), something like this (Illust. 6):[119]

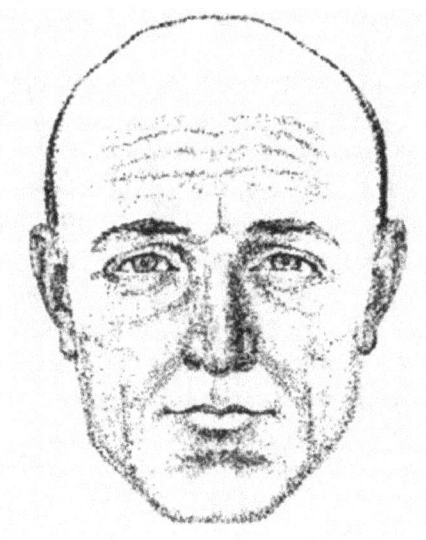

Abbreviations

AfED: *Antifeodal'nye ereticheskie dvizheniia na Rusi XIV-nachala XVI veka*. Edited by N.A. Kazakova and Ia.S. Lur'e. Moscow-Leningrad: Akademii nauk SSSR, 1955.*ChOIDR*: *Chteniia v Imperatorskom Obshchestve istorii i drevnostei rossiiskikh*.

DRIU: *Drevnerusskie inocheskie ustavy. Ustavy rossiiskikh monastyre-nachal'nikov* (expanded reissue of *Istoriia Rossiiskoi ierarkhii*. Compiled and edited by Metropolitan Evgeni Bolkhovitinov and Bishop Amvrosii A. Ornatskii. 6 vols in 7. Moscow: Holy Synod, 1807-1815; 2nd ed.,1822). Edited by T.V. Suzdal'tsev. Moscow: Severnyi palomnik, 2001.

KTsDRIVM: *Kniznye tsentry Drevnei Rusi: Iosifo-Volokolamskii monastyr' kak knizhnyi tsentr*. Edited by Dmitrii S. Likhachev. Leningrad: "Nauka," 1991.

MRIV: *The Monastic Rule of Iosif Volotsky*, rev. ed. = Cistercian Studies 36. Translated and edited by David Goldfrank. Kalamazoo: Cistercian Publications, 2000.

NSAW: *Nil Sorsky: The Authentic Writings* Translated and edited by David Goldfrank. Cistercian Studies 221. Kalamazoo: Cistercian Publications, 2008.

PIV: *Poslaniia Iosifa Volotskogo*. Edited by Ia. S. Lur'e and A. A. Zimin. Moscow-Leningrad: Izdatel'stvo Akademii nauk SSSR, 1959.

PIVO: *Prepobodnyi Iosif Volotskii i ego obitel'*. Vol. 1: *Materialy nauchno-prakticheskoi konferentsii, posviashennoi piatietiiu obreteniia Sviatykh moshchei Prepodobnogo Iosifa, 520-letiiu osviashcheniia pervogo monastyrskogo kamennogo khrama – Uspenskogo sobora – i 80-letiiu so dnia rozhdeniia Mitropolita Volokolamskogo i Iur'evskogo Pitirima*. Vol 2: *Materialy nauchno-prakticheskoi konferentsii, posviashennoi 530-letiiu osnovaniia Iosifo-Volotskogo monastyria i 20-letiiu vozrozhdeniia v nem monasheskoi zhizni*. Moscow: Iosifo-Volotskii stavropigial'nyi muzhskoi monastyr'/Istoriko-Arkhitekturno i khudozhvestvennyi muzei "Novyi Ierusalim", 2008, 2013.

PSRL: *Polnoe sobranie russkikh letopisei*. 41 vols. to date. St. Petersburg-Petrograd-Leningrad-Moscow:Arkheograficheskaia komissiia, Nauka, and Arkheograficheskii tsentr, 1841–

	1995.
SKKDR:	*Slovar' kniznikov i knizhnosti Drevnei Rusi.* 8 vols. to date. Edited by D. S. Likhachev, et al. Leningrad, St. Petersburg: Nauka, Dmitrii Bulanin, 1987-2012.
VMCh:	*Velikiia Minei chetii, sobrannye vserossiiskim Mitropolitom Makariem.* 22 vols. St Petersburg: Arkheograficheskaia komissiia, 1868-1917.
VPW:	Smith, T. Allen. *The Volokolamsk Paterikon. A Window into a Muscovite Monastery.* Studies and Texts 160. Toronto: Pontifical Institute, 2008.

Notes

1   *VMCh*, Sept., col. 561; and *DRIU*, 110: trans. *MRIV*, 240—attributed to Ephrem the Syrian.
2   *Prosvetitel', ili oblichenie eresi zhitovstvuiushchikh: Tvorenie prepodobnago ottsa nashego Iosifa, igumena volotskago*, 4th ed. (Kazan: Tipo-litografiia Imperatorskogo universiteta, 1903); see the list of manuscripts in *AfED*, 461–466.
3   *VMCh*, Sept., cols. 499–615; and *DRIU*, 57–157: trans., *MRIV*, 163–308. Iosif's earlier and hardly regulatory "Brief Rule" is found in *PIV*, 296–319; and *DRIU*, 187–215; trans., *MRIV*, 117–161: see below, note 20.
4   Ludwig Steindorff, *Memoria in Altrußland. Untersuchungen zu den Formen christlicher Totensorge* = Quellen und Studien zur Geschichte des östlichen Europa 38 (Stuttgart: Steiner, 1994), 164–166, 172, 195–196; for the text, as well as further analysis, T. I. Shablova, *Sinodik Iosifo-Volokolamskogo monastyria (1479-1510-e gody)* (Moscow: Dmitrii Bulanin, 2004), 97–207 (texts); and I. V. Dergacheva, *Drevnerusskii Sinodik: issledovaniia i teksty* = Pamiatniki drevnerusskoi mysli. Issledovaniia i teksty 6. (Moscow: "Krug," 2011), 154–163.
5   A. A. Zimin, *Krupnaia feodal'naia votchina i sotsial'no-politicheskaia bor'ba v Rossii konets XV- XVI v.* (Moscow: "Nauka," 1977), 281–314; idem, *I. S. Peresvetov i ego sovremenniki. Ocherki po istorii russkoi obshchestvenno-politicheskoi mysli serediny XVI veka* (Moscow: Izd. ANSSR, 1958), 71–101; Tom E. Dykstra, *Russian Monastic Culture. "Josephism" and the Iosifo--Volokolamskii Monastery, 1479-1606* = Slavistische Beiträge 450 (Munich: Otto Sagner, 2006), 83–193; Zhmakin, *Mitropolit Daniil i ego sochineniia* (Moscow: 1881) (also *ChOIDR*, 1881.1, rpt. Moscow: "Kniga po trebovaniiu," 2012), 110–750; B. M. Kloss, *Nikonovskii svod i russkie letopisi XVI-XVII vekov* (Moscow: Nauka, 1980), 96–103; David Miller,

"The *Velikie Minei Chetii* and the *Stepennaia kniga* of Metropolitan Makarii and the Origins of Russian National Consciousness," *Forschungen zur osteuropäishen Geschichte* 26 (1979): 263-382; David Goldfrank, "Nil Sorskii's Following among the Iosifo-Volokolamsk Elders," in *The New Muscovite Cultural History. A Collection in Honor of Daniel B. Rowland*, edited by Valerie Kivelson et al. (Bloomington IN: Slavica, 2009), 207-222; and Arkhimandrit Makarii (Veretennikov), *Moskovskii Mitropolit Makarii i ego vremia. Sbornik statei* (Moscow: Izdatel'tsvo Spaso-Preobrazhenskogo Valaamskogo monastyria, 1996), 132–133.

6   Zimin, *Krupnaia feodal'naia votchina*, 314–318.
7   A. I. Alekseev, *Sochineniia Iosifa Volotskogo v kontekste polemiki 1480-1540-kh gg.* (St. Petersburg: Rossiiskaia natsional'naia biblioteka, 2010), 16, 152n24 for 1439; *Iosif Volotskii* (Moscow: Molodaia Gvardiia, 2014), 25; but see below, note 21.
8   A. I. Pliguzov, "Letopischik Iosifa Sanina," in *Letopisi i khroniki. Sbornik statei.1984 g.*, edited by V.I. Buganov (Moscow: Nauka, 1984), 184.
9   Pliguzov, "Letopischik," 184–185; Zimin, *Krupnaia feodal'naia votchina*, 53.
10 Shablova, *Sinodik*, 46; Dergacheva, *Drevnerusskii sinodik*, 149.
11 *Akty feodal'nogo zemlevladeniia i khoziaistva XIV-XVI vekov*.3 vols., edited by L. V. Cherepnin and A. A. Zimin (Moscow: ANSSSR, 1951-1961), 2: 10–65; and Pliguzov, "Letopischik," 185.
12 Iu. V. Ratomskaia, "Stolpoobraznyi khram ikony Bogoroditsy Odigitrii Iosifo-Volotskogo monastyria 1510-x godov i pamiatniki arkhitektury vremeni pravleniia Vasiliia III," in *PIVO*, 2: 240–41.
13 S. Z. Chernov, "Nekropol' Iosifo-Volotskogo monastyria v svete arkheologicheskikh issledovanii 2001 g. Staryi i novyi predely," in *PIVO*, 1: 292.
14 See the diagrams and pictures in I. A. Shalina, "Zakhoronenie prepobodnogo Iosifa Volotskogo i simvolicheskaia traditsiia mesta pogrebenii russkikh chudotvortsev," in *PIVO*, 1: 135; Chernov, "Nekropol' … Staryi i novyi predely," in *PIVO*, 1: 305; idem, "Nekropol' Iosifo-Volotskogo monastyria v svete arkheologicheskikh issledovanii 2001 goda. Pogrebenii 'za tserkov'iu' i 'za starym pridelom'," in *PIVO*, 2: 393–395; L. A. Belova, "Trapeznaia tserkov' Bogoiavleniia," in *PIVO*, 1: 391–392; idem, "Tserkov' Odigitrii pod "kolokolami" Iosifo-Volotskogo monastyriam," in *PIVO*, 2: 119.
15 *Dukhovnye i dogorvornye gramoty velikikh i udel'nykh kniazei XIV-XVI vekov*, edited by L. V. Cherepnin and S. V. Bakhrushnin (Moscow: ANSSSR, 1950), 353; L. V. Cherepnin, *Russkie feodal'nye arkhivy XIV-XV vekov*, 2 vols. (Moscow: ANSSSR, 1948-1951), 1: 216–219—excellent timing in light of the vicious church and state politics of the time: see,

inter alia, Ia. S. Lur'e, *Ideologicheskaia bor'ba v russkoi publitsistike kontsa XV-nachala XVI veka* (Moscow-Leningrad: ANSSSR, 1960), 407–427.
16 *AfED*, 305–309, 320–373, 391–510.
17 *Akty istoricheskie sobrannye i izdannye Arkheografichskoi komisseiui*, 5 vols. (St. Petersburg, 1841-1842), 1, no. 288 (p. 524): trans., *VPW*, 183: not to be confused with Iosif's later testamentary Rule (our term, not his) for the monastery.
18 *PIV*, 187–221. Iosif's chief hagiographer subsequently relied on these letters but also papered over Iosif's truculence and what others saw as his unreasonable and offensive actions in this affair and depicted him as more conciliatory than his letters showed him to have been: *VMCh*, Sept., cols. 475–482: trans., *VPW*, 167–175.
19 A. G. Avdeev, "Epigraficheskie pamiatniki kontsa XV-XVI v. Vozmitskogo monastyria 'Prechistoi Bogoroditsi chestnago Eia Rozhdestva i sviatago prepodobnago ottsa nashego Kirila chiudotvortsa'," in *PIVO*, 1: 335n1. Aleksei Pil'emev's attempt to build up Vozmitskii with Fëdor's support and at Iosif's expense (enticing away monks with their icons, according to Iosif) included rededicating the cloister to Iosif's proclaimed model cenobiarch, Kirill Belozerskii, as well as to the Birth of the Theotokos. So it would seem that towards the very end of Nil Sorskii's life or soon afterwards, potential or real opponents of Iosif connected to Nil and to Kirillov Monastery (maybe German Podol'nyi and Vassian Patrikeev, but less likely the genuinely conciliatory Gurii Tushin), as well as opponents connected to Troitse–Sergiev Monastery and either Novgorod (Archbishop Serapion), or the city of Moscow and its Simonov Monastery (ex-Metropolitan Zosima), became involved in a web of intrigue associated with Pil'emev, Vozmitskii, and Fëdor. On the leading Kirillov elders connected with Nil, see *NSAW*, 37–44, 58–61.
20 *PIV*, 296–297. For suggested dates of *Prosvetitel'* and its component parts, see David Goldfrank, "The Anatomy of the Key Codices and the Ontogeny of *Prosvetitel'*," *Canadian-American Slavic Studies* 49, no. 2-3 (2015): 159-172; for the Rule, *MRIV*, 51–52. Note that what Soviet scholars called the "brief redaction of Iosif's Rule," and I have called his "Brief Rule" is much more homiletic than regulatory and never could function as a genuine monastic rule.
21 "… and he died on September 9 … . And all of his years of the life of Iosif to his dormition from his birth—70 and 6 years—and he died in the year 7024 [1 Sept 1515 to 3 August 1516], …and after he founded the Monastery of the Immaculate [*Prechistyia*, as substantive] 36 years:" Pliguzov, "Letopischik," 185. Since the monastery was founded on June 1489 ("6997"), reckoned as "36 years" before 9 Septem-

ber "7014," Iosif would have been born forty years earlier in "6967" (1438/1439) as well as 76 years before "7024 (1439/1440).
22 According to Alekseev (*Sochineniia Iosifa Volotskogo*, 42), codex Vol. 564, folia 79–80, notes that Daniil was hegumen for 11 years (i.e., 1511/1512-1522). This also contains Bishop Leonid's 1584/1585 list of eminent Pafnutiev and Iosifov monks in codex No. 92 (P. Stroev's original enumeration): *Akty istoricheskie*, 1, no. 216 (pp. 410–411). On the correlation of these Iosifov codex enumerations, see Zimin, "Iz istorii, sobraniia rukopisnykh knig Iosifo-Volokolamskogo monastyria" in *Zapiski otdela rukopisei GBL* 38 (1977): 24.
23 *PIV*, 101–116.
24 *PIV*, 144–145.
25 *PIV*, 143–152; see also David Goldfrank, "Litigious, Pedagogical, Redemptive, Lethal: Iosif Volotskii's Calculated Insults," *The Russian Review* 75, no. 1 (2016), 90-91.
26 *PIV*, 160–229, passim; and *AfED*, 305–309, 323–325, 419–438, 513–520; Goldfrank, "Insults," 91-92.
27 *VMCh*, Sept., cols. 552–559; and *DRIU*, 102–109: trans., *MRIV*, 230–238.
28 *VMCh*, Sept., cols. 586; and *DRIU*, 131: trans. *MRIV*, 269.
29 *VMCh*, Sept., col. 464: trans., *VPW*, 156.
30 *Drevnerusskie pateriki*, edited by L. A. Ol'shevskaia and S. N. Travnikov. (Moscow: Nauka, 1999), 213–222: trans., *VPW*, 194–201: see also 137–140.
31 *VPW*, 32–137.
32 *Zhitie prep. Iosifa Volokolamskogo sostavennoe neivestnym*, edited by S. A. Belokurov, in *ChOIDR*, 1903, 2: 1-46; see Ia. S. Lur'e, "Zhitie Iosifa Volotskogo," in *SKKDR*, 2.1: 273-276., and L. P. Dmitrievskii, "Lev Filolog," In *SKKDR*, 2.2: 3-6, representing, respectively, Lev Filolog and 'Anonymous' as the author: the issue is not yet resolved.
33 *VMCh*, Sept., col. 455: trans., *VPW*, 145.
34 Pliguzov, "Letopischik," 178, noting that the very entry of this "Little Annal" textually influenced the analogous one in the "Little Annal of Iosif;" see also G. V. Popov, "Drevneishie monastyrskie ikony. Dionisii ikonnik i prepodobnyi Iosif," in *PIVO*, 1: 182-186.
35 Pliguzov, "Letopischik," 185.
36 *KTsDRIVM*, No. 357 (pp. 369–370).
37 *KTsDRIVM*, 55–56.
38 *VMCh*, Sept, col. 457: trans., *VPW*, 146.
39 *VMCh*, Sept., cols. 502–520, 528–519, 530–542; *DRIU*, 61–75, 82–83, 84–94; and *PIV*, 297–306, 309–310, 311–317; trans., *MRIV*, 120–134, 142–143, 146–154, 169–188, 199–200, 203–216 (*slova* 1, 2, 4, 6 of Iosif's actual, testamentary Rule, and *slova* 1, 2, 3, 6, 8 of his programmatic

"Brief Rule").
40 *VMCh*, Sept., col. 474: trans., *VPW*, 165; there is the slightest possibility that this stems from a chronicle alteration, as in the mid-17th century Shumilovskii recension of the *Nikon Chronicle*, where both synods remain, but Vasilii opens the earlier one: *PSRL* 12: 225; on the dating, see Kloss, *Nikonovskii svod*, 20, 270.
41 *VMCh*, Sept., cols. 472–482: trans., *VPW*, 168–175.
42 "Zhitie ... neizvestnym," 30; cf. *NSAW*, 46–47.
43 *NSAW*, 44–46.
44 Goldfrank, "Nil Sorskii's Following," esp., 221–222.
45 B. M. Kloss, "Nil Sorskii i Nil Polev-'spisateli knig'," in *Drevnerusskoe iskusstvo: Rukopisnaia kniga*, 3 vols., edited by O. I. Podobedova et al. (Moscow: Nauka, 1972-1983), 2: 155; and G. M. Prokhorov, "Avtografy Nila Sorskogo" in *Pamiatniki kul'tury. Novye otkrytiia. 1974 g.* (1975): 52–53.
46 "Zhitie ... neizvestnym," 35–39.
47 Ostrowski has been promoting this argument in various writings since his dissertation appeared in 1977 — most recently in debunking the veracity of a source also regarding Iosif: Donald Ostrowski, "The *Letter concerning Enmities* as a Polemical Source for Monastic Relations of the Mid-Sixteenth Century," in *Essays in Russian Monasticism*, edited by David Goldfrank = *Russian History* 39, nos. 1-2 (2012): 77-105; see also, Pliguzov, *Polemika v russkoi tserkvi pervoi treti XVI stoletii* (Moscow: Indrik, 2002), 253–277, exposing pseudo-Vassian Patrikeev's "Dispute with Iosif," as well as Ostrowski's contribution to this volume.
48 Pliguzov, *Polemika*, 295–304.
49 G. M. Prokhorov, *Prepodonbyi Nil Sorskii i Innokentii Komel'skii. Sochineniia* (St. Petersburg: Oleg Abyshko, 2005), 27–28; N. V. Sinitsyna, "Spornye voprosy istorii nestiazhatel'stva ili o logike istoricheskogo dokazatel'stva," in *Spornye voprosy otechestvennoi istorii. XI-XVII vekov: tezisy dokladov i soobshcheniia Pervykh chtenii, posviashchennykh pamiati A. A. Zimina*, edited by Iu. N. Afanas'ev and A. P. Novosel'tsev (Moscow: Institut istorii SSSR, 1990), 250-254; R. G. Skrynnikov, *Gosudarstvo i tserkov' na Rusi XIV-XVI vv. Podvizhniki russkoi tserkvi* (Novosibirsk: "Nauka," Siberskoe otdelenie, 1991), 156–173; and A. I. Alekseev, *Pod znakom kontsa vremeni. Ocherki russkoi religioznosti kontsa XV-nachala XV vv.* (St. Petersburg: Aleteiia, 2002), 245–303, the only one of these who attempts a source by source analysis.
50 David Goldfrank, "Recentering Nil Sorskii: The Evidence from the Sources," *Russian Review* 66, no. 3 (July 2007): 359-376, and *NSAW*, 44–55; Pitirim (Nechaev), Mitropolit, "Estetika prepodobnogo Iosifa Volkotskogo," in *PIVO*, 1: 11-18. (Reprint from *Zhurnal Moskovs-*

koi patriarkhii, 1989, 1: 60-65); note also, T. L. Aleksandrova, and T.V. Suzdal'tseva, "Traditsii prepobodnogo Iosifa Volotskogo vo vzgliadakh Mitropolita Volokolamskogo i Iur'evskogo Pitirima, in *PIVO*, 1: 19-28.

51 E. V. Romanenko, *Nil Sorskii i traditsii russkogo monashestva* (Moscow: Pamiatniki istoricheskoi mysli, 2003), 124; and Fairy von Lilienfeld and E. M. Vereshchagin, *Zhizn', tserkov', nauka i vera: Professor Feri fon Lilienfel'd rasskazyvaet o sebe i svoem videnii pravoslaviia i liuteranstva. Besedy s prof. E. M. Vereshchaginy, sostoiavshiesia v Germanii v 1996-2002* (Moscow: Indrik, 2004), 162.

52 *AfED*, 310, 466, 475–476, et al.

53 *AfED*, 438–466; and Lur´e, *Ideologicheskaia bor'ba*, 102–111, 459–470.

54 A. P. Pliguzov, "'Kniga na eretikov Iosifa Volotskogo." *Istoriia i paleografiia* 1 (1993): 90-139.

55 Jana Howlett (Khoulett, Ia. R.), "Svidetel'stvo arkhiepiskopa Gennadiia o eresi," *Trudy otdela drevnerusskoi literatury* 46 (1993): 53-73.

56 Anatolii Grigorenko, *Dukhovnye iskaniia na Rusi kontsa XV v.* (St. Petersburg: "Eidos," 1999), 18–79.

57 N. N. Lisovoi, "Prepodobnyi Iosif Volotskii i ego vremia v istorii bogoslovskoi mysli," in *PIVO*, 1: 32.

58 Moshe Taube, "The Fifteenth-Century Ruthenian Translations from Hebrew and the Heresy of the Judaizers: Is There a Connection?" in *Speculum Slaviae Orientalis: Muscovy, Ruthenia and Lithuania in the Late Middle Ages*, edited by Vyacheslav V. Ivanov and Juia Verkholantsev, (Moscow: Novoe izdatel'stvo, 2005), 185-208; idem, "The 'Poem on the Soul' in the *Laodicean Epistle* and the Literature of the Judaizers," in *Kamen' Kraeug"l'n". Rhetoric of the Medieval Slavic World. Essays Presented to Edward L. Keenan on his Sixtieth Birthday by his Colleagues and Students*, edited by N. S. Kollmann et al. = *Harvard Ukrainian Studies* 19 (1995): 671-685.

59 Alekseev, *Sochineniia Iosifa Volotskogo*, 213–310; idem, *Religioznye dvizheniia na Rusi poslednei treti XIV-nachala XVI v.: strigolniki i zhidovstvuiushchie* (Moscow: Indrik, 2012), 306-378.

60 Alekseev, *Sochineniia Iosifa Volotskogo*, 109.

61 A. V. Shcherbakov, "Zarozhdenie ideologii iosiflianstva: Prepodobnyi Pafnutii Borovskii i sviatitel' Gennadii (Gonozov)," in *PIVO*, 2: 309, indicates that he continues, fearfully: "—this is a device which more than once would still be employed in our history by the enemies of Russia."

62 See, inter alia, David Goldfrank, "Adversus Haereticos Novgorodensos: Iosif Volotskii's Rhetorical Syllogisms," in *Dubitando: Studies in History and Culture in Honor of Donald Ostrowski*, edited by Brian J. Boeck,

Russell E. Martin, and Daniel Rowland (Bloomington, IN: Slavica), 254-274; Goldfrank's contribution to this volume; and his forthcoming "Iosif 'Ritorikos-Sillogistkos': k izucheniiu *Prosvetitelia*," within the projected third *PIVO volume*.

63 *AfED*, 468, 472; and *Prosvetitel'*, 31, 41.
64 *VMCh*, 505, 507, 509, 510, 514, 522, 529–530, 531, 537, 540–41, 545; *DRIU*, 63–64, 66–67, 70, 77, 82, 84, 89, 93, 96; and *PIV*, 298–299, 300, 302, 310–311, 312, 315, 316, 318–319: trans., *MRIV*, 122, 124–125, 126, 127, 137, 144–145, 146, 152–153, 158–159, 170–171, 175–176, 181, 191, 201–202, 203, 210, 212, 214, 221.
65 Thomas M. Seebohm, *Ratio und Charisma. Ansätze und Ausbildung eines philosophischen und wissenschaftlichen Weltverständnisses im Moskauer Russland* = Mainzer Philosophische Forschungen 17 (Bonn: Bouvier, 1977), 485.
66 *VMCh*, 562–563; *DRIU*, 111; and N. A. Kazakova, *Vassian Patrikeev i ego sochineniia* (Moscow-Leningrad: ANSSSR: 1960), 355–356: trans., *MRIV*, 241, 310.
67 *AfED*, 342; *Prosvetitel'*, 158-159, 166, 168, 274–275; Kazakova, *Vassian Patrikeev*, 357; *VMCh*, Sept., cols. 549, 559; and *DRIU*, 100, 108–109: trans., *MRIV*, 227, 237, 311.
68 *PIV*, 230–231; *Prosvetitel'*, 535–536.
69 *AfED*, 498–503; *Prosvetitel'*, 503–509.
70 *AfED*, 505–508; *Prosvetitel'*, 510–551.
71 *AfED*, 346; *Prosvetitel'*, 287.
72 *PIV*, 184; *Prosvetitel'*, 547.
73 Among them, M.A. D'iakonov; Ia. S. Lur'e, and Marc Szeftel.
74 Among them, Vladimir Val'denberg and Ihor Ševčenko. On the conflicting pre-1917 positions, see Marc Szeftel, "Joseph Volotsky's Political Ideas in a New Historical Perspective," *Jahrbücher für Geschichte Osteuropas*, New Series.13, no. 1 (April, 1965): 19–23.
75 Note "*Slovo 16*" of *Prosvetitel'* esp. pp. 541; also "*Slovo 11*" on the superior and "*Slovo 13*" (misnumbered as "14") on the council and council elders of Iosif's testamentary Rule: *VMCh*, Sept., cols. 563–566, 570–587; and *DRIU*, 112–115, 118–131: trans., *MRIV*, 242–246, 252–270.
76 For example, the *Nikon Chronicle*, *Stepennaia kniga*, and Metropolitan Makarii's and Archbishop Feodosii's epistles to Ivan IV: see, inter alia, Kloss, *Nikonovskii svod*; David Miller, "The *Velikie Minei Chetii* and the *Stepennaia kniga*;" and Zimin, *I. S. Peresvetov*, 80–81.
77 For example, the 1512 *Khronograf*: *PSRL* 22: 241, 260–261, 274–275, 302–303 (on the emperors Nero, Diocletian, Julian the Apostate, and Phocas). Cf. Nils Sorskii's autograph version of the "Life" of Theodore of Sykeon, who personally reproved Emperor Phocas for murdering

subjects, while six others of Nil's subjects risked their lives to oppose heresy: *NSAW*, 28–29, found in a codex Nil Polev donated to Iosifov Monastery.
78 *AfED*, 419–430, 471–472, 473, 488–498; *VMCh*, Sept., cols. 548–549; and *DRIU*, 99–109: trans., *MRIV*, 227–238.
79 *VMCh*, Sept., cols. 485–488: trans., *VPW*, 178–180. Keeping the chronological order of incidents as in the *Nikon Chronicle*, Savva might have been inspired by Iosif's known ties to Iurii and the latter's brother's Semën's fear for his life and then reconciliation with Vasilii III soon after the trial of Serapion: *PSRL* 13: 13; cf. *PIV*, 232–236.
80 Note Iosif's titles or introductions, and closes to his major works and many of his discourses: *AfED*, 474–477, 483–486; *VMCh.*, Sept., cols. 499, 501–502, 546, 605, 615; and *DRIU*, 57, 59–60, 97–98, 147, 154–155: trans., *MRIV*, 163, 166–167, 233–234, 295, 307–308. On the primacy of these writings for Iosif, see Seebohm, *Ratio und Charisma*, 485.
81 See below, the contribution of Kevin Kain to this volume. One can add Metropolitan Ignatii Korsakov of Siberia and Tobolsk to the Nikonians who utilized Iosif's writings: V. M. Kirillin, "Literaturnoe nasledie prepobodnogo Iosifa Volotskogo," in *PIVO*, 1: 50; see also S. K. Sevast'ianova, "Traditsii isikhastskoi literatury v monastyrskoi ustava prepodobnogo Iosifa Volotskogo i ikh razvitie v trudakh Patriarkha Nikona," in *PIVO*, 1: 87-100.
82 E. V. Emchenko, *Stoglav. Issledovanie i tekst* (Moscow: Indrik, 2000), 328–338, 339–343, 381–385 (maybe); and Zimin, *I. S. Peresvetov*, 178, and note 282.
83 Pliguzov, *Polemika*, 330–384, for a total rejection of authenticity of Iosif's authorship of the (putative) "Synodal Response of 1503" on monastic lands. For a counter-argument, which this author rejects, see Alekseev, *Pod znakom*, 249–255; and for the document itself, *PIV*, 293–294, 323–329.
84 Hugh Olmsted, "Modeling the Genealogy of Maksim Grek's Collection Types. The 'Plectogram' as Visual Aid in Reconstruction," in *Medieval Russian Culture*, 2 vols., edited by Michael Flier et al. (Berkeley-Los Angeles: University of California Press, 1984-1994), 2: 107-131.
85 David Goldfrank, "Sisterhood Just Might Be Powerful: The Testament-Rule of Elena Devochkina," in *A Festchrift for Richard Hellie*, Part 1, edited by Lawrence L. Langer and Peter B. Brown = *Russian History* 34, nos. 1-4 (2007): 189-205.
86 See below, Kevin Kain's contribution to this volume.
87 *NSAW*, 104; David Goldfrank, "Nil's and Iosif's Rhetoric of *Starchestvo*," in *Essays in Russian Monasticism*, 75-76.
88 Lur'e, *Ideologicheskaia bor'ba*, 10–21.
89 See, inter alia, Ostrowski, "The *Letter concerning Enmities*," 78n1.

90 *Pravila blagoustroistva monastyrskoi zhiznii*, edited by Sviateishii Sinod (Kazan: 2010); Ieromonakh Serafim, *Muzhskoi obshchezhitel'nyi ustav* (Nizhnii Novgorod: 1910); idem, *Zhenskie monastyrskie ustavy*, vol. 3 (Kungur: 1910); on the direct Studite influence on Iosif's Rule, see *MRIV*, 265, 295–296.

91 Zimin, "Iz istorii," 15–18; see Arkhimandrit Iosif, *Opis' rukopisei perenesennykh iz biblioteki Iosifova monastryia v biblioteku Moskovskoi dukhovnoi akademii.* Moscow, 1882. = *ChOIDR*, 1882, 3; P. Stroev, *Opisanie rukopisei monastyrei Volokolamskogo, Novyi Ierusalim, Savvina Storozhevskogo, i Pafnutieva Borovskogo* (St. Petersburg, 1891).

92 *KnTsDRIVM*; Zimin gives both a concordance of Stroev's enumeration with the State Library (Volokolamsk) and Historical Museum (Eparchial) collections and listing of the other manuscripts, some of which were sent elsewhere earlier or lost during World War II: "Iz istorii," 18–28. See also V. V. Kashirina, "K istorii biblioteki Iosifo-Volokolamskogo monastyria, in *PIVO*, 2: 340-362.

93 Ivan Kologrivov, *Essai sur la sainteté en Russie* (Bruges: Ch. Beyaert, 1953), 214–243; George Fedotov *The Russian Religious Mind*, 2 vols. (Cambridge, Mass: Harvard University Press: 1946-1966), 2: 285–315.

94 Ia. S. Lur'e, Vassian Sanin, " in *SKKDR*. 2: 125-126.

95 For example, B. A. Rybakov, "Rybakov, B.A. "Voinstvuiushchie tserkovniki XVI v.," *Antireligioznik*, 3-4 (1934): 21-31, 31-40, who is not reliable here.

96 I. U. Budovnits, *Monastyri na Rusi i bor'ba s nimi krestian v XIV-XVI vv.* (Moscow: Nauka, 1966), 226–258.

97 Lur'e in *AfED, PIV*, and *Ideologicheskaia bor'ba*; and Zimin in *Krupnaia feodal'naia votchina*.

98 Seebohm, *Ratio und Charisma*, 244–249 et al., vastly surpassing in analytical depth the critically sympathetic, quite insightful Thomas Špidlik, S.J., *Joseph de Volokolamsk, Un chapitre de la spiritualité russe* = Orientala Christiana Analecta 146 (Rome: Pont. Institutum Orientalium Studiorum, 1956).

99 Kloss, "Nil Sorskii i Nil Polev;" and Prokhorov, "Avtografy."

100 Lilienfeld and Vereshchangin, *Zhizn', tserkov', nauka i vera*, 161.

101 Sergii, Igumen, "O vybore posviashcheniia," 173; the exterior floor plan is about 16.83m x 15.17m: see the diagram in Chernov, "Nekropol' ... Staryi i novyi predely," 305.

102 Ratomskaia, "Stolpoobraznyi khram," 255–257. The exterior of the octagonal is about 5.35m across and 2.3m per side: see diagram in Belova, "Tserkov' Odigitrii," 119.

103 Ratomskaia, "Stolpoobraznyi khram," 257–259.

104 *Istoriia russkogo iskusstva*, edited by I. E. Grabar, 13 Vols. (Moscow:

ANSSSR, 1953-1964), 3: 362, 365, 369. The interior dimensions of the refectory were about 22m x 20m: see the diagram in Belova, "Trapeznaia," 391.
105 V. V. Kashirina, "Osobennosti sviazi v litsevom shit'e Anny Volotskoi," in *PIVO*, 2: 191-205.
106 M. S. Serebriankova, "O nekotorykh osobennostiakh posviashcheniia tserkovnykh prestolov Drevnei Rusi IX–serediny XVI vekov (po letopisnym istochnikam)," in *PIVO*, 1: 155. This characterization of Theophany, she claims, holds for other aspects of Christ and also for the Trinity. She does not discuss the Hodigitria, with its obvious path-directing symbolism, but it is interesting that the presumed architectural model was dedicated to John Climacus, whose *Ladder of Divine Ascent* served as the most popular spiritual handbook and as a path-indicator to perfect prayer and to heaven for Russia's ascetics.
107 Sergii (Voronkov), Igumen, "O vybore posviashcheniia glavnogo monastyrskogo khrama Iosifo-Volotskogo monastyria," in *PIVO* 1: 167: see *AfED*, 337; and *Prosvetitel'*, 259.
108 From viewer's left to right: St, Peter, Archangel Michael, the Theotokos, Jesus, John the Forerunner/Baptist, Archangel Gabriel, and St. Paul.
109 See *AfED*, 356; *Prosvetitel'*, 319–320.
110 Sergii, Arkhimandrit, "Sobranie ikon Uspenskoi tserkvi XV veka kak vyrazhenie bogosloviia prepodobnogo Iosifa," in *PIVO*, 2: 219–230.
111 *Prosvetitel'*, 439; cf. Eph 4:11-12 (the words from Scripture in the text to this note in italics).
112 L. P. Medvedeva, "Prepodobnyi Iosif Volotskii i 'inzhenernoe myshlenie': K voprosu o perevodakh," in *PIVO*, 2: 66; for the translation, http://www.wco.ru/biblio/books/iosifv1/Main.htm (accessed 4 February, 2015).
113 *PIVO*: so far in this essay eighteen *PIVO* contributions by fifteen scholars have been cited, and five more follow.
114 T. V. Suzdal'tseva, "Drevnerusskie inocheskie ustavy i ikh mesto v russkoi monasheskoi traditsii," in *PIVO*, 140–144. The specific terms, as used in the Eastern Church, refer chiefly to the liturgical order, not to the disciplinary aspects of a monastic rule, which also may be called *ustav* or *tipik*. See, for example, Spock, "Regarding the Good Order of the Monastery: The Tipik Solovetskago and the Integration of the Spiritual with the Temporal in the Early 17th Century," in *Rude and Barbarous Kingdom Revisited: Essays in Russian history and Culture in Honor of Robert O. Crummey*, edited by Chester S. L. Dunning, Russell E. Martin and Daniel Rowland, (Bloomington, IN: Slavica, 2008), 251-267.

115 L. A. Ol'shevskaia, "Vassian Koshka – redactor Volokolamskogo paterika," in *PIVO*, 2: 68-73.
116 O. V. Chevela, Allegoricheskaia i tipologicheskaia ekzegeza v tvoreniiakh prepobodnogo Iosifa Volotskogo ee otnoshenie k vizantiiskoi traditsii," in *PIVO*, 2: 80-85.
117 Lipakov, "Izuchenie prepodobnogo Iosifa Volkotskogo v Kazanskoi dukhovnoi akademii," in *PIVO*, 2: 44-46.
118 Ágnes Kriza, "Vizantiiskie istochniki bogosloviia ikony v 'Poslanii ikonopistsu'," *Studia Slavica Hungarica* 54.1, 2 (2009): 161-87, 407-27; "Isikhazm i ikonopochitanie. Analogicheskaia funktsiia v bogoslovskikh trudakh Moskovskoi Rusi i Kievskoi mitropolii v XV-XVI vv.," *Pravoslavie Ukrainy i Moskovskoi Rusi v XV-XVII vekakh: obshchee i razlichnoe*, edited by M. V. Dmitriev (Moscow: Indrik, 2012), 14-34; "Slavonic Translations of Greek Iconophile Texts: the Problem of Reception of Byzantine Theology in Medieval Rus'," in *Fontes. Studies Presented to Róbert Sikon on the Occasion of his 75th Birthday*, edited by Monika Pesthy-Simon (Budapest: Corvina, 2014), 134-143.
119 V. N. Zviagin, M.E. Berezovskii, and M.A. Grigor'eva, "Identifikatsiia moshchei prepodobnogo Iosifa Volotskogo" (in Table of Contents: "O rezul'tatakh mediko-kriminalisticheskogo issledovaniia po identifikatsii chestnykh ostankov prepobodnogo Iosifa Volotskogo"), in *PIVO*, 1: 114-12.

PART I

Antecedents

Antecedents: Introduction

Christopher D.L. Johnson

One might assume that the following four chapters on late antique Eastern Christianity simply serve as a chronological prelude to the more central period commemorated by the title of this book: the medieval period in which Iosif Volotskii lived. While this is true in an obvious sense, the degree of intellectual overlap between these vastly removed periods and contexts is also quite striking. Not only do the events and personages covered in this section 'go before' Iosif chronologically, but they set the conceptual stage and provide the props for him: many of the assumptions, categories, and rhetorical strategies Iosif employs were shaped during this period, which makes it essential to understand Iosif's antecedents in order to understand Iosif himself. Among the themes that resonate down from this early period to Iosif's are 1) the selective and creative use (or abuse) of the past to address changing social and intellectual conditions, 2) the long-range power of language to shape the perceptions of a text's contemporary and future audiences especially when coupled with a tendency toward the extremes of panegyric and polemic, and 3) the relationship between civil and religious authorities and their views on the importance of ecclesiastical orthodoxy or ecclesiastical unity.

As Goldfrank pointed out in the previous chapter, Iosif was a "masterful pedagogue-polemicist" whose writings often had an "anti-heretical emphasis" that divided the world into the right-believing Orthodox and those who were led by Satan. There was little middle ground for him between these two extremes. These two options called for the use of either panegyric or polemic, the latter of which included using "every trick in the book to expose such dissidents" and establish correct belief as authoritative. Iosif employs the power of rhetorical language not only to determine contemporary public opinion on a given issue but also to shape the perception of all future readers to his side. One can see Iosif's use of guilt by association in labeling some of his critics 'Judaizers', though it seem highly questionable to describe their actual position with this term. The authority of the past was applied to force his critics into the role previously occupied by earlier heretics. Here "there is nothing new under the sun" (Eccl 1:9), only new versions of primordial truth and falsehood. This binary division of the world that warranted such hostile denunciation of dissenters also justified the authority of civil leaders in Iosif's eyes: the litmus test for divinely-guided civil leaders was their faithfulness to right belief. A tsar had the 'mandate of heaven' as long as he continued to be a champion for orthodox Christian belief, which also involved carefully monitoring and swiftly stamping out heresy within his sphere of influence. He "must remain steadfast in the faith and vigilant against heresy, lest the realm perish as other Orthodox realms have fallen." Rome and Constantinople might have served as instructive examples for Iosif with his modified Deuteronomistic view of history: when orthodoxy fell, the empire fell. Civil unity and religious orthodoxy were closely linked. These three themes of the power of the past, the power of language, and the power of unity and orthodoxy can be found throughout the following four chapters to varying degrees.

Commencing the focus on early Christian antecedents to Iosif, Fr. Joshua Lollar's chapter "The World as Cenobium" marshals patristic evidence to show a conception of the contemplation of nature in the Greek Fathers that conflicts with recent criticisms that Christian theology is responsible for shaping views that have led to the destruction of the environment. His chapter is an example of how the past can be successfully brought to bear on present issues, in this case the use of quotations from early Eastern Christian authors to complicate a sweeping modern narrative about Christianity as a whole. In other words, Lollar gives us an instructive counter-example to the previous two chapters of how the past can be used in innovative ways while being intellectually honest and faithful to tradition. Some recent authors have argued that the anthropology and doctrine of creation in Christianity have disenchanted the natural world of sacred meaning, alienated humanity from nature, given rise to a mechanistic view of nature, and made nature simply material to be exploited for human needs. Rather than rejecting that there is any truth at all to this critique, Lollar goes back to early Eastern Christian sources to show that they present a Christianity that is "deeply at home in, and not at war with, its environment" which offers an "aesthetic, sacramental, personal, nondualistic, integrated, nonexploitative, and reverent orientation to the natural world." The chapter surveys the writings of many patristic authors, but especially Clement, Origen, Gregory of Nazianzus, Gregory of Nyssa, Basil of Caesarea, Evagrius, Pseudo-Dionysius, Maximus, and even considers the contribution of the current Ecumenical Patriarch, His All-Holiness Bartholomew of Constantinople. Though each author has his own perspective, the many citations add up to show that "the whole of the Christian spiritual project can be, and was, described in terms of contemplating nature," with the natural world not only as 'scripture,' but as sacrament such that contemplation of the natural world as revelation of the presence of God is linked to the reception of God in the Eucharist. In this sacramental view, ritual blessings of the natural world "do not, in this view, make things into something they were not already as though sanctifying what was originally profane, but rather articulates what things are in themselves." The notion that in general Greek patristic authors see "the world as 'habitation,' as 'home,' as *oikoumenê*, rather than as object or as resource" and as cenobium or place of common life comes across strongly in Lollar's chapter.

Our next three chapters leave the realm of community and contemplation and critically analyze the rhetorical and sometimes polemical use of texts to further particular early Christian theological agendas. Edward Mason goes back into the history of Christological debates to the failed attempts of Emperor Constantius II to subdue controversy about the exact relationship of the nature of Christ as Son of God with the divine nature of God the Father. In Chapter II, Mason shows that, while Constantius has often been denigrated as a betrayer of orthodoxy and contrasted with his father Constantine I, his council at Sirmium actually followed many of the precedents set by his father at Nicea. At Sirmium, it was proposed that divisive Christological terms such as *homoousios* ('of the same nature') should be abandoned from theological discussion, but wording from the council also promoted an "undeniably subordinationist," though not explicitly Arian, doctrine of Christ in relation to the Father. Yet, Mason argues that theological formulation was not Constantius's primary aim. By comparing Nicea and Sirmium, Mason argues that Constantius was more concerned with the unity of the church than the subtleties of Christ's nature just as his father had been when he called the *homoousios* controversy "exceedingly trivial." Despite this, due to the rhetoric and polemic that followed the council, Constantius has been seen by posterity as disregarding the standard set by his father rather than following it. Both Athanasius and Hilary of Portiers shaped later readers' perceptions of Nicea and Sirmium by downplaying Constantine's involvement in Nicea when comparing it to Constantius at Sirmium so that the prior was viewed as essentially theological and the latter as an imperial over-reach. In linking Constantius to Arianism, we again see the rhetorical use of the past to easily categorize people and ideas based on previous types but also the conflict between the imperial drive to unity and the clerical drive to orthodoxy. For Constantius, as for Constantine, unity was prioritized over doctrine, which primarily operated in the service of ecclesiastical and civil unity. We may want to neatly differentiate between the religious and political motivations behind the council but Mason insists that these two aspects were viewed as "two side of the same imperial coin." Because of this, no imperial motive is likely to be exclusively religious in our terms, but neither can one "reduce every action of the emperor into a mere act of statesmanship" or dismiss their piety or sincerity just because there are also other imperial aims at work. As with Iosif Volotskii over eleven centuries later, in the era of Constantine and Constantius "[i]t was divine favor that legitimated the ruler and emperor" and "it was devout Christian religious observance in which the prosperity of the empire rested." There was a practical need to determine proper belief and observance and deal with heretical ideas and those who promoted them. Doctrine served ecclesiastical unity, which ensured security in the empire, both physical and spiritual.

Joshua Powell's Chapter 3 continues the study of how imperial politics often affected the reception and spread of ideas, this time during the time of Justinian in the sixth century. Powell attempts to explain Justinian's dramatic reversal of opinion regarding the doctrine of theopaschism promoted by a group of monks from Scythia Minor. These monks were attempting to appease both miaphysite and dyophysite parties after the council of Chalcedon by proposing the simple confession that "one of the Trinity suffered." This was meant to both affirm the Chalcedonian position that Christ had two natures and appease the miaphysites who focused on the unity of the person of Christ and worried that Chalcedonian definition was excessively 'Nestorian'. As the monks left Constantinople for Rome, Justinian, who was the likely heir-apparent at the time, initially sent a letter harshly denouncing their ideas and recommending their immediate expulsion from Rome but followed this only weeks later with a plea to Pope Hormisdas to welcome them and treat them honorably, urging that the peace of the church was at stake. Powell argues that this was not a result of the emperor's capriciousness, as some have suggested, but an effect the sources of information available to him regarding the band of monks. Rome had earlier sent a delegation to Constantinople that included the deacon Dioscorus who authored many of the letters sent to Rome about the Scythian monks. Dioscorus seems to have used his position as a middleman between Rome and Constantinople to shape the reaction to the monks in Rome. He thought the Christological formulation of Chalcedon was sufficient and that this novel formula would only cause more dissension and scandal to "put the unity of the church at risk." The task of his delegation to ensure the upholding of Chalcedon in the East may have also been seen as jeopardized by the innovation. Powell draws the reader's attention to the overlooked authority of those such as Dioscorus who are strategically positioned as an essential link between two centers of power; his authority in shaping perception and opinion is less from his charisma or ecclesiastical rank but due to his position as gate-keeper between Rome and Constantinople. This chapter, along with the other three, shows that all authors are to some degree gate-keepers that selectively filter the past and present for readers to shape their perceptions and reactions. They also show us how the authority of the past is often used to reform the present through the use of rhetoric to argue for different conceptions of right-belief, highlighting the inevitable challenge of applying the past to changing circumstances in a way that does not warp either past or present beyond recognition.

Finally, in "Pious Forgeries," Ryan W. Strickler focuses on the text *Disputatio cum Pyrrho* to show how disputants in seventh century Christological controversies over the number of operations and wills of Jesus Christ were able to discredit opponents by accusations of using forgeries while relying on forgeries themselves. Both sides in the debates shared a sense of the authority of the past and a fidelity to it rather than to the creativity of their argument. Yet despite their protests and efforts to the contrary, both sides of the argument couldn't help but be innovative since these topics were largely new conceptual territory for Christology. The tension between new issues and old sources of authority often led to creative interpretations over the history of theology but, occasionally, as in this case, it seems to have led to the use of 'pious forgery' where a venerable author's name was attached to a document that more directly addressed the topic at hand. Just as Iosif's use of the negatively-connoted term 'Judaizer' could tarnish the reputations of his critics by association, the name of a 'select father' such as Clement or Athanasius could give a disputant a critical edge in a Christological debate when applied to one's own position. Though it may strike modern readers as anachronistic, opponents during these debates were seen as intellectual descendants of earlier heresies such as Apollinarianism and Arianism. Strickler refers to the difficulty of trying to apply old texts to new issues in the light of patristic proof texts, but the same can be said of biblical hermeneutics and of textual interpretation in general. While closely focused on late antique Christological debates, Strickler's chapter highlights the perennial problem of trying to force writings from the past into current debates and the temptation to force a fit by any means necessary to make one's point, even if this involves misattribution of texts.

1. The World as Cenobium
Greek Patristic Foundations of the Contemplation of Nature in Eastern Christianity

Rev. Dr. Joshua Lollar

7 – Coptic Icon of Macarius the Great in front of his monastery at Wadi al-Natrun (Scetis)

I. Iosif Volotskii and the Environment of Spiritual Life

The Russian Orthodox Church remembers St. Iosif Volotskii as a great monastic organizer and reformer, as the most forceful advocate of large-scale monastic possession, and as a staunch opponent of heresy in his day.[1] He sought to found monasticism on the patristic heritage of the Orthodox Church and so provide for the spiritual enlightenment of his monks. As this volume is dedicated to the 500th anniversary of Iosif's repose, I would like to place this essay on the Greek patristic foundations of the contemplation of nature in Eastern Orthodoxy under his patronage. Iosif is not to be found amongst the typical patrons of Orthodox ecology,[2] and one might indeed expect his non-possessing contemporary Nil Sorskii and his woodland retreat to be a more natural witness to the Orthodox consciousness of the natural world than Iosif in his well-endowed monastery at Volokolamsk. It is, however, precisely Iosif's advocacy of monastic possession, and the activities that attended it—elaborate and well-organized liturgical practice in particular— that provide a most interesting frame for the consideration of nature, conceived as "environment," that which surrounds us, but also as "habitation," a place we precisely *have* as a dwelling, in Eastern Christianity. As Iosif's English-language translator puts it, "Iosif understood salvation in this world and the next as a state of serving God in a pleasing environment."[3] Now, "environment" here is not the Environment of modern environmentalism but rather the world of the monastery's labor, prayer, and asceticism and the objects that went along with them, and so I have no intention of making Iosif into an "environmentalist" in our sense of the term, but his attention to the importance of his surroundings, to what formed the world of his monastic community, does make him an environmentalist in the fundamental sense of the term.

Iosif understood that the environment of spiritual life, the collection of external experiences of his monks and their organizing rationale, was of crucial importance to their progress. Referring to liturgical observance, he writes in the *Rule*, "Let us be concerned first over physical elegance and good order and then over internal observance" (1.12), and then, referring to St. John Chrysostom, he writes, "Let us be concerned first for the good order of sensations and then for the good posture of the inner thoughts" (1.13). The experience of beautiful and well-ordered phenomena, both within church and without, was for Iosif the guiding principle of the life of the monastery. Moreover, its possessions, while serving to support the liturgical commemorations requested by the people and to provide resources for those in need, also had as a fundamental function the provision of an environment in which the monks could cultivate the fundamental monastic virtues of non-acquisitiveness and Christ-like poverty: "It is not easy for those who are not in a cenobium, where we have security regarding our most basic needs, to exercise this virtue" (3.16). Iosif's understanding of spiritual advancement is thus thoroughly environmental; balance, harmony, and virtue flow from a well-ordered, disciplined, and splendid surrounding into the inner life of the monk. It is by "possessing" communally that the monk learns to "have" nothing (2 Cor. 6:10). In honor of St. Iosif Volotskii, then, I use the well-ordered cenobium—a place of "common life"—as a guiding image for an Eastern Christian contemplation of the environment, of what surrounds us, as we see it in some foundational texts of the patristic era.

II. Christianity's Problem with Nature

It has become something of a pious obligation for anyone who would write about Christianity and ecology to cite Lynn White's well-known essay on "The Historical Roots of Our Ecological Crisis," published in the journal *Science* in 1967. White indicts the Christian tradition as primarily responsible for framing an abusive relationship between humanity and nature in which man stands transcendent over a disenchanted natural world, which is there simply to submit to human mastery and exploitation.[4] This, for White, is what enabled the development of humanity's aggressive and technologically enhanced posture toward nature, whose consequences were already bleak when he wrote in the late 1960s and are all the more so now. Years later, Pierre Hadot summed up the sentiment with concision: "It is correct to say that Christianity contributed to the development of the mechanistic representation of Nature, and to the desacralization of Nature. ... From a Christian creationist perspective, Nature is an object fashioned by an artisan who is distinct from her and transcends her. As God's work, she is no longer divine. There is no longer a divine presence in Nature."[5] Small wonder, then, that the West, with this as its spiritual inheritance, should lead human civilization into the plundering of the abandoned temple that is the world. The particular form of Christian anthropocentrism, which makes human salvation of central, if not exclusive, importance in the world-process is, on this reading, primarily responsible for the suffering of the rest of the nonhuman world (to say nothing of its effect *also* on humankind), and must be replaced, according to some, by a "biocentric or geocentric norm."[6]

However, White excepts the Eastern Orthodox churches from this assessment and, in what turns out to be something of a compliment within the context of his essay, notes that the Greek Christian world shows little evidence of any technological advancement after the seventh century. He attributes this, and the sharp contrast in technological advancement with the Latin West, to "a difference in the tonality of piety and thought": where Latin theology viewed salvation primarily in moral terms, the Greeks viewed it in terms of the acquisition of illumined knowledge. "The Greek saint contemplates," he says, "the Western saint acts." Moreover, according to White, for Eastern Christianity, nature symbolically reveals God; the view of nature is "essentially artistic rather than scientific."[7] As such, it is no wonder that the menace of modern technology, which is an offspring of Christianity, was born in the West and not in the East.

It is not my concern to analyze this tidy distinction between the so-called practical West and contemplative East; in fact, Lynn White himself advocated a return to Francis of Assisi, a rather prominent Western saint, as the patron saint of ecology. Moreover, the relationship between praxis, supposedly the West's forte, and contemplation lies at the heart of Eastern Orthodox spirituality from the early fathers to the present, so the contrast requires considerable nuance, if not outright rejection. Indeed, there is much to be said from a geopolitical point of view to help explain hindrances in Byzantine technical development. However, I do want to take up the question of Eastern Orthodox approaches to the natural world, and I use White's observation as an entryway to the topic because the positive aspect of White's intuition, that Eastern Christianity has shown itself to be deeply at home in, and not at war with, its environment is born out by the sources. There are many who work in the intersection of religion and ecology who see Eastern Christian approaches to nature as being distinctively hopeful, and there are indeed many Orthodox voices who are intent upon distancing the Eastern Christian tradition from what they acknowledge to be Western Christian culpability for the loss of the sense of the sacred—both in terms of piety and in metaphysics—in the natural world.[8] What these voices want to say is that the Orthodox tradition offers an aesthetic, sacramental, personal, non-dualistic, integrated, non-exploitative, and reverent orientation to the natural world, a perspective that is summed up nicely in the words of a 20th-century Athonite monk, Elder Paisios:

> Look at what God has created with just one word! What harmony, what variety! Wherever one turns, one sees the wisdom and the grandeur of God. Look at the celestial lights, the stars; with what simplicity His divine hand has scattered them in the sky, without using a plumb line and level! They give such comfort to people, whereas man-made lights tire the eyes even though they are placed in regular distances. You see, trees planted by man in a forest resemble an army battalion, whereas natural forests, made of trees of different colors and sizes, comfort the human eye. Natural forests are so peaceful and restful! Some trees are small and others are big, and each one has its own colour. One of God's small wild flowers has more grace than a pile of fake paper flowers.[9]

The elder here echoes a common theme of Christian thought, that the wisdom of God is inscribed within the created order, that contemplating the creature is to contemplate the glory of the Creator. But Paisios is also attentive to the dynamics of our experience of our surroundings: naturally growing forest versus trees planned and planted by human beings, natural light versus artificial lights, wild versus artificial flowers. The world as it is in itself, nature as it arises from itself, is most salutary and pleasant, whereas the artificial works against the faculties of sense. Moreover, for the elder, God creates without tools; his mode of creating is non-mechanistic and even without the kind of planning and deliberation we typically associate with production.[10]

In response to Hadot, we might say with Elder Paisios that, from the Eastern Christian point of view, there is no interval between nature and art in God's fashioning of the world. The sublimity of the world just is the fact that its artifactuality is nature itself, and as such there is a fundamental disanalogy between human and divine artistry: human fashioning is opposed, or perhaps in its better moments supplemental to, nature, whereas divine "fashioning" just is nature itself. As John of Scythopolis has it in his scholia on

Dionysius the Areopagite's *Divine Names*, "as an established state (*kath' exin*), nature is divine art (*technê*) coming into being."[11] At its best moment, human artifice follows Hamlet's instruction and holds "the mirror up to nature," catching its light in the clarity of its own surface. The cenobium, then, as a constructed and "artificial" world, is a sort of mirror, a reflection of the natural world and of the society that inhabits it.

In what follows I would like to present some of the roots of this approach to the question of nature in the Greek fathers. Greek philosophy as such begins with the question of nature, with the attempt to elaborate the coherence of the phenomenal world as it arises before us—what Socrates called *peri physeôs istoria* ('an account of nature').[12] The Greek fathers of the church inherited this movement in the form of *theôria physikê*, "the contemplation of nature" or "natural philosophy," which, along with ethical philosophy and mystical theology, provided ancient Christians a spiritual itinerary of practical and contemplative life. Although the Greek fathers do not figure prominently in the history of natural science and are not often considered to be leading players in the history of natural philosophy—as one mid-20th-century commentator puts it, "with edification always in view, [the fathers of the church] produce moralized and sometimes illustrated animal stories which exhibit no intelligent observation and are often childish to the verge of imbecility"[13]—many of them were actually quite attentive to the themes of natural contemplation in ways that were of the utmost significance for their various understandings of spiritual life. As I shall show in this brief elaboration of Greek patristic views of the cosmos, the whole of the Christian spiritual project can be, and was, described in terms of contemplating nature.[14]

III. The Contemplation of Nature in the Greek Fathers of the Church

Christ and Nature

The monastic life has been presented by the Eastern Christian tradition as a unique way of living in Christ, or of "putting on Christ." Evagrius of Pontus, the great fourth-century monastic philosopher, found this symbolically inscribed in the very habit of the monk. "The hood," he writes, "is a symbol of our Savior God, which shelters their governing faculty (*hegemonikon* = the mind) and surrounds their youthfulness in Christ with warmth..." and "the scapular that is wrapped around their shoulders in the form of a cross is the symbol of faith in Christ."[15] In our endeavor to contemplate the natural world as cenobium, as monastic enclosure and habitation of spiritual life, it is essential that we begin with the relationship between Christ and nature in the Greek fathers, for reflection upon Christ is the fundamental way in which they worked out their natural philosophies.

For Clement of Alexandria (died c. 215), one of the principal figures in the early formation of Eastern Christian approaches to the contemplation of nature, Christ is the high priest of the natural world, who has clothed himself with the universe, symbolized by the vestments of the Levitical priest, which "prophesy the incarnation by which [the Word] was seen to be in closer proximity to the world."[16] The stones on the priestly garment represent the planets, and its bells the days of the year. It is Christ who teaches divine providence—a standard topic of ancient natural philosophy—as well as the nature of the elements:

> The teaching that is consistent with Christ considers the Fashioner to be God, recognizes providence in particular events, knows that the nature of the elements is changeable and generated, and teaches the way of life that is directed to the power that assimilates us to God and teaches us to prefer the economy as the guiding principle of all learning.[17]

Clement contemplates Christ in relation to basic topics of natural philosophy—the concept of divine providence and the nature of the elements—and links them to the basic understanding of philosophy as a way of life which, for the Christian, is directed toward assimilation to God.

For Origen, Clement's successor in Alexandria, the center of the contemplation of nature is to be found in its relationship to the other branches of spiritual or philosophical life—praxis or ethics and theology. King Solomon is, for Origen, the great scriptural philosopher, who wrote his Proverbs as a guide to the practical life of virtue, Ecclesiastes as a philosophy of nature, and the Song of Songs as the summit of mystical theology or vision, whose consummation is union with the Word of God:[18]

> Eager longing for the reality of things is natural to us and implanted in our souls... The mind burns with unspeakable longing to learn the design of those things which we perceive to have been made by God... Our mind cherishes a natural and appropriate longing to know God's truth and to learn the causes of things.[19]

The natural philosophy of Solomon's Ecclesiastes has as its aim the directing of this natural desire toward the eternal and unchanging realities of the divine by teaching it not to become fixated upon the changing appearances of the natural world, though it is precisely desire to understand the world that motivates the transcendent movement toward God.

Despite the vanity of the world—"vanity of vanities, saith the preacher"—it is bound to the reality of Christ for Origen. He writes in his homilies *in Genesim*,

> "In the beginning God made heaven and earth"[Gen. 1:1]. What is the beginning of all things if not our Lord and "Savior of all"[1 Tim. 4:10], Jesus Christ, "the firstborn of all creation"[Col. 1:15]? For it is in this beginning, that is, in his Word, that "God made heaven and earth," just as the Evangelist John has also said at the beginning of his Gospel: "In the beginning was the Word, and the Word was with God and the Word was God. He was in the beginning with God. All things were made through him and nothing was made without him"[John 1:1–3].[20]

The point for Origen here, as he goes on to say, is not the location in time of the creation of the world, but rather the fact that the heavens and the earth exist within the salvation of God, within God the Savior himself, so all contemplation of nature is the contemplation, at the same moment, of nature and of nature's ultimate

Source, which transcends it, so that the contemplation of nature as a spiritual exercise draws the one contemplating ever upward.

Finally, we see in Evagrius a continuation of the basic insights of Clement and Origen. It is in Evagrius that the basic unity of the three phases of spiritual development—that is, ethical, natural, and theological philosophy, which are "the teaching of Christ our Savior"[21]—were coherently systematized and given a definitive articulation. For Evagrius, love, the goal of the ascetical life, is "the doorway" to the knowledge of nature, which is, in turn, followed by knowledge of God in a coherent progression of intellectual purification:

> Child, the fear of God establishes faith, self-mastery establishes this fear, and endurance and hope make self-mastery unwavering. From these dispassion is born, whose offspring is love. Love is the doorway of natural knowledge, which is followed by theology and the final blessedness.[22]

The life of ascetical striving for the establishment of the virtues leads to the *apatheia* and love that open the door of knowledge of the world, which then gives the purified intellect over to the contemplation of God.

Evagrius identifies Christ with the knowledge of nature in his *Scholia on Ecclesiastes*, which, we recall, Origen saw as Solomon's book of nature:

> The church (*ekklêsia*) of pure souls is true knowledge of the ages and worlds and of the judgment and providence in them. The preacher (*ekklêsiastês*) is Christ the begetter of this knowledge. Or, the preacher is the one who purifies souls through ethical contemplations and leads them to natural contemplation.[23]

For this tradition of spiritual progress, the figure of Christ, the one in whom Creator and creation are joined, is the center of the contemplation of nature. Just as the monk puts on Christ with the monastic habit, it is Christ, in a putting-on that mirrors that of the monk, who puts on nature in the incarnation and is therefore both the teacher and that which is taught.

Sacred Space, Cosmic Worship

The central structural point of reference in a typical monastery is its church, where the primary work of the monastic community takes place. For the seventh-century theologian and monastic philosopher Maximus the Confessor, the church building is a "type and image" of the world in its visible and invisible aspects, because, he says, the church, like the world, "admits of both unity and distinction."[24] The one church building is divided into sanctuary and nave, just as the natural world is divided into the intellectual or mental (noetic) cosmos, with its intellectual and bodiless realities, and the sensual cosmos, which is bodily and is "woven" together of diverse "forms and natures." The church is also a symbol of the sensual world itself, where the sanctuary and the pleasing appearance of the nave correspond to the sky (heaven) and the splendor of the earth.[25]

Clement has a similarly cosmic view of the liturgical rites that take place within the cosmic temple. Moses the law-giver is the scriptural paradigm of the *physikos*, the master of the contemplation of nature, and Clement takes the laws relating to liturgical rites as veiled teachings about the natural world. The altar in the tabernacle is the earth in the midst of the universe; the seven-branched candle stand is the seven planets (as they were numbered in the ancient world); the two cherubim on the ark of the covenant are the constellations Ursa Major and Ursa Minor or perhaps the two hemispheres; the total of twelve wings of the two cherubim are the twelve signs of the zodiac.[26]

While Clement is referring here to the rites of Hebrew worship in the tabernacle, his basic orientation to liturgical worship as a manifestation of the contemplation of nature is taken up by Maximus once again. Within the world-as-church, the creatures of the world form a choir. Considering the verse "The heavens declare the glory of God" (Ps. 18:2), Maximus says, "[David] received from soulless creatures the *logoi* [ideas; rational or structural principles; pronouncements; words] that pertain to theology in what is heard by the intellect and thoroughly learned the modes of providence and judgment[27] as far as these are accessible for human beings."[28] The song of the celestial hosts of nature, as does all Orthodox hymnography, proclaims the theology of the church.

Maximus also considers the central act of worship within the church, the Eucharist, in cosmic terms in a series of chapters of his *Ambigua to John*. Here Maximus is interpreting how it is that the Son of God is referred to as "the Sun of Righteousness" in the prophet Malachi.[29] Maximus says that it is an exercise of the contemplation of nature that will reveal the meaning of this title.

He begins his analysis with a description of the "uninterrupted motion of time." The fourth-century Cappadocian theologian Gregory Nazianzen had said that the Lord was "one year old as the Sun of righteousness," and, starting from this idea, Maximus defines one year as "the restoration of the sun from a sign to the same sign."[30] The year proceeds regularly through its hours, days, weeks, months, and seasons. Maximus then applies this cycle to the Lord, writing that

> the whole duration of the ages must be, as it is written, the "acceptable year of the Lord" [Isa. 62:2], taken allegorically, from the beginning of which God thought it good to bring beings into being and to give existence to what did not have being, and through providence, like an intellectual sun, with power holding the universe together in stability, [B] by rising up to send forth rays of light in a way adapted to each reality, having thought it fitting to diversify the ways for their full maturation, he sowed his own goodness in beings, until the completion of all the ages when he will gather the fruits of his own seed, unmixed with weeds and pure of all chaff-like residue and anything else that might be mixed in, and the whole *logos* of the motion of moving things will be completed, for those who are worthy will have received the final blessedness of deification that has been promised.[31]

God creates the world by sowing the seeds of his own goodness in beings and then "shining" upon them like the sun to make them grow.[32] He has "diversified the ways for their full maturation" by sending down his rays upon the seeds of his own goodness, which he has planted within creatures. "Thus," writes Maximus,

> the Lord is called "the sun of righteousness" as the maker and perfecter of the ages, as the source and final end of all

things, as the fashioner of the wise five-fold order[33] of those things foreknown by providence, and as the one who fills all things with everlasting light by the unfailing bestowal of goodness, and who ripens and makes edible for God the Father those who widen their own intellectual pathways for the reception of his blessed ray of light.[34]

The Word as the Sun of righteousness "being born of the Father, light from light, true God from true God,"[35] inseminates his goodness in created things and shines upon them to cause them to grow, which is to cause himself to grow in them, and then brings the fruit of that growth, which again is the fruit of his own goodness, to the Father, thus completing the "cycle of the year," "the acceptable year of the Lord." For Maximus, the year of the Lord is completed in the gathering of "the spiritual knowledge of intellectual realities through the rigorous natural contemplation of the *logoi* of phenomena."[36] Thus the contemplation of nature is the fruition of the very divine Word himself in created things, as they fill the mind of the contemplative.

In a closely related text, Maximus uses the image of the Passover sacrifice to consider how each person encounters the one unified Christ in many individual ways, in accordance with each person's faith and level of spiritual life. Because the imagery of the Passover was associated with the passion of Christ from the very beginning of the Christian era, Maximus poses the question of why many lambs were sacrificed at Passover when Christ is one:

> Since there is one Christ Who is proclaimed mystically through the law, the prophets, and the magnificence of creation to those who are able to hear and see spiritually, how does the law, which presents a complete type of Christ, order that many sheep be sacrificed at the houses of the patriarchs?[37]

In response, Maximus says that each person has been given a certain measure of grace and power, and so each person partakes of the sacrifice, which is a symbol of partaking of Christ, in different ways and to different degrees in proportion to this measure. Accordingly, Maximus applies the stages of philosophy, which we have observed here in earlier fathers, to the different aspects of Christ's being. The one engaged in asceticism or praxis partakes of Christ's body; the one involved in the contemplation of nature partakes of His soul; the theologian passes beyond the soul of Christ and the "symbolic contemplation of beings," which characterizes the contemplation of nature, and comes to the intellect of Christ; and the one who transcends the discourse of theology comes to Christ's divinity "through an all-encompassing apophasis."[38] In the language of the Passover sacrifice, each person "sacrifices the lamb and partakes of its flesh and takes his fill of Jesus"[39] in a way that is proper to oneself so that the Word who has diversified himself in and as the world maintains his unity even as he "becomes all things for all" (1 Cor. 9:22; 15:28; Col. 3:11).[40] Moreover, each part of the Passover lamb signifies a particular aspect of the spiritual life. The faithful theologian eats the head; the one who receives the principles of theology with knowledge eats the ears; the one who "considers creation spiritually" and unifies sensual and intellectual reality partakes of the eyes; the one who proclaims his theological knowledge eats the breast, and so forth.[41]

The Word nourishes those who partake of him and "becomes the substance in the entirety of things," even as he is "beyond nature."[42] Maximus has here taken the doctrine of the presence of the Word in all things and has transposed it into the eucharistic imagery of feeding on the Word. This reflection speaks of the contemplation of nature in terms of insemination, growth, fruition, and finally offering and partaking. Even though the metaphors shift from the planting and growth of grain (bread for the Eucharist) to the partaking of the Passover lamb, this sequence of thought in the *Ambigua* clearly holds together as a reflection upon partaking of the presence of the divine Word in all things. In this understanding of natural contemplation, partaking of the world in natural contemplation and partaking of the incarnate Word of God are one and the same, and to partake of the Word is to partake of the substance of all things, that is, the very essence of the world.

The World as School

The Christian church in general and the monastery in particular have been presented from the very beginning as schools. The teacher-disciple relationship is inherent to the Gospels and carries through the tradition, from the school of Justin the Philosopher in Rome, to the catechetical school (however defined) in Alexandria with Clement and Origen, to the mystagogical catechesis of Cyril of Jerusalem, and to the monasteries throughout the Christian world. For some of the Eastern fathers, the world itself was a school, the place where divine instruction was given to the attentive student.

The fourth-century Cappadocian Gregory of Nyssa, who showed himself to be very interested in the minute details of the workings of the natural world, believed that the human mind is perfectly suited to acquire knowledge of the world because its diversity of senses is perfectly arranged to perceive the diversity of creation and is, in fact, the place where the world attains unity.[43] The world is, for Gregory, essentially an intellectual reality, and mind is therefore connatural with the world and gives it unity in its understanding of it. Because of the mysterious nature of much of the natural world, and of the scriptures that describe it, Gregory conceives this process of understanding as a sort of school exercise for the mind and not as the fashioning of a dogmatic account of the nature of the world:

> We freely admit that we are giving only our own views on the ideas that are before us as a sort of exercise; we are by no means setting down a fully explanatory teaching in what follows. So when I weave together unconventional ideas with the starting points that are available to us from holy scripture and from what we learned while sitting at the feet of our teacher,[44] let no one question my discourse, for it is not my task to contrive some sort of justification for the obstacles that seem to be at hand, but let me be granted the authority to scrutinize the meaning of the words in accordance with their own purpose, if somehow it should be possible for me, with the help of God, to put together a coherent and consistent study of the creation of what has come into being in such a way that my speech remains consistent with how [scripture's meaning] appears to us.[45]

Accounts of the natural world are essays assigned to train the soul's powers of scrutiny and understanding.

Maximus also considers the training of the ascetic in cosmic terms, where the world serves (as it did for Origen) as a school for the education of the soul, and the soul itself, with its various powers and virtues, becomes a world. In his interpretation of Gregory of Nazianzus's phrase "For the exalted Word plays in all kinds of forms, making determinations in his world as he wishes, this way and that," Maximus wonders what it means to say that the Word of God "plays," as this relates to his "making determinations in" or "judging" (*krinas*) his world. His response is to describe the world as a sort of interactive classroom for children:

> just as parents…by providing enticements to their children to shake off their slowness, seem by the mode of condescension to engage indulgently in childish play – such as, say, playing with nuts and indulging in dice games with them, or even presenting multi-colored flowers to them and clothes dyed with many colors that are enchanting for the senses –, they divert or amaze them, since children do not yet have any other work, and after a little while, the parents hand them over to the schools, and thereby impart to them a complete education and tasks proper to them,[46]

in a similar way,

> the God over all casts us as children in His care into a state of amazement or even diversion through the as yet story-like aspect of the nature of created phenomena when we see and come to know them, then he also introduces the contemplation of the more spiritual *logoi* that are within them, and finally leads us to a more mystical knowledge of himself through theology, as far as this can be attained, which knowledge is absolutely pure of all multiplicity and synthesis in form, quality, shape, and quantity, which are in magnitude and mass, in the preparatory teachings, since in relation to the culmination of contemplation it is called "playing" by the God-bearing Gregory."[47]

The appearances of worldly phenomena are a game that God the teacher plays with his children to teach them about reality, which is himself.

Similarly, the world of nature is a scripture to be read. The paradigmatic monk of the Eastern tradition, St. Anthony the Great, famously said that the nature of creatures was a book where he could read the words of God.[48] For Maximus, the contents of the world–scripture correspond precisely to the written scripture:

> the natural law, since it is organized in an exceedingly rational way, coherently holds together the harmonious web of the universe by means of the visible realities that naturally arise in it, like a book, and the contemplation of nature has bodies, which are the first things most proximate and particular to us and are compacted by the conjunction of their many qualities, as letters and syllables, and as words it has beings that are far more universal than these and more refined, from which the Word, having wisely shaped them and having ineffably been engraved in them, is composed when he is read there, though providing only a certain concept that he is, not what, whatever he may be.[49]

This text of nature reveals, for Maximus, the basic threefold structure of Christian spiritual life we have observed in earlier thinkers: ethics, the true nature of reality, and mystical theology, culminating in union with God.[50]

8 – (11th-12th c.) Chios Nea Moni mosaic of Anthony the Great (c 251/2-356), by tradition the immensely authoritative founder of desert monasticism, as well as a staunch supporter of Orthodox Trinitarianism against Arianism.

The World as Cenobium

9 – Chios Nea Moni mosaic of Maximus the Confessor.

Just as for Gregory of Nyssa the mind is perfectly suited to intuit the world, which corresponds to its intellectual powers, so in Maximus the formation of the individual soul is itself the formation of a world, where each element in the world corresponds to a virtue of soul:

> For that which is, as they say, the ether, that is, the fiery element in the sensory cosmos, this is intelligence in the mental cosmos, since intelligence is the habit that brings to light and demonstrates the spiritual *logoi* particular to each being, unfailingly making manifest the cause in all things, through them it also draws the soul's inclination about the divine.
>
> That which is air in the sensual cosmos, this is courage in the mental cosmos, since courage is the habit that moves, constitutes, and effects the natural life of the spirit and is also the habit of the soul that strengthens its continual motion about the divine.
>
> And that which is water in the sensual cosmos, this is moderation in the mental cosmos, since moderation exists

as the habit that produces the vital power of generation in the spirit and generates the ever-bubbling erotic enchantment of the impulse about the divine.

And that which is the earth in the sensual cosmos, this is righteousness in the mental cosmos, since righteousness exists as the habit that, in virtue of its form, gives birth to all the *logoi* in beings and equally distributes the life-giving endowment in spirit to each being and is the unchangeable foundation of each thing's own stable position in the beautiful.[51]

The human soul exemplifies and articulates the elemental realities of the world so that the formation of the human being in spiritual life is nothing less than the creation of a cosmos.

Sacred Presence

This pedagogical approach to the world does not, however, imply that it is somehow unreal or "merely" an exercise. On the contrary, the pedagogy of the world leads the disciple to the understanding that the world's deepest meaning is its very presence and that this presence is the revelation of the presence of God. The fourth-century Cappadocian Basil of Caesarea (Gregory of Nyssa's older brother) gave a renowned series of homilies on the Genesis account of the six-day creation, the *Hexaemeron*, to a mixed congregation of unlettered craftsmen, intellectuals, women, and children in Caesarea. Basil was unconcerned with the quest for the abstract essences of things, which, he says, characterized philosophical speculation. His concerns were ethical in the broadest sense, as seeking to learn virtue from the natural environment and as seeking a pious disposition toward the world as it is in its ineffable presence, as the creation of God.[52] This led Basil to direct his attention to the sensory experience of the objects of creation as they appear to human perception and to the rejection of the search for essences that, he says, had characterized Greek metaphysics before him:

> Let us resolve, with respect to the things on earth, not to busy ourselves with trying to define the earth's essence, or to wear out our capacity for thinking by seeking out its under-

> lying substance; neither let us seek out any nature devoid of all qualities and existing completely unqualified in its own *logos*. Rather, let us be well aware that all of the things we see surrounding a particular reality are employed when we give an account of that thing's being and complete its essence. If you try to remove with reason each reality from the qualities that are inherent to it you will come up with nothing in the end. For if you should set aside, for example, black, cold, weight, thickness, and its qualities pertaining to taste, or anything else like these that we see to pertain to it, then there will no longer be any underlying substance left.[53]

It is the presence of things in their appearance that guides Basil's contemplation of the world, and it is for this reason that he does not seek to dispense with the poetry of biblical descriptions of the natural world; these descriptions bring the world itself before us with such immediacy that we are taught both virtue and reverence. For example, the prophet Isaiah describes the heavens as "smoke" (Isa. 51.6) and as a "curtain" (Isa. 40.22), and these poetic descriptions are, for Basil, more adequate to the reality than a more "scientific" description because they convey the heavens to us as they actually appear, as fashioned by God, and are transparent to the mystery of divine presence that they represent. Basil's friend and sometime companion Gregory of Nazianzus said that to handle Basil's *Hexaemeron* was to be "brought into the presence of the Creator,"[54] an apt description, for this is how Basil himself understood the scriptures and the world about which they speak.

So the world appears as a sacred presence to the human mind through the senses. The world is also a manifestation of moral guidance for humanity. Within nature "red in tooth and claw," it is the human being who is the exemplar of rapacity and should learn from the fish, for example, how to stay content in one's own allotted space.[55] The dynamics of human ascetical striving are also inscribed within the natural world, where the rose is endowed with thorns, indicating that pleasure and pain circle around one another as a result of human sin.[56]

While Basil's predominant emphasis was on the practical instruction and experience of presence to be gleaned from the contemplation of nature, Gregory of Nazianzus focused on the relationship of the contemplation of nature to mystical theology. For Gregory, the contemplation of the created world admitted of open-ended speculation, in which, he says, valid discovery is not without value and mistakes pose no threat.[57] Fundamentally, however, an authentic contemplation of nature for Gregory conditions one's orientation toward the mysteries of theology. Gregory interprets the back of God, which Moses saw when he requested to see God (Exod. 33:18ff.), as the created world itself, and although Moses was allowed to see it, as are we, it, like God, is incomprehensible to the human mind.[58] So again, as in Basil, it is the simple apprehension of natural things in their givenness that allows human beings to become like the angels, who watch over creation and constantly praise God, and the incomprehensibility of the world itself opens a way to the world's incomprehensible source. Gregory continues the Christological focus of patristic contemplation of nature and identifies the rock where Moses was set when God passed by and showed him his back with Christ the incarnate Word.[59]

Similarly, for Dionysius the Areopagite, the mysterious pseudonymous sixth-century Christian philosopher, the contemplation of the world is really inseparable from the contemplation of the divine, for the world just is the visual manifestation of divine goodness. The names that are given to the divine are taken from created things, for God is the cause of all that is and can be called "all things," though God is "not one thing among others":

> They say he is in intellects, in souls, in bodies, in heaven, on earth, that in his own self-identity he is at once within the cosmos, the enclosure of the cosmos, beyond the cosmos, beyond heaven and beyond being; he is sun, stars, fire, water, wind, dew, cloud, cornerstone, and rock. He is all things and not one being among other beings.[60]

As with his predecessors among the Greek fathers, the naming of God with the names of the world, which we might regard as the height of the contemplation of nature, is ultimately a mode of doxology for Dionysius and once again draws the contemplation of nature, the contemplation of God in nature, into the realm of liturgical celebration.[61]

Holy Habitation: Ecology and the Oikoumenê

We find echoes of these Greek patristic voices in statements from the Ecumenical Patriarch, His All-Holiness Bartholomew of Constantinople. Patriarch Bartholomew is, of course, well known throughout the world as an outspoken advocate of ecological awareness, and this is quite fitting for the "Ecumenical" Patriarch, for this honorary title refers to the patriarchate's care for the *oikoumenê*, the 'inhabited world,' which is the focus of "ecology." In 1994, at the reception of an honorary degree at a university in Greece, he referred to "the significance of the Eucharistic and ascetic ethos of our tradition, that manifests our most important and most crucial unique contribution toward the proper and universal struggle for the protection of the natural environment as a Divine Creation and shared inheritance."[62] He defines ecology here in terms of love and participation in God. Similarly, in 2008, on the occasion of the ecclesial new year of September 1, which the Ecumenical Patriarchate had designated as a day of prayer for the natural environment, he wrote, "The use of the world and the enjoyment of material goods must be Eucharistic, accompanied by doxology toward God; by the same token, the abuse of the world and participation therein without reference to God is sinful both before the Creator and before humanity as creation."[63]

Knowing the world as "habitation," as "home," as *oikoumenê*, rather than as object or as resource, has a profound influence on how we are aware of ourselves in the world. The world in this awareness becomes a cenobium, the place of common life, the place where every experience is informed by the divine ground from which all things spring forth. All of the various liturgical blessings of the Eastern Christian tradition—at the sowing of seeds and at harvest; blessings for cattle, bees, honey, vineyards, and new wine; the blessing of rivers, lakes, seas at Theophany; and preeminently the blessing of bread and wine and the liturgy—do not, in this view, make things into something they were not already as though sanctifying what was originally profane, but rather articulates what things are in themselves, members of a sacred cenobium, an all-encompassing monastic enclosure that ensures the stability of all because it is the private possession of none.

IV. Conclusion

In the spirit of St. Iosif Volotskii, we have traced some basic features of Greek patristic attention to the environment, to the surroundings in which we "live, move, and have our being." From the centrality of Christ, the incarnate Word of God, who is the teacher of natural philosophy and also its ultimate content, to the liturgical, pedagogical, and participatory facets of attention-to and being-in the World, the wealth of nature, which provides for all its inhabitants, who bear their flesh as a monastic habitus, gives to them the possibility of acquiring the traditional monastic virtues of dispassion, nonpossession, and humility, which are essential to the preservation of the earth as a habitation and place of common life.

Abbreviations

FC: Fathers of the Church. Washington, DC: The Catholic University of America Press: 1947--.

NPNF: *Nicene and Post-Nicene Fathers*. Second Series.14 vols. Edited by Philip Schaff and Henry Wace. New York: The Christian Literature Company, 1890-1899.

PG: *Patrologia Cursus Completus, Series Graeca*. 161 vols. Edited by Jacques-Paul Migne. Paris: Imprimerie Catholique, 1857–1866.

SC: Sources chrétiennes. Paris: Cerf, 1941–.

Notes

1   My remarks on Iosif's life and quotations from his *Rule* follow David M. Goldfrank, *The Monastic Rule of Iosif Volotsky* (Kalamazoo, MI: Cistercian Publications, 1983; rev. ed., 2000).
2   For a useful summary of the literature on ecology and Christian theology, both Eastern and Western, see Christina M. Gschwandtner, "The Role of Non-Human Creation in the Liturgical Feasts of the Eastern Orthodox Church: Towards an Orthodox Ecological Theology" (Ph.D. dissertation, Durham University, 2012), 164–183.
3   Goldfrank, *Monastic Rule* (1983 ed.), 48.
4   Lynn Townsend White, "The Historical Roots of Our Ecological Crisis," *Science* 155 (March 10, 1967): 1203–1207; see also Elizabeth A.

Johnson, "Losing and Finding Creation in the Christian Tradition," in *Christianity and Ecology: Seeking the Well-Being of Earth and Humans*, edited by Dieter T. Hessel and Rosemary Radford Ruether, (Cambridge, MA: Harvard University Press, 2000), 3-21.

5   Hadot, *The Veil of Isis: An Essay on the History of the Idea of Nature*, translated by Michael Chase (Cambridge, MA: Belknap Press, 2006), 84–85.

6   Thomas Berry, *Evening Thoughts: Reflecting on Earth as Sacred Community*, edited by Mary Evelyn Tucker (San Francisco: Sierra Club Books, 2006), 43; see also idem, *The Dream of the Earth* (San Francisco: Sierra Club Books, 1988).

7   White, 1206.

8   See many of the essays in *Toward an Ecology of Transfiguration: Orthodox Christian Perspectives on Environment, Nature, and Creation*, edited by John Chryssavgis and Bruce V. Foltz (New York: Fordham University Press, 2013).

9   Paisios of Mt. Athos, *Spiritual Councils*, vol. 1, *With Pain and Love for Contemporary Man*, translated by Cornelia A. Tsakiridou, edited by Peter Chamberas (Thessaloniki, Greece: Holy Monastery Evangelist John the Theologian, 2007), 135.

10 This echoes an important aspect of Plotinus's understanding of the productivity of nature; cf. *Enneads* 3.8.2; *Plotini Opera*, Vol. 1, edited by Paul Henry and Hans-Rudolf Schwyzer (Oxford: Oxford University Press, 1964); cf. translation in *The Enneads of Plotinus*, Vol. 3, edited and translated by A.H. Armstrong (Cambridge, MA: Harvard University Press, 1966).

11 John of Scythopolis, *Scholia* 294.3, cited in Elizabeth Theokritoff, *Living in God's Creation: Orthodox Perspectives on Ecology* (Crestwood, NY: St. Vladimir's Seminary Press, 2009), 60.

12 Plato, *Phaedo* 96a; *Platonis Opera* Vol. 1, edited by John Burnet (Oxford: Oxford University Press, 1967); cf. translation by G.M.A. Grube, *Plato: The Complete Works*, edited by John Cooper (Indianapolis: Hackett, 1997).

13 Quoted in D. S. Wallace-Hadrill, *The Greek Patristic View of Nature* (Manchester: Manchester University Press,1968), 3.

14 For an elaboration of the following material, see Joshua Lollar, *To See into the Life of Things: The Contemplation of Nature in Maximus the Confessor and his Predecessors* (Turnhout: Brepols Publishers, 2013).

15 Evagrius, *Praktikos*, In *Traité pratique ou Le moine*, edited by Antoine and Claire Guillaumont, 2 vols, SC 170-171 (Paris: Cerf, 1971), 2: Prologue 2.4.

16 Clement of Alexandria, *Stromata* 5.6.39.2, in vol. 1 of *Les stromates*, 7 vols. in 6 to date, edited by Marcel Caster et al., SC 30, 38, 278, 279,

428, 446, 463 (Paris: Cerf, 1951--); translation in vol. 2 of *Ante-Nicene Fathers*, edited by Alexander Roberts, James Donaldson, and A. Cleveland Coxe, 10 vols. (New York, 1885–87).

17 Ibid.,1.11.52.
18 For a discussion of this theme in Origen and later authors, see Sandro Leanza, "La classificazione dei libris salomonici e i suoi riflessi sulla questione dei rapporti tra Bibbia e scienze profane, da Origene a gli scrittori medioevali," *Augustinianum* 14 (1974): 651–666.
19 Origen, *De principiis* 2.11.4, in vol. 5 of *Origenes Werke*, 5 vols., edited by Paul Koetschau, Die griecheschen christlichen Schriftsteller der ersten Drei Jahrhunderte (Leipzig: Hinrichs'sche Buchhandlung, 1899-1913), 5: 186.23–24 and 187.9–10, 13–15. Translated by G. W. Butterworth as *Origen: On First Principles* (New York: Harper and Row, 1966).
20 Origen, *Homilae in Genesim* 1.1.1–9, in *Homélies sur la Genèse*, edited by Henri Louis Doutreleau, SC 7 (1976); translation by Ronald Heine, FC 71 (1982).
21 Evagrius, *Praktikos* 1.
22 Evagrius, *Praktikos*, Prologue 8.
23 Evagrius, *Scholia in Ecclesiasten* 1, in *Scholies à l'Ecclésiaste*, SC 397, edited by Paul Géhin (Paris: Cerf, 1993), Scholia 1.
24 Maximus, *Mystagogia* 2.14.206–2.15.209, in *Maximis Confessoris Mystagogia*, edited by Christian Boudignon, Corpus Christianorum Series Graeca 69 (Turnhout: Brepols, 2011).
25 Ibid., 3.17.258–3.18.263.
26 Clement of Alexandria, *Stromata* 5.6.32–39.
27 The pairing of "providence and judgment" was a *topos* of the contemplation of nature in the Greek fathers.
28 Maximus, *Ambigua ad Ioannem* 10, PG 91: 1121A.
29 Cf. Gregory of Nazianzus, *Oration* 45.13 in NPNF 7: 427.
30 Maximus, *Ambigua* 46, PG 91: 1356D7–8.
31 Ibid., PG 91: 1357A9–B9.
32 Echoing the common theme of *spermatikos logos*, or "inseminated" principle, from the Stoics and earlier Christian fathers.
33 Probably a reference to the fivefold division of created things in Maximus, *Ambigua* 41.
34 Ibid., 46, PG 91: 1357B9–C4.
35 Ibid., PG 91: 1357C12–14.
36 Ibid., PG 91: 1357C8–10.
37 Ibid., 47, PG 91: 1357D7–1360A4.
38 Ibid., PG 91: 1360C6–D2.
39 Ibid., PG 91: 1360D9–11.
40 Ibid., PG 91: 1361A4.

41 Ibid., 48, PG 91: 1364C1–1365B3.
42 Ibid., PG 91: 1365C4–5.
43 See Gregory of Nyssa, *De hominis opificio* 2, PG 44: 131D-134C.
44 Referring to St. Basil of Caesarea's *Hexaemeron*; see below, text to note 52.
45 Gregory of Nyssa, *Apologia in Hexaemeron* 6, in *Gregorii Nysseni. In Hexaemeron, opera exegetica in Genesim, Pars I*, edited by Hubertus R. Drobner (Leiden: Brill, 2009), 13.21–14.12.
46 Maximus, *Ambigua* 71, PG 91: 1413B9–C7.
47 Ibid., 1413C7–D6.
48 Evagrius, *Praktikos* 92.
49 Maximus, *Ambigua* 10: 1128D8–1129A8).
50 Ibid., 1129B3–6.
51 Ibid., 21: 1245B1-C7.
52 Basil of Caesarea, *Homilae in Hexaemeron* 1.8, in *Basile de Césarée. Homélies sur l'Hexaéméron*, edited by Stanislas Giet, SC 26 (1968), 118–120; translation by Agnes Clare Way, FC 46 (1963).
53 Ibid.
54 Gregory Nazianzen, *Oration* 43.67, in *Grégoire de Nazianze: Discours 42-43. (Discours Théologiques)*, edited by Paul Gallay, SC 405, trans. NPNF. vol. 7.
55 Basil, *Hexaemeron* 7.3–4.
56 Basil, *Hexaemeron* 5.6.
57 Gregory Nazianzen, *Oration* 27.10, in *Grégoire de Nazianze: Discours 27-31. (Discours Théologiques)*, edited by Paul Gallay, SC 250, trans., NPNF, vol. 7.
58 Idem, *Oration* 28.3.
59 Ibid.
60 Dionysius the Areopagite, *De divinis nominibus* 1.6, 119.5–9, in *Corpus Dionysiacum*, vol. 1, edited by Beate Regina Suchla, Patristische Texte und Studien 33 (Berlin: Walter de Gruyter, 1990).
61 Ibid., 1.7.
62 Ecumenical Patriarch Bartholomew, *On Earth as in Heaven: Ecological Vision and Initiatives of Ecumenical Patriarch Bartholomew*, edited by John Chryssavgis (New York: Fordham University Press, 2012), 71.
63 Ibid., 61.

2 "No one can doubt that the Father is greater"
Constantius II and the Council of Sirmium

Edward Mason

10 – Bust of Emperor Constantius II.

In 379, reflecting upon the trinitarian turmoil that had engulfed the church in the flames of discord, Jerome commented that "the word *ousia* was abolished: at that time the Nicene faith was condemned. The whole world groaned and was amazed that it was Arian."[1] Despite the hyperbolic nature of his statement, Jerome highlighted an important aspect of imperial policy during the fourth century. Both Constantine and Constantius II would have delighted to think that the *totus orbis* ascribed to a single theological formula. The history of early Christianity was certainly, to a large degree, the development of theology; in few places is this more clear than the debates over the relationship of the Son to the Father in the fourth century.

Church historian Socrates stated the entire debacle was "not unlike a nighttime battle, as neither side fully understood the grounds on which they fought each other."[2] The terms of this battle as well as imperial strategies for enforcing doctrinal resolution were being defined, to a large degree, ad hoc. In the fourth-century church there was a proclivity for church councils; and the council convened by Constantius in Sirmium in 357 provides a unique avenue by which to explore the development of imperial policy and institutional evolution.

By the year 357 Constantius had been confounded at every turn: he faced usurpers in the West, Germanic tribes along the Danube border, a looming war with the Sassanids in the East, and all around a church embroiled in disputes about the relationship of the Son to the Father. The major theological problem facing the church, presumably resolved by Constantine at Nicaea in 325, remained disputed. Because of the ongoing discord within the church, the emperor convened a council at the imperial residence in Sirmium. The result of this council was the production of a creed that unequivocally subordinated the Son to the Father and explicitly forbade discussion of terms of *ousia/substantia*. To pro-Nicene polemicists, the Council of Sirmium stood in direct contrast to the establishment of doctrine at Nicaea. To be certain, Constantine himself had suggested temporary solution to the trinitarian problem at Nicaea—the term *homoousios*—and himself directly had overseen the enforcement of church unity. The evidence, however, indicates that the situation was far more complex. Constantius's solution to the Trinitarian debate was not a novelty. He followed precedent—just like his father before him did—in his interactions with the church. For Constantius, his father, with the steps taken at Nicaea, provided a ready precedent for doctrinal solutions. Sirmium continued and appropriated the recent imperial policy. Examining the approaches toward church unity taken by Constantine and Constantius allows scholars the opportunity to understand the role of church councils in ecclesiastical politics, imperial authority, and the development of institutional structures aimed at creating and enforcing imperial orthodoxy in the earliest stages of late antique Christianity.

To say that scholars have neglected study of the Council of Sirmium would be *somewhat* of an understatement. The phenomenon is a symptom of the overall lack of scholarly work on the reign of Constantius. As Chantal Vogler stated, "Surrounded by the reigns of Constantine the Great and Julian, both famous for their religious policy, that of Constantius II has not captivated historians."[3] In addition to this problem, the portrait of the emperor that remains today is one utterly tainted by polemic. A. H. M Jones famously noted how the sources portrayed him as "a conscientious emperor but a vain and stupid man, an easy prey to flatterers ... timid and suspicious."[4] Despite this problem, scholars have not completely disregarded Sirmium. "The uncompromising character of its creedal statement," Carl Beckwith recently acknowledged, "made it clear to everyone where they stood on the debate over the Trinity."[5] However, much remains to be examined in regard to enigmatic nature of this oft-disregarded council. Nearly every scholar who deals with Sirmium treats the event as a mere historical footnote.[6] It is no surprise that the council has generally been regarded as a dead end considering that Arian theology was eventually defeated.

Scholars must approach the Constantinian dynasty with the understanding that religion and politics are inherently connected by an unshakeable symbiotic relationship. As Hans-Georg Beck stated, "Imperial history is at the same time church history, and decisive impulses of politics are of a religious or even of a theological nature."[7] The Constantinians should be seen as men of their time, viewing religion and politics as merely two sides of the same imperial coin. Additionally, they must be viewed as the continuation of the traditional Hellenistic political philosophy.[8] In the end, the Donatist controversy was as much of a political issue for Constantine as the usurpation of Magnentius was a religious problem for Constantius. In the fourth century *Kirchenpolitik* was *Reichspolitik* and vice versa.

The influence of Jacob Burckhardt, who famously stated, "There can be no question of Christianity and paganism, of conscious religiosity or irreligiosity; such a man is essentially unreligious, even if he pictures himself standing in the midst of a churchly community," permeated scholarship for many years.[9] Certainly, Constantine was irrefutably influenced by political considerations, and the German tradition certainly raised valid points. However, one cannot reduce every action of the emperor into a mere act of statesmanship.

Most notably, Timothy Barnes and H. A. Drake have described the deficiencies in the aforementioned tradition of scholarship. Speaking of terms such as *Reichskirche*, Barnes has argued that these scholars tell us far more about *Realpolitik* and Bismarck than any of the realities of the fourth century.[10] The Constantinians certainly were shrewd politicians heavily invested in maintaining their own imperial power, but this did not in any way discount the profound sincerity of their religious experiences. Barnes stated that, at Nicaea, "Constantine deliberately emphasized his role as a Christian emperor bringing unity and concord to a divided Church."[11] As Drake argued, Nicaea was more about fostering the unity of the church than it was about theology. Thus, the idea of Nicaea as reflecting the battle over an already developed orthodoxy in reality reflects the doctrinal positions developed decades and centuries later.[12] Building upon the work of these scholars, a closer examination of the patterns of imperial policy and institutional operation can take place.

The sources for the Council of Sirmium are problematic. They contain no narrative, no extensive list of those present, and no detailed explanation of the role of the emperor. To further complicate matters, most of the sources are polemical in nature.[13] The sources for Nicaea, on the other hand, are far more descriptive. We have been left with Eusebius's detailed account of the proceedings and the involvement of the emperor as well as a handful of other useful sources.[14] For this reason, it is imperative to examine fully the role of the emperor and his imperial policy at Nicaea in order to understand Constantius's policy at Sirmium. I will begin by examining in detail the Eusebian narrative of Nicaea to uncover how the emperor viewed the council. After revealing the overt imperial nature of the council, I will then deconstruct the religious polemic of Hilary of Poitiers and Athanasius of Alexandria to reveal the imperial policy of Constantius. It is my intention to show that Constantius was actually following the precedent set by his father rather than disregarding it.

The exact proceedings of Nicaea are difficult to ascertain, and reconstructing the events is like trying to assemble a puzzle that is missing half its pieces. The texts we are left with today reflect how certain churchmen wished to present the council rather than what actually happened. The council left no *acta*, no concrete description, and the accounts that remain are couched in either polemic or panegyric. As a result, scholars have arrived at highly different reconstructions of Nicaea.[15] As many scholars have noted, in the end it is highly unlikely that we will ever accurately be able to reconstruct the proceedings at Nicaea.[16] There does remain evidence, though, and with that, the hope that something can be uncovered. By far the fullest account of the proceedings comes to us from Eusebius's *Vita Constantini* (2.6–23). It should be noted, however, that one cannot place full trust in the Eusebian account either. Steps must be taken to disconnect the actions of Constantine from how Eusebius wished to portray the emperor. Obviously, placing too much weight on any particular piece of evidence is dangerous, and certainly any construction of Nicaea is open to interpretation.

To begin examining the emperor's actions, we must understand that the emperor's imprint is on every aspect of the council. Even before the council began, the emperor was involved, as Constantine chose the location for the council.[17] Certainly, Nicaea—the location of the imperial palace—was strategically advantageous for the emperor. He thus was able to make certain that his agenda—ecclesiastical unity, not adjudicating orthodoxy—was fulfilled. The sheer fact that Constantine himself made provisions for bishops to travel to Nicaea demonstrates the importance of location.[18] Due to the emperor's presence, Nicaea was different. When the emperor convened the council and chose its location, he was setting a dramatic precedent for his son and future emperors.

Although Constantine's main motive for calling the council was to encourage agreement within the church, ostensibly the council was convened to deal with two major theological problems: the trinitarian controversy between Arius and Alexander, and the date of Easter. Eusebius is strangely silent about the debates that took place. He did not relate the extent to which the bishops interacted with each other or the emperor. The description he did leave has indicated that Constantine himself played a decisive role, though. Eusebius simply stated that, after the exhortation to concord, Constantine intently listened to the complaints of each bishop until he at last exhorted all to unity. Constantine demanded, "Do not delay, friends and servants of God, the Lord and Savior, in bringing the causes of the disagreements between you into the open here, and in casting off the fetter of dispute among yourselves through the laws of peace."[19] Following the "agreement concerning the faith" and the date of Easter, the general decisions were written down and signed. Philostorgius related that Constantine even had imperial notaries go around to collect the signatures.[20] Finally, before the official close of the council, Constantine initiated a victory feast dedicated to God (*epinikion eortēn tō theō*).[21]

A victory over whom, though? Although the nominal cause for celebration was Constantine's twentieth year of rule, Constantine himself deemed this a celebration for "the second victory over the enemy of the church." Certainly this was Licinius, Constantine's adversary in a rather bloody civil war that had recently come to an end, in 324.[22] The battle between Constantine and Licinius was framed as a religious war between Christianity and the ravaging forces of paganism.[23] Indeed, the city of Nicaea was in territory taken from the fallen co-*augustus*. In order to understand the importance of this evidence, we must acknowledge that "before Constantine was a Christian emperor, he was a typical emperor."[24] For the emperor, religion had clear and identifiable material effect. It was divine favor that legitimated the ruler and emperor, and being victorious in battle was contingent upon maintaining the favor of the divinity. Constantine was not alone in this sentiment.[25] Indeed, it was the Christian God who—after giving the famous command *en toutō nika* (in this, conquer)—bestowed favor upon Constantine, thus allowing him to be victorious at the Battle of the Milvian Bridge against Maxentius in 312.[26] Constantine himself echoed the sentiment in his correspondence. Writing to the Palestinian provincials, Constantine warned that it was devout Christian religious observance in which the prosperity of the empire rested. "For who would happen upon anything good, if he is willing neither to acknowledge that God is the source of good things nor to worship him properly? Indeed, the results give confirmation."[27]

As Drake noted, the Constantine of Nicaea aimed at bring the church together, and he intended to do this by whatever means would most decisively cement ecclesiastical unity.[28] In the Donatist controversy, Constantine's major concern was not the validity of sacraments performed by *traditores* but rather the divine favor that a united church granted him. The same was true about Nicaea: the trinitarian debate itself was only a means to the end of ecclesiastical unity. Eusebius related that Constantine held a central role in the debates: "Persuading some, and convincing others by reason, and praising those who spoke well, urging all to come to unanimity (*homonoian*), he at last made them of one mind (*homognōmonas*) and of one opinion (*homodoxous*) concerning every disputed issue."[29] Indeed, it was the emperor himself who produced the crowning achievement of the council, giving the resolution with the solitary utterance of the word *homoousios*.[30]

Perhaps the most interesting aspect of Nicaea is the use of imperial ceremony. Eusebius tells us that when all the bishops were assembled at the imperial palace, the emperor appeared in a high ceremonial fashion. Constantine, being the emperor, did not make any attempt at subtlety. Eusebius elegantly wrote:

> On each side [of the palace] seats were arranged in order, and all who were summoned took their seat. When the entire assembly (*synodos*) had seated themselves with clear orderliness, a silence held them all in expectation of the emperor. The first of the emperor's entourage entered, then a second and then a third. Then others were led in, not those of his soldiers and bodyguards, but those of his friends in the faith. Everyone stood upon the signal that the emperor was entering, and he walked between them, as if some messenger of god from heaven, his bright garment shining as if with rays of light, reflecting with the radiance of a purple robe, and adorned with decorations of gold and gems... Upon reaching the upper end, he stood in the middle and a small chair made of gold was placed before him. He did not seat himself until the bishops assented. After this, the entire council sat down with the emperor.[31]

Immediately following this ceremonial display, one of the bishops rose and delivered a panegyric on behalf of the emperor. Then, once again, "silence fell upon everyone concentrating intently upon the emperor."[32] The entire event up to this point focused on the majesty of the emperor. Constantine was the focus of the bishops, and indeed the marked feature of the ceremony was the reverent silence of the bishops.

To be certain, this scene bears a striking resemblance to the *adoratio* of Diocletian.³³ Constantine, being a member of the tetrarchy, would certainly have been aware of the characteristic way in which imperial audiences took place. Nicaea, especially as envisioned by the emperor, was a court event for ecclesiastical actors. Perhaps the peculiar detail of the missing *acta* was simply due to the fact that there were no notes produced. Scholars have long noted that the early councils bore a striking resemblance to imperial gatherings. Francis Dvornik compared the council to a senate meeting: "Its procedure was the usual senatorial one used by both Church and state, which the Churches in Rome and Africa had made their own. Judging from the description of the first oecumenical council left us by the author of the *Vita Constantini*, Nicaea proceeded in the same way."³⁴ Certainly, the council seemed to have proceeded in just such a manner; the emperor announced the topic at hand (agreement on the date of Easter and the dispute between Arius and Alexander), and the opinions of the bishop were stated. Following this, perhaps a vote was taken. It was a moot point because Constantine saw to it that those not in agreement were exiled from the church. Finally, the council produced a proclamation, from the hand of the emperor no less, which was to be sent out those not present.³⁵ The edict promulgated by the emperor demonstrated that Constantine did not view Nicaea as simply a suggestion to the church; the decisions made were imperial law. Constantine did give the bishops an arena in which to air their grievances, but he was quite determined about the eventual outcome of the council: everyone would agree. The most unique aspect of Nicaea was not the emperor's transformation into a church figure but rather the transformation of the bishop into a court figure.

The idea of an "ecumenical council" did not spring forth fully formed as did Athena from the head of Zeus. Nicaea represented precedent and evolution. It was over a decade later before Eusebius referred to Nicaea as *synodon oikoumenikēn* (ecumenical council).³⁶ It was only after decades of experimentation and evolution that any universally accepted idea of what a church council, let alone an "ecumenical council," truly was.³⁷ To be certain, there were *synodoi* before Nicaea.³⁸ Yet, having the emperor present and active, as occurred at Nicaea, unquestionably altered the dynamic of a council.

Thus the traditional narrative, in which the bishops gather in a solemn meeting to *clarify* orthodoxy, tells us more about later events like the Council of Chalcedon than it does Nicaea. Furthermore, this narrative robs Nicaea of its historical value by refusing to acknowledge the council on its own terms.

Nicaea fell apart almost as quickly as it materialized, in part because the emperor himself refused to enforce it. As Barnes wrote, "The Council of Nicaea failed to bring harmony to the eastern Church. On the contrary, it sharpened divisions and inaugurated a new phase of ecclesiastical politics."[39] Exactly what Constantine envisioned theologically at Nicaea should at the very least be called into question by the events that transpired toward the end of his life: he recalled exiled bishops such as Eusebius of Nicomedia, Theognis of Nicaea, and even Arius himself. Constantine even went as far as to threaten Athanasius with exile for refusing to accept Arius back into the fold.[40] Before his death Constantine was even baptized by an Arian bishop.[41] The legacy that Constantius inherited from his father upon Constantine's death in 337 is, at the very least, complex. He did not develop a fully developed doctrinal position but rather precedent for providing temporary solutions through imperial decree.

In the autumn of 357, on his victory circuit after defeating Magnentius and Silvanus, Constantius arrived at Sirmium. He must have felt the overwhelming gravity of the situation. Just as his father had defeated Maxentius and Licinius, Constantius had recently defeated Magnentius and Silvanus, and found himself, for the time being, unopposed.[42] His brothers were dead, and old challengers to the imperial position had been neutralized.[43] Constantius had completed his military victory over the enemy of the church—his adversary Magnentius—and now it was time, like his father, to establish the unity of the church whose prayers had secured his victory.

Nowhere was the continuity between father and son more apparent than in Constantius's patterns of institutional operation. His father had given him a grave command: the imperial office would mean nothing to him unless he could establish concord in the church.[44] Constantius was so disposed to harmony in the empire that he refused to take action against the meddlesome Athanasius despite the latter's repeated attempts at undermining Constantius's every move. Athanasius reported that Constans and Constantius almost came to civil war over Athanasius's deposition.[45] In the end, Constantius yielded to his brother rather than run the risk of civil war. This event was likely exaggerated by Athanasius, but it does underscore the extent to which Constantius shared in his father's regard for the harmony of the empire. Sirmium was a clear and direct attempt at creating ecclesiastical unity despite its blatant lack of success. Hilary's *Contra Constantium* uncovered another interesting point about the emperor's involvement in church affairs. Hilary himself argued that Constantius did not have the right to intervene in the affairs of the church, despite holding the imperial power.[46] Constantius, like his father, believed that in his capacity as emperor he had the right to become involved in church affairs. Indeed, even though the Athanasian polemicists disagreed, it was just as if Constantine still reigned.[47]

Anti-Constantian bishops seized upon the council as a means to label Constantius a heretic and an unworthy heir to the dynasty of his father. The accounts we are left with are predominantly from Athanasian polemicists who viewed the emperor as a violent persecutor who aimed at destroying the church. Hilary even famously issued the following invective against the emperor: "You wage war against God, you rage against the church, you persecute the saints, you hate those who proclaim Christ, you destroy religion (*religionem*), and you are a tyrant in not only the affairs of men, but in the affairs of the divine (*divinorum*) as well."[48]

The Anti-Constantians had a far more nefarious plot in mind than simply denigrating the emperor, though; they wished to invalidate Constantius's claim to his father's legacy. Through their tireless efforts to manufacture a break in the piety of the Constantinian dynasty with the reign of Constantius, they seemed to succeed in large part. Athanasius, seemingly forgetful of Constantine's involvement at Nicaea, wrote, "Since when was the decision of the church validated by the emperor? When was the decree of the emperor ever recognized by the church, for that matter? There have already been many councils and many decisions made by the church, but the emperor's consent was never sought, nor did the emperor involve himself in the decisions of the church."[49] In order to give this statement validity, Athanasius was forced to change the narrative of Nicaea. We see this revision more fully developed in *De Decretis*: Constantine was a puzzling omission. The text transformed the event into a purely theological disputation aimed at quelling the spread of Arian heresy. By the time Hilary had finally become openly hostile to the emperor in 360/361, he boldly declared, "Hear your father's faith professed ... and know that you are an enemy of the divine religion, an enemy of the memory of the saints, and a rebel against the inheritance of your father's duty (*pietas*)."[50] Only by deconstructing the rhetorical nature of these attacks can we view Constantius's ecclesiastical work in its proper context. His conciliar policy was not contrary to his father's, it was identical.

Despite attempts to sever the dynastic connection, the Council of Sirmium must be seen in light of Constantius's connection to the Constantinian dynasty and its policy of organizing court events in which the emperor was the focus of ecclesiastical unity. Brennecke has correctly suggested that, through Sirmium, Constantius was attempting to highlight the dynastic link to his father.[51] As Pedro Barceló stated, "Therefore, Constantius II's chief concern was to finally end the long-simmering religious controversy."[52] The event was no innovation or novelty; Constantius had the same imperial policy in mind with Sirmium as Constantine did with Nicaea. Constantius convened the bishops, and his presence at the council dictates that he almost certainly played a pivotal role.[53] There has been some debate regarding Constantius's presence in Sirmium; however, Barnes's reconstruction of the imperial itinerary from Ammianus Marcellinus and laws included in the *Codex Theodosianus* have shown that the imperial residence was in Sirmium from autumn 357 to spring 358.[54]

The creed produced at Sirmium was unique. It went to great lengths to avoid theological vocabulary. Clearly, the adoption of a seemingly clear, concise term (*homoousios*) at Nicaea had not resolved anything. The next step for the imperial policy was a move backward; the church was to disregard all theological language that possessed the potential to create division. Together with a collection of Western bishops, the emperor issued a creed that stated,

> Since questions concerning substance (*de substantia*), called *ousia* in Greek, were disturbing some or many people, or

what is more properly understood as *homousion*, or what is called *homoeusion*, no mention should be made of them. Nor should anyone discuss these questions because they are not contained in divine scripture and they are above human knowledge. Nor can any man declare the birth of the Son, about whom the scripture says, "Who will declare his generation [Isa. 53:8]? For it is clear that only the Father knows how he generated his Son, and only the Son knows how he was generated by the Father. It is not ambiguous that the Father is greater. No one can doubt that the Father is greater than Son in honor, dignity, renown, majesty, and in the very name of the Father, with the Son himself testifying, "The one who sent me is greater than I [John 14:28]."[55]

The accounts that provide this information are full of invective. Hilary himself, objecting to the creed on theological grounds, deemed this creed the *apud Sirmium blasphemia* ("blasphemy at Sirmium"). For those who supported the Nicene definition of faith, this creed was not reconciliatory or compromising. Rather, it was an unabashed, blatant attempt at promoting Arianism. Phoebadius of Agen even argued that the creed was an attempt to delude the church with a "subtle heresy" (*haeretica subtilitate*), just as honey may be used to disguise poison.[56] However, in this statement, he did acknowledge the potential for reconciliation that the creed offered.

All the sources agree that the aged bishop Ossius, Constantine's close theological adviser at Nicaea, played an important role in drafting the creed. The sources, however, greatly disagree about the exact nature of Ossius's role. Athanasius stated that Constantius detained Ossius in Sirmium for an entire year, subjecting him to threats and coercion in order to force his approval of Sirmium's creed and his denunciation of Athanasius. Conveniently for Athanasius, Constantius was appeased by Ossius's agreement with Sirmium and seemingly dropped the latter issue.[57] The church historians Sozomen and Socrates related a similar narrative, perhaps relying upon Athanasius as a source.[58] Hilary paints the picture in a different way. He believed that Ossius, aided by the bishops Polamius, Valens, and Urascius, was the major contributor to the *blasphemia*.⁵⁹ Although today it is probably impossible to uncover the exact nature of Ossius's involvement, all accounts recognize his importance to the imperial cause. The agreement of one bishop did not make orthodoxy, but having the support of possibly the most notable of the Nicene bishops was a boon to Constantius's policy.

The second, and most important, item all the sources agreed upon was that the chief concern with Sirmium was a prohibition on divisive theological terminology. At Sirmium, as well as at Nicaea, the problem was not Arianism per se, no matter how much seemed to be the case. Part of deconstructing the polemical texts is disregarding the traditional model of the Nicene struggle against Arianism. "The removal of polemical labels like 'Arian' or 'Nicene,'" as David Gwynn recently stated, "and the abandonment of the polarization inherent in such language" have the potential to prompt new questions about church councils.⁶⁰ Constantius's imperial policy was to foster unity within the church, not to promulgate specific theological views.

The ban on discussion of the terms *ousia* and *substantia* seems to have been the emperor's primary concern. While Constantine's famous utterance of *homoousios* at Nicaea may have driven enmity from the church for a short while, it must have become apparent to Constantius by the final years of his reign that it was in fact the trinitarian vocabulary itself that proved problematic. Constantine himself had stated that *both* Arius and Alexander were frivolously wasting their time in idle exercises and that the quarrel between them was *tē lian euēthei* ('exceedingly trivial').⁶¹ It was no surprise that Constantius would address the problem in a similar manner. While the creed produced at Sirmium was undeniably subordinationist, it cannot be labeled an inherently divisive statement. The creed did not seek to employ an Arian theology but rather avoided the problem entirely. It was a solution that did not throw anyone overboard, although some chose to leave on their own volition. If Constantius wished to endorse Arianism outright, he could have produced a more theologically developed formula rather than an explicitly inclusive one. In this way, Constantius's removal of Nicene trinitarian vocabulary was not a reversal of his father's policy but an extension of it. Despite any thought to the contrary, Sirmium, just as Nicaea before it, did not come to bring the sword.

Due to the vague nature of the sources, it has proven nearly impossible to reach any solid conclusion about Sirmium. However, Constantinian dynastic continuity must be considered a, if not the, primary determinant in interpreting the failed ecumenical council; knowing that Constantius viewed his reign as a seamless continuation of his father's and that the imperial agenda was *exactly* the same for both councils has provided us with a great deal to work with. The irrefutable nature of Sirmium as an attempt to foster doctrinal unity indicates that a similar procedure was being followed. Thus it can reasonably be concluded that Sirmium was also a court event. Given the extent to which Constantius followed in his father's footsteps, there can be absolutely no reason to conclude that he would have employed a different program for his church councils.

Obviously, there is much left to be said, as Nicaea and Sirmium were only two instances of imperial policy during the Constantinian dynasty. Additionally, understanding both councils as court events and the bishops involved as court figures is in no way an endorsement of caesaropapism. Because both councils have often been viewed as explicitly *theological* events, their *imperial* nature has gone unexplained. Nicaea has been seen as divinely inspired orthodoxy expressed in collaboration with a pious emperor, whereas Sirmium is seen as violent Arian incursion upon the church by a tyrant. In reality, though, both councils followed the exact same imperial policy—the creation of unity. To be sure, imperial policy cannot be separated from church policy. Indeed, "What is good for the church is also good for the empire."[62] Constantine never had the opportunity to wield a caesaropapist imperial policy because the church, as a whole, never forced his hand. The decisions of Nicaea were taken as orthodoxy, and rabble-rousers were never able to present a clear and present danger to Constantine's vision of the church. Constantius, on the other hand, did not enjoy his father's luck. His entire ecclesiastical policy was challenged and disregarded at every turn. Yet, as he was the continuation of the dynasty and keeper of Constantine's imperial policy, overt state compulsion was not a part of the program. Had Constantius innovated and employed the use of force, the situation could have been entirely different. As it stands, Nicaea and Sirmium had the exact same goal—imperial harmony—and both emperors used the exact same means to achieve it—imperial ceremony.

"No one can doubt that the Father is greater" 79

11 – Modern Orthodox icon by Aidan Hart of the First Ecumenical Council (I Nicea, 325), depicted as essentially Eastern.

12 – Sistine Chapel late 1590s painting the First Ecumenical Council, depicted as essentially papal and Roman Catholic.

Abbreviations

AW: *Athanasius Werke*. Edited by H. G. Opitz. Berlin: De Gruyter, 1934--
CCAC: *Cambridge Companion to the Age of Constantine*. Edited by Noel Lenski. New York: Cambridge University Press, 2006.
GCSEDJ: Die griechischen christlichen Schriftsteller der ersten drei Jahrhunderte. 53 vols. Leipzig: Hinrichs'sche, 1897-1969.
PL: *Patrologia Cursus Completus, Series Latina*. 221 vols. Edited by Jacques-Paul Migne. Paris: Imprimerie Catholique, 1841–65.
SC: Sources chrétiennes. Paris: Cerf, 1941--.

Notes

1 Jerome, *Dialogus contra Luciferianos* 19, PL 23: 172C. (All translations of primary source material are my own.)
2 Socrates, *Historia Ecclesiastica*, 1.23.6, in *Histoire ecclésiastique*, 4 vols. to date, edited by P. Maraval and P. Périchon, SC 477, 493, 505, 506 (2004--).

3 Chantal Vogler, *Constance II et l'administration impériale* (Strasbourg: AECR, 1979), 5; Pedro Barceló, *Constantius II. und seine Zeit: Die Anfänge des Staatskirchentums* (Stuttgart: Klett-Cotta, 2004), 2. For works that have examined the reign of Constantius in detail, see Vogler and Barceló, as well as Richard Klein, *Constantius II. und die christliche Kirche* (Darmstadt: Wissenschaftliche Buchgesellschaft, 1977); Hanns Christof Brennecke, *Hilarius von Poitiers und die Bischofsopposition gegen Konstantius II.* (Berlin: Walter de Gruyter, 1984); Mary Michaels Mudd, *Studies in the Reign of Constantius II* (New York: Carlton Press, 1989); Timothy Barnes, *Athanasius and Constantius: Theology and Politics in the Constantinian Empire* (Cambridge: Harvard University Press, 1993).

4 A. H. M. Jones, *The Later Roman Empire, 284–602* (Norman, OK: University of Oklahoma Press, 1964), 116.

5 Carl Beckwith, *Hilary of Poitiers on the Trinity: From* De Fide *to* De Trinitate (New York: Oxford University Press, 2008), 56. Others boil the events of Sirmium 357 down to a purely theological debate as well. See also J. N. D. Kelly, *Early Christian Doctrines* (New York: Harper, 1958), 238; idem, *Early Christian Creeds* (London: Longman, 1972), 285ff., 291ff.; H. M. Gwatkin, *Studies of Arianism* (New York: AMS Press, 1978), 110–196; R. P. C. Hanson, *The Search for the Christian Doctrine of God. The Aruan Controversy, 318-381* (Edinburgh: T&T Clark, 1988), 347; Lewis Ayres, *Nicaea and Its Legacy: An Approach to Fourth-Century Trinitarian Theology* (Oxford: Oxford University Press, 2004), 137.

6 For discussions of Sirmium, see most notably Hanson, *Search for the Christian Doctrine*, 343-347; Leo Davis, *First Seven Ecumenical Councils, Their History and Theology* (Wilmington, DE: M. Glazier, 1983), 94-95; Brennecke, *Hilarius von Poitiers*, 312–319; Charles Pietri, "La politique de Constance II: Un premier 'césaropapisme' ou *l'imitatio Constantini?*" in *L'Église et l'Empire au IVe siècle*, edited by Friedrich Vittinghoff and Albrecht Dihle (Geneva: Fondation Hardt, 1989), 165-167; Beckwith, *Hilary of Poitiers*, 54–68.

7 Hans-Georg Beck, *Kirche und theologische Literatur* (Munich: C. H. Beck, 1959), 1.

8 Francis Dvornik, *Early Christian and Byzantine Political Philosophy*, 2 vols. (Washington, DC: Dumbarton Oaks, 1966), 2: 611ff.; Johannes Straub, "Constantine as ΚΟΙΝΟΣ ΕΠΙΣΚΟΠΟΣ: Tradition and Innovation in the Representation of the First Christian Emperor's Majesty," *Dumbarton Oaks Papers* 21 (1967): 39ff.; R. F. Price, *Rituals and Power: The Roman Imperial Cult in Asia Minor* (New York: Cambridge University Press, 1984), 15–19; H. A. Drake, *Constantine and the Bishops* (Baltimore: Johns Hopkins University Press, 2000), 3ff.; Raymond Van Dam, *The Roman Revolution of Constantine* (New York: Cambridge University

Press, 2002), 226.
9 Jacob Burckhardt, *The Age of Constantine the Great*, trans. Moses Hadas (New York, 1949), 292. Also notable are Eduard Schwartz, *Kaiser Constantin und die christliche Kirche* (Leipzig: Teubner, 1913); Wilhelm Schneemelcher, *Kirche und Staat im 4. Jahrhundert* (Bonn: Hanstein, 1970); Klaus Girardet, *Kaisergericht und Bischofsgericht* (Bonn: R. Habelt, 1975). For a more recent scholarly discussion of the continued influence of Burckhardt's ideas, see Pietri, "Politique de Constance II," 115; Klein, *Constantius II.*, 1–15.
10 Barnes, *Athanasius and Constantius*, 168; Hanson, *Search for the Christian Doctrine*, 153; Drake, *Constantine and the Bishops*, 13. For a more complete overview of Constantinian historiography, see Barnes, *Athanasius and Constantius*, 1–9; Drake, *Constantine and the Bishops*, 12–34.
11 Timothy Barnes, *Constantine and Eusebius* (Cambridge: Harvard University Press, 1981), 219.
12 See Drake, *Constantine and the Bishops*, 250-272, esp. 256-257.
13 For specifically the Council of Sirmium, 357, see Athanasius, *Apologia de Fuga* 5, in *Apologie à L'empereur Constance. Apologie pour sa fuite*, edited by J.-M. Szymusiak, SC 56 (1958); idem, *Historia Arianorum*, in *AW* 2.1: 45; Hilary, *De Synodis* 11, PL 10: 487A-489B; Phoebadius, *Contra Arianos* 3, PL 20: 15A-C; Sozomen, *Historia Ecclesiastica* 4.6.1–16, and 12.6, in *Sozomenus. Kirchengeschichte*, GCSEDJ 50, edited by J. Bidez and G. C. Hansen (Berlin: Akademie Verlag, 1960); Socrates, *Historia Ecclesiastica* 2.29.
14 Eusebius, *Vita Constantini* 2.6–23, in *Eusebius Werke*, 9 vols., GCSEDJ. (Leipzig/Berlin: J.C. Hinrichs et al., 1902--).; vol. 1, pt. 1, second ed., edited by F. Winkelmann (Berlin: Akademie Verlag, 1975); Athanasius, *De Decretis*, in *AW* 2, pt. 1; Socrates, *Historia Ecclesiastica* 1.8–13; Sozomen, *Historia Ecclesiastica* 1.17–24; Theodoret, *Historia Ecclesiastica* 1.7.1–9, in *Theodoret. Kirchengeschichte*, 2nd ed., edited by L. Parmentier and F. Scheidweiler, GCSEDJ 44, (Berlin: Akademie Verlag, 1954).
15 Beckwith, *Hilary of Poitiers*, 17–53; Robert Grant, "Religion and Politics at Nicaea," *Journal of Religion* 55, no. 1 (1975): 1–12; Hanson, *Search for the Christian Doctrine*, 181–207; Peter L'Huiller, *Church of the Ancient Councils* (Crestwood: St. Vladimir's Seminary Press, 1996), 17–30; A. H. M. Jones, *Constantine and the Conversion of Europe* (Toronto: University of Toronto Press, 1978), 148-165; Kelly, *Early Christian Creeds*, 231-262; Charles Odahl, *Constantine and the Christian Empire* (New York: Routledge, 2004), 196–201; Christopher Stead, *Divine Substance* (Oxford: Oxford University Press, 1977), 233-242.
16 Barnes, *Constantine and Eusebius*, 216; Hanson, *Search for the Christian Doctrine*, 172; Kelly, *Early Christian Creeds*, 211ff.

17 Eusebius, *Vita Constantini* 6. See also Drake, *Constantine and the Bishops*, 251; L'Huiller, *Church of Ancient Councils*, 18; Henry Chadwick, "Ossius of Cordova and the Council of Antioch," *Journal of Theological Studies* 9, no. 2 (1958): 301-304.
18 Eusebius, *Vita Constantini* 3.6.1.
19 Ibid., 3.12.5.
20 Philostorgius, *Historia Ecclesiastica* 1.9, in *Philostorgius. Kirchengeschichte*, 3rd ed., edited by F. Winkelmann, GCSEDJ (Berlin: Akademie Verlag, 1981).
21 Eusebius, *Vita Constantini* 3.15.2.
22 For Constantine's civil war with Licinius, see Barnes, *Constantine and Eusebius*, 62–77.
23 Lactantius, *Divinarum Institutionum* 1.1, PL 10: 116A-117C ; Socrates, *Historia Ecclesiastica* 1.3–4.
24 Van Dam, *Roman Revolution of Constantine*, 11. For Constantine's connection to the tetrarchic understanding of religion and victory, see Simon Corcoran, "Before Constantine," in *CCA C*, 51; Bill Leadbetter, *Galerius and the Will of Diocletian* (New York: Routledge, 2009), 48–80; Sabine MacCormack, *Art and Ceremony in Late Antiquity* (Berkeley: University of California Press, 1981), 169–177, esp. 170.
25 Eusebius, *Historia Ecclesiastica* 9.9; idem, *Vita Constantini* 1.36; Lactantius, *De Mortibus persecutorum* 34, PL 7: 249A-250A; Sozomen, *Historia Ecclesiastica* 1.7.3; Zosimus, *Historia Nova* 2.16, in *Zosimi comitis et exadvocata fisci historia nova*, edited by Ludwig Mendelssohn (Leipzig: Teubner, 1887).
26 Eusebius, *Vita Constantini* 1.28.2.
27 Ibid., 2.24–42, esp. 2.24.1–3. See also idem, *Historia Ecclesiastica* 10.7.1.
28 Drake, *Constantine and the Bishops*, 270ff. One of the *few* aspects of the Constantine's reign that scholars agree upon is his desire for church unity. See also Barnes, *Constantine and Eusebius*, 212ff.
29 Eusebius, *Vita Constantini* 3.13.2
30 Athanasius, *De Decretis* 33.17. Even if Constantine was actually the one to propose the term *homoousios* at the council, its origins lie elsewhere. The emperor was likely given the suggestion by one of his advisors. Philostorgius, *Historia Ecclesiastica* 1.7, suggests that Ossius and Alexander met beforehand to craft the agenda for Nicaea. For more theories, see Hanson, *Search for the Christian Doctrine*, 235; Rowan Williams, *Arius: Heresy and Tradition* (Grand Rapids: Eerdmans, 2002), 68–70.
31 Eusebius, *Vita Constantini* 3.10.2–5.
32 Ibid., 3.11.
33 Ammianus Marcellinus, *Res Gestae* 16.5.18, in *Rerum gestarum libri qui supersunt*, edited by Wolfgang Seyfarth, 2 vols. (Leipzig: Teubner,

1978). For a more detailed description, see H. Stern, "Remarks on the *'Adoratio'* under Diocletian," *Journal of the Warburg and Courtsuld Institutes* 17, nos. 1–2 (1954): 184–189.

34   Dvornik, *Early Christian and Byzantine Political Philosophy*, 2: 640. See also Hamilton Hess, *Early Development of Canon Law and the Council of Serdica* (New York: Oxford University Press, 2002), 25; Heinrich Gelzer, *Ausgewählte kleine Schriften* (Leipzig: Teubner, 1907), 144; Pierre Batiffol, *Études de liturgie et d'archéologie chrétienne* (Paris: J. G. Gabalda, 1919), 84–153; Elisabeth Herrmann, *Ecclesia in re publica: Die Entwicklung der Kirche von pseudostaatlicher zu staatlich inkorporierter Existenz* (Frankfurt am Main: Bern, 1980), 61–70. For more on the senate procedures themselves, see Hermann Sieben, *Die Konzilsidee der alten Kirche* (Munich: Schöningh, 1979), 478–481; Richard Talbert, *The Senate of Imperial Rome* (Princeton: Princeton University Press, 1984), 221–302. Perhaps Nicaea was a step in the evolution of the *silention* given form by Justinian. See A. Christophilopoulu, "Silention," *Byzantinische Zeitschrift* 44 (1951): 79ff.; Otto Treitinger, *Die oströmische Kaiser- und Reichsidee nach ihrer Gestaltung im höfischen Zeremoniell* (Darmstadt: Wissenschaftliche Buchgesellschaft, 1956), 52ff.

35   Eusebius, *Vita Constantini* 3.17–20.

36   Ibid., 3.6.1. Socrates, on the other hand, refers to Nicaea as *megalēn kai agian synodon* (*Historia Ecclesiastica* 1.9.1).

37   Grant, "Religion and Politics," 5, argues that the word "ecumenical" means nothing more than "Roman imperial."

38   See Hess, *Early Development*, 5–34; Davis, *First Seven Ecumenical Councils*, 30; L'Huiller, *Church of the Ancient Councils*, 18.

39   Barnes, *Constantine and Eusebius*, 225.

40   Sozomen, *Historia Ecclesiastica* 1.16, 1.27; Socrates, *Historia Ecclesiastica* 1.14, 1.26–27.

41   Sozomen, *Historia Ecclesiastica* 2.34; Socrates, *Historia Ecclesiastica* 1.39.

42   Mark Humphries, "In Nomine Patris: Constantine the Great and Constantius II in Christological Polemic," *Zeitschrift für Alte Geschichte* 46, no. 4 (1997): 451; Brennecke, *Hilarius von Poitiers*, 315. For more about the usurpation of Magnentius, see Barnes, *Athanasius and Constantius*, 101–8; Brennecke, *Hilarius von Poitiers*, 65–71.

43   In 337, upon the ascension of Constantine II, Constans, and Constantius, there was a bloody purge of all possible imperial claimants. There is confusion as to who exactly was involved in the massacre. For more see Robert Frakes, "The Dynasty of Constantine Down to 363," in *CCAC*, 98–99; Mark Humphries, "From Usurper to Emperor," *Journal of Late Antiquity* 1, no. 1 (2008): 99ff.; Barnes, *Athanasius and Constantius*, 34–35; Noel Lenski, "The Reign of Constantine," in

CCAC, 62; and most notably R. W. Burgess, "The Summer of Blood: The 'Great Massacre' of 337 and the Promotion of the Sons of Constantine," *Dumbarton Oaks Papers* 62 (2008): 5–51.

44 Sozomen, *Historia Ecclesiastica* 3.19.5.
45 Socrates, *Historia Ecclesiastica* 2.22; Sozomen, *Historia Ecclesiastica* 3.20.2. Constantius, however, claimed that Athanasius plotted against him with not only his brother but even with the usurper Magnentius. See Athanasius, *Apologia ad Constantium* 2–9.
46 Hilary, *Contra Constantium* 1.27, PL 10: 603A.
47 Julian, Éloge de Constance 1.7, in vol. 1, pt. 1 of *L'empereur Julien. Oeuvres complètes*, 2 vols. in 4, edited by J. Bidez (Paris: Les Belles Lettres, 1924-[vol. 1, pt. 1]1932).
48 Hilary, *Contra Constantium* 1.7; later in the venomous text Hilary even declares the emperor as the Antichrist (1.11): PL 10: 583B, 589A.
49 Athanasius, *Historia Arianorum* 52. As Humphries noted, "In Nomine Patris," 456, "It is also in the *Historia Arianorum* that we first encounter the dramatic opposition of Constantius and Constantine" See also Barnes, *Athanasius and Constantius*, 19–33; David Gwynn, *The Eusebians: The Polemic of Athanasius of Alexandria and the Construction of the 'Arian Controversy'* (New York: Oxford University Press, 2007),147-158.
50 Hilary, *Contra Constantium* 1.27, PL 10: 603A.
51 Brennecke, "Die sirmische Synode von 357 und ihre theologische Formel," in *Hilarius von Poitiers*, 312–25; Paul Burns, "Hilary of Poitiers' Road to Béziers," *Journal of Early Christian Studies* 2, no. 3 (1994): 277; Dvornik, *Early Christian and Byzantine Political Philosophy*, 2: 729; W. H. C. Frend, *Rise of Christianity* (Philadelphia: Fortress Press, 1984), 536.
52 Barceló, *Constantius II.*, 169.
53 The bishops Valens, Ursacius, and Germinius unquestionably played an important role at the council as well. See Athanasius, *De Synodis* 2.28; Phoebadis, *Contra Arianos* 3.1.
54 See Barnes, *Athanasius and Constantius*, 219-222, for a detailed explanation of the imperial itinerary. Socrates, *Historia Ecclesiastica* 2.30, stated that the creed was published in the presence of the emperor. However, both Socrates and Sozomen seem to have combined the Councils of Sirmium in 351 and 357 into one account. However, the presence of the creed and the insistence that the emperor forced Ossius to sign the document demonstrate that their accounts do contain information about Sirmium. For more on this, see Barnes, *Athanasius and Constantius*, 231–232.
55 Hilary, *De Synodis* 11; Athanasius, *De Synodis* 2.28–29.
56 Phoebadius, *Contra Arianos* 3.3.
57 Athanasius, *Historia Arianorum* 6.45.

58 Socrates, *Historia Ecclesiastica* 2.31; Sozomen, *Historia Ecclesiastica* 4.6.
59 Hilary, *De Synodis* 10.
60 Gwynn, *Eusebians* (New York: Oxford University Press, 2007), 249. Cf. Dvornik, *Early Christian and Byzantine Political Philosophy*, 2: 731; Klein, *Constantius II.*, 67.
61 Eusebius, *Vita Constantini* 2.64–72.
62 Barceló, *Constantius II.*, 177.

3   The Deacon Dioscorus and Justinian's Indecision

Joshua Powell

13 – Emperor Justinian I, Bishop Maximian of Ravenna, and court officials, depicted in the late Roman clothing of the time on the choir mosaics of San Vitale Basilica in Ravenna.

This paper will address a pair of strange events occurring in the year 519. This year saw the growth of a theological controversy around a group of monks from Scythia Minor, modern-day Dobruja. These Scythian monks had proposed as a solution to the theological ills of the day a common confession that "one of the Trinity suffered" (*unus de trinitate passus est*). The confession produced an unusual reception indeed. First, the monks faced hostility when presenting their ideas in Constantinople. Seeking some confirmation, they then departed for Rome. There, they were initially welcomed along with their ideas. But this would not remain the case.

With the departure of the monks from Constantinople, dispatches were sent to warn Rome that little good would come from giving them a hearing. Among these dispatches was a letter from the theologically active Justinian, then the emperor's nephew and likely already the heir-apparent. Justinian had a decidedly negative view of the meddlesome monks and their confession and urged Pope Hormisdas to expel them quickly.

And now we come to the strange part. In contrast to Rome's earlier reception of the monks, Hormisdas soon changed his mind and came to reject them, causing them to leave Rome and seek allies elsewhere. Yet Justinian, within days of sending the initial and hostile letter to Rome, wrote again arguing in the monks' favor and even indicating that the peace of the church itself depended upon their ideas. Neither Hormisdas nor Justinian offers any explanation for his swift reversal. It is under these circumstances that the notion of network position, so important to modern network theory, will become particularly helpful. As we shall see, the position of certain actors within the network connecting Rome and Constantinople gave them an unusual degree of informal influence over major players such as the pope and Justinian.

Before we begin discussion of the subject, we will do well to consider its importance, as it may not be immediately evident. After all, although Hormisdas and Justinian changed opinions concerning the Scythian monks and their formula, this need not be more than a curiosity, worthy perhaps of a footnote and little else. Yet the event takes on an importance all its own in the historiography of Justinian's reign and his relationship to the church and theology. Whatever one's view of Justinian's reign as a whole, his approach is often seen as erratic and even capricious.[1] Few events in his reign are more frequently used as evidence for this fact than his sudden reversal on the matter of the Scythian monks. Patrick Gray, for example, chose to highlight this event as a paradigm for Justinian's attitude toward ecclesiastical policy in the *Cambridge Companion to the Age of Justinian*:

> This about-face is extremely instructive: for one thing, it reveals that Justinian's fundamental agenda was – an emperor could have no other – to restore the peace of the church. It also reveals that Justinian was not concerned about the theological issues *per se*, since he seems to have been willing to move from one position to its opposite in mere days, and with no sign of a theological justification, simply because

he suddenly realized the potential of the monks' initiative. The incident thus shows Justinian to be a pragmatic power broker looking for a deal that would do the job.[2]

Likewise, in a recent and more comprehensive treatment of Justinian's ecclesiastical policy, Volker L. Menze sees something fundamental to Justinian's modus operandi in this reversal. After denying that one can really analyze the personal faith of another, at least so long as the other neglected to write a work such as Augustine's *Confessions*, Menze proceeds to consider Justinian's image as a theologian on the throne. This image, as Menze has it, was shrewdly crafted for political purposes. As evidence for an ability and willingness to use theological artifice to political ends, Menze cites Justinian's reversal on the Scythian monks:

> It cannot be excluded that Justinian had become a connoisseur of Christian discourses over the years and tried to force personal persuasions onto his subjects. However, it is more conclusive to regard his treatises first of all as works of a statesman who wished to reach a universally accepted dogma for the Christian *Oecumene* over which he ruled. Within a couple of weeks during the summer of 519, Justinian switched his dogmatic position from opposing the theopaschite formula to strongly encouraging Pope Hormisdas to accept it. Obviously this could mean a speedy personal theological development, but it rather demonstrates Justinian's political far-sightedness that the theopaschite position could be useful. Similarly, political shrewdness should be assumed as the reason why Justinian presented himself as a theologian on the throne.[3]

In a still more recent work, Richard Price seems to echo Gray's interpretation directly as he acknowledges that the "suddenness of the change may suggest that [Justinian] was a pragmatic broker, indifferent to theological niceties but keen to propitiate miaphysite opinion."[4] Price does offer some modification of this view, however, suggesting that Justinian would have been motivated chiefly by competition with Vitalian at this stage rather than by interest in conciliating the non-Chalcedonians.[5]

While these are examples of broader conclusions that scholars have drawn from Justinian's sudden change in opinion, some attempts have also been made to explain the change itself. A. A. Vasiliev, for instance, attributes the change to the influence of the prominent Chalcedonian and master of soldiers, Vitalian.[6] Regrettably, however, he only offers this attribution as a suggestion and does not propose a detailed argument in its defense. A similar suggestion is made by Aloys Grillmeier, who focuses rather on Justinian's first opinion, attributing it to the passing influence of papal legates in Constantinople.[7] These suggestions do not need to be considered mutually exclusive, as we shall see. For now it is only important to emphasize that the matter has been given little attention beyond the suggestions. This leaves us in a position where great significance is placed on a relatively minor change in Justinian's opinion, but little detailed explanation is given for the change. The remainder of the paper will seek a detailed explanation and, in so doing, will consider a new way of looking at the problem as a whole. We will turn now to the background of the theopaschite controversy.

Ecclesiastical relations between Rome and Constantinople had been under some strain for the past few decades. The first major schism between old and new Rome began in 484 during the reign of the patriarch Acacius. Only under the new pro-Chalcedonian emperor Justin did negotiations to heal this Acacian schism begin in earnest. To this end, Pope Hormisdas sent a delegation to Constantinople to oversee the reunion that, with the aid of imperial court, would be effected by 519. Among the group sent by Rome were two bishops, Germanus and John; a priest, Blandus; the deacon Felix; and, most prominent in our sources in spite of his formally low rank, the deacon Dioscorus.

The theopaschite controversy of the sixth century was short-lived and in many ways uneventful enough that it scarcely merits the term "controversy."[8] Yet it offers some important insights into the development of religious policy during the period. The controversy arose in response to the formula proposed by the Scythian monks as a possible solution to the divisions over Chalcedon, which had greatly disturbed the East. The fresh approach came in the form of the Scythian monks' suggestion that all confess together, "*Unus ex Trinitate passus est carne.*"⁹ While the Scythians believed Chalcedon was essentially correct, they thought this theopaschite confession would address the concerns of non-Chalcedonians that the fourth council was Nestorian at heart.¹⁰

Much of what we know about the beginnings of the controversy must be gleaned from the reports of the papal delegation contained in a collection of document known as the *Collectio Avellana*.¹¹ In a way, this places us in a situation similar to that of Pope Hormisdas, who depended primarily upon the witness of the deacon Dioscorus and his colleagues. From his earliest reports on the Scythian monks, Dioscorus is kind enough to the historian to make his biases clear. His first mention of the monks comes in Letter 216 of the *Collectio Avellana*:

> And since these things are being advanced, and in them the catholic church daily prevails, the ancient plotter has stirred up the monks of Scythia, who are of the house of the master of soldiers Vitalian, enemies of the prayers of all Christians, whose disturbance begets not a few obstacles to the unity of the church and a great many to the ordination in the aforementioned Antiochian church.¹²

That the devil is responsible for the activities of the Scythian monks cannot be doubted if we are to take Dioscorus's word. For when one discusses the Council of Chalcedon, these obscurantist monks, enemies of Christian prayers, only showed it to be "doubtful and unsound and opened to the error of all heresies."¹³ In his first letter on the Scythian monks, both in tone and in content, Dioscorus does not so much attempt to report events at Constantinople as to shape perceptions in Rome.

The letter as a whole reads as a series of charges against the monks. Dioscorus warns that the monks "hasten to Rome hoping to have a number of *capitula* confirmed by your beatitude. It is in these, among other things, where they want to say, 'One of the Trinity [was] crucified,' which is said neither in the holy synod nor in the letter of holy Pope Leo nor in ecclesiastical custom."¹⁴ If the monks' formula were approved, it seemed "that it would produce no small number of dissensions and scandals among the churches."[15] What is worse, even the emperor Anastasius and the "disciples of Eutyches" would have found such a formula amenable. For Dioscorus, Chalcedon alone should suffice and he would brook no deviance from this point. What is evident in Dioscorus's accusations is a kind of inflexibility that makes negotiation impossible, and perhaps this is intentional. It is important to note that the delegation was sent with strict instructions, the slightest deviation from which would undoubtedly seem to risk the project as a whole. Indeed, the deacon indicates as much, warning against a failure of all they had tried to accomplish if anything at all is added to the Chalcedonian synod and the epistles of Leo.[16] Acting under strict instructions from Rome as ambassador to a penitent Constantinople, it is little surprise that Dioscorus should be so hardened in his position.[17]

The reader comes away with an image of the Scythians as meddling, undiplomatic troublemakers. This is seconded by a letter, number 217, addressed to Hormisdas from the whole papal delegation. Yet the language of this letter presents us with an interesting comparison. On the one hand, Letter 217 has less tendency to attach unnecessary invective to its complaints about the Scythian monks and offers more details in its stead. On the other hand, a careful look at the language hints that, although it was addressed from the whole delegation, the main author of Letter 217 may have been none other than Dioscorus.

The first evidence for this claim comes from Dioscorus's habitual use of certain vocabulary that is also paralleled in Letter 217.[18] The close verbal parallels between several passages, however, provide the strongest evidence. One may point, for example, to such parallels in each letter's description of the Scythian monks' immediate plans.[19] Some of the similarity can be accounted for by the like circumstances each letter describes. Even so, several similar passages may be cited, and, taken together with the other aspects of the letters mentioned above, they build a plausible case that Dioscorus is largely responsible for this letter written in the name of the whole delegation.[20]

If Dioscorus is responsible for drafting reports written in the name of the whole committee, we begin to get a clearer picture of him and his position. Whatever his clerical rank and whatever his formal position, this deacon is the most influential member of the delegation. Of those letters sent between the delegation and Hormisdas which that survive in the *Collectio Avellana*, the majority are to and from the delegation as a whole. It is only with Dioscorus, however, that we find letters to and from an individual member.[21] The slight change in tone between Letters 216 and 217, may also reflect the difference between the informal relationship between Dioscorus and Hormisdas, on the one hand, and the official mission of the delegation, on the other. Though a member of a larger delegation, Dioscorus is also acting as a personal adviser to the pope.

There is a further detail about the Scythian monks contained in Letters 216 and 217 that can be confirmed with certainty, and this detail elucidates Dioscorus's portrayal of them. As we have already seen, both letters are anxious about the fact that the Scythian monks are on their way to Rome. If the Scythian monks had already departed, it was uncertain that the delegation's letters would precede the monks to Rome. It is unlikely, therefore, that the delegation wrote merely to inform Rome that the monks were coming. Again, if the monks were bearing texts, it would have been superfluous for the delegation to write to supply Rome with notes on the texts' contents. Still, there are several reasons for the delegation to write. The delegation would have been remiss in its duty as representative of Rome had it not informed of affairs that would soon spill over in the West. But the expectation that the delegation should relate relevant information cannot by itself account for much of what we have seen. This is especially true of the invective, the accusations of heresy, and the attempts to explain the consequences of approving the monks' views. Also, the delegation likely believed it their duty to inform Rome that the monks had objected to the appointment of Paul as bishop of Antioch. This still does not explain the elements for which the first reason did not account, but it is suggestive. The letters are not satisfied merely to report the Scythian monks' objections—indeed, they say little about the actual objections the monks made—but they do take the opportunity to portray the monks as unnecessarily troublesome. This points us to a third reason and possibly the chief goal of the letters. They were written not only to relate some information to Rome, as one expects of a representative, but also to shape the way Rome would receive the monks and their writings. Rather than acting merely as a conduit for information, Dioscorus is working carefully to stay in control of the flow and content of information. It is his position, as a crucial link in a network connecting Rome and Constantinople, that makes this possible. This point is especially well illustrated by how events played out upon the arrival of the Scythians in Rome.

The Scythians were fortunate to precede Dioscorus's letter to Rome. The delegation's letters were dated June 29, 519, and the monks had already arrived sometime in July or early August.[22] There they seem to have received as strong a welcome as could be hoped, both for themselves and their ideas. The *libellus* which that comes down to us claims to have been rejected in Constantinople, only to be approved by the pope, Senate, and all the Church of Rome.[23] The Scythian monks seemed, therefore, to have attained the advantage in Rome where they failed in Constantinople. If the monks successfully managed to present themselves as defenders of Chalcedon, it is little surprise the Rome should receive them well.

Yet Dioscorus's report eventually did arrive in Rome, and it seems the mood changed accordingly.[24] One of the monks, John Maxentius, later complained of being detained in Rome for nearly fourteen 14 months.[25] It is clear that the monks were detained on account of Dioscorus's influence. For one thing, we know that Hormisdas quickly sought further council from Dioscorus after receiving Letter 216. This may be deduced from Letter 224 of the *Collectio Avellana*, which presents itself as a reply to a papal request for advice.[26] Before we consider the contents of Dioscorus's reply, however, our attention must be given to another aspect of the theopaschite controversy.

Dioscorus was not the only one who saw fit to write Hormisdas upon the Scythian monks' departure for Rome. Justinian wrote two letters, the first of which was sent along with Letters 216 and 217 and is dated with them at June 29, 519.[27] The second followed closely on the heels of the first, being dated sometime at the beginning of July in the same year.[28] The strangeness of these two letters, indeed of the whole situation, lies in the sudden contrast between them.

The first, Letter 187, resembles the contemporary dispatches of the delegation in important ways. Dioscorus had described the Scythian monks as men whose restlessness would put the unity of the church at risk.[29] The same description is found in Justinian's letter.[30] Dioscorus had warned that the Scythians were attempting to introduce novelties not to be found in the Council of Chalcedon or in the epistles of Leo.[31] Justinian shared this same complaint.[32] After this complaint, Justinian may even make a direct reference to the opinions of the delegation on the matter, though a lacuna in the text obscures certainty here. It is probable, therefore, that Letter 187, sent with Letters 216 and 217, was drafted under the advice of the delegation. All the letters build the same argument, use similar language, and have the same agenda: to undermine the Scythian monks' appeal to Hormisdas. In addition to warning the pope of the coming monks, Justinian's letter even suggests that they be thrown from Rome upon their arrival.[33] The second letter, number 191 of the *Collectio Avellana*, is altogether different. It is so different, in point of fact, that it presents us with a puzzle. Making no reference to his earlier letter or to the Roman delegation, Justinian introduces the subject of this letter with an emphasis on unity and some important references:

> Whatever is more prudent, whatever more secure, so it be carried out for the holy faith and for the concord of the sacred churches, that we desire. Whence our brother, the most glorious Vitalian, [......] wrote to your beatitude and ...[...] we too have undertaken to indicate that your beatitude ought to bring about those things which would permit the peace and concord for the holy churches. And so to your sanctity we have immediately sent with letters of our most pious emperor [the messenger] who may bring back a rather more settled answer [...].[34]

The important question to which Justinian refers, as we will see momentarily, is none other than the status of the theopaschite confession. It is instructive, however, to notice at once the stress Justinian places on his connection to the master of soldiers Vitalian, a relative of at least one of the Scythian monks and their chief patron in Constantinople. That Vitalian should be mentioned in the first favorable letter Justinian writes concerning the Scythian monks, and that the same should be excluded from a hostile letter in favor of the delegation, hints that Vitalian may be responsible for Justinian's change of heart. The letter continues:

> Wherefore we ask that, if it is possible, with a swift reply given and the religious monks satisfied, you send [them] back to us. For if that question is not solved by your prayers and attentiveness, we fear that the peace of the holy churches will be unable to come forth. Therefore, knowing that the reward and risk of that affair is watched over by you, carefully discuss and send back to us a very substantial answer by the aforementioned monks, if it is possible, before our legate reaches your beatitude; for the whole effort depends on this alone.[35]

Within a very few days, Justinian had moved from viewing the Scythian monks as a threat to treating them as indispensable allies. Indeed, he even implies by his positive treatment of the monks that the unity of the church depends on a positive response from the pope. This is the exact opposite of what he had claimed in the previous letter. Accounting for this sudden change is not easy and can never be certain. But we are not without hints.

As we have seen, Letters 216, 217, and 224 all make explicit mention of Vitalian's involvement in the case of the Scythian monks. That he acted as their advocate has already been mentioned. But while these earlier letters speak of Vitalian's presence at the hearing held for the monks, they are altogether silent about Justinian. It is almost a truism at this point to say that Justinian was more personally involved in theological controversies than his royal uncle. But it is Justin who appears in Letter 217, involved in the hearing and reconciling the opponent of the Scythian monks, Paternus of Tomis, and their patron, Vitalian.[36] Justinian's absence from the letter certainly does not indicate his absence from the hearing, but it opens the possibility.

We can say for certain that not all the hearings concerning the Scythian monks involved all those who were part of this controversy. At one point, Dioscorus makes this complaint:

> Afterward without us, the *vir magnificus* Vitalian, master of soldiers, and the bishop of Constantinople called the aforementioned Victor among themselves; they spoke with him: what they settled among themselves, we do not know. Afterward, neither Victor came to us nor was the case pled.[37]

Vitalian and the patriarch thought a solution to Victor's objections to the Scythian monks could best be achieved without the presence of the Roman delegation, who had come to dislike the monks intensely. Up to that point, we have no evidence of Justinian's involvement in the controversy in any capacity. After this incident, however, we find Justinian writing against the Scythian monks with the very delegation who had fallen so far out of favor with Vitalian and the patriarch.[38]

This combination of circumstances presents us with an enticing explanation for Justinian's sudden reversal. Justinian's initial hostility to the Scythian monks may be credited to his source of information about them. From what we have seen in Letter 187, Justinian was clearly aware of the version of events that Dioscorus and the delegation gives in Letters 216 and 217. Indeed, this seemed to have shaped his view of the monks. If Justinian were not present at the hearing, then it is only the more certain that he would have depended on Dioscorus for information. His new-found appreciation for the monks in Letter 191 is accompanied by an acknowledgment that he was by then aware of the same information Vitalian sent to Rome. By the time Justinian writes Letter 191, he has at least two sources of information, and he now favors the position of Vitalian. The likeliest explanation for Justinian's reversal, therefore, is that through his contact with Vitalian he was given a perspective on some events that Dioscorus could not have, because of his absence, and a perspective on other events that Dioscorus did not want to give, because of his opposition to the monks.

This is the exact inverse of what we see with Hormisdas. His apparent early acceptance of the Scythian monks was conditioned by his ignorance of Dioscorus' position. Dioscorus's letter put that early acceptance in doubt. This shows how very important the control of information was to Dioscorus in his ability to control the views of his ostensible superiors.

Justinian changed his views on the Scythian monks, and the preponderance of evidence points to his connection to Vitalian, if as nothing more than a source of information, as the best explanation for this change. Likewise, Hormisdas's shifting opinion about the Scythian monks and their formulations may be attributed to shifting sources of information. As discussed earlier, the Scythians were initially welcomed in Rome. But when Letters 216, 217, and 187 arrived in Rome, they gave Hormisdas reason to doubt. After his change of mind, Justinian wrote Hormisdas, requesting a response on the matter of the theopaschite formula, but found himself frustrated. Hormisdas's reply in Letter 190, dated September 2, 519, reveals his dependence on Dioscorus. In this letter, Hormisdas avoids giving any direct answer to the theopaschite question. Instead, he claims that the Scythian monks themselves refuse to leave Rome, fearing that they might be ambushed on the road.[39] They had not yet been expelled from Rome, however, because Hormisdas awaited further information from the delegation.[40]

Dioscorus's advice arrived in the form of Letter 224, dated October 15, 519. We have already noted several of the more aggressively anti-Scythian aspects of this letter and need not belabor the point. If Hormisdas had begun to hesitate with the arrival of the delegation's letters, an equally if not more important event was the return of the delegation itself. We know that the Scythian monks had come to Rome sometime in July or early August, 519. Thereafter, they were detained for fourteen 14 months while Hormisdas considered their case. This would place their expulsion sometime around September or October of 520. In spite of Justinian's repeated requests for a response on the theopaschite question, we have no evidence of any other changes in this period save one. Letter 192, written by Justin, was carried on the return trip of the delegation to Rome. Its date of reception is September 17, 520, precisely at the time when the Scythian monks were finally expelled by Rome. Having left Constantinople on account of their conflict with Dioscorus, the Scythian monks now found they were unwelcome at Rome as well.

At the center of the apparent indecision of both Hormisdas and Justinian is the influence of Dioscorus. Influence can, at times, seem a difficult thing to define. In some cases, it can derive from individual charisma, in others, from a formal and ritualized office. Dioscorus had neither. But the case of Dioscorus reveals how a position within a network as gate-keeper of information can grant one an otherwise unexpected amount of control over events. The papacy had little choice but to rely upon a delegation to represent its interests in Constantinople. But even as the pope used the delegation to project papal influence, papal policy toward the Scythian monks was shaped by the information that the delegation could provide and the way in which the delegation chose to spin that information. This can be a difficult fact for historians to accept because it has unfortunate consequences for our ability to reconstruct events. Our sources tend to focus on those who are most able to shape events through their exercise of formal positions of power. But institutional behavior and policy making can often be shaped by the actions of individuals with vastly less formal power. In this case even Justinian, who himself already exercised a great deal of informal influence in the empire, was subject to the sources of information available to him. This also draws into question any picture of Justinian as capricious or indecisive during the theopaschite controversy. The case as a whole has offered us a rare opportunity to see just how much influence may be exercised by those who could occupy the spaces between acknowledged centers of power.

Abbreviations

CCSL 85A: *Maxentius, Ioannes Tomitanus Opuscula; Capitula sancti Augustini*. Edited by F. Glorie. In *Corpus Christianorum Series Latina* 85A.Turnhout: Brepols, 1978.

CSEL 35B: *Collectio Avellana (Epistulae imperatorum pontificum aliorum inde ac a. XVII usque ad a. DLIII datae)*. Edited by Otto Guenther. *Corpus Scriptorum ecclesiasticorum Latinorum* 35.B. Vienna: Akademie der Wissenschaften in Wien, 1897.

Notes

1   Thus one finds William Frend, borrowing from Eduard Schwartz, offering this as a given: "The zigzag policy of Justinian towards the

Monophysites in the first half of his reign is well known" (*Rise of the Monophysite Movement* [Cambridge: Cambridge University Press, 1972], 255). Of course, there are exceptions. One thinks of the portrayal of Justinian, by Milton V. Anastos, as both consistent Cyrillian Chalcedonian and consistent despot. See Milton V. Anastos, "Justinian's Despotic Control over the Church as Illustrated by His Edicts on the Theopaschite Formula and His Letter to Pope John II in 553," in *Mélanges G. Ostrogorsky*, edited by Franjo Barisic, 2: 1–11, rpt. in *Studies in Byzantine Intellectual History*, edited by Milton V. Anastos (London: Variorum, 1979), passim.

2. Patrick T. R. Gray, "The Legacy of Chalcedon: Christological Problems and Their Significance," in *The Cambridge Companion to the Age of Justinian*, edited by Michael Maas, 215–338 (New York: Cambridge University Press, 2005), "The legacy of Chalcedon", 228. This is also roughly equivalent to Gray's earlier statement on the matter in Patrick T. R. Gray, *The Defense of Chalcedon in the East (451–553)* (Leiden: Brill, 1979), 49–50.

3. Volker L. Menze, *Justinian and the Making of the Syrian Orthodox Church* (Oxford: Oxford University Press, 2008), 252.

4. Richard Price, *Acts of the Council of Constantinople of 553* (Liverpool: Liverpool University Press, 2009), 9.

5. Price also cautions against regarding Justinian as a mere politician on religious matters, pointing to the "consistency with which he subsequently defended Cyrillian Chalcedonianism:" Ibid., 9-10.

6. A. A. Vasiliev, *Justin the First: An Introduction to the Epoch of Justinian the Great* (Cambridge, MA: Harvard University Press, 1950), 193.

7. "Where did Justinian stand? When Pope Hormisdas demanded from his legates a report of success, Vitalian and Justinian seized the opportunity to report to Rome about the monks, concerning whom the papal legates themselves made some very critical remarks. No doubt influenced by the negative attitude of the papal legates, in the heat of the moment Justinian wrote a letter, in which the names of the monks are mentioned and clearly warned against." See Alois Grillmeier, *Christ in Christian Tradition,* translated by John Bowden, vol. 2.2, *The Church of Constantinople in the Sixth Century* (Louisville, KY: Westminster John Knox Press, 1995), 322.

8. By "theopaschite controversy of the sixth century" I mean, of course, to distinguish it from the much larger fifth-century controversy surrounding the trisagion and certainly from the unrelated patripassianist controversy of the third century. "The designation ''Theopaschite' originated as an insult among their enemies (notably the pro-Roman Acometae monks at Constantinople), but it is particularly misleading in so far as it suggests some form of theological connection with the

third-century Patripassions, when there is no such relation whatsoever." See John A. McGuckin, "The 'Theopaschite Confession' (Text and Historical Context): a Study in the Cyrilline Re-interpretation of Chalcedon," *Journal of Ecclesiastical History* 35, no. 2 (April 1984): 239. The former is related to but distinct from the sixth-century theopaschite controversy.

9   "One of the Trinity suffered in the flesh."

10 Thus Gray, *Defense of Chalcedon*, 51: "In effect, a new type of reconciliation was being proposed. Previous emperors had attempted to reconcile the Chalcedonians to the anti-Chalcedonians and vice-versa by variations on the approach of the Henoticon. Such an approach had always implied an unacceptable by-passing of Chalcedon. Justin and Justinian proposed, instead, to reconcile the anti-Chalcedonians to Chalcedon ; the attempt to reconcile, rather than to correct or neglect, was the new feature of their policy."

11 The paucity of primary sources on the subject is bested only by the paucity of secondary sources. The most complete narrative summary of events remains Émile Amann, "Scythes (Moines)," in *Dictionnaire de théologie catholique*, 14, pt. 23, ed. Émile Amann, Eugène Mangenet, Alfred Vacant (Paris: Letouzey et Ané, 1941), 1746-1753.

12 CSEL35.B, 216.5. "Et quia ista aguntur et in his cotidie proficit ecclesia catholica, insidiator antiquus excitauit monachos de Scythia, qui de domo magistri militum Uitaliani sunt, omnium Christianorum uotis aduersarious, quorum inquietudo non pauas moras generauit unitat iecclesiarum et magnopere de praedictae ecclessiae Antiochenae ordinatione."

13 CSEL 35.B, 216.9: "Non, quasi non intellegentes, nisi conantes per subtilitatem ad hoc nosa dducere, ut disputetur de synodo Calcedonensi. Quod si factum fuerit, dubia et infirma ostenditur et haereticorum omnium patuit errori."

14 CSEL 35.B, 216.6: "Isti monachi [...]... Romam festinant sperantes aliquanta capitula a beatitudine uestra confirmari."*Capitula*, literally '"chapters'," are enumerated points to be argued.

15 CSEL 35.B, 216.6: "Quod si permittitur fieri, mihi uidetur dissensiones aut scandala non mediocria nasci inter ecclesias."

16 CSEL 35.B, 216.10: "Inter alia si post synodum Calcedonensem, si post epistolas papae Leonis, si post libellos, quos dederunt et dant episcopi et per ipsos satisfecerunt sedi apostolicae, iterum aliquid nouum addatus, sic mihi uidetur, quia quicquid factum est destruitur."

17 CSEL 35.B, 216.4: That Dioscorus was anxious make clear to Hormisdas how closely he was adhering to the instructions is evident from an earlier passage concerning the choice of Paul for the See of Antioch: "Uuolerunt et temptauerunt hic eum ordinare; ego iussionis uestrae non immemor contradixi dicens "iussit domnus noster beatissimus

papa secundum antiquam consuetudinem ibi eum episcopum ordinari'. hoc obtinuit, quod praecepistis."

18 For example, *magnopere*, which also makes an appearance also in *CSEL*35.B, 217; see also 216.1, 216.5, 216.7., 217.8. Likewise, *intentio* is frequently used in both letters to cover a relatively wide range of circumstances where any number of other expressions could have been chosen: see 216.4, 216.8, 217.7, 217.11. (Here and in notes 19-22 below, all references are likewise to *CSEL* 35.B.)

19 Compare Letters 216.6: "Isti monachi, inter quos est Leontius, qui se dicit parentem esse magistri militum, Romam festinant sperantes aliquanta capitula a beatitudine uestra confirmari. est in ipsis *inter cetera*, ubi volunt dicere unum de trinitate crucifixum [...]" and 217.7--8: "Magnopere praedicti monachi ad Italiam uenientes *aliquanta capitula* proponere habent, *inter quae* et ''unum de trinitate crucifixum' continetur, *sperantes ita confirmari ex auctoritate beatudini suestra*."

20 For other parallels, cf., e.g., the almost nervous insistence that the papal instructions were followed (at 216.4 and 217.6) and the circumlocuitous manner of naming the Antiochian priest (216.4 and 217.4).

21 By my count there are seven letters to (170, 219, 221, 226-229) and seven letters from (185, 213, 214, 217, 218, 223, 225) the delegation. There are two letters each to (173, 175) and from (216, 224) Dioscorus personally.

22 Thus F. Glorie says, "Interea Paulinus et ipsi Scythae monachi Romam aduenerunt mense VII siue VIII ineunte." See *CCSL*85A, xxix. In this context, the term *libellus*, literally a "little book," is a petition advocating for a specific doctrinal position.

23 *CCSL* 85A, 5: "Libellus fidei quem legati apostolicae sedis Constantinopolim accipere noluerunt, susceptus est Romae a beato papa Hormisda, et, in conuentu episcoporum siue totius ecclesiae nec non etiam omnium senatorum lectus, catholicus est per omnia approbatus." Translated, the passage reads, "*Libellus* of the faith, which the legates of the apostolic seat would not accept in Constantinople, was received by the blessed Pope of Rome, Hormisdas, and, read in an assembly of the bishops of the whole church and even of all the senators, it was approved as catholic by all."

24 So too Amann, 1748: "Les dépêches des légats refroidirent les bonnes dispositions d'Hormisdas."

25 This complaint appears in the "Responsio Maxentii Iohannis servi Dei adversus epistulam quam ad Possessorem a Romano episcopo dicunt haeretici destinatam," in *CCSL* 85A, 132.270.

26 *CSEL* 35.B, 224.1. Letter 190, which we will soon examine, provides an even stronger indication.

27 *CSEL* 35.B, 187.

28 *CSEL* 35.B, 191.

29 *CSEL* 35.B, 216.5: "[...] Quorum inquietudo non paruas moras generauit unitati ecclesiarum [...]"

30 *CSEL* 35.B, 187.4: "Haec nostra est maxima sollicitudinis causa, ne unitas, quam uester labor orationque perfecit, per inquietos homines dissipetur [...]"
31 *CSEL* 35.B, 216.6.
32 *CSEL* 35.B, 187.2: "[...] Quoniam uaniloquia ipsorum festinatium nouitates introducere in ecclesia, quod neque quattuor synodi uenerabiles neque sancti papae Leonis epistolae continere noscuntur, in omni loco turbas excitare uidentur."
33 *CSEL* 35.B, 187.2: "Quos beatitudo uestra praesentibus scriptis causam liuoris eorum cognoscensita, ut merentur, suscipere et a se longe pellere dignetur"
34 *CSEL* 35.B, 191.1-2:"Quicquid est cautius, quicquid firmius, ut pro sancta fide et concordia sacrarum ecclesiarum geratur, optamus. Unde ad beatitudinem uestram et frater noster gloriosissimus Uitalianus per Paulinum u. s. Defensorum uestrae ecclesiae rescripsit et nos per eundem significare curauimus illa debere beatitudinem uestram perficere, quae pacem et concordiam sanctis concedant ecclesiis. Subinde tamen, qui certius responsum ad sanctitatem uestram referat, cum litteris piissimi nostri imperatoris destinauimus; nam quanta quaestio in partibus nostris orta est, potestetiam antefatus uir religiosus defensor sanctitatem uestram instruere."
35 *CSEL* 35.B, 191.3-4: "Unde petimu sut, si est possibile, celerrimo dato responso et satisfactis religiosis monachis Iohannem et Leontium ad nos remittatis. Nisi enim precibus et diligentia uestra ista quaestio soluta fuerit, ueremur, ne non possit pax sanctarum ecclesiarum prouenire. Ergo congnoscentes, quia et mercees et periculum istius rei uobis seruatur, diligenter tractate et firmissimum responsum per antefatos religiosos monachos, si est possibile, antequam legatus noster ad beatidinem uestram perueniat, nobis remittite; in hoc enim solo omnis pendet intentio."
36 *CSEL* 35.B, 217.7.
37 *CSEL* 35.B, 224.6: "Postea sine nobis magnificus uir Uitalianus magister militum inter se et epscopum Constantinopolitanum uocauerunt praedictum Uictorem; locuti sunt cum eo: quid definierunt inter se, nescimus. postea nec Uictor ad nos uenit necesta causa dicta." *Vir magnificus* is an honorary title.
38 After the humiliation of having to condemn his predecessor, the patriarch can have had little love for the Roman delegation. But the delegation had proven themselves poor at making friends generally, as Frend, 247, notes.
39 *CSEL* 35.B, 190.2.
40 *CSEL* 35.B, 190.3: "Quapropter necesse habebimus uenientibus legatis nostris inquirere, qua re uera faciente causa inter eos fuerit commota discordia."

4 Pious Forgeries
The Simultaneous Use and Critique of Spurious Texts in the Disputatio cum Pyrrho

Ryan W. Strickler

14 – 14th-c. illustrated Bulgarian translation of the 12th c. Chronicle of Constantine Manasses depiction of the severing of the tongue and right hand of Maximus the Confessor in 662 for his opposition to imperial support of Monothelitism (the 'compromise' doctrine that 'Christ has two natures, but one will).

In his study on the practice of forgery in the sixth century, Patrick Gray made two keen observations, namely that "forgery was no respecter of party divisions, and the phenomenon of simultaneous use of forgery and critique of forgery in an opponent can be observed on both sides of the central Chalcedonian–Monophysite debate."[1] I would suggest that Gray's thesis is equally applicable in the seventh–century Christological controversies over the number of operations and wills of Christ, or the monenergist and Monothelete controversies respectively. The present paper examines the practice of simultaneous use and critique of spurious texts in the seventh century, using as a case study the *Disputatio cum Pyrrho*, a late seventh–century document that purports to be the account of theological debate that took place in North Africa between Maximus the Confessor and Pyrrhus, the former Patriarch of Constantinople, in 645. Of interest are the ways in which the document both employs forgery and critiques its use by Pyrrhus, and in particular its critique of apparent forgeries that would be pivotal in the Sixth Ecumenical Council held at Constantinople in 680–81, which took place 35–36 years after the historical disputation. However, before discussing these specifics, it is necessary to discuss briefly seventh–century conceptions of doctrinal authority and the widespread practice of producing "pious forgeries."

Forging Authority in Seventh–Century Byzantium

In order to understand the widespread practice of forgery in the seventh century and why one would forge or manipulate a text, it is necessary to discuss what sort of documents provided doctrinal authority in seventh–century discourse. Jaroslav Pelikan described the theoretical notion of authority when he stated, "What was required of a theologian was not that he be independent or productive or original, but that he be faithful to the authority of Christian dogma as this has been set down in Scripture, formulated by the fathers, and codified by the councils."[2] The notion of a need to appeal to outside authority is certainly evidenced in the *Disputatio cum Pyrrho*. However, as Patrick Gray has established, by the sixth century the authority of a canon of "select fathers" had gained such traction that it became essential for a theologian to demonstrate that his doctrine was in strict conformity to the teachings of these fathers.[3] In other words, while scripture was nominally the final authority, as theological arguments increased in sophistication and became increasingly difficult to prove by scripture, the "select fathers" began to surpass the scriptures as a source of authority.

With the increased importance placed on these "select fathers" as a litmus test for orthodoxy, it became increasingly important for theologians to demonstrate that their doctrines conformed to patristic tradition. This could prove problematic when previous generations had never before considered a particular theological position. Under such circumstances theologians increasingly resorted to the practice of "pious forgery" to demonstrate a canonical author's conformity to their conception of orthodoxy.

The use of the "select fathers" as an authority became particularly problematic when seventh–century theologians began to speak of the "operations" and "wills" of Christ, concepts that were nearly foreign to Greek theology until that time. As Susan Wessel has observed, literary forgery was widely employed in the Monothelete controversy.[4] Forgery became so widespread in the second half of the seventh century that significant effort was expended during the Sixth Ecumenical Council to determine the authenticity of proof texts. According to Daniel Larison,

> Checking contemporary claims against the established patristic tradition was well–established practice by 680, but at the sixth ecumenical council there was a particular focus on verification and authentication of documents, comparison with official records, and an "archival" mentality that defined the validity of certain claims by their official recognition in an archived collection...Rather than simply judging potentially spurious texts against the standard of a patristic author's corpus or according to the standard of contemporary orthodoxy, the council also considered the physical state of manuscripts presented to them and tested controversial (typically Monothelete) documents against the archival deposit to determine whether the claimed authorship of the document could be sustained.[5]

This devotion to proving authenticity demonstrates that the practice of forgery had become widespread, and that in many ways one's position could be vindicated or defeated on the basis of textual authentication rather than soundness of doctrine.

Despite the fact that Larison and Wessel independently demonstrated the extensive nature of forgery in light of the Sixth Ecumenical Council, few scholars have examined specific instances of forgery in the seventh century before the council met in 680–81. The two notable exceptions are both related to Maximus the Confessor, namely Rudolf Riedinger and John D. Madden. Riedinger in his landmark study of the *Acta* of the Lateran Synod of 649, demonstrated convincingly that the Greek *Acta* were actually composed by Maximus and did not represent an actual deliberation which had taken place, going so far as to say that the entire synod was a ruse and never actually met.[6] Although many scholars question Riedinger's latter conclusion, his demonstration of Maximus's authorship of the *Acta* is widely accepted.[7] Madden's work, which focuses primarily on early definitions of the "will" leading to Maximus the Confessor and not forgery per se, specifically discusses the *Disputatio cum Pyrrho* among other works of Maximus.[8] Madden's work will be discussed in greater detail below, but it is sufficient at this point to note that while he stops short of a full conviction, he raises the possibility that Maximus himself was guilty of forgery.

The above discussion of particular instances of forgery and the broad discussion of forgery as a phenomenon in late antique Byzantine culture are both instructive in themselves. They have demonstrated the way in which theological discourse is often constructed was in many ways rhetorical. Likewise, the studies by Gray, Wessel, and Larison in particular have demonstrated that documents are often created for a specific purpose, either to force "canonical fathers" to conform to theological norms, or, as is often the case, to fuel polemic.

The present study applies Gray's theory of forgery as an instrument of progress, or the production of documents fabricated to progress a particular agenda, and builds upon Larison and Wessel's discussion of forgery in to the seventh century by applying it specifically to the *Disputatio cum Pyrrho*. This will be accomplished by examining three instances in which spurious texts are applied, and three instances in which Pyrrhus is accused of using forged or altered texts. Ultimately, this paper will suggest that the *Disputatio cum Pyrrho* is proof that the practice of simultaneous use and critique of forgery described by Gray was alive and well in the seventh century, and was employed to progress the agendas of the opponents of Monotheletism and monenergism.

Forgery within the *Disputatio cum Pyrrho*

The *Disputatio cum Pyrrho* employs a number of dubious citations. These chiefly include an appeal by Maximus to the Fifth Ecumenical Council of Constantinople in 553, and citations attributed to Clement of Alexandria by both parties. One particular instance of a dubious appeal is made by Maximus in answer to Pyrrhus's objection that it is best to pass over in silence subjects not discussed by ecumenical councils, including the question of the number of wills in Christ. In this appeal the author associates Pyrrhus and the Monotheletes with the "arch–heretics" Apollinarius and Arius, and associates dyotheletism with the Fifth Ecumenical Council. However, this appeal is highly problematic.[9]

The author does not provide any specific references from the authors whom he cites, which is unusual considering that generally Maximus, as portrayed in the document, is able to give specific books and chapters within individual works, even if the works themselves are spurious. It seems that the author is unable to provide specific references; otherwise he would not miss an opportunity to disprove his opponent in a targeted fashion.

Moreover, it seems that the author is attempting to conflate *thelēma*, or simply one's will, with *thelēsis*, the faculty of willing, equivalent to the Latin *voluntas*. As John D. Madden has demonstrated, this particular understanding does not appear until Maximus who transforms the word *thelēsis*.[10] Thus if indeed the authors cited above discussed the number of wills in Christ, which itself is unlikely, it is nearly impossible that they could be referring to the will in the sense of *thelēsis*, which is the way in which the author would have us believe. In other words the author, through clever deception, turns Monotheletism into a rebirth of Arianism and Apollinarianism, and associates dyotheletism with Athanasius, Gregory, and Basil, none of whom addressed the problem at hand. In so doing, the author enforces his position with the authority of the select fathers and an ecumenical council, an authority that could not be provided with extant witnesses, while simultaneously associating his opponent with figures whom both sides recognized as heretical.

However, the *Disputatio cum Pyrrho* did not limit itself to broad appeals to spurious authority. Indeed, a significant incidence of likely forgery within the text of the *Disputatio* involves references to specific texts attributed to Clement of Alexandria. Both references are included in succession and begin as a response by Maximus to Pyrrhus, who references a problematic citation from Athanasius. For context, I have included the exchange as follows:

> **Maximus**: ... For if, according to the Father [Athanasius], "The mind of the Lord is not the Lord," his mind is clearly something different from the Lord, that is to say, the mind of the Lord is not Lord by nature, that is to say, it is not God; it is believed that it became his according to his hypostasis; and clearly this is from the teaching that it is either a will, or wish, or energy toward something; for this, he is using the rule of he who was **the** Philosopher of Philosophers, Clement, in his sixth book of the Stromateis, *which defines the will, on the one hand, as "an appetitive mind", and wishing as "reasonable desire," or "the will for something." And the same divine teacher says that "an energy toward something," because for all the things which happened divinely from Him, he employed a mind and logical soul united to him according to a hypostasis.*
> **Pyrrhus:** In truth, through those things by which they seem attack the blessed, they have unknowingly set up the refutation against themselves. And it is necessary to investigate another example, which they introduce from the Father, so that we may leave no motive for them against the truth.
> **Maximus:** What example is this? For I do not know.
> **Pyrrhus**: That which that wonderful man said: *"He was begotten from a woman, having raised up the form of man from the first formation in himself, in the appearance of flesh, apart from the fleshly wills and thoughts of men, in the image of commonality. For the will is only proper to divinity (thelēsis theotētos monē)."*[11]

The first citation attributed to the sixth book of Clement's *Stromateis* has been clearly demonstrated to be a false attribution by Madden, who notes "The Sixth book is extant in its entirety, and there is no such definition in it...at best Maximus is guilty of gross negligence in citing Clement, at worse he may be a forger."[12] Considering the prolific nature of forgery in the seventh century and within this document specifically, it is safe to confirm Madden's suspicion that the author, who is likely not Maximus, did forge the passage in question. The antiquity of Clement would have certainly have been a boon to the anti-Monothelete party. Moreover, this reference is interesting because it is very specific, and not only convinces Pyrrhus, but provokes him to quote another text of "Clement" that itself is falsely attributed.

There are several observations worth mentioning about the second reference, which has not yet been studied at any length. The text is quoted by Pyrrhus as a counter–example from Clement. However, the citation is not an authentic Clementine quotation but rather is taken from a pseudo-Athanasian author.[13] Maximus claims not to know the reference, and rather than taking the opportunity to correct Pyrrhus, simply explains how the reference in fact supports his own position, leaving the attribution to Clement intact.

On the surface this seems incidental; it would not be unusual in the heat of a "debate" for a disputant to misattribute a source. However, Maximus was particularly familiar with this reference and quoted it in his so-called *Dogmatic Tome* to Marinus the Priest.[14] Polycarp Sherwood, in his seminal date-list of the works attributed to Maximus the Confessor, dates this document to 640.[15] In it Maximus gives the entire reference with an additional line, and attributes it to Athanasius as follows:

> As is expressed by the great Athanasius, writing such things against the ungodly Apollinarius: "He was begotten from a woman, having raised up the form of man from the first formation in himself, in the appearance of flesh, apart from the fleshly wills and thoughts of men, in the image of commonalty. *For there is a single will of divinity (thelēsis theotētos monē), since the whole nature is also of divinity (tou theotētos).*[16]

Thus it is clear that Maximus was entirely familiar with the citation Pyrrhus attributed to Clement in the *Disputatio cum Pyrrho*. Yet Maximus, as depicted in the text, chose not to take an opportunity to correct Pyrrhus's "ignorance"; rather, he accepted the former patriarch's attribution. He chose simply to correct Pyrrhus's "misunderstanding" of the text to suit his own purposes.

Beyond the discrepancy of attribution, there are some philological notes worth considering. Not only do the two texts vary from one another, they also vary from the actual pseudo-Athanasian, text which is as follows:

> He was begotten from a woman, having raised up the form of man from the first formation in himself, in the appearance of flesh, apart from the fleshly wills and thoughts of men, in the image of commonalty. *For the will is only of divinity (thelēsis theotētos monēs), since the whole nature is also of the Logos (tou Logou)*.[17]

Thus the following variations are present between the three documents:

(1.) The text of the *Disputatio cum Pyrrho* includes the Greek particle *de*, which is not included in either the *Dogmatic Tome* to Marinus, or the actual pseudo-Athanasian text. Likewise, the final clause of the quotation does not appear in any form in the *Disputatio cum Pyrrho*.

(2.) The *Disputatio cum Pyrrho* preserves the pseudo-Athanasian text "The will is only of divinity (*thelēsis theotētos monēs*)." However, the *Dogmatic Tome to Marinus* changes this clause to "There is a single will of divinity (*thelēsis theotētos monē*)." Thus the genitive adjective *monēs*. (alone, only) is changed to the nominative adjective *monē*, and is changed from modifying *theotētos* (divinity) to *thelēsis* (will).

(3.) The *Dogmatic Tome* replaces the pseudo-Athanasius *tou Logou* with *tou theotētos*. Thus Maximus changes the specific reference to the Logos into a generic reference to "divinity."

A number of conclusions can be reached based on this evidence. First, it is noteworthy that the version of the quotation found in the *Disputatio cum Pyrrho* varies significantly from that found in the *Dogmatic Tome*, a document that itself appears to have been purposefully altered. Taken together, these two quotations attributed to Clement represent significant liberties taken by the author with textual evidence. The first has been demonstrated by Madden to be a whole cloth fabrication by the author of the *Disputatio cum Pyrrho*. The other appears to be a purposefully altered and misattributed citation from another text which, though it was ironically proven to be a forgery, was frequently used and widely accepted at the time as authentic.

The first example can be understood in terms of Gray's concept of forgery as an instrument of progress. In order to advance his agenda, the author needed to prove his position with a patristic citation. However, when one could not be found, he created a new reference and attributed it to one of the most ancient authors in the patristic canon. This served to demonstrate the continuity of the theology with patristic thought while providing added the bonus of an ancient pedigree.

The pseudo-Athanasian quote is more troubling. This was an extant document and though it was forged, neither disputant would have been aware of this. It is a citation that Maximus is on record as having an intimate knowledge of, knowledge confirmed by apparent alterations to the original text; yet Maximus is depicted as denying such knowledge in the *Disputatio cum Pyrrho*. What could account for this bizarre textual problem?

I would suggest that this is evidence of an interpolation by a disciple of Maximus. Such an interpolation would allow for the citation to be presented as evidence and for Maximus to claim the evidence without the exchange appearing contrived. If Pyrrhus had simply attributed the quotation properly, or if Maximus himself had cited it, it would have been understood to be cliché and called the disputation's authenticity into question. Pyrrhus would have presumably been aware of Maximus's familiarity with the citation, so it is unlikely that Pyrrhus would have used it in an actual debate. By using this technique, the interpolator would have brought the citation to the reader's attention without compromising the appearance of a real debate. The fact that this text, attributed to Athanasius, is used by the fathers of the Sixth Ecumenical Council can possibly be traced to this clever use of deception.

Forgery Detection in the *Disputatio cum Pyrrho*

Perhaps more interesting than the use of forgery by the author of the *Disputatio cum Pyrrho* is the critical examination and refutation of proof texts employed by Pyrrhus. Included in this examination are the *Libellus* attributed to Patriarch Menas, which would become infamous at the Sixth Ecumenical Council; the letter of Pope Honorius to Patriarch Sergius, and interpretation of the formula "a new theandraic energy" by pseudo-Dionysus the Areopagite.

This textual examination begins with a discussion of the *Libellus* of Menas. This exchange begins when Pyrrhus makes the following assertion:

> **Pyrrhus:**...But how could Vigilius, the bishop presiding over the Romans at that time, accept the *Libellus*, which held one will, from Menas, who was the imperial bishop, when he was shown these things in the Imperial Privy Chamber of Council of the Emperor of the Romans at the time?[18]

Here Pyrrhus not only attempts to introduce the *Libellus* as proof of the Monothelete position, but goes a step further by suggesting the details of the letter's reception. Thus Pyrrhus is portrayed as attempting root the text in a particular moment in time and to promote the *Libellus* as a legitimate authority. The exchange takes a dramatic turn when Maximus counters as follows:

> **Maximus:** I am amazed how both of you, who are patriarchs, tell brazen lies! Your predecessor [Sergius], writing to Honorius, said that "he received [the *Libellus*], on the one hand, but it was not given nor clearly shown;" and you yourself, to Pope John who is now among the saints, said that "it [the *Libellus*] was given and shown clearly, having been read by Constantine the Quaestor." Whom are we to believe, you or your predecessor? For it is not possible for both to be true.[19]

Thus Maximus accuses both Pyrrhus and his predecessors of speaking falsely, and accuses Pyrrhus in particular of countering Sergius' own account. Sergius, he asserts, admitted to never actually seeing the *Libellus* whereas Pyrrhus said that he did, citing Pyrrhus's own correspondence as poof. As the account continues Pyrrhus, per the usual, concedes to Maximus' accusation and quickly changes the subject. In other words, Maximus calls both Pyrrhus and his predecessor Sergius liars, and manages to convince Pyrrhus to admit that the *Libellus* of Menas was a forgery!

It is difficult to overemphasize the importance of this particular passage. The *Libellus* was a significant weapon in the Monothelete arsenal. If it were authentic, it would have provided a link between a respected patriarch, whose orthodoxy had never been questioned and the pope, which attested that Christ had one will. This particular document was of unique importance to legitimizing the Monothelete cause, and disproving its authenticity was critical to the anti-Monotheletes' strategy during the Sixth Ecumenical Council. According to Larison:

> Proving the Menas forgery was vital in two ways: it was necessary to show that the Monotheletes were using unreliable sources, but more than that it was necessary to prevent Monotheletism from partaking of the reputation of a venerated Constantinopolitan patriarch whose orthodoxy had never been in doubt.[20]

Forgery in some cases could prove to be a double-edged sword. If the *Libellus* had been accepted, it would have provided a great victory for the Monothelete cause, both as a documentary source of authority and by suggesting the continuity of Monotheletism with traditional orthodoxy. However, proving the document to be a forgery would render the remaining Monothelete *florilegia* suspect.[21]

Understanding the importance of the *Libellus* places this exchange in perspective. This is the first extant reference to the possibility of the *Libellus* being a forgery that I am aware of, and it does not merely raise the possibility, but rather records a key Monothelete proponent acknowledging that it is a forgery. In addition to this, it offers an insider argument against the authenticity of the *Libellus* well before it was dramatically declared to be a forgery during the proceedings of the Sixth Ecumenical Council.

Immediately after Pyrrhus concedes that the *Libellus* of Menas is a forgery, he offers up another critical document as evidence of his position. This is infamous letter of Pope Honorius to Patriarch

Sergius, in which the latter employed the phrase "one will in our Lord and Savior Jesus Christ," which initiated the rise of Monotheletism. After Pyrrhus suggests that Honorius "clearly taught one will of our Lord Jesus Christ to my predecessor (*eipein phanerōs pros ton pro emou hen dogmatisantos thelēma tou kyriou hemōn Iēsou Christou*)," Maximus makes a rebuttal which appeals to the anonymous amanuensis who composed the letter on Honorius's behalf. After Pyrrhus agrees that this individual would be the best witness to the truth, rather than the reader of the letter, Maximus states:

> **Maximus:** This same man who, writing to Constantine, who is among the saints, who was Emperor, again for Pope John, who is among the saints, concerning the same letter, said that "We said one will for Christ, not for his divinity and humanity, but only his humanity. For with Sergius having written that some say that the two wills of Christ are in opposition, we write against this, that Jesus did not have two opposing wills, I speak of flesh and spirit, as we have after the fall, but one, characterized by his humanity according to his nature."...Then in anticipation of the reply being made, he said "If one says: 'thinking about something concerning the humanity of Christ, do you make mention of his divinity?' We say that the answer was made for a specific question; and after, according to the custom of scripture, as in all things, we have spoken in this; sometimes with the scripture speaking of divinity..."[22]

The passage ends with Pyrrhus's concession that Sergius understood the text "simplistically (*proseschēkōs*)" and concedes, once again, to Maximus's argument.

Maximus's support for Pope Honorius was well documented. He wrote in defense of Honorius in his *Dogmatic Tome to Marinus the Priest* and in a letter to Peter the Illustrious, the Strategos of Numidia.[23] However a comparison of the *Disputatio cum Pyrrho* with these two documents reveals the unique nature of its appeal. In the *Dogmatic Tome* Maximus wrote,

> And indeed I do not think that Honorius pope of the Romans opposes the two inborn wills of Christ, in that letter that was written to Sergius to speak about the one will, but I think that rather he agrees, and I think it is reasonable to affirm this, that he was not speaking in rejection of the human and natural will of our Savior, but that the will of the flesh by no means ruled over his unbegotten conception, or his uncorrupt birth, or was subject to desire.[24]

In this passage Maximus defends Honorius by suggesting that he was misunderstood by Sergius in his letter. In other words this defense is based on explaining Honorius "real" meaning, as opposed to the Monothelete "misinterpretation."

In his letter to Peter the Illustrious, which is dated by Sherwood to about 643,[25] Maximus offers a different sort of defense for Honorius:

> Concerning all of these things they are wretched, nor has the opinion of the Apostolic See been done, and that which is laughable, nay it is better that we say, most deserving of lament, in as much as it is demonstrative of the audacity of these men, nor did they hesitate to rashly lie to that very Apostolic See: but as if they had taken the counsel of that see, and just as if a decree had been received from that see, *these men usurped the great Honorius for their own purposes in their own continuous actions on behalf of the impious Ekthesis,* making the most eminent man in the cause of piety a witness of their presumption to others.[26]

In this text, Maximus accuses the Monotheletes, Pyrrhus and Sergius in particular, of "usurping" Honorius for their own purpose. Thus Maximus suggests that rather than simply misunderstanding Honorius's letter, the patriarchs willingly usurped the letter, and concealed their usurpation. Unfortunately, because the letter only survives in an excerpt, it is difficult to determine to what extent Maximus believes they "usurped" Honorius, but it is clear that, from Maximus' perspective, Honorius is innocent in the affair.

Both of these defenses differ significantly from the defense offered in the *Disputatio cum Pyrrho*. All three are interested in absolving Honorius of any belief in a single will as the Monotheletes understand it. However, unlike the other two, the *Disputatio* appeals not to Honorius's words but to words of the papal copyist! In the *Disputatio* the author portrays Maximus as saying that the same person composed both Honorius's letter to Sergius and John IV's letter in defense of Honorius, which explicitly opposed the doctrine of Monotheletism. Thus, he concludes that Honorius' letter could not possibly be interpreted the way in which Sergius and Pyrrhus were attempting.

This appeal is particularly interesting in light of its context within the document, namely as a discussion of the legitimacy of authoritative documents. Maximus, rather than attempting to redeem Honorius per se, is attempting to delegitimize the Monothelete claim to this crucial piece of evidence. Although Honorius is redeemed as a result, it seems that the validity of the letter as a support for Monotheletism is the author's chief concern rather than an apology for the late pope. Again I would suggest that this is best understood in light of the Sixth Ecumenical Council's emphasis on textual authenticity. Ultimately the council decided, despite this attempt to demonstrate otherwise, that Pyrrhus's interpretation of the letter was correct, though it only served to condemn Honorius rather than vindicate the Monothelete position. Although it was ul-

15 – The Bulgarian 'Manasses' depiction of the Sixth Ecumenical Council (681), which among other things, vindicated Maximus.

timately unsuccessful, this exercise reflects the efforts to critique the documentary evidence offered in support of the Monothelete position, an effort not evidenced in the letters discussed above, and which would reach its zenith at the Sixth Ecumenical Council.

Pseudo-Dionysius the Areopagite

In addition to epistolary evidence, the *Disputatio cum Pyrrho* addresses the monenergist use of pseudo-Dionysius the Areopagite.[27] The discussion focuses on the proper interpretation of the Dionysian phrase "a new theandric energy (*kainēn tina tēn theandrikēn energian*)." Pyrrhus argues that "newness (*kainotēs*)" refers to the "quantity (*posotēs*)" rather than the "quality (*poiotēs*)" of the energies of Christ. In other words, newness is synonymous with oneness. Likewise, he suggests that adjective "theandric (*theandrikē*)" implies a unity and therefore requires that Christ had one energy. Maximus offers the following rebuttal:

> **Maximus:**...When the Apostle says "behold, all things become new," no one says he means "something else" or that he meant "behold all things become one"; whether you wish to call this nature, or energy.... But if the newness is a quality, then it is clearly not one energy, but a new and mysterious mode of the exhibition of the natural energies of Christ, mingling the natures of Christ into one another as is fitting, and his participation as man, being foreign and paradoxical, and unknowable by the nature of everything that exists, and a means of exchange according to the mystical union.[28]

The use of pseudo-Dionysius the Areopagite in the Sixth Ecumenical Council is one of the greater ironies of the seventh century. With all of the focus on authenticating texts, both sides appealed to pseudo-Dionysius as a source, and neither realized that the Dionysian corpus was itself a forgery. The phrase "a new theandric energy" was of particular importance to the monenergist position. It was one of the primary proofs employed at the Union at Alexandria in 633.[29] While the rise of Monotheletism would cause this particular reference to lose some of its importance, the desire of the fathers of the Sixth Ecumenical Council to condemn monenergism along with Monotheletism created a need to address the use of this text.

Pyrrhus raises the primary interpretation of this citation against those who opposed monenergism, that "newness" was synonymous with "oneness." Maximus proceeds to object that newness refers to the quality of the energy, not a number. Pyrrhus objects to both interpretations suggesting instead that newness is an essence. The conversation continues, and Pyrrhus eventually concedes.

This exchange is interesting in its wider context of a discussion about the energies, a matter that would have been moot by this time and would only regain relevance again in 680–681 at the Sixth Ecumenical Council. It is also important as it provides in brief an answer to questions that would most certainly be raised, and were raised in the context of the eventual Sixth Ecumenical Council. This exchange, like the passages examined above, suggests that this discussion may not have actually taken place at the disputation in 645, but may have been added later for a greater purpose.

Conclusion

The nature of seventh-century theological discourse compelled its participants to appeal to a set of canonical, or "select," fathers as proof of doctrinal orthodoxy. This measure of authority, which had its roots in the previous century, became an increasingly difficult standard to meet as subjects like the "wills" and "energies" of Christ dominated intellectual inquiry. As in previous centuries, disputants were forced to resort to tampering with or fabricating authoritative texts to advance their ideological agenda, a process that Gray has referred to as "forgery as an instrument of progress." This practice became so widespread that the fathers of the Sixth Ecumenical Council found a useful strategy in devoting significant time and theatrics to disproving the authenticity of opposing proof texts. This strategy was effective in part because of the admittedly widespread practice of "pious forgery" by disputants on both sides.

This paper has taken the discussion of forgery out of the realm of general, theoretical discussion and applied it to a particular document, the *Disputatio cum Pyrrho*. The effect has been to show that "forgery as an instrument of progress" was a practice that continued into the seventh century, and that this is evidenced not only in the study of extraordinary events such as ecumenical councils but in theological and polemical treatises as well.

The present study has drawn a number of similarities between the *Disputatio cum Pyrrho* and the Sixth Ecumenical Council. Such similarities go beyond a mere focus on documentary authentication; they extend into the specific documents used and critiqued, critiques that did not occur elsewhere between the historical disputation that took place in 645 and the council proceedings of 680–681. This, I would argue, is not mere coincidence, but reflects the purpose of the composition of the *Disputatio cum Pyrrho*.

This paper, while answering a number of questions, ultimately raises even more problems for investigation. Questions such as the nature and extent of influence played by communities of forgers in advancing theological and political discourse cannot be answered here. Moreover while this paper has essentially denied the authenticity of the *Disputatio cum Pyrrho*, a possibility raised–though not definitively answered–by Jacques Noret, that is, the question of authorship and audience needs to be addressed in greater detail.[30] Unfortunately the limitations of this paper do not permit the in depth analysis that these questions deserve.

However at this juncture it is safe to conclude that the forgeries and critiques found within the *Disputatio cum Pyrrho* were created to advance the position of the anti–Monothelete party in the run up to the Sixth Ecumenical Council. This document both created a body of evidence and set the standard for the eventual critique of Monothelete and monenergist evidence, and though some critiques, such as the dismissal of the Letter of Honorius, fell short of their intended goal, on the whole they were a resounding success.

I hope that the strong connections demonstrated by this paper between the *Disputatio cum Pyrrho* and the Sixth Ecumenical Council will lay the groundwork for future study and publications on these and other questions, which I intend to pursue and refine in the process of dissertation research. Ultimately, this paper will satisfy its author if it stimulates further inquiry into these questions and provokes scholars to discover in concrete terms the role played by forged documents in theological discourse.

Abbreviations

BZ: *Byzantinische Zeitshrift.* 106 vols. to date. Berlin: Walter de Gruyter: 1892–1914, 1919–43, 1949–present.

MCAS: *Maximus Confessor: Actes du Symposium sur Maxime le Confesseur, Fribourg 2-5 Septembre, 1980.* Edited by Fritz Heinzer and Christoph von Schönborn. Fribourg: Éditions Universitaires, 1982.

PG: *Patrologia Cursus Completus, Series Graeca.* 161 vols. Edited by Jacques-Paul Migne.Paris: Imprimerie Catholique, 1857–1866.

PL: *Patrologia Cursus Completus, Series Latina.* 221 vols. Edited by Jacques-Paul Migne.Paris: Imprimerie Catholique, 1841–1865.

Notes

1 The present paper had its genesis in my M.A. thesis, "A Dispute in Dispute: Forgery, Heresy, and Sainthood in Seventh–Century Byzantium." I would like to thank Prof. David M. Olster for suggesting that the *Disputatio cum Pyrrho* would be a subject worthy of study. Without his encouragement and strong hand this paper would not be possible. I would also like to thank Prof. David G. Hunter and Prof. Daniel Gargola, whose service on my thesis committee and sound advice allowed me to hone the arguments found in the present paper. Finally I would like to thank the members of ASEC, especially Prof. Jennifer Spock, Prof. Joshua Lollar, and those present at the March 8–9 2013 meeting at Georgetown University, where an early version of this paper was presented, for their helpful comments, and the Hilandar Library at the Ohio State University, whose generous stipend facilitated my participation in the conference.
Patrick Gray, "Forgery as an Instrument of Progress: Reconstructing the Theological Tradition in the Sixth Century," *BZ* 81 (1988): 284.

2 Jaroslav Pelikan, "'Council or Fathers or Scripture': The Concept of Authority in the Theology of Maximus the Confessor," in *The Heritage of the Early Church*, edited by D. Neiman and M. Schatkin, Orientalia Christiana Analecta (Rome: Institutum Studiorum Orientalium, 1973), 278.

3 Patrick Gray, "'The Select Fathers': Canonizing the Patristic Past," *Studia Patristica* 23, edited by E. A. Livingstone (Leuven: Peeters, 1989), 284–289.

4 Susan Wessel, "Literary Forgery and the Monothelete Controversy: Some Scrupulous Uses of Deception," *Greek, Roman and Byzantine Studies,.* 42, no. 2 (2001): 201–220.

5 Daniel Larison, "Return to Authority: The Monothelete Controversy

and the Role of Text, Emperor and Council in the Sixth Ecumenical Council" (Ph.D. dissertation, University of Chicago, 2009), 235.
6   Cf. Rudolf Riedinger, "Aus den Akten der Lateransynode von 649," *BZ* 69 (1976): 17–38; idem, "Die Lateransynode von 649 und Maximos der Bekkener," in MCAS, 111–121.
7   Cf. Andrew Louth, *Maximus the Confessor* (London: Routledge, 1996), 222, completely affirming Reidinger; Larison, "Return to Authority;" and Cyril Hovorun, *Will, Action and Freedom: Christological Controversies in the Seventh Century* (Leiden; Brill, 2008), 83-84.
8   John D. Madden, "The Authenticity of Early Definitions of the Will," in *MCAS*, 61–79.
9   Marcel Doucet, "Dispute de Maxime le Confesseur avec Pyrrhus: introduction, texte critique, traduction et notes" (Ph.D. dissertation. Université de Montréal, 1972), 300D–301A. All citations of the *Disputatio cum Pyrrho* are from this edition and follow its numbering. All translations of primary sources provided herein are my own.
10 Madden, "Authenticity of Early Definitions," 62ff.
11 Doucet, "Dispute," 317B-320B. Emphasis mine.

M. ... Εἰ γὰρ κατὰ τὸν Πατέρα «Νοῦς Κυρίου οὕτω Κύριος» ἄλλο πάντως παρὰτὸν Κύριον ἔσται ὁ νοῦς αὐτοῦ, τουτέστι οὐ φύσει Κύριος ἤγουν Θεὸς ὁ νοῦς τοῦ Κυρίου· καθ᾽ ὑπόστασιν γὰρ αὐτῷ γεγενῆσθαι πιστεύεται. Καὶ τοῦτο δῆλον ἐκ τοῦ ἐπαγαγεῖν «ἢ θέλησιν ἢ βούλησιν ἢ ἐνέργειαν πρός τι» αὐτὸν εἶναι, κανόνι χρώμενος πρὸς τοῦτο τῷ ὄντι φιλοσόφῳ τῶν φιλοσόφων Κλήμεντι ἐν τῷ ἕκτῳ τῶν Στρωματέων λόγῳ τὴν μὲν θέλησιν «νοῦν εἶναι ὀρεκτικὸν» ὁρισαμένῳ, τὴν δὲ βούλησιν «εὔλογον ὄρεξιν» ἢ «περί τινος θέλησιν». «Πρός τι δὲ ἐνέργειαν» ὁ θεῖος οὗτος ἔφη διδάσκαλος διότι πρὸς πάντα τὰ θεοπρεπῶς παρ᾽ αὐτοῦ γενόμενα τῇ κατ᾽ ὑπόστασιν ἑνωθείσῃ αὐτῷ νοερᾷ καὶ λογικῇ ἐχρήσατο ψυχῇ.

Π. Τῷ ὄντι δι᾽ ὧν ἀντιστρατεύεσθαι τῇ εὐσεβείᾳ δοκοῦσι δι᾽ αὐτῶν τὸν ἔλεγχον ὑπομείναντες ἠγνόησαν. Χρὴ δὲ καὶ τὴν ἑτέραν ἣν ἐκ τοῦ Πατρὸς παράγουσι ἐπεξεργάσασθαι χρῆσιν πρὸς τὸ μηδεμίαν αὐτοῖς ὑπολείπειν πρόφασιν κατὰ τῆς ἀληθείας.

Μ. Τίς αὕτη; ἀγνοῶ γάρ.

Π. Ἡ φησιν ὁ θαυμαστὸς ἐκεῖνος ἀνήρ· «Ἐγεννήθη ἐκ γυναικός, ἐκ τῆς πρώτης πλάσεως τὴν ἀνθρώπου μορφὴν ἐν ἑαυτῷ ἀναστησάμενος, ἐν ἐπιδείξε ἰσαρκὸς δίχα δὲ σαρκικῶν θελημάτων καὶ λογισμῶν ἀνθρωπίνων, ἐν εἰκόνι καινότητος. Ἡ γὰρ θέλησις θεότητος μόνης».

12 Madden, "Authenticity of Early Definitions of the Will," 69.
13 Ps.-Athanasius, *De incarnatione Domini Nostri Jesu Christii, contra Apollinarium*, bk. 2, (PG 26: 1148).

14 Maximus the Confessor, *Tomus Dogmaticus ad Marinum Presbyterum*, PG 91: 228–245.
15 Polycarp Sherwood, "Date-List of the Works of Maximus the Confessor," *Studia Anselmiana* 30 (1952): 41–42.
16 Maximus, *Tomus Dogmaticus*, 240A-B, emphasis mine: συμφθεγγόμενος τῷ μεγάλῳ Ἀθανασίῳ, γράφοντι τάδε κατ' Ἀπολιναρίου τοῦ δυσσεβοῦς, «Ἐγεννήθη ἐκ γυναικὸς, ἐκ τῆς πρώτης πλάσεως τὴν ἀνθρώπου μορφὴν ἐν ἑαυτῷ ἀναστησάμενος, ἐν ἐπιδείξει σαρκὸς δίχα σαρκικῶν θελημάτων καὶ λογισμῶν ἀνθρωπίνων, ἐν εἰκόνι καινότητος. Ἡ γὰρ θέλησις θεότητος μόνη ἐπειδὴ καὶ φύσις ὅλη τοῦ θεότητος.»
17 Ps-Athanasius, *De incarnatione* 2: 1148C: καὶ ἐγεννήθη ἐκ γυναικὸς, ἐκ τῆς πρώτης πλάσεως τὴν ἀνθρώπου μορφὴν ἐνέαυτῷ ἀναστησάμενος, ἐν ἐπιδείξει σαρκὸς δίχα σαρκικῶν θελημάτων καὶ λογισμῶν ἀνθρωπίνων, ἐν εἰκόνι καινότητος. Ἡ γὰρ θέλησις θεότητος μόνης· ἐπειδὴ καὶ φύσις ὅλη τοῦ Λόγου.
18 Doucet, "Dispute," 328: Π. ...Πῶς οὖν τὸν ἐπιδοθέντα λίβελλον ὑπὸ Μηνᾶ τοῦ γενομένου ἐπισκόπου τῆς βασιλίδος ἓν θέλημα ἔχοντα ἐδέξατο Βιγίλιος ὁ τῆς Ῥωμαίων τηνικαῦτα πρόεδρος καὶ ταῦτα ἐμφανισθέντος αὐτοῦ ἐν τῷ βασιλικῷ σεκρέτῳ τοῦ τηνικαῦτα τῶν Ῥωμαίων βασιλεύοντος καὶ τῆς συγγλήτου;
19 Ibid.: Μ. Θαυμάζω πῶς πατριάρχαι ὄντες κατατολμᾶτε τοῦ ψεύδους. Ὁ προηγησάμενός σε πρὸς τὸν ἐν ἁγίοις Ὀνώριον γράφων εἶπεν ὅτι «Ὑπηγορεύθη μὲν οὐκ ἐπεδόθη δὲ οὔτε ἐνεφανίσθη». Αὐτὸς δὲ ἐν τοῖς πρὸς τὸν ἐν ἁγίοις Ἰωάννην τὸν πάπαν ἔφης ὅτι «Καὶ ἐπεδόθη καὶ ἐνεφανίσθη ἀναγνωσθεὶς διὰ Κωνσταντίνου κοιαίστωρος». Τίνι οὖν πιστεύσωμεν; σοὶ ἢ τῷ πρὸ σοῦ; Οὐ γὰρ δυνατὸν ἀμφοτέρους ἀληθεύειν.
20 Larison, "Return to Authority," 269.
21 Ibid., 277.
22 Doucet, "Dispute," 328B-329C: Μ. Αὐτὸς οὖν πρὸς τὸν ἐν ἁγίοις Κωνσταντῖνον τὸν γενόμενον βασιλέα ἐκ προσώπου πάλιν Ἰωάννου τοῦ ἐν ἁγίοις πάπα περὶ αὐτῆς γράφων ἔφη ὅτι «Ἓν θέλημα ἔφημεν ἐπὶ τοῦ Κυρίου οὐ τῆς θεότητος αὐτοῦ καὶ τῆς ἀνθρωπότητος ἀλλὰ μόνης τῆς ἀνθρωπότητος. Σεργίου γὰρ γράψαντος ὡς τινες δύο θελήματα λέγουσι ἐπὶ Χριστοῦ ἐναντία, ἀντεγράψαμεν ὅτι Ὁ Χριστὸς δύο θελήματα ἐναντία οὐκ εἶχε– σαρκός φημι καὶ πνεύματος–ὡς ἡμεῖς ἔχομεν μετὰ τὴν παράβασιν ἀλλ' ἓν μόνον τὸ φυσικῶς χαρακτηρίζον τὴν αὐτοῦ ἀνθρωπότητα». ... Εἶτα καὶ προκατάληψιν ἀνθυποφορᾶς ποιούμενος φησίν «Εἰ δέ τις λέγοι καὶ τίνος χάριν περὶ τῆς ἀνθροπότητος τοῦ Χριστοῦ διαλαβόντες περὶ τῆς θεότητος αὐτοῦ μνήμην οὐκ ἐποιήσατε;

φαμὲν ὅτι πρῶτον μὲν πρὸς τὴν ἐρώτησιν ἡ ἀπόκρισις γέγονεν. ἔπειτα δὲ καὶ τῷ τῆς γραφῆς ἔθει ὡς ἐν πᾶσι καὶ ἐν τούτῳ ἑπόμενοι ποτὲ μὲν ἀπὸ τῆς θεότητος αὐτοῦ διαλεγομένης.

23 Maximus, *Tomus dogmaticus*, 237C-240C; idem, *Diffloratio ex epistola ejusdem S. Maximi ad Petrum Illustrem*, PL 129: 568–574. The letter survives only in the Latin translation by Anastasius Bibliothecarius, and even then only as excerpts that he used in his *Collectanea*. Migne included a version in both his collected works of Maximus (as in PG 91: 141A-146A) and his edition of Anastasius' *Collectanea*. Strangely enough there are textual variants between the two editions; however, the text of the present section is identical in both. I have chosen to cite the PL version.

24 Maximus, *Tomus dogmaticus*, 237C-D: Τὸν δέ γε τῆς Ῥωμαίων πάπαν Ὀνώριον, οὐ κατα γορεύεινοῖμαι τῆς τῶν ἐμφύτων θελημάτων ἐπὶ Χριστοῦ δυάδος, ἐν τῇ γραφείσῃ πρὸς Σέργιον ἐπιστολῇ διὰ τὸ ἓν θέλημα φάναι, συναγορεύειν δὲ μᾶλλον, καὶ ταύτῃ νῶς εἰκὸς συνιστᾶν, οὐκ ἐπ' ἀθετήσει τοῦτό γε λέγοντα τοῦ ἀνθρωπίνου καὶ φυσικοῦ τοῦ Σωτῆρος θελήματος, ἀλλ' ἐπὶ τοῦ μηδαμῶς τῆς ἀσπόρου συλλήψεως αὐτοῦ καὶ τῆς ἀφθόρου γεννήσεως προκαθηγεῖσθαι θέλημα σαρκός, ἢ λογισμὸν ἐμπαθῆ.

25 Sherwood, "Date–List," 52.

26 Maximus, *Diffloratio*, 575A, emphasis mine: De quibus omnibus miseri nec sensus apostolicae facti sunt sedis, et quod est risu, imo ut magis proprie dicamus, lamento dignissimum, utpote illorum demonstrativum audaciae, nec adversus ipsam apostolicam sedem mentiri temere pigritati sunt: sed quasi illius effecti consilii, et veluti quodam ab ea recepto decreto, in suis contextis pro impia ecthesi actionibus secum magnum Honorium acceperunt, suae praesumptionis attestationem ad alios facientes viri in causa pietatis maximam eminentiam.

27 Doucet, "Dispute," 345C-348C

28 Ibid.: M. ...ὅταν λέγῃ ὁ Ἀπόστολος· «Ἰδοὺ γέγονε τὰ πάντα καινὰ» οὐδὲν ἕτερον λέγει, ἢ ὅτι Ἰδοὺ γέγονε τὰ πάντα ἕν· εἴτε δὲ φύσει εἴτε ἐνεργείᾳ τοῦτο καλεῖν βούλεσθε... Εἰ δὲ ποιότης ἐστὶν ἡ καινότης, οὐ μίαν δηλοῖ ἐνέργειαν ἀλλὰ τὸν καινὸν καὶ ἀπόρρη τον τρόπον τῆς τῶν φυσικῶν τοῦ Χριστοῦ ἐνεργειῶν ἐκφάνσεως, τῷ ἀπορρήτῳ τρόπῳ τῆς εἰς ἀλλήλας τῶν Χριστοῦ φύσεων περι χωρήσεως προσφόρως καὶ τὴν κατὰ ἄνθρωπον αὐτοῦ πολιτείαν ξένην οὖσαν καὶ παράδοξον καὶ τῇ φύσει τῶν ὄντων ἄγνωστον καὶ τὸν τρόπον τῆς κατὰ τὴν ἀπόρρητον ἕνωσιν ἀντιδόσεως.

29 Larison, "Return to Authority," 273.

30 Jacques Noret, "La rédaction de la *Disputation Cum Pyrrho* (CPG 7698) de Saint Maxime le Confesseur serait–elle postérieure à 655?" *Analecta Bollandiana* 117 (1999): 291–296.

PART II

Iosif and Russia

Iosif and Russia: Introduction

David Goldfrank

Moving from the preceding, intriguing aspects of Late Ancient antecedents of some of the issues the Russian Orthodox confronted in the late Middle Ages and early moded period, the contributions to this section touch upon numerous aspects of Iosif's activities and overall influence. We commence with the practical. From the time Iosif founded his rapidly successful Volokolamsk monastery in 1479, he initiated his *sinodik* and other "profitable and salvific books" to record and regularize the commemorations, which he contracted to execute, and which proved both essential for monastic economies and central to the psychological security of many Orthodox believers of the time—hence the numerous and varied donations to Iosifov and other cloisters.[1]

For over a quarter of a century, Ludwig Steindorff has been researching, analyzing, and publishing about Muscovite commemorative practices and, having become profoundly knowledgeable about the manuscript sources, he has been pivotal in our cracking the codes of the extant donation books and monastery customaries relative to these services.[2] Focusing to a great extent on Iosif and his monastery, Professor Steindorff has argued cogently that they played a central role in rationalizing and standardizing these practices in the late 15th and early 16th centuries. His present contribution, "What Was New about Commemoration in the Iosifo-Volokolamskii Monastery? A Reassessment," represents his latest breakthrough in linking Iosif's seminal mode of commemorative financing and bookkeeping to how this practice operated in various parts of Rus' before 1479 and to the modified modus operandi that developed in Muscovy, due in part to Iosif's efforts. Linking the types of commemorations to the theology of both the small and great eschatologies (the immediate fate of the soul after death and the Last Judgment), the author explains the key terminology and his very useful table clarifies the standard sixteenth-century sliding scale of payments and services.

We turn next to Iosif the writer and polemicist. He was a singularly argumentative individual, when such suited his purposes, and our next two contributions focus on polemics in the form of disputes—one composed by Iosif and one crafted by another writer, ostensibly directed against Iosif and his disciples. The author of this introduction, one of a small number of active specialists in Iosif's thought, has recently analyzed the syllogistics contained within his logically tightest discourse,[3] then prepared another essay concerning the logical structures and dialectical schemes of his major theological work,[4] and also published an analysis of his use of insults.[5] Continuing in this vein for the present volume with "Iosif Volotskii's Disputational Technique (*Ars Disputandi*)," Goldfrank examines Iosif's use of a variety of polemical devices. As the title suggests, the author does this partially through the lenses of the Classical heritage and formal Western medieval disputes. Elucidating some of Iosif's argumentative rhetoric in his monastic homiletics, practical affairs, and celebrated quarrel with Archbishop Serapion of Novgorod, Goldfrank focuses here chiefly on Iosif's defense of the doctrine of the Trinity in an imagined dispute with a "Jewish-reasoning heretic." In passing, this exposition also gives the reader a taste of Iosif as a positive, didactic theologian, linking abstract doctrine to individual salvation. In addition, several of Goldfrank's notes point to the differences between the original Hebrew and the Judaic-Greek versions of key Old Testament passages utilized as Christian proof texts.

Unrivaled as Iosif seems to have been in his day among Russian churchmen in his possession of so many talents, neither he nor his disciples enjoyed a smooth path in promoting their policies. Rather, several figures disputed forcefully against the Volokolamsk hegumen and his ecclesiastical faction. These opponents included the fallen and involuntarily tonsured magnate Vassian Patrikeev, who posed as a devotee of Iosif's ally, the hesychastic master Nil Sorskii, and protested the execution of heretics and some of the practices of monks in wealthy monasteries. For about forty years, Donald Ostrowski, practitioner of his own *sui generis ars dubitandi*,⁶ has been at the forefront of source and historical analysis of some of these Church polemics. His dissertation made a convincing case that no reliable contemporary source points to a genuine Nil-Iosif rivalry or to the raising of the question of secularization of church and monastic lands at Moscow's late 1503 Synod. Rather such traditionally widely accepted sources stem from the mid-16th century, when the question of regulating the acquisition of monastic estates was being discussed.⁷ Subsequently, Ostrowski questioned whether there were such Church parties as "Possessors" and "Nonpossessors."⁸ In his contribution here, "The *Debate with Iosif* (*Prenie s Iosifom*) as a Fictive Disputation," Professor Ostrowski continues his analysis of those polemical sources,⁹ and he suggests here that the *Debate* was probably written in the early 1560s at Solovki by Artemii, the former hegumen of the Trinity St. Sergius Monastery. Framing this discussion with an admirably learned survey of the formal disputation, Ostrowski goes one step further than Goldfrank and argues that the *Debate* follows the general principles of such contests as they had developed in the Middle Ages in the Islamic lands before spreading to the West. Though differently framed and conceived, these two analyses are compatible, and Goldfrank's contains a chart indicating how the genres of both of these fictive disputations could have deep Ancient origins and even South Asian connections.

Following the mid-16th century disputes, our volume leapfrogs over the crucial contributions of Iosif's 'school' to the expansion of the Russian church into newly conquered Kazan after 1552, to the establishment of the Russian patriarchate in 1589, and to the recovery of Muscovy during the Time of Troubles,¹⁰ and takes us to the mid-17th century, Patriarch Nikon, and one of the latter's nemeses, the Old Believers. For over a dozen years, Kevin Kain has been working on Nikon and adding his voice to the Russian scholars who have been rescuing our understanding of that crucial figure from the clutches of hostile, one-sided Old Believer narratives.¹¹ Here, though, Professor Kain's contribution, "*The Enlightener* and Feodor Ivanov's Screed, 'About the Wolf and Predator ... Nikon,'" thrusts us smack into the cauldron of Old Believer polemic against the redoubtable patriarch. Affirming the conclusions of those of us, who have put paid to the myth, stemming in part from the Old Believer Feodor, that Nikon reviled Iosif, and, rather, having demonstrated his direct influence on Nikon, Kain now takes the next step. By careful textual comparisons and analysis, he proves that Iosif likewise directly influenced Feodor. For our Volokolamsk hegumen provided models not only for the Old Believers' repudiation of a "heretical" bishop, but also for their valuing monasticism, icon veneration, and church fathers and lambasting Nikon for allegedly not doing so. Kain's work here thus deepens our understanding of the degree to which Iosif's mentality lived on among both sides of the dramatic schism within the Russian church with even greater influence than has hitherto been asserted.

Our specialists have argued that Iosif's defense of icon veneration constituted his initial theological-polemical discourses, which eventually blossomed into his *Enlightener*.[12] It is therefore fitting that our section's final contribution focuses on this all-important devotional practice. In fact, precisely because the controversies between the Old Believers and the official church were symbolic and devotional rather than doctrinal, externals came to the fore in this conflict and marked both sides. Accordingly and, for this phenomenon, appropriately informed by recent anthropological approaches to the material culture of devotion, Evgeny Grishin's pioneering contribution, "'Their Prayer Is Reaching God …' – Old Believers and Icons in 18th-Century Russia," opens up new vistas for analyzing the lived religion of Orthodox and Old Believer alike. Having already studied and published in Russia about the nature of the ecclesiastical changes in the 17th century,[13] and now having engaged in meticulous research into the regional Kirov archival holdings relative to two South Viatka Old Believer communities, Grishin elucidates not only their theology concerning the need for the iconographer to hold to a proper ethical as well as correct ritual practices in order that his product be efficacious, but also the contradiction in some Old Believers' strangely claiming that copper icons and only copper icons could be non-"Nikonian," while their churches in fact also contained some icons painted on wood. The key to resolving this contradiction, so asserts the author, lies in the physical purity of both objects and people.

To attempt any direct linkage to Iosif stands beyond the scope of Grishin's already massive archival research and the problems he has posed about lived religion, but he certainly paves the way for seeking connections between the more purely patristic based monastic homiletics of Iosif's day and the infusion of popular legend into the admonitory literature circulating among 18th-century Russian peasants. As Grishin has found among the Viatka papers, the Old Believers considered alcohol consumption and mother-cursing (along with tobacco) to be signs of impiety, while the available apocrypha against these habits claimed to cite both Basil the Great and John Chrysostom. It turns out that for the former, the folk version of this alleged Basil, "Heady spirit keeps off the Holy Spirit as smoke keeps off bees,"[14] is a variant of a venerable passage in Iosif's Rule: "Just as smoke drives away bees, so drunkenness drives away the Holy Spirit."[15] And though differently from the apocrypha cited by Grishin,[16] Iosif too used Chrysostom to enjoin against a "holy mouth" using "filthy and disgraceful words."[17]

Yet also, in the real life of the monastery, at least according to Fatei the Old, a bookman-disciple of Iosif's co-founding comrade Kassian Bosoi:[18]

> We now see and hear not only some of the lesser brothers who are similar to me in boorishness, but also some of the preeminent ones saying filthy and abominable words, such that other brothers have learned that filthy expression from them. And the elder Iosif [*in his writings- DG*] forbids these abominable words with a great penance. At that time in the monastery there was never uttered that filthy and abominable expression, to call one's brother or any other human being of our holy Christian faith: "whoreson!"

This is certainly an honest formulation of the ethical legacy of someone who insisted that "we bow down to one another because in the beginning God created humans in His image," but, regarding heretics, "we hate them with perfected hate."[19] And Evgeny Grishin, with his thorough research into the South Viatka Old Believers, has provided us with interesting material for analyzing the distant ties between these schismatics, who, as sectarians, lacked access to punitive public authority, and our formidable, redoubtable, and venerable Iosif, who faced no such constraints.

Notes

1. See, in addition to the sources utilized by Professor Steindorff in his contribution to this volume, Tom Dykstra, "*Zapisnaia kniga* (Donation Records) of Volokolamsk Monastery, for 1550-1607," in *Essays in Russian Monasticism*, edited by D. M. Goldfrank = *Russian History* 39.1-2 (2012): 106-147.
2. His first such publication was his ground-breaking monograph, *Memoria in Altrußland. Untersuchungenzu den Formenchristlicher Totensorge*, Quellen und Studienzur Geschichte des östlichen Europa 38 (Stuttgart: Fritz Steiner Verlag, 1994). Numerous articles and a superb critical and annotated edition with a German translation of the Iosifov commemorative "Feast Book" followed: *Das Speisungsbuch von Volokolamsk. Kormovaia kniga Iosifo-Volokolamskogo monastyria. Eine Quelle zur Sozialgeschichte russischer Klöster im 16. Jahrhundert* = Bausteine zur Slavischen Philologie und Kulturgeschichte, NF 12 (Cologne/ Weimar/Vienna: Böhlau Verlag, 1998); most recently: "Equality under Reserve: Men and Women in Donations and Commemoration in Muscovite Russia," *Canadian-American Slavic Studies* 49 (2015): 193-210, and "Desirable ubiquity? Family strategies of donation and commemoration in Muscovy," *Cahiers du monde russe* 57, no. 2-3 (April-September 2016): 641-665
3. David Goldfrank, "Adversus Haeriticos Novgorodensos: Iosif Volotskii's Rhetorical Syllogisms," in *Dubitando: Studies in History and Culture in Honor of Donald Ostrowski*, edited by Brian J. Boeck, Russell E. Martin, and Daniel Rowland (Bloomington, IN: Slavica, 2012), 254-274.
4. Idem, "'Iosif Ritorikos-Sillogistikos': k izucheniiu 'Prosvetitelia," accepted for the third volume of *Prepodobnyi Iosif Volotskii i ego obitel'*.
5. Idem, "Litigious, Pedagogical, Redemptive, Lethal: Iosif Volotskii's Calculated Insults," *Russian Review*, 75.1 (Jan. 2016): 86-106.
6. See above, note 3.
7. Donald Ostrowski, "A 'Fontological' Investigation of the Muscovite Church Council of 1503," 2 vols. (Ph. D. dissertation. The Pennsylvania State University, 1977()). See also his "500 let spustia: Tserkovnyi Sobor 1503 g.," *Palaeoslavica* 11 (2003): 214–239.
8. Idem, "Church Polemics and Monastic Land Acquisition in Sixteenth-Century Muscovy," *Slavonic and East European Review* 64 (1986): 355–379 (reprinted in *Major Problems in Early Modern Russian History*, ed. Nancy Shields Kollmann [New York: Garland, 1992], 129–153).
9. See Ostrowski's "Direction of Borrowing: The Relationship of the *Life of Iosif* by Lev Filolog and the *Life of Serapion, Archbishop of Novgorod*," *Palaeoslavica* 13, no. 1 (2005): 109–141; and "The *Letter concerning*

Iosif and Russia – Introduction   135

Enmities as a Polemical Source for Monastic Relations of the Mid-Sixteenth Century," in *Essays in Russian Monasticism,* 77–105.
10 See A. A. Zimin, *Krupnaia feodal'naia votchina* (Moscow: Nauka, 1977), 305-307, 314-318.
11 In addition to Kain's works listed in the bibliography to his volume contribution, See, inter alia, "Izobrazhenie patriarkha Nikona v iskusstve XVII-XIX vekov," *Nikonovskie chteniia v muzee "Novyi Ierusalim:" Sbornik statei,* edited by G. M. Zelenskaia (Moscow: Severnyi Palomnik, 2002), 82-87; *From Peasant to Patriarch: Account of the Birth, Upbringing, and Life of His Holiness Nikon, Patriarch of Moscow and All Russia Written by His Cleric Ioann Shusherin,* translated and edited by Kevin M. Kain and Katia Levintov (Lanham, MD et al.: Lexington Books/Rowman and Littlefield, 2007); Kevin A. Kain, "Before New Jerusalem: Patriarch Nikon's Iverskii and Krestnyi Monasteries," in *Essays in Russian Monasticism,* 173-231. For a sense of Nikon's wide-ranging activities, see S. K. Sevast'ianova, *Materialy k "Letopisi zhizni i literaturnoi deiatel'nosti patriarkha Nikona,"* (St. Petersburg: Dmitrii Bulanin, 2003).
12 *Antifeodal'nye ereticheskie dvizheniia na Rusi XIV-nachala XVI veka,* edited by N. A. Kazakova and Ia. S. Lur'e (Moscow-Leningrad: Akademiia nauk SSSR, 1955), 325-360 = *Prosvetitel', ili oblicheni eresi zhidovstviushchikh: tvorenie prepodobnago ottsa nashego Iosifa, igumena volotskago,* 4th ed.) Kazan: Tipo-litografiia Imperatorskogo universiteta: 1903), 7: 219-283; Goldfrank, "The Anatomy of the Key Codices and the Ontogeny of *Prosvetitel',*" *Canadian-American Slavic Studies* 49, no. 2-3 (2015): 162, 170.
13 "'Reforma' ili 'ispravlenie'? K ponimaniiu tserkovnykh izmenenii serediny XVII veka," in *Pravoslavie: Konfessiia, instituty, religioznost' (XVII-XX vv.),* edited by M. Dolbilov and M. Rogoznyi (St Petersburg: Izdatel'stvo EUSPb, 2009), 15-29.
14 See Grishin's contribution, below, text to note 56.
15 *The Monastic Rule of Iosif Volotsky,* rev. ed., Cistercian Studies 36, translated and edited by David Goldfrank (Kalamazoo: Cistercian Publications, 2000), 155, 217: actually found in Antiochus's *Pandectes.*
16 Grishin, Chapter 9 below, text to note 53.
17 *Monastic Rule of Iosif Volotsky,* 150: the commentary on *Ephesians,* as found in Nikon of the Black Mountain.
18 "Pouchenie Startsa Fotiia. Startsa Fateia, uchennika velikago startsa Kassiana Bosago, sobrano ot bozhestvennykh pisanii, zelo polezno, ezhe ne skvernosloviti iazykom vsem pravoslavnym khristianom, pachezhe nam inokom, nizhe paki reshchi maternee laianie bratu svoemu: bliadin syn, kakovu libo cheloveku krest'ianskiia nasheia

very sviatia," in *Pamiatniki starinnoi russkoi literatury*, 4 vols in 2., edited by N. I. Kostomarov and A. N. Pypin (St. Petersburg: Tipografiia P. A. Kulisha, 1860-1862), 4: 189-191.

19 *Antifeodal'nye ereticheskie dvizheniia*, 345, 466; *Prosvetitel'*, 28 ("Account"), 7: 283.

5 What Was New about Commemoration in the Iosifo-Volokolamskii Monastery? A Reassessment

Ludwig Steindorff

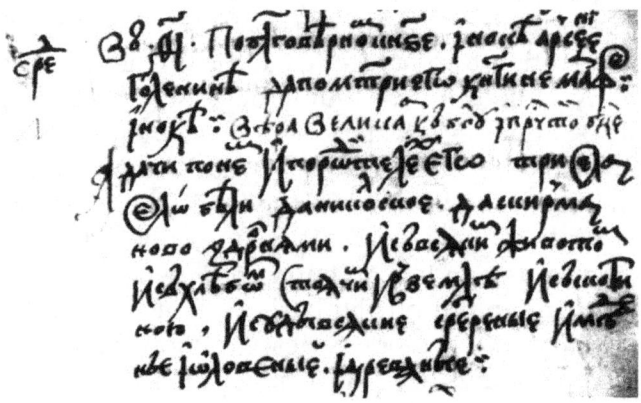

16 – Iosifov Monastery 1581/2 *Obikhodik* (Table Customary) page with the Arsenii and mother "Marfa" (Maria) Golenin "middle" size commemorative feast and mention of their "great faith in God and the Immaculate Theotokos" and also the family's gifts and burial location.

There exists among historians of Russia and Russian Orthodoxy, a general consensus that there was something new about liturgical commemoration in Muscovy at the turn from the 15th to the 16th century. The traces of this innovation are most visible in the monastery founded by Iosif Sanin in 1479 not far away from the city of Volokolamsk, about 70 miles west of Moscow. However, a little later we can trace the innovation in other big monasteries also.[1] Only from the 16th century do we dispose of a richer tradition of preserved para-liturgical books for the purpose of commemoration and its administration, and normative texts referring to the implementation of commemoration. Starting at that time, more and more regularly property deeds contained the stipulation to enter the name of the donor, and/or the donor's relatives, in two different lists for commemoration, and we are able to prove the existence of two types of lists for that purpose.

The names of the two lists varied.[2] Just for convention I shall use in the following pages the most frequent pairings of names in the documents from the Iosifov Monastery: *vechnyi sinodik*[3] and *povsednevnyi spisok* ("eternal synodicon" and "daily list"). The layers of names in these lists reach back, in general, no further than to the end of the 15th century.

Notwithstanding, I would like to stress in advance, that the practice of donating to monasteries and churches has older roots; we have only to look at the numerous charters in favor of the older Troitse-Sergiev Monastery and the Simonov Monastery in Moscow, which were analyzed by Boris Kloss, Pierre Gonneau, Marina Cherkasova, and Liudmila Ivina.[4] Obviously, before the end of the 15th century, a donation was not yet bound to the expectation and demand of an entry in a memorial book, or of a regular commemoration on the basis of that book. Interestingly, from medieval Western monasteries we know of a similar delay between the beginnings of a flourishing practice of donating and a regular fixation of the names in the necrologies.[5]

According to the extant sources, only from the beginning of the 16th century was a donation regularly accompanied by an entry in memorial lists. At the same time, a stable relation was established between the amount of the donation either in money or in corresponding movable or immovable values and the liturgical gift in return. A donation of a quarter of a ruble allowed the entry of a whole family in the eternal *sinodik*. But the liturgical "value" of that counter gift was low, since the long list was read during the course of the day independently of ongoing church services. An entry in the daily prayer list (*povsiadnevnyi spisok*) could be limited to a certain period, the price being one ruble for one year. Only after a donation of fifty rubles was the entry "forever," thereby providing daily commemorative prayers for the deceased for as long as the monastery lasted. Because of the high price, this list grew much more slowly and could be read at the corresponding stations of the liturgical cycle within one day. The highest liturgical return gift was a *korm*, a feast meal on the day of death or saint's day of the person to be commemorated. The price of one feast a year was a hundred rubles.[6]

Value of the donation	Entry in the *vechnyi sinodik*	Entry in the *povsiadnevnyi spisok* for one year	Entry in the *povsiadnevnyi spisok* for ever	*korm*, 'Feast'
¼ ruble	X			
1 ruble	X	X		
50 rubles	X		X	
100 rubles	X		X	X

Table 1 The tariff: Levels of commemoration and corresponding minimal value of the donation

We may enumerate a cluster of reasons for the rise of that system:

- Processes of individualization caused a growing interest in one's own name.
- The optimistic conviction of salvation only on the basis of baptism immediately after Christianization had faded away long ago. Instead, salvation depended on good deeds by oneself or on prayers, as well as alms and donations of others. The fear of the Last Judgment was internalized, maybe to a certain degree also under the effects of previous expectations of the end of the world in the year "7000," that is, 1492.[7]
- Sufficient skills had developed only since the 15th century to produce and handle complex pragmatic literacy.
- The establishment and preservation of the rules concerning commemoration were aspects of social learning and discipline.

There is no doubt about the innovative character of this system at the beginning of the 16th century, but we cannot neglect the fact that there are numerous traces of an earlier practice of liturgical commemoration in Old Russia.[8] Already the Patericon of the Kievan Cave Monastery mentioned a *pominanie*, a memorial book in which the names of brethren were written. The early 12th century Russian pilgrim, Hegumen Daniil, thanked God for the opportunity to write down the names of Russian princes, their female relations (wives, sisters, mothers), and children in the Sabbas Monastery in Jerusalem to be mentioned in *ekteny* (litany) prayers. During the excavation of the territory of a priest's house in Novgorod, numerous birch bark pieces with short lists of names were discovered in layers from about 1200. Most probably, these lists served for liturgical commemoration for a limited period, and then they were thrown away. One of the accusations against the anti-simoniac *strigol'niki* at Novgorod consisted of the assumption that they denied the necessity of a regular care for the deceased through services, gifts to the church, or through alms. Independently of the circumstance that we do not dispose of any reliable information about this allegedly heretical movement, the accusation serves as a proof for the regular practice of care for the dead.[9]

Starting in the 15th century, deeds occasionally contained the provision to enter the name of the donor or relatives in the *sinodik* or the *pominanie*.[10] In the charter about the church courts, about the people and the measures on the market at Novgorod ostensibly sanctioned by the Prince Vsevolod Mstislavich (d. 1138) the prince confirms that he was given a *vseden'nik senanik,* a *sinodik* for all days, for the altar of the Saint Sophia Cathedral.[11] Generally, this charter is not accepted as a text from the time of Vsevolod Mstislavich (1135), but it is regarded as a compilation from the end of the 13th century. According to Aleksei Alekseev, an even later dating of the charter is confirmed simply by the statement about the *vseden'nik senanik*, since the term refers to memorial practice, as it was formed only at end of the 15th century. He suggests a compilation of the actual version only in the second half of the 15th century, which coincides with the fact that the first manuscripts containing this charter, derive from that time.[12] It is also possible to suppose that just the paragraph about the *vseden'nik senanik* belonged to a later layer in a charter which was really connected with Vsevolod Mstislavich, since there are no grounds to attribute this paragraph to a ruler from such an early period. For my point, it is not important to determine the age of this paragraph; it is enough to state that the relevant information derives from a text not younger than the 15th century.

Consciousness about the necessity of care for the deceased and about the helpfulness of commemoration was certainly well developed already in the 15th century. This is obvious from the history of the tripartite *predislovie* (foreword), which we encounter for the first time in the oldest *sinodik* of the Iosifo-Volokamskii Monastery from 1479. The first two *slova* (discourses) of the foreword are certainly older. According to S. B. Sazonov, they were composed, at the latest, in 1448.[13] But, as we should stress, neither contained hints of an elaborated system of two types of lists for commemoration. These *slova* do not even exhibit knowledge of the term *sinodik*. The first *slovo* spoke only about *siia kniga spasena i dushepolezna*—"this salvific and soul-profiting book."

It is obvious that there is an inconsistency between my statement about the innovative character of the elaborated system as we know it from about the year 1500, on the one hand, and the numerous hints of a vivid memorial practice, including in former times, on the other hand. I was conscious of this inconsistency long ago, but I was not able to reconcile it. So in my book *Memoria in Altrußland* (1994), and in later publications, I simply abstained from discussing the problem. Vladislav Nazarov was the first colleague who, in the discussion after my public lecture in the German Historical Institute at Moscow in March 2010, noted the contradiction between the thesis about an innovation and the proofs of an older practice he knew from the article by Aleksei Alekseev.[14] At that time, I was unable to offer a firm explanation for how the new system developed from the older practice and stated only a tendency towards specialization and differentiation. Only some months later I discovered a convincing solution when I worked with a group of students on the translation of central texts on the Muscovite memorial practice from Old Russian to German.[15]

Before I turn to the text which offered the key to me, I would like to specify the two Russian meanings of the central term *sinodik*— because the distinction is not always made clear enough in modern research, and sometimes the two types are confused.[16] Let us start with the older meaning: *sinodik pravoslaviia*, corresponding to the Greek term "*synodikon* of Orthodoxy" (in Russian, s*inodik pravoslaviia*). The name of this book is a metonym, which recalls a *synodos*, specifically, the church council in 843 at

Constantinople, when the iconoclasts were condemned and the veneration of icons was confirmed. The book which was then composed, i. e., the *synodikon*, contains the resolutions of the seven ecumenical councils, lists of anathematized people, and lists of especially honorable people, both dead and alive. The *synodikon* was and is read only once a year, on the first Sunday of Great Lent. Besides the Greek version there are different Slavic versions and a Georgian one with partly varying lists of names corresponding to the specific circumstances in the different countries and the time of the composition of the *synodikon*. The *sinodik pravoslaviia* does not serve for commemoration, and its reading is not a means of care for the deceased. It serves for the self-identification and self-assurance of the Orthodox community on earth and for the definite exclusion of other groups.[17] Only in Russian did the word *sinodik* obtain a second meaning, which corresponds to the Greek term *diptykha* or the South Slavic term *pomenik*.[18] The second meaning obviously arose as a metonymic shift on the basis of the meaning "long list of names." These lists are to be read within the liturgical cycles over the entire year and serve to aid the salvation of the deceased. It is easy to distinguish the two types of *sinodiki*. The names in the *sinodik pravoslaviia* were written in the dative case corresponding to the appeals: *vechnaia pamiat'* (eternal remembrance) or "Mnogo let!" ("Many years!") The names in the *sinodik*, which corresponds to the diptychs, were written in the accusative case, corresponding to the appeal "pomiani, Gospodi!" ("Remember, Lord!").

For our purposes, only *sinodiki* of the second type are of interest. In this regard, the system of the 16th century proves to have been a differentiation of the former practice of commemoration of the deceased. But how did this differentiation take place? The key is to be found in the letter by Iosif Volotskii to the Princess Mariia Golenina, written between 1506 and 1510.[19] The princess sent a letter to Iosif which was not preserved, but from which Iosif took numerous quotations. She complained that she donated very much to Iosif's monastery, but that the names of her husband and her two sons were not commemorated in the expected way.[20] Iosif explained to her how the system of commemoration worked, and that her expectations rested upon misunderstandings.

First of all, Iosif informed her, it was impossible to organize individual services for each donor's relatives, but the commemoration of all persons took place in common within the different services during the week. Then Iosif turned the attention of the princess to the existence of two types of lists. One was the *sinodik*, in which the names of the husband and the sons were written, and here they were commemorated forever. The second list was called by him "*godovoe pominanie*." The commemoration in this list could be limited to one year; in this case the person obtained *godovoe pominanie v god*, as was said in the letter. The entry in this list forever was bound to big donations, and for illustration Iosif enumerated numerous well known persons and their gifts.[21] As he stressed, the entry for an unlimited period, *v godovoe pominanie v vek*, was bound to a special agreement between the donor and the brethren in all monasteries and churches. Thanks to these agreements we dispose of the deeds about land donations or at least of the entries in the donation books (*vkladnye knigi*) of the Iosifov Monastery and many other communities,[22] and we can easily verify that Iosif's information in the letter about the practice fits exactly with the normative texts.

The term *godovoe pominanie* is undoubtedly synonymous with the *povsednevyi spisok*, as we know it from the regulations in the foreword to the oldest *sinodiki* and in the *obikhod*, the specific daily rules of the monastery.[23] The term refers to a previous, no longer extant version of a list of names from about 1600, which can be easily identified as a copy of the *povsednevyi spisok*, the "daily list" by comparison with the names in the monastery's Donation Book.[24] How precisely do we understand the term *godovoe pominanie*? One explanation could be "commemoration throughout the year," but this interpretation is not convincing, since the commemoration on the basis of the *sinodik* also takes places throughout the entire year. It is much more reasonable to explain the term as "one year-long daily commemoration," which means that the term refers to the special commemoration during the first year after death.

Finally, we are now in a position to explain what was new at the turn from the 15th to the 16th centuries. For centuries in the Christian world, the first year after death was a period of special care for the deceased person to help secure peace for the soul during the small eschatology from the separation of the soul from the body to its accommodation in a peaceful place, until the Last Judgment.

This care is bound to certain dates, namely the third, the ninth and the fortieth days, half a year, and the first anniversary day, as well as to two periods: the *sorokoust* – a series of forty daily liturgies —and exactly one year. Obviously, churches and monasteries were accustomed to recording the persons to be commemorated every day for a whole year in special lists or books, that is, in the *godovoe pominanie* following the terminology of Iosif. The *vseden'nik senanik* on the altar of Saint Sophia in Novgorod, which was either really or allegedly donated by Vsevolod Mstislavich in 1135, can be identified as a book for this purpose, too.

We can only guess when it became customary to enter the names forever in a *sinodik* that was read independently of the ongoing service, and not from the altar, but in the *kliros* (choir), as described in sources from Iosif's monastery.[25] This practice was already well established by the early 16th century in all monasteries and churches, according to Iosif's letter to the princess. As the desire for commemoration rose, and as the *sinodiki* became overcrowded with names, the commemoration in the *godovoe pominanie* was prolonged, no longer only *na god* ("for one year"), but for several years or even forever, as called by Iosif *godovoe pominanie v vek*, "year-long [daily] commemoration forever," a contradictory expression in itself and understandable only in the broader context. To a certain degree there was a shift in the function of the *godovoe pominanie*: now it was no longer a form of commemoration for the first year after the death, but was integrated into the permanent liturgical cycles and orientated towards the Last Judgment following the great eschatology. On the one hand, we are certainly justified in visualizing a correspondence between the rise and prolongation of the *godovoe pominanie v vek* and the *povsednevnyi spisok* according to the later terminology; and on the other hand, we see the marginalization of the *sinodik* as a book for small donations by anybody.

Outside the territory of the Muscovite state, a similar development had taken place in the memorial practice of the Kievan Cave Monastery. There were those whose names were written in the *sluzhebnitsi*, the liturgical service books, and commemorated every day—about 150 names.[26] Although this was not indicated explicitly, most probably the instruction referred to commemoration within the Divine Liturgy. Alternatively, there was the huge number of names in the *Pominanie*, the memorial book from shortly after 1482, which was read within the special memorial services after the *utrenia* (Matins) and *vechernia* (Vespers) services. Because of the size of this book, the names were certainly not read all at one time, but successively during numerous services. As noted in the prescriptions to the *Pominanie*, after reading all the names written there in a low voice, the priest read the names from two or three pages of the *sorokoustnyi* list,[27] the composition of which, maybe, corresponded to the list of names in the *sluzhebnitsi*. Despite the differentiation of two kinds of lists, the practice in the Kievan Cave Monastery was significantly different from the established system in Muscovy: there was no reading of the *pominanie* throughout the day as in the case of the *vechnyi sinodik*, and we do not know about any traces of a tariff of prices to pay for commemoration, similar to the Muscovite practice.

Is it still justifiable to speak about an innovation at the beginning of the 16th century, now that we can prove that the commemoration from two different book types developed within a longer process and was also known, though in a less elaborate form, in the Kievan Cave Monastery on Polish-Lithuanian territory? At this time, I would prefer to address the consolidation and standardization of a practice which was worked out during the previous century, accompanying the entrenchment of monasteries as centers of care for the deceased, including the rise of their roles as receivers of donations and as centers of prayer that was given as a gift in return. In this sense, there are sufficient grounds to attribute a central role in the stabilization of the new system to Iosif Volotskii's monastery, despite the fact, that Iosif himself argued in his letter to the princess, that all monasteries follow the same practice. As Aleksandr Aleksandrovich Zimin put it: "Not one [other] Russian monastery disposed of such a neatly elaborated system of commemoration of the dead as Volokolamsk."[28]

The central normative text for when to read the two lists within the daily liturgical cycle is extant in the three oldest *sinodiki* from Volokolamsk; only later was this text transferred also to the Kirillo-Belozersk Monastery.[29] Even if Iosif was not the composer himself, certainly the text derived from his close surroundings. In the larger version of his Rule,[30] Iosif stresses the necessity to read the lists carefully, and he refers explicitly to his "Account (*Skazanie*) of the Salvific and Soul-Profiting Books" within the oldest *sinodik* from Volokolamsk. Here again he gives short hints about the reading practice and, more importantly, he stresses the role of monasteries as centers of care for deceased. He justifies the rich possessions of the monastery, since they are necessary to ensure the fulfillment of the liturgical obligations, and he obliges the brethren to take this task as seriously as possible.[31]

Also in later decades of the 16th century, the Iosifov Monastery maintained its leading role in pragmatic literacy concerning commemoration. We do not know of any other monastery's book matching the preciseness of the Iosifov *obikhodnik* in explaining the daily practices of the monastery, the extant version of which was composed about the year 1580. Chapter Five of this book contains a detailed description of the relations between the amount of the donations and the liturgical gifts in return. It enumerates all books that were kept to assure a reliable administration of the names to be commemorated.[32] And as we can prove, this description corresponded exactly to the practice in the monastery, or as we may say equally: the practice corresponded to the norm, as it had been established since the beginning of the 16th century.[33]

The practice of commemoration, based on oral tradition and experience, was obviously very similar in many other monasteries, but only in the Iosifov Monastery was this practice described in detail and in written form, so that these texts gained a norm-setting function. In many monasteries the practice did not correspond to the norms. We simply have to look at the conclusions of the Stoglav Council in 1551 in which the monasteries are ordered to take care of donations, and respect the will of the donors. Almost certainly Ivan IV (r. 1533–1584, as of 1547, "Tsar"), while reprimanding the monasteries, was not thinking about the Iosifo-Volokolamsk Monastery, this model of memorial practice.[34]

Finally, we are accustomed to seeing the Russian church father Iosif Volotskii in traditional historiography as the figure who diverted Russian monasticism from the path of poverty and modesty, but we should also acknowledge that he was convinced that the wealth of the monasteries carried an obligation. He attributed to the monasteries a role which corresponded to the demand of the society to have prestigious centers of care for the deceased.[35]

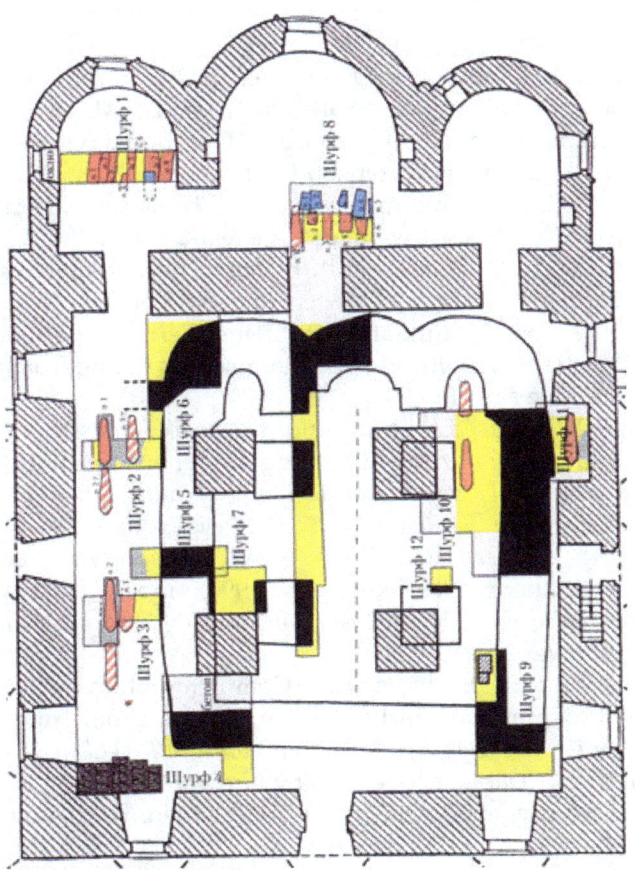

17 – Iosifov Monastery Uspenskii Sobor diagram with two later enlargements and excavation shafts of 16th c. elite burials. Iosif was located in Shaft (шурф) 11, and the male Golenins in Shaft 5. Note that the 17th century enlargement of the church enclosed and covered a goodly number of burial sites that originally were outside the walls

Abbreviations

DRVM: *Drevniaia Rus'. Voprosy medievistiki.*
GIM: Gosudarstvennyi istoricheskii muzei, Moscow.
RGADA: Rossiiskii gosudarstvennyi arkhiv drevnikh aktov, Moscow.
RGB: Rossiiskaia gosudarstvennaia biblioteka, Moscow.
RNB: Rossiiskaia natsional'naia biblioteka, St. Petersburg.

Notes

1. For instance, S. B. Veselovskii, *Issledovaniia po istorii oprichniny* (Moscow: Izdatel'stvo Akademii nauk SSSR, 1963), 328; *The Monastic Rule of Iosif Volotsky*, translated and edited by David Goldfrank, rev. ed., Cistercian Studies 36 (Kalamazoo: Cistercian Publications, 2000), 28–29; and A. I. Alekseev, *Pod znakom kontsa vremeni. Ocherki russkoi religioznosti kontsa XIV–nachala XVI vv.* (St. Petersburg: Aleteia, 2002), 138, 152.
2. Ludwig Steindorff, *Memoria in Altrußland. Untersuchungen zu den Formen christlicher Totensorge,* Quellen und Studien zur Geschichte des östlichen Europa 38 (Stuttgart: Fritz Steiner Verlag, 1994), 252–254, lists the various terms employed in 59 manuscripts dating from as early as 1507 and as late as 1713.
3. Any English term used as a translation of *sinodik*, for instance, "memorial book," would be confusing within the further argumentation.
4. Pierre Gonneau, *La maison de la Sainte Trinité. Un grand-monastère russe du moyen-âge tardif (1345–1533)* (Paris: Klincksiek, 1993); M. S. Cherkasova, *Zemlevladenie Troitse-Sergieva monastyria v XV–XVI vv.* (Moscow: Arkheograficheskii tsentr, 1996); and L. I. Ivina, *Krupnaia votchina Severo-Vostochnoi Rusi kontsa XIV–pervoi poloviny XVI v.* (Leningrad: Nauka, 1979).
5. Ludwig Steindorff, "Donations and Commemorations in the Muscovite Realm—a Medieval or Early Modern Phenomenon," in *Religion und Integration im Moskauer Russland. Konzepte und Praktiken, Potentiale und Grenzen. 14–17. Jahrhundert*, edited by Ludwig Steindorff, Forschungen zur osteuropäischen Geschichte 76 (Wiesbaden, Harrassowitz Verlag, 2010), 487–488.
6. The basic normative sources for commemorative prayer are: 1) The liturgical regulations "O ezhe vnegda i kako chesti Sinodik podobaet" ("When and How to Read the Sinodik") and "O ezhe kogda i kako chesti Pominanie povsiadnevnoe" ("When and How to Read the Daily Commemoration") in: GIM, Fond Eparkhial'noe sobranie, No. 411 (829), folia 3–6; RGB, Fond 113, № 571, ff. 31v –34; and RGADA, Fond 1192, Opis' 2, No. 559, folia 30–32v.; RNB, F. Kirillo-Belozerskii monastyr', No. 759/1016, folia 36v–38. A published version can be found based upon the manuscript of RGB, *Sinodik*, "Prilozhenie 2," 211–215 and in the above manuscript from RNB: *Shablova*, 62–63. 2) *Obikhodnik* Iosifo-Volokolamskogo monastyria. "Glava 5," in: GIM, F. Sinodal'noe sobranie, No. 403 (829), ff. 38–44; RGADA, Fond 1192, Opis' 2. No. 556, ff. 35–42; and RGB, F 113, No. 681, folia 1–6. For a publication of this chapter following the manuscript from RGB see: E. E. Golubinskii, *Istoriia russkoi tserkvi*, 2 vols. in 4 (Moscow: Universitetskaia tipografiia,

1900–1919; rpt. The Hague and Paris, Mouton, 1969), 2.2: 577–580; and note also Ludwig Steindorff, "Sravnenie istochnikov ob organizatsii pominaniia usopshikh v Iosifo-Volokolamskom i Troitse-Sergievom monastyriakh v XVI veke," in *Arkheograficheskii ezhegodnik za 1996* (Moscow: Nauka, 1998), 65–67.

7   Alekseev, *Pod znakom*, 51–55; Steindorff, "Donations and Commemorations," 480–481.
8   Cf. the documentation of the sources in Steindorff, *Memoria*, 146–156
9   For the sources cf. Steindorff, *Memoria*, 146–156; A. I. Alekseev, "O nachale gosudarstvennogo pominaniia praviashchikh dinastii Riurikovichei (XIV–XV vv.)," in *Drevneishie gosudarstva Vostochnoi Evropy. 2005 god. Riurikovichi i rossiiskaia gosudarstvennost'*, edited by M. V. Bibikov, E. A. Mel'nikova, and V. D. Nazarov, (Moscow: Indrik, 2008), 426–435.
10 Steindorff, *Memoria*, 156.
11 Ia. N. Shchapov, *Drevnerusskie kniazheskie ustavy* (Moscow: Nauka, 1976), 155, article 8; for the manuscripts and development of the redactions, 153-154.
12 Alekseev, "O nachale," 429–430.
13 S. V. Sazonov,"K rannei istorii sinodichnykh predislovii," *Soobshcheniia rostovskogo muzeia*, 1 (1991): 8-28, see http://rostmuseum.ru/publication/srm/001/sazonov01.html (last accessed 28 May 2014); ; see also Alekseev, *Pod znakom*, 140–141; *Sinodik Iosifo-Volokolamskogo monastyria (1479–1510 gody)*, edited by T. I. Shablova (St. Petersburg: Dmitrii Bulanin, 2004) 7–10 ("Introduction"); I. V. Dergacheva, *Drevnerusskii sinodik: Issledovaniia i teksty* (Moscow: Krug, 2011), 21–25, 125–127.
14 Alekseev, "O nachale."
15 Iosif Volotskii, "Poslanie Kniagine Goleninoi," in *Poslaniia Iosifa Volotskogo,* edited by Ia. S. Lur'e and A. A. Zimin (Moscow-Leningrad : Nauka, 1959), 179-183, trans. https://www.histsem.uni-kiel.de/de/abteilungen/osteurpaeische-geschichte-1/materialen/stiftung-und-totengedenken (last accessed 17 Dec. 2016).
16 For instance: *Pamiatniki literatury Drevnei Rusi. Konets XV–pervaia polovina XVI v.*, edited by L. A. Dmitrieva and D. S. Lichachev (Moscow: Khudozhestennaia literatura, 1984), 740 (commentary on the letter of Iosif Volotskii to Princess Mariia Golenina); and Hans Rothe, *Religion und Kultur in den Regionen des russischen Reiches – Erster Versuch einer Grundlegung* (Opladen: VS Verlag für Sozialwissenschaften, 1984), 43–44.
17 Recent publications about the *Sinodik pravoslaviia:* V. V. Dergachev, "K istorii russkikh perevodov *Vselenskogo Sinodika,* in *Stanovlenie povestvovatel'nykh nachal v drevnerusskoi literature XV–XVII vekov (na*

materiale sinodika), Specimina Philologiae Slavicae 89, edited by Irina Dergacheva (Munich: Otto Sagner, 1990), 165–188; Steindorff, *Memoria*, 60–62; V. V. Dergachev, "Vselenskii sinodik v drevnei i srednevekovoi Rossii," in *DRVM* 1, no. 2 (2001): 18–29; K. A. Maksimovich, "K utochneniiu korpusa drevnerusskikh domongol'skikh perevodov s grecheskogo: Sinodik v nedeliu pravoslaviia," in *DRVM* 4, no. 46 (2011): 77–86; Dergacheva, *Drevnerusskii Sinodik*, 9–11; and Vera Shevzov, "Resistance and Accommodation: The Rite of Orthodoxy in Modern Russia," in *Religion and Identity in Russia and the Soviet Union. A Festschrift for Paul Bushkovitch*, edited by N. Chrissidis, C. J. Potter, D. Schimmelpenninck van der Oye, and J. B. Spock (Bloomington, IN: Slavica, 2011), 165–190.

18 There are no proofs of this development on the territory under Polish-Lithuanian rule; see, for instance, S. T. Golubev, *Drevnii pomiannik Kievo-Pecherskoi Lavry*, 1, Chteniia v istoricheskom obshchestve Nestora letopistsa, no. 6, III (Kiev: 1892). This book corresponds to a Muscovite *sinodik*, but the term *sinodik* does not appear at all. The self-designation of the book in the headline is *Pominanie (Commemoration)*. It starts with the first half of the first *slovo* of the tripartite *predislovie* to the *sinodik*, mentioned above. Following to the next passage, pp. 1–2, the book was composed shortly after the heavy damage of 1482, when the troops of Crimean Khan Mengli-Girei sacked Kiev.

19 Iosif, "Poslanie kniagine Goleninoi," dating following A. I. Pliguzov, "O khronologii poslanii Iosifa Volotskogo," in *Russkii feodal'nyi arkhiv* 5 (1992): 1052-1053, different from Lur'e's dating of 1508–1513 (*Poslaniia*, 259). According to Shablova (*Sinodik*, 202–203), the letter was written at the latest in 1505, since Iosif wrote about the intention of the monastery to use the money from the donation of Prince Semen Ivanovich Bel'skii for the purchase of land. We know from other sources that the construction of the Church of the Epiphany in the monastery was finished 9 May, 1506, thanks to donations of Bel'skii and Boris Vasil'evich Kutuzov. The phrase in the letter, *[Bel''skii] velel pytati, gde by zemlia kupiti monastyriu* ([Bel'skii] asked to find out where he could buy land for the monastery), indicates that beside his donation of 200 rubles, the prince was ready to buy land which the monastery would choose.

20 Thanks to the information in the *Kormovaia kniga* (the *Feast Book* of the monastery) about the location of graves, S. Z. Chernov succeeded in identifying three graves in the new *pridel* (annex) as graves of the Goleniny: Nekropol' Iosifo-Volokolamskogo monastyria v svete arkheologicheskikh issledovanii 2001 god. Staryi i novyi pridely" in *Prepodobnyi Iosif Volotskii i ego obitel'*, edited by Heguman Sergii (Vo-

ronkov), Monakh Panteleimon (Dementenko), and G. M. Zelenskaia (Moscow: Severnyi palomnik, 2008), 292. Chernov suggests that Ivan and Semen (mentioned in the letter) and their brother Andrei Andreevich, the Monk Arsenii, were buried here, and Ivan and Semen had become monks under the names Antonii and Trifon, since these names appear in the entries in the *Donation Book* and in the *Feast Book*. However, we do not possess any information that Ivan and Semen took the monastic vow. In the *povsiadnevnyi spisok* (the "everyday list") they are written in the chapter for princes who had died as laymen. The information about the burial of Ivan and Semen is taken from the quite unreliable "Tale about the Princess Mariia Golenina" in the *Volokolamsk Patericon* from the middle of the 16th century. It is more convincing to suppose that Antonii and Trifon were sons of Andrei Andreevich, and that they were buried together with their father in the annex: see Steindorff, "Princess Mariia Golenina," 568; *Das Speisungsbuch von Volokolamsk. Kormovaia kniga Iosifo-Volokolamskogo monastyria. Eine Quelle zur Sozialgeschichte russischer Klöster im 16. Jahrhundert*, edited and translated by Ludwig Steindorff in cooperation with Rüdiger Koke, Elena Kondraškina, Ulrich Lang and Nadja Pohlmann, Bausteine zur Slavischen Philologie und Kulturgeschichte, NF 12 (Cologne/ Weimar/Vienna: Böhlau Verlag, 1998), 349 (Nos. 61, 62, 64).

21 See Steindorff, "Princess Mariia Golenina," 552–565, 576–577, where I prove that all information in Iosif's letters about donations corresponds exactly to the information about them in deeds, in the donation books, and in the *Feast Book* of the monastery.

22 Donations of money and movable values were registered only in a donation book, not in special charters.

23 See above, note 6.

24 RGADA, Fond 1161, Opis' 2, No. 561. For the structure of that manuscript, see Steindorff, *Memoria*, 190–192, and the additions in Steindorff, "Commemoration and Administrative Techniques," *Russian History* 22 (1995): 439–441.

25 See Golubinskii *Istoriia russkoi tserkvi*, 2.2: 579, and above, note 6.

26 Golubev, *Pomiannik Kievo-Pecherskoi Lavry*. 86–87. The editor stresses, in the introduction (p. X), the important role the entries in the *Pominanie* played for the monastery as a source of income, and in this connection how much the role of the monastery as center of care for the deceased was accepted also in the Orthodox Polish-Lithuanian society.

27 Golubev, *Pomiannik Kievo-Pecherskoi Lavry*. 2–3. The *Pominanie* is a good source for contacts across state borders. Following the entry on

p. 30, Grand Prince Ivan Vasil'evich of Muscovy had ordered the entry of his father, Vasilii II Vasil'evich Temnyi (†1462), his mother Mariia, who died as nun Marfa (†1484), and his first wife, Mariia (†1467). This entry serves as the proof that the basic text of the *Pominanie* was not finished before 1484. The name of the donor was added only later after his death (†1505). There are further donations from Muscovy, even including Novgorod. A large majority of entries came from families of the Polish-Lithuanian territory.

28 A. A. Zimin, *Krupnaia feodal'naia votchina i sotsial'no-politicheskaia bor'ba v Rossii (konets XV–XVI v.)* (Moscow: Nauka, 1977), 103.
29 See above, note 6.
30 *Monastic Rule*, 277 (Discourse 13, Tradition 1).
31 *Sinodik*, 127–133, also Kazakova, *Vassian Patrikeev i ego sochineniia* (Moscow and Leningrad: Izdatel'stvo Akademii Nauk SSSR, 1960), 355–357; trans., *Monastic Rule*, 309–311.
32 See above, note 6; at that time also the *Kormovaia kniga* was composed: *Speisungsbuch*, XIII–XIV.
33 The unique *Godovaia kormovaia kniga* (*Feast Book for One Year*) (GIM, Eparkhial'noe sobranie, No. 417 [683]), served for the verification of this practice. For the period from 1 September 1566 until 17 April 1567, it registers for every day what was actually served on the table and for whose commemoration the *kormy* (feast meals) were intended; these were moved back to earlier days or forward to later days to avoid collisions with other monastery regulations concerning fasts and feasts: see Ludwig Steindorff "Realization vs. Standard: Commemorative Meals in the Iosif Volotskii Monastery in 1566/67," in *Rude & Barbarous Kingdom Revisited. Essays in Russian History and Culture in Honor of Robert O. Crummey*, edited by Chester S. L. Dunning, Russell E. Martin, and Daniel Rowland (Bloomington, IN: Slavica, 2008)," 231–249.
34 "Stoglav," in *Zakonodatel'stvo perioda obrazovaniia i ukrepleniia russkogo tsentralizovannogo gosudarstva*, edited by A. D. Gorskii (Moscow: Iuridicheskaia literatura, 1985), 271 (Question 15), 351–352 (Chapter 75).
35 A former version of this article has appeared in Russian under the title "Chto bylo novogo v kul'ture pominaniia v Iosifo-Volotskom monastyre? Peresmotr voprosa." in *DRVM* 1, no. 55 (2014): 25–32.

6 Iosif Volotskii's Disputational Technique (*Ars Disputandi*)

David Goldfrank

And if it had not been fitting to venerate a church, the Prophet would not have said: *I shall worship toward your holy church* [Ps 5:7/8; *LXX* 137:2] Does David really lie, saying this, and bowing to the church says: *I shall worship toward your holy church?* If David lies, then who indeed tells the truth? How could David himself say: *You will destroy all who speak a lie?* [Ps 5:6/7] And if David tells the truth, saying: *I shall worship toward your holy church,* and he does not say it once, but often, then how can anyone dare to say, that it is not proper to venerate a church?[1]

18 – Late 1560s-1570s Illustrated Chronicle (*Litsevoi letopisnyi svod*) depiction of Iosif composing *Prosvetitel'*.

Disputes of various kinds may have abounded in Old Rus', but not formal "questions in dispute" (*quaestiones disputatae*) or "obligations" (*obligationes*) as they developed the medieval West with their own special rules, whereby two equally orthodox contestants jousted over philosophical and theological matters.[2] Nor, so far as we know, did Rus' know of the pedagogical "sophisms" (*sophismata*), whereby one had to argue the pros and contras of a given reasonable or absurd proposition,[3] or any other of the developed systems of disputation spread across Afro-Eurasia.[4] The skilled Klim Smoliatich might show off his rhetorical and exegetical prowess at the prince's court in Kiev in the twelfth century,[5] but structured debates on level playing fields did not constitute part of the early Rus' intellectual-pedagogical experience.

Nevertheless, in the century before Iosif's era, Russia/Eastern Rus' experienced, in literary or actual form, at least five types of dramatic disputes. Epifanii Premudryi's late 14th century Life of Stefan of Perm relates an unlikely but colorful, bravado-filled entertaining debate, where 700 miles east of Moscow the missionary hero defeats the pagan Zyrian (Komi) shaman Pam by challenging him to walk through fire unharmed.[6] After the death of Vasilii I in 1425, the supporters of his son Vasilii II out-argued (or out-bribed) those of the latter's uncle Iurii at the court of Khan Ulug Makhmed for the succession to Moscow's throne.[7] In 1438-39, Russian clerics attending the Council of Ferrara-Florence witnessed Roman Catholic dialectical prowess, where, in the words of a sarcastic Moscow annalist, three languages were spoken: "Greek, Frankish (Church Latin or Italian), and 'Philosophy'."[8] In the 1370s-1420s, the simony-attacking, priest- and sacrament-rejecting *Strigolniki* of Novgorod and Pskov evoked a polemical screed attributed to Stefan and addressed them and their alleged doctrines in turn, just as Kozma Presviter did against the Bogomils four centuries earlier.[9] Finally, among the translated apologetics appearing in Russia in the early 15th century sits, among other less elaborate disputes, the doctored, Old Testament-based debate between the sixth-century Bishop Grigentios "the Himyarite" of Taphar (Yemen) and Rabbi Herban, who stands his own ground before he surrenders, even while the bishop levels mild rhetorical insults.[10]

The chart on the next page, with the relationships among some of

Scheme of Development of Disputations, Antiquity to 16th Century Muscovy

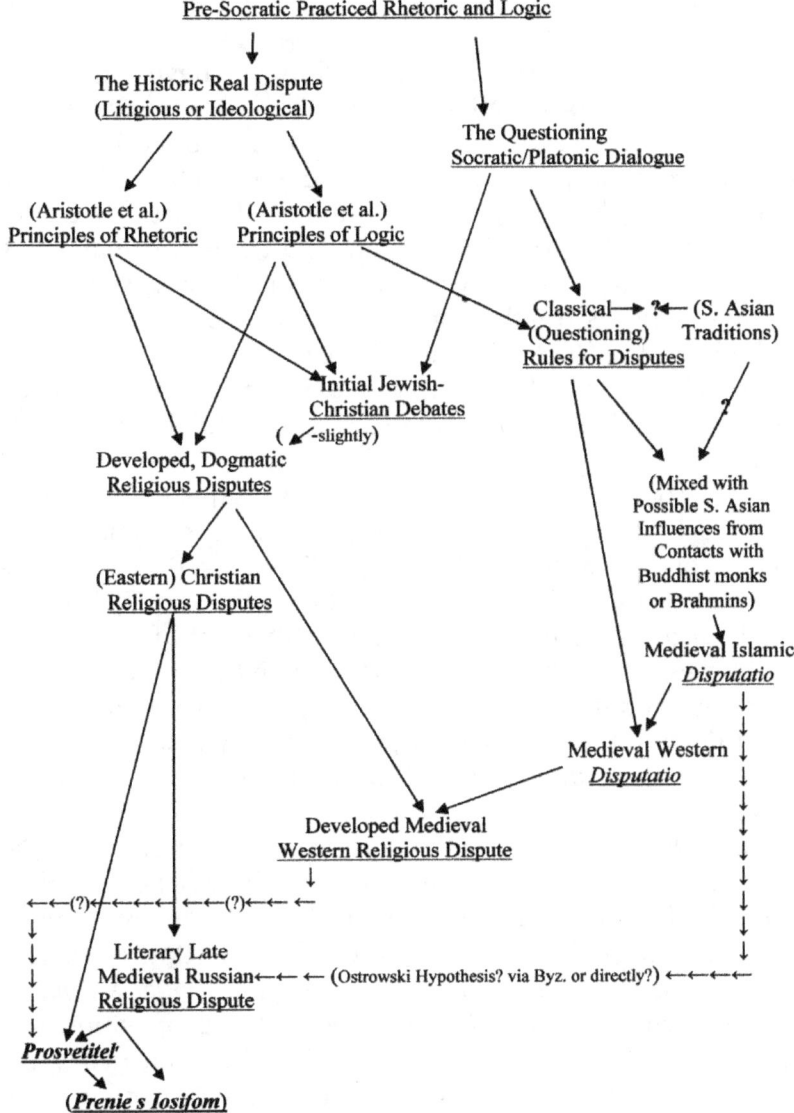

the broad categories of Classical, early Christian, Eastern Christian, South Asian, Islamic, medieval Western, and Russian genuine and literary disputes, shows how Iosif and fellow Muscovites may have acquired such knowledge.

Iosif himself is known from his writings to have employed disputational techniques in all three major arenas of his activities: monastic leadership, real life conflicts; and his most celebrated and extensive polemical theater: theological-apologetic activism. With an intellect capable of discerning the logical structure behind the Bible's and Orthodoxy's innumerable parables and maxims, Iosif could always argue effectively by rhetorically and syllogistically adapting from his treasury of available sources—for example, allegedly from the Desert Fathers:[11] Once a demon ... saw boys in a coenobium, and said: "I do not need to be here, because they will be much more troublesome here than I." This is actually an enthymeme or rhetorical syllogism,[12] here with an unstated first premise, that the listener or reader is expected to supply: that one role of demons is to cause trouble for monasteries [A]. When combined with the stated second premise concerning devilish boys [B], the conclusion follows logically: "I do not need to be here [$A \wedge B \rightarrow C$]." Were Iosif actually arguing against the position that it is okay for boys to be in monasteries, as he implies by his discourse (*slovo*) title, "That it is not proper for boys to live in the cloister,"[13] we would then have, as an enthymeme rather than as a dry syllogism, a simple polemical argument (*argumentum*) or position (*positio*) within a disputation (*obligatio*).

Likewise, without any known formal training in logic or disputation, Iosif seems to have grasped the essence of the three standard classical forms of dispute: the deductive-expository (*methodus syllogistica* or *scholastica*), the questioning (*methodus erotematica* or *socratica*), and the less common Megarian (*methodus megarica*), which reduces the opponent's proposition to an absurdity.[14] Iosif mostly employs the first two, but his Extended Rule (*Dukhovnaia gramota* = "Spiritual Testament") contains a biting homiletic-enthymematic modulation of the Megarian method. Here the requirements of a corps of responsible senior elders and monastery officials to enforce needed decorum serve as the unstated (actually earlier stated), premises that are granted, and then Iosif skips several deductive steps:[15]

If someone says: "there is no need for so many council brothers," he is really saying: 'there is no need for good order, reverence, and a peaceful administration in the monastery, but everything shall be irregular and perverse.

In this manner, using very few words, Iosif has reduced the proposition of his real or imagined opponent within his monastery to a damnable absurdity. Of course his goal is not to win laurels in a debate, but to shut down any the opposition to his structural arrangements and innovations

One of Iosif's specialties is his mixing threatening homiletics and syllogistic, as in his practical epistles, where a degree of informal, litigious-procedural 'discovery' operates in material disputes. In one case Iosif has augmented his brotherhood by tonsuring a prince's young bondsman (*domashnoe chado*). Iosif's first epistle on this matter emphasizes the positive, salvific value of allowing a bondsman to become a monk, but the prince replies to the messenger: "He has cut off my head," and berates monasteries over their alleged contingent of phony ascetics. Iosif in turn not only reminds the prince that virtue-oriented groups normally include a few deviants, but also, as if by logical necessity, though with an argument that any skilled logician could demolish by parsing the details, imputes a fatal *a minore ad maius* (inference from lesser to greater) analogy with this warning:[16]

If someone blasphemes monasteries or the holy monastic habit, since many dress in the monastic habit, but not all are saved, they blaspheme our Lord Jesus Christ, since there were many disciples but not all were saved.

The prince likewise stands in danger of blaspheming baptism, with an implied loss much greater than the material or prestige value of the bondsman—the original ground for the dispute. In common parlance, Iosif's real message is: "Shut up or burn!" And this being so, he has implicitly, in the lingo of the obligatory dispute, converted his mode of argumentation to "a second-person discursive demand" (*petitio*).[17]

Iosif's embrogio with the prestigious former hegumen of

Troitse-Sergiev (1495-1505) Serapion, who became Archbishop of Novgorod (1505-1509), serves as the one example where we have both sides of a literary dispute before the court of elite public opinion, and the opponents appear remarkably similar and reciprocal. Without the approval of his spiritual superior Serapion, Iosif had transferred his cloister from his *udel* (territorial-appanage) prince's legally indeterminate overlordship to that of his cousin Grand Prince Vasilii III. Iosif's two lengthy apologetic epistles paint himself as a threatened victim acting canonically or practically within the confines of real possibilities, the *udel* prince Fëdor of Volok as anomic and rapacious, and Serapion as the tool of ruthless intriguers, effecting an uncanonic excommunication of Iosif, and then speaking improperly when so indicted at the Moscow Synod. This evidence of illicit behavior allows Iosif to draw damning moral conclusions regarding the now deposed archbishop.[18] In turn, a likewise lengthy epistle-response has Serapion acting canonically and properly, the synodal trial proceeding as a travesty of justice, and Iosif standing as a mega-liar, all around scoundrel, and chronic violator of diocesan boundaries and rules. And this evidence of impermissible behavior allows Iosif's foes to draw their own damning moral conclusions regarding him.[19] Aristotle, whose analysis of the syllogism and rhetoric owes a lot to the litigious practices of the Greece of his day,[20] might have found confirmation of some of his observations in this colorful controversy. But from the standpoint of formal dispute analysis, in the Iosif-Serapion conflict character assassination and polemical homiletic seem to overshadow reasoned argumentation regarding the church canons, civil law, and the discretionary authority of prelates and princes.

Iosif's *Book Against the (Novogorod) Heretics* or *Prosvetitel'*, the first such original theological treatise produced by any East Slav, stands as the chief source for his art of disputation. As a literary religious dispute with the highest (and hottest) of stakes for this life and eternity, *Prosvetitel'* does not have to follow the same format as an intellectual contest between two Orthodox or a 'fair' debate with established ground rules between spokesmen of rival creeds. Rather, as a treatise aiming to condemn and anathematize the opponent, the writer is free to 'play dirty' with rhetoric.

Among the striking paradoxes of this work, produced in stages over time, with additions and subtractions as fit a given moment or purpose,[21] are his utilization of at least one disputation source and his claims to write his discourses to prepare readers to debate heretics, while in fact he allows his hypothetical opponents only to raise objections, but not engage in any extensive parsing of his own or the Orthodox position. The genre is the apologetic-polemical discourse that accuses and damns as well as refutes the opponent, while it contains varying amounts of positive homiletic. The initial *Skazanie o novoiavivsheisia eresi novogorodskikh eretikov* ("Account of the Recent Heresy of the Novgorod Heretics") provides the dramatic backdrop. Instead of the debate stage or place of possible execution, we have the historical tableau with a drama of cosmic forces represented by heroically pious Orthodox combating the heretics' satanic doctrines and actions. The goal, he admits, at the close of "Discourse" 11 ending the Brief Redaction—the sole complete version known from his lifetime—is not to correct the incorrigible, but to "rescue those in the Orthodox faith."[22]

In my own terminology, Iosif's typical polemical discourse is simultaneously a running refutation of a false proposition and an affirmation of the truth. Each discourse commences with a summary title, some brief positive doctrinal or attitudinal pedagogy, and the heretical position and main points to be opposed, all spiced with his rhetorical insults and admonitions, as well as a promise of proof "from the divine writings" of the Orthodox doctrine in the exposition that follows.[23] Thereupon comes the refutation of the chief heretical proposition and of the trapping arguments attempted by the imagined opponent. Iosif certainly writes as if he understands the Aristotle-cum-Boethius-based rules of the obligatory disputation, whereby only the possible follows logically from the possible, and genuine contradictions therefore represent either a fallacious premise or faulty argumentation.[24] The four or five discourses with the greatest number of such objections (six to thirteen) may be the closest to a genuine disputation, though I would leave such a judgment to experts in medieval Western dialectic.

This brief essay lacks the space to review Iosif's sources, but we can note here five generically distinct works that provided partial models for him. The above-mentioned, extended Grigentios-Herban dispute contains quite a few Jewish objections to Christian doctrine, including one which Iosif ascribes to the Novgorod Heretics concerning propriety for God of the Incarnation,[25] and all allowing the archbishop, typically for this genre, to expound positively on doctrine. Both sides use syllogistic rhetorical questions, and Grigentios has an informal enthymeme-syllogism similar to one of Iosif's:[26]

> Therefore if the temple is addressed completely as holy and as the house of the Lord Almighty, it proves that also the things of it, being sacred and holy, are worthy of honor and worship.

Kozma Presviter's earlier known 10th-century treatise against the Bogomils, of which the oldest extant full manuscripts circulated in Russia in the 1490s in connection with the campaign against the Novgorod Heretics, has a title akin to a Iosif discourse: *Dialogue*

19 – Illustrated Chronicle depiction of Ivan III and Metropolitan Zosima looking on as the accusing bishop confronts the monk Zakhar and other "Novgorod Heretics" at the 1490 Moscow synod; the opponents are dumbfounded and cannot respond.

against the Recent Heresy of Bogomil (*Beseda na noviavivshuiu eres´ Bogomilu*).[27] Since the Bogomils rejected much of basic Christianity, Kosma, just as Iosif in *Prosvetitel'*, refutes a series of heretical or Judaic positions. Literarily addressing and dialoguing with the imagined audience as well as with the imagined Bogomils,[28] Kozma combines insulting rhetorical questions and informal syllogism, as here with the second premise at the end:[29]

> Who are you, O heretic, judging him, and judging him before God's judgment? For if a priest is sinful, he still is not a heretic. Indeed heresy is worse than any sin.[30]

The *Vita Constantini*, excerpted in the essay which follows, contains a brief spirited debate between the future "Apostle to the Slavs" and John the Grammarian over icon and cross veneration with some standard arguments later employed by Iosif.[31] Of a different nature is John of Damascus's *Exposition of the Orthodox Faith*, which disputes certain heretical positions in passing, but serves as Iosif's didactic model for setting forth doctrinal premises, such as what is knowable about God,[32] or the necessary identity both of the mutable and the created and of their inverses regarding the immutable, uncreated creator.[33]

And finally of another type are John Chrysostom's *Six Sermons against the Jews*, constituting part of *The Pearl* (*Margarit*), a Russian compilation of this 'golden-mouthed' prelate, who also influenced Kozma.[34] Here not systematic arguments against Jewish doctrines, but moral invective to create a wall separating the Christian faithful from these principled adherents of the Old Testament and their attractive Passover celebrations was the chief purpose.[35] Typical of Chrysostom's polarizing reasoning is:[36]

> Nothing is more wretched than they, who strive all over to alienate their own salvation: for when it was proper for them to observe the Law, they trashed it; and now that the Law has ceased, they argue in favor of observing it.

or the more enthymematic-syllogistic:[37]

For if the Judaic are honorable and great, ours are false. And if these are true, then theirs are full of deceit.

Iosif's first discourse, in defense of the Trinity, will serve as our chief example of his mode of argumentation. His title forecasts both the rebutting and the catechizing aspects of the contents that follow:[38]

Discourse 1 against the recent heresy of the Novgorod Heretics, who say that God the Almighty Father does not have a Son or a Holy Spirit, and that there is no Holy Trinity. Here is an exposition from the divine writings that God the Almighty Father does have a Son and a Holy Spirit of same-essence and co-enthroned with Himself, and that the Holy and life-creating and omnipotent Trinity has testimony from the beginning, from the patriarchs, and from the prophets, and from all the divine writings.

The title itself signals that for Iosif, as for his polemical sources, the chief argument for anything is the "testimony" found in sacred literature. Indeed the next discourse, in defense of Jesus's being the messiah prophesied in the Old Testament, contains only structured proof texts, whose historical accuracy Iosif defends, but no rhetorical questions with their implied syllogistic, not to say any "if ... then ..." statements or other forms of the syllogism.

Discourse 1, more characteristically for Iosif, mixes testimony and logic and starts by applying the latter to the former, where Paul's statement concerning the Son has been augmented in the Slavic version of *First Corinthians* with the Spirit, and thereby creates an imperative:[39]

The blessed and great apostle, the mouth of the Lord, Paul, says: *If there are many gods and many lords, yet for us there is one God the Father, out of whom is everything, and we are in Him; and one Lord Jesus Christ, by whom is everything, as we by Him* (1 Cr 8:5-6), *and one Holy Spirit, in whom also is everything, and we are in Him.*[40] And therefore it is proper for every Christian to believe, as he was baptized, in the Father, the Son and the Holy Spirit, in the same essence and nature and divinity, ...

After elaborating on the nature of the Trinity with definitions and analogies adapted from Gregory of Nazianzus and John the Damascene (among others),[41] Iosif bridges with an explicit command dictum cum argumentative principle, "Let faith precede and not proof (*pokazanie*),"[42] again demands belief in the credo, and, with damning insults, anathematizes his opponents:[43]

And so we hold, and so we confess with every breath. And we anathematize every heresy, especially that which now has appeared, of Aleksei—*by myriads anathematized*,[44] called the soul-corrupted archpriest, Satan's first-born—, Denis the priest of the Antichrist, and Fëdor Kuritsin, and all who so reasoned and reason, and who sowed many Jewish doctrines among men. And on this account much harm came unto life, and into many heresies, and similarly deceits spread—evil and darkened Jewish traditions.

Only at this point, 800 words (nine per cent) into the discourse and immediately following the above bridge that closes the topical-pedagogical and credo-affirming introduction, stands the full statement of the major proposition [A – *my division, DG*] and its four-part elaboration [B, C, D, E] to be opposed:[45]

Of one of these we shall now speak, which they evilly say and define,[46] and deny, and [A] do not confess in verity and truth the holy, one-essence, and life-creating and inseparable Trinity, but say [B] that God the Almighty Father does not have a Son or a Holy Spirit of same-essence and co-enthroned with Himself, and that there is no Holy Trinity; and [C] that what Scripture says, that God has a Word and a Spirit, God indeed does have a word, but it is pronounced by the spirit via the mouth and spread onto the air; and [D] what the prophets said of the Son of God, this is Jesus Christ, and the Son of God not by essence, but by grace, like the holy prophets Moses and David and others;

and [E] what they write of the Holy Spirit, they do not say that according to hypostasis (*s"stav*)[47] or according to essence this is God, but that it proceeds out of God's mouth and disperses throughout the air.

The remainder of the discourse refutes propositions [B], [C], [D], and [E] in turn, and then refutes [C] and [E] on the Word and the Spirit together, segueing to a positive elucidation of the Trinity. Iosif's proofs combine syllogistics and straightforward scriptural exegesis with the latter lending itself to positive exposition of doctrine.

Iosif also sprinkles his argumentation with some generalizing principles, in part, it seems, to ward off potential objections. Even before the start of the refutation of [B], he claims that the prophets "concealed the prophesies by means of hermeneutic difficulties (*neudobstvo tolkovaniia*)" in order to avoid being killed and having their books destroyed,[48] something he backs up with a conceptually clever *a minore ad maius* syllogism:[49]

> Therefore the great Moses not only in a certain way obscurely revealed the Holy Trinity by means of shadows and images and enigma, but also did not write about the holy angels, but adduced rather such a multitude of those incorporeal heavenly forces, which is the second light after the divine and first light, therefore allegorizing these, so that the Judaeans not apotheosize that heavenly and bright army. For if they worshiped the calf and Baalpeor and Chemosh and Astarte, they much more would have served that fearsome heavenly army, like unto God. Therefore Moses also first started to write of the creation of heaven and earth and all created things, and not of angels, of whom all the divine writings, old and new, testify that they exist.

And he lays the ground rules, similar to Grigentios's, of this literary dispute: since Jews accept only the Old Testament, and he is arguing against Jewish-reasoning heretics, he will argue only from the Old Testament.[50] Further discreet exegetical principles appear as Iosif requires them.

An initial refutation of [B], "that God the Almighty Father does not have a same essence Son or a Holy Spirit enthroned with himself, and that there is no Holy Trinity," occupies the next 13.8% of Discourse 1 and focuses on only one issue: to whom did God speak when He said: "Let us create man in our own image" (Gn. 1:26)[51]—the Son and Spirit, himself, or angels. After reaffirming the Trinitarian position, Iosif introduces the first alternative with a rhetorical insult:[52]

> But the Judaeans resist, saying: To whom did he speak? Ah, God said this to himself. Lo the heretics rage, the Judaeans resist, and the truth is twisted.

He dismisses the last one with an anthropomorphic *ad maius* syllogism in the form of a rhetorical question:[53]

> It is the custom of a mindless person, not a wise one, to sit by himself and talk to himself, and to meditate [*out loud – DG*] to himself at work. And if this is unbefitting of a wise man and improper to do, how much more improper is this for God!

Having so proven that God when creating humanity, though not during his other acts of creation, must have been speaking to someone else, Iosif invokes Isaiah 9.6/9.5[54] in those Septuagint versions that read: "... son given us ... called angel of great counsel ... mighty god, master, prince of peace, father of the future age,"[55] in order to show this is the "counselor" is the Son, and cannot be Moses or David who lack such attributes.[56]

With the running commentary of a partisan sportscaster of this one-sided intellectual joust, Iosif further abuses his opponent in bridging to the second alternative explanation:[57]

> We saw just recently, that the heretic fell mute, for he comprehended that it is unfitting not only for God, but for a wise man to sit at work alone and speak to himself. Yet the Jew once more is shameless and says that God is speaking to the angels: *"Let us create man in our image and likeness."*

Here Iosif finds appropriate Scripture for the angels to praise God when He created the stars (Jb. 38:7) to augment his enthymematic directive to the audience:[58]

> Respond to him: If He spoke to the angels, then it would not be written that *"God created man, in the image and likeness of God He created him,"* for man would have been both in the likeness and in the image of God and in the likeness and in the image of the angels.

He concludes this initial section on the Trinity with three more proof texts, which he simply interprets more kerygmatically than deductively, for example: "Isn't it clear that He speaks to His Son and the Holy Spirit?"[59]

Iosif next seamlessly introduces more such Old Testament proof texts with commentary, enough to fill more than a third of the discourse, to demonstrate chiefly the prophets' revelation of the Son, but, where convenient, also of the Spirit and the entire Trinity.[60] His expository exegetical style addresses the audience, such as with:[61]

> David says from the face of God: ... *"I shall not accept a young bull from your house or a goat from your flocks."* (Ps 49:9-*LXX*) And again: *"Do I eat the meat of a calf or drink the blood of a goat'? Rather sacrifice unto God a sacrifice of praise."* (Ps 50:13-14-*LXX*) Being God himself, to which God does he command to sacrifice a sacrifice of praise? Do you see that the Father here reveals the Son and the Holy Spirit and directs to sacrifice a sacrifice of praise to them, and not a sacrifice of the blood of a calf or a goat?

And Iosif likewise continues to berate his opponents and barbs them with rhetorical questions:[62]

> Also Daniel speaks similarly: *"I saw in a nighttime vision, and lo, on the heavenly clouds, that the Son of Man was going, and he approached the Ancient of Days; and he was given all the authority and honor and kingship, and all the people, and tribes,*

and tongues will serve him. And his authority is eternal authority and shall not pass, and his kingship will not disintegrate" (Dn 7:13-14). So shame on you, Jews, who say that the godhead is of one person and one hypostasis and that God the Father Omnipotent does not have a Son of one essense, and co-enthroned with Himself, and that the Christ, whom the prophets preached, He is the Son of God not by essence, but by grace, like David and Solomon. If this were so, then who approached the Ancient of Days? And to whom was given the eternal authority and honor and kingship?

Soon afterwards introducing the argumentative principle that "the testimony of enemies is most genuine," Iosif mixes syllogism and analogy to prove a prophesy:[63]

For he [Balaam – DG] says: *A star will shine from Jacob, and a man shall rise from Israel* (Nm 24:17). Star means godhead because a star is fire, and fire is destructive of matter and a wicked nature, just as the godhead purifies the transgression of the believers.

Iosif is even more syllogistic in his argument that the indirect object of the psalmist's *The Lord said to my Lord: 'Sit at my right'* (Ps 110:1/109:1)[64] is the Son and not a high priest, as a Jew would contend:[65]

But hear again what David says in that psalm: *From the womb before the morning star I begat you* (Ps 110:3/109:3), and *You are a priest forever, according to the order of Melchisedek* (110:4/109:4). If he had said this to a high priest, he would not have said: *From the womb before the morning star I begat you*, and also *You are a priest forever*, nor would he have said *according to the order of Melchisedek*. For nowhere is it said that a king begat a high priest before the morning star, and high priests do not abide forever, because they are prevented by death from abiding, and are not according the order of Melchisedek, but according the order of Aaron, as everyone recognizes.

This deduction is of the type $(C \rightarrow \neg A \wedge \neg B) = (A \wedge B \rightarrow \neg C)$, where C is a high priest, A is physical conception from a king "before the morning star," and B is of "the order of Melchsedek. Iosif here, as elsewhere, has put in own words and logical exposition traditions of Christian thinking hearkening back to St. Paul's use of logic and Hebrew Scripture.

Iosif continues with syllogistic exegesis:[66]

> And again he says: *God Lord, make manifest to us* (Ps 118:27/117:27). *Blessed is he who comes in the name of the Lord* (Ps 118:26/117:26). And indeed this *in the name of the Lord. God and Lord* means no other coming one, except our Lord Jesus Christ, who says: *I have come in the name of my Father* (Jn 5:23). And if Christ were not the Son of God by essence, but like David and Solomon, then why would David state: *God* and *Lord coming in the name of the Lord*?

Iosif's next exegesis to refute the Jewish position ends with a syllogistic refutation containing another *ad maius* deduction:[67]

> And again he says: *Like rain on the fleece, and like a drop dropping on the land, justice will shine forth in his days and an abundance of peace, until the moon is removed* (Ps 72/71:6-7), *and let his name be blessed forever, his name abide before the sun* (Ps 72/71:17). The Jews say that this was said of Solomon,[68] but this speech has nothing to do with Solomon. For Solomon is not like rain falling upon a fleece, but as his father David says: *Surely I was conceived within lawlessness, and my mother bore me in sins* (Ps 50:7-LXX). And if David was conceived in lawlessness, how much more so Solomon, since he was born of a fornicating woman, and his name is not blessed forever, nor does he abide before the sun, nor with the moon will he be removed; nor do all the earthly kings worship him, nor do all the nations serve him.

Iosif continues here with some historical arguments identifying Jesus with the characteristics so prophesied, but also intersperses a classical argument from the physics employed the Church fathers:[69]

And again he says: *Forever, Lord, your word will abide in heaven* (Ps 119:89/ 118:89). A pronounced word disperses into the air and does not abide forever.

Soon comes another if-then rhetorical question exegesis to prove the Son of same essence and, in passing, reaffirm the virgin birth:[70]

And again Isaiah says: *Lo a virgin shall receive in the womb, and give birth to the Son, and they shall name Him Emmanuel, which means God is with us.*[71] If the godhead were one person and one hypostasis, and if Christ were not of same-essence with God the Father, but like David and Solomon and Moses: then whom did the Prophet show being *born of the virgin* and being *God with us*?

This string of logically and historically interpreted Old Testament citations, augmented by Jeremiah and Zechariah and evincing a homiletic-triumphal ring, ends with a refutation of a final objection:[72]

Micah says: *And you, Bethlehem, the house of Ephrath, you are in no way lesser among the Judaean chieftans. For out of you shall go forth a leader, who shall pastor my people, Israel: his goings forth are from the beginning, from days eternal* (Mi 5:2). If someone says that this is said of David: but it has not been said of David. For David was many generations before Micah, and no king can have *goings forth from the beginning, from days eternal*, except our Lord Jesus Christ.

Iosif follows with an initial summary concerning the Son, and then adds first a chronological argument for "Christ the Leader" from Daniel (9:25-*LXX*),[73] and a lexical argument that God's allegedly using "God" instead of "I" in a threat to Moses as proof that "God the Father, conversing, recalls the Son, and God the Word, conversing, recalls the Father."[74]

At this point, roughly two thirds (65%) through his 9200-word discourse, Iosif shows his pedagogical and organizational savvy, as he sums up his earlier points and bridges into the section on the Spirit [E], which comprises the next sixth of the text:[75]

> Lo, we have explained a little and partially from the divine and prophetic writings of our Lord Jesus Christ, that He is He who by humanity is called 'the Christ' and 'Son of Man', and by divinity the 'Son of God', the same-essence and co-enthroned 'counselor' to the Father, and 'mighty God', and 'Master', and 'Prince of the World', and 'Father of the future age', and 'Creator' and 'Maker; of the visible and invisible with the Father and the Holy Spirit, and not as Moses and David and all the prophets. Next we shall speak from the divine prophetic writings of the Holy and life-creating Spirit, who is of same-essence and co-enthroned and counselor to the Father.

Iosif then goes onto another refutational attack with rhetorical insults accompanying his questionable use of the Megarian method, since the opponents' position is absurd only to the believer in a hypostatic Holy Spirit, but not at all to the Antitrinitarian or Jew:[76]

> The heretical cadets reason contrary to this, for they say that God the Father Omnipotent has a spirit, which proceeds out of Him and flows through the air. But look, inane and impudent ones! What is more inane than these words? And what is greater than this blasphemy? You have not likened the Holy Spirit to an angel or to a soul. For if an angel also is incorporeal, yet he does not flow through the air, but has eternal being, and so the soul.

Polemically logical exegesis now follows, again based on physics as understood in the sacred tradition:[77]

> And to what do you liken? Wind? Smoke? These flow through the air and come to non-being. If the Holy Spirit of God flows through the air, then how can the prophet Isaiah say of Him and call Him *Spirit of God, Spirit of wisdom,* Spirit *of knowledge, Spirit of light,* Spirit *of strength, Spirit of testimony, Spirit of piety, Spirit of fear of God*?[78] For a spirit flowing through the air does not grant wisdom, nor knowledge, nor light, nor strength, nor testimony, nor piety, nor fear of God, but when it occurs, it soon comes to non-being.

And Iosif similarly concludes his next proof text with a rhetorical syllogism equating the Holy Spirit and God:[79]

> And again, the saintly Job says: *The Spirit of God, it having created me* so (Jb 33:4). We seek out the force of the word, and we see with knowledge that Job says: *The Spirit of God, it having created me* so, and Scripture says that to Job, God is the one *having created* him *so*. And there is a great deal in the Scriptures, which is about Job, but all Scripture says *God, having created* him so. Job says that *the Spirit of God, it having created me* so. Are the statements of Righteous Job ever contrary to Divine Writing? This shall in no way be. But as there is one force and one essence and one divinity of the Father and the Holy Spirit, that righteous, and blemishless, and great, true man, says: *the Spirit of God, it having created me so.*

Iosif then once more barbs his opponents: "Where are the heretical statements, saying that the Spirit of God proceeds out of the God and flows throughout into the air?" and restates his positive proposition to give the force of repetition.[80] Indeed he seems to enjoy ending his proof texts with such syllogistic taunts, as with this string of extracts from the Psalms:[81]

> ... and again he says: *Your good Spirit will direct me to level ground* (Ps 143/142:12)–*Level ground* is where the righteous dwell in the heavens–; and again: *With the word of the Lord*[82] *the heavens were made firm up by the Lord, and by the Spirit of his mouth, all of their force* (Ps 33/32:6).[83] With a word and a spirit pronounced and flowing through the air, how could *the heavens* be *made firm* and *all of their force*? And indeed, if David speaks of the Holy Spirit as creator and maker and *directing* to *level ground, making firm with His word the heavens and all of their forces*, then how can the heretics say that the Spirit flows through the air?

Or the following from Isaiah:[84]

And again, Isaiah says: *the Lord sent me and His Spirit,*[85] and *the Spirit of the Lord*[86] *is upon me, and for His sake has anointed me* (Is 61:1). And again: *The house of Jacob*[87] *made wroth the Spirit of the Lord* (Is 63:10),[88] and again says about the Judaeans: *they were disobedient and made wroth His Holy Spirit, and it turned towards them in enmity* (Is 63:10).[89] And if the Holy Spirit sends prophets, and rests on prophets, and is wroth with the house of Jacob, with disobedient Judaea, which irritated Him, then how can the heretics say that the Spirit of God flows through the air?

Continuing in this vein with glossed proof text evidence from eight more prophets,[90] Iosif climaxes and concludes this section with a directly addressed, pleonastic rhetorical question, partially answered again with his physics:[91]

And if the Holy Spirit granted to Elisha to make miracles (2/4 Kg 2:9), instructed Ezekiel (Ez 11:5, 36:26, 37:1) and showed the resurrection of the dead (1/3 Kg 17:17-24), and filled Joshua the son of Nun full of wisdom (Dt 34:9), and filled Bezalal with knowledge and craftsmanship (Ex 35:30-31), and upon 70 elders descended and granted them to prophesy (Nm 11:25), and made Moses a lawgiver (Nm 11:26-29), and according to Joel's prophesying in the last days is flowing out and granting to prophesy (Jl 2:28-29/3:1-2), and made Daniel most wise (Dn 4:6/9), and sanctified Isaiah and made him into a prophet (Is 61:1), and chose Jeremiah from within the maternal womb (Jr 1:5)—speak, O heretic—and did still more such great and kindred and likewise terrifying and ineffable things, then how can it be flowing through the air? Everything that flows through the air comes to non-being.

Iosif devotes the last sixth of the discourse to a positive elucidation of the Trinity with anthropomorphic comparisons and distinctions, reminiscent of John of Damascus's treatment of these issues, with the distinction that Iosif is more polemically hostile and insulting than John, who gives Judaic theology and Hellenic philosophy credit for their contribution to a correct understanding of the godhead.[92]

Iosif begins this by creating a thesis-antithesis sequence to affirm Orthodoxy and set up his final counterpunch:[93]

> And this suffices for us to know for salvation, that the Father has a Word and Spirit, which is the Son and the Holy Spirit, of same-essence and enthroned with Himself. For God's Word is not like my word … . But again the heretic says: just as a human, who has a soul, which gives birth to a word conveyed out through the lips by spirit [breath] and invisible among humans, but only solely the soul is constituted within the body, while the word and the spirit proceed out and perish flowing throughout into the air, so also the Father, the Creator of all things, has a pronounced word and a spirit flowing throughout into the air. …

This is the last we hear from Jews or heretics in Discourse 1, as Iosif moves to finish them off with more insult, analogy, and logic:[94]

> To them one is to answer: So that is how you opine, mindless ones, simply that being *in the image* means inalterable and like unto the one by whose image one is? … If one had the totality, which the king has, that would not be the image of the king, but the king himself. Accept also the same concerning the human: if he also was created in the image of God, but still, what is similar and what he can contain, he receives.

Iosif's exposition on the difference between God and humans now continues with some key, salvific homiletic, still mixed with syllogism:[95]

> And as the Father and the Son and the Holy Spirit is immortal and infinite, so a human, who is created in the image of God, bears within himself the likeness of God, a soul, a word, and an intellect.[96] And if a human passes from his body, yet that trinity within him which *is in the image* of

God–the soul, the word, and the spirit–sing and glorify God, as it knew within the body how piously to do supplications and prayers and other good actions, and not as in a reverie, but in truth. And furthermore, *in the image* means the self-determining and governing faculty of the human. As no one is higher than God, so on earth no one is higher than the human: God created him governing everything. And to be *in the likeness*, this is to be merciful and generous to all, and especially to enemies, just as God, who shines the sun on the evil and the good. This is to be *in the image and the likeness* of God. And if it were not so, but one were completely in the likeness of God, then man would not be the image of God, but God Himself.

Iosif's last 575 (printed) words (6% of the discourse) finish up this argument with a few more explanations of the godhead and close with a typical invocation of the Trinity.[97]

So how to sum up Iosif's peculiar *ars disputandi*? Like every other art and skill, which he mastered sufficiently to suit his needs, whether it be reading, chanting, and choral directing; teaching with apothegms, homiletics, or treatises; targeted oratory; iconographic theory and patronage; application of law; pastoral care; or monasterial entrepreneurship,[98] Iosif subordinated any craft to immediately practical or higher salvific goals. Beyond deploying his argumentative skills to advance and protect his cloister and himself, he mobilized his own and his followers' intellectual assets in defense of Orthodoxy and the promotion of his specific brand that envisioned a sacralized Russian monarchy, a pious laity, coenobitic liturgy- and commemoration-centered monasticism for most ascetics, hesychastic-minded elderhood (*starchestvo*) for the select few, and no tolerance at all for religious dissidence.[99] Never engaged, to our knowledge, in either a formal inner-Orthodox dispute or one with heretics or heterodox, Iosif made extensive use of the monologue-dispute as a literary genre within *Prosvetitel'*, whose discourses ranged from the almost exclusively homiletic-didactic (Discourse 7), to the largely historical (Discourse 11, chapter 1), to the tightly enthymematic-syllogistic (Discourse 12), to the nearly exclusively proof text-filled (Discourse 2), and to an apologetic-expository mixed type embedding created dialogue as a pedagogical device (Discourse 1).[100] If at the end of the Brief Redaction depicting the contemporary "Novgorod Heretics" as terminally obstinate and incapable of being corrected, even by angels, and hence himself as having directed the entire work towards confirming the Orthodox,[101] still, at the close of his introductory "Account," where he lists the titles of each discourse, Iosif advertises his work as providing the necessary disputational ammunition for the reader:[102]

> And if it is necessary for someone to have something against a speech of heretics, then, with the grace of God, he will find it readied without toil in each discourse, which are these:
> ... .

20 – Illustrated Chronicle (*Litsevoi letopisnyi svod*) depiction of the 1490 Synod affirming the Trinity Doctrine, followed by its depiction of Iosif composing his "denunciatory discourses against the Novgorod Heretics ... which comprise an entire book for the firming up of the Orthodox" (Illustr. 18)

We can therefore envision *Prosvetitel'* partially as a pedagogical handbook for a verbal champion of Orthodoxy, who may or may not have the occasion to employ his skills in a formal or informal dispute. Whatever the case, he will be prepared, if only for cogitation, conversation, or homiletics, with an array of systematic exposition, Scriptural proof texts, exegetical principles, enthymematic-syllogistic paradigms, and other rhetorical devices to utilize as needed. From reading *Prosvetitel'* one can imagine Iosif himself employing these argumentative methods, with a ready justification for anything he wanted to prove, spiced by devastating invective against his opponents. So able at this was he, aided no doubt by disciple-colleagues, that at one point in the aftermath of his clearly troubling ecclesio-political victory over the well-respected and perfectly Orthodox Serapion, the Grand Prince silenced our controversial giant, as if a sports league commissioner were suspending a star player or penalizing a team.

In the inherited genre of homiletics, apologetics, and literary disputes against Jews and heretics, some of the church fathers 'played dirty.' We see this as well in such comparable medieval Western successors and masters of learned dispute as the remarkable Cluniac reformer and reconciler of St. Bernard with Abelard's methods, Peter the Venerable (1092-1156), who combated Judaism and Islam—the latter with a good deal more concrete knowledge from targeted and recently translated Arabic texts than Iosif ever had of late medieval Judaism. But just as Ioann the Bulgarian Exarch against the Bogomils and other heretics a century before Peter, and Iosif almost four hundred years later against "Jewish-reasoning Novgorod Heretics," Peter's expository refutation of Judaism mixed proof texts and enthymematic-syllogistic, spiced with barbing and insulting rhetorical addresses and questions, all without a live opponent.[103] Curiously, of all of the anti-Jewish treatises or disputes this researcher has seen, Peter's monologue seems most akin to Iosif. In fact, Iosif's originality may lie in the rhetorical sphere, via his adaptation, in line with Nil Sorskii's "On Mental Activity" (his so-called *Ustav*) of the *Taktikon* of Nikon of the Black Mountain, creating the diverse multi-discourse composition,[104] but here as a disputational treatise against "Jewish-reasoning" heretics, introduced by a biting historical indictment to set the stage for the reader to learn, for the synodal court to convict, and for the state to eradicate. After all, Iosif's applying syllogistics to sacred proof texts was no matter for jests or for jousts,[105] but a deadly serious endeavor, whereby the rulers over society were required to liquidate "Satan's army" of heretics, lest Orthodox souls, and maybe even the realm itself, perish.[106]

И яже оубо о сихъ до здѣ.

Abbreviations

AfED: *Antifeodal'nye ereticheskie dvizheniia na Rusi XIV-nachala XVI veka.* Edited by N. A. Kazakova and Ia. S. Lur'e. Moscow-Leningrad: Izd. Akademii nauk SSSR, 1955.

CHLMP: *The Cambridge History of Later Medieval Philosophy. From the Rediscovery of Aristotle to the Disintegration of Scholasticism 1100-1600.* Edited by Norman Kretzmann, Anthony Kenny, Jan Pinborg. Cambridge, ENG: Cambridge University Press 1982/1989 rpt.

John Dam.: *The Orthodox Faith*, in *Saint John of Damascus Writings*.

LXX: The *Septuagent*–the pre-Christian, Judaic-Greek version of the Old Testament.

MRIV: *The Monastic Rule of Iosif Volotsky*, rev. ed. Cistercian Studies 36. Translated and edited by David Goldfrank. Kalamazoo: Cistercian Publications, 2000.

NSAW: *Nil Sorsky: The Authentic Writings.* Cistercian Studies 221. Translated and edited by David Goldfrank. Kalamazoo: Cistercian Publications, 2008.

PG: *Patrologiae cursus completus, series graeca.* Edited by Jacques-Paul Migne. 161 vols. in 166. Paris: Migne, 1857-1866.

PIV: *Poslaniia Iosifa Volotskogo.* Edited by Ia. S. Lur'e and A. A. Zimin. Moscow-Leningrad: Izdatel'stvo Akademii nauk SSSR, 1959.

PSRL: *Polnoe sobranie russkikh letopisei.* 41 vols. to date. St. Petersburg-Petrograd-Leningrad-Moscow: Arkheograficheskaia komissiia, Nauka, and Arkheograficheskii tsentr, 1841-1995.

TSL 73: Troitse-Sergieva lavra, Fond Glavnoi biblioteki, number 73 (*Apostol*) (= http://old.stsl.ru/manuscripts/book.php?col=1&manuscript=73, last accessed 18 August 2013).

VMCh: *Velikiia Minei chetii, sobrannye vserossiiskim Mitropolitom Makariem.* 22 vols. St Petersburg: Arkheograficheskaia kommissiia, 1868-1917.

Notes

1. *AfED*, 327 = *Prosvetitel', ili oblichenie eresi zhitovstviushchikh: tvorenie prepodobnago ottsa nashego Iosifa, igumena volotskago*, 4th ed. (Kazan: Tipo-litografiia Imperatorskogo universiteta: 1903), 6: 127.
2. Anthony Kenny and John Pinbourg, "Medieval Philosophical Literature, In *CHLMP*, 21-26; Eleanore Stump, "Obligations. From the beginning to the early fourteenth century," in *CHLMP*, 315-334.
3. "Sophismata:" http://plato.stanford.edu/entries/sophismata/ (last accessed 2 February 2014).
4. In addition to the medieval Western modes presented here, and the Classical Greek and medieval Islamic and Western modes discussed the in the following essay in this volume by Donald Ostrowski, one must never neglect the South Asian (Brahmin/Hindu and Buddhist) as a possible source of Hellenistic, Persian, Muslim and hence Christian learning.
5. On the elusive Klim, see *Sermons and Rhetoric of Kievan Rus'*, edited and translated by Simon Franklin, Harvard Library of Early Ukrainian Literature, English Translations, vol. 5 (Cambridge, MA: Harvard University Press, 1991), xlv-lxxiv.
6. *Zhitie Sv. Stefana Episkopa Permskogo*, edited by V. Druzhinin (The Hague: Mouton, 1959), 39-55.
7. *PSRL*, 10: 15-16.
8. *PSRL*, 10: 26-27.
9. *AfED*, 236-243; *Kozma Presviter v slavianskikh literaturakh*, edited by Iurii K. Begunov (Sofia: BAN 1973), 297-392.
10. *Grigentios*, 450-803; *VMCh* December: 1225-1438.
11. *PIV*, 318-319; *VMCh* September: 544; *MRIV*, 158, 221.
12. Aristotle, "Analytikon Proteron," in *Aristotelis Opera ex recensione Immanueis Bekkeris*, 11 vols. (Oxford: Academic Press, 1837), 1: B27: 70a; idem., *The "Art" of Rhetoric*, edited and translated by John Henry Freese (New York: Putnam, 1926), I.ii.8 (1356b24): 18-19. In a simple enthymeme, the reader or listener is expected to supply one of the premises or the conclusion.
13. *PIV*, 318; *MRIV*, 158.
14. See Ignacio Angelelli, "The Techniques of Disputation in the History of Logic," *The Journal of Philosophy* 67 (October 22, 1970): 800-815: http://www.ditext.com/angelelli/dispute.html (last accessed 1 January 2014).

15 *VMCh* September: 583; *MRIV*, 267.
16 *PIV*, 151. Note as well that accomplished Western scholastics also proffered inventive arguments when they syllogized Old Testament metaphors containing anthropomorphic analogies: for example, *I will be your death, O Death* (Hosea 13:14) applied to Christ's redeeming execution/self-sacrifice: *Guillelmi Alverni Sermones de Tempore CXXXVI-CCCXXIV*, edited by Franco Morenzoni (Turnhout: Brepols, 2011), 158 (*Sermo* 173, lines 165-170): my gratitude to Eric Nemarich (BA Georgetown University, 2014) for bringing this passage to my attention.
17 Stump, "Obligations," 320.
18 *PIV*, 191-93, 202-205.
19 *PIV*, 331-333, 336-366.
20 *Aristotle: The "Art" of Rhetoric*, xvii et al.
21 See Goldfrank, "The Anatomy of the Key Codices and the Ontogeny of *Prosvetitel'*," *Canadian-American Slavic Studies* 49.2-3 (2015): 159-172.
22 *Prosvetitel'*, 11: 464.
23 Note the discourse titles: *Prosvetitel'*, 48-54 ("Account") = *AfED*, 484-486.
24 Stump, "Obligations," 318-319.
25 *Life and Works of Saint Grigentios, Archbishop of Taphar. Introduction, Critical Edition, and Translation*, edited by Albrecht Berger = Millenium Studies, Vol. 7 (Berlin-New York: Walter de Greuyter, 2006), 468-471, 698-699, 724-725, 760-761, 766-767, 768-769; *VMCh* December: 1233-1234, 1372, 1391, 1412-1413, 1416, 1418; *Prosvetitel'*, *Slovo* 4.
26 *Life and Works of Saint Grigentios*, 711; *VMCh* December: 1380; *AfED*, 329 = *Prosvetitel'*, 6: 231. This is just one among a large anti-judaic corpus available in Slavic translation: see Alexander Iwan Pereswetoff-Morath, *A Grin without a Cat*, 2 vols. (Lund: Department of East and Central European Studies, Lund University, 2002), esp. 1: 113-198.
27 *Kozma Presviter*, 74-80, 297; *AfED*, 320.
28 See *Kozma Presvter*, 259-260.
29 *Kozma Presvter*, 317; on Kozma as writer, 257-281.
30 Cf. Iosif: *AfED*, 346.
31 See Donald Ostrowski's essay which follows, text to note 60, and *AfED*, 325-326, 337-338.
32 John of Damascus, "The Orthodox Faith," in *Saint John of Damascus, Writings*, translated by Frederic H. Chase, Jr. = Fathers of the Church, vol. 37 (New York: Fathers of the Church, Inc., 1958), 1.3: 168-170; *Prosvetitel'*, 1: 89-90.
33 John of Damascus, "The Orthodox Faith," 1.4: 170-71; *AfED*, 394 = *Prosvetitel'*, 8: 333-334.

34 *Kozma Presvter*, 261-63.
35 These six omit No. 2-3 of Chrysostom's eight: PG 48: 843-856, 871-942; *VMCh* September 846-962; see Pereswetoff-Morath, *Grin*, 1: 71-83, esp. 75.
36 *VMCh* September: 849; PG 48: 845.
37 *VMCh* September: 858; PG 48: 852.
38 *AfED*, 475, 484 = *Prosvetitel'*, 1: 55.
39 *Prosvetitel'*, 1: 55.
40 Not in Greek New Testament, but in the Russian *Apostol* (Acts and Epistles) from that time toward the end of its Incipit (*Zachalo*) 139 (right before 1 Cr 8:7): TSL 73, folia 232-232v.
41 *Prosvetitel'*, 1: 55-58.
42 Cf. Hb 11:1: from the overall context of *Hebrews*, I read Hb 11:1 as asserting *"faith is"* both the operational undergirding *"substance"* (*hupostasis* = s˝*stav*; Vulgate: *substantia*—see below, note 45) enabling realization *"of things hoped for,"* and the indicting/convincing/ convicting *"proof-evidence* (*elegchos* = *oblichenie*; Vulgate: *argumentum*) *of the unseen,"* which justifies using Biblical citations as valid premises in syllogistic argumentation. On some possibilities for translating *elegchos* and *hupostasis* here, see *A Greek-English Dictionary of Early Christian Literature*, 2nd ed. (Chicago/London: University of Chicago Press, 1957/1979), 249, 487.
43 *Prosvetitel'*, 1: 58-59.
44 Cf. *Taktikon ... Nikon Chernogortsa* (Pochaev, 1795), Forward, 7v.
45 *Prosvetitel'*, 1: 59-60.
46 *ustavliaiut*—alt. transl.: decree, establish, determine.
47 s˝*stav*, the usual, non-calqued translation of the Greek *hupostasis*.
48 *Prosvetitel'*, 1: 61.
49 *Prosvetitel'*, 1: 61.
50 *Prosvetitel'*, 1: 62.
51 Cf. *Deanie sviatago Silvestra, episkopa rim'skago pri Kostiatine, tsesarem rimstem*, in *VMCh* January: 104.
52 *Prosvetitel'*, 1: 62.
53 *Prosvetitel'*, 1: 63.
54 The Hebrew OT enumeration precedes the *LXX* (Greek Septuagint).
55 See *Septuaginta*, edited by Afred Rahlfs, 9th ed. (Stuttgart: Württembergische Bibelanstalt, 1971), 2: 578, and the variants in the notes.
56 *Prosvetitel'*, 1: 63-65.
57 *Prosvetitel'*, 1: 65.
58 *Prosvetitel'*, 1: 65-66: Iosif never explicitly states the syllogistic conclusion: *therefore God did not speak to angels.*

59 Gn 11:7 (the confounding of tongues); also Gn. 18:1-3 (the hospitality of Abraham), Gn. 19:24 (raining fire over Sodom): *Prosvetitel'*, 1: 66-67.
60 *Prosvetitel'*, 1: 67-80.
61 *Prosvetitel'*, 1: 68.
62 *Prosvetitel'*, 1: 70-71.
63 *Prosvetitel'*, 1: 71-72.
64 The subject *Lord* in the Hebrew is the tetragram *YHWH*; the direct object in Hebrew is *adonai* (= *Lord*). Over time *YHWH* became unutterable, and *adonai* was substituted, which explains the *LXX* Greek *kyrios* and subsequent translations here and elsewhere as Lord or its equivalent.
65 *Prosvetitel'*, 1: 69-70.
66 *Prosvetitel'*, 1: 74.
67 *Prosvetitel'*, 1: 74-75.
68 Cf. *Life and Works of Saint Grigentios*, 476-479; *VMCh* December: 1237-1238, where Herbano also claims the psalm speaks of Solomon.
69 *Prosvetitel'*, 1: 7; cf. John Dam. 1.7: 175.
70 *Prosvetitel'*, 1: 77.
71 Is 7:14 adapted as in Mt 1: 23.
72 *Prosvetitel'*, 1: 79-80.
73 In the original Greek it could be just *the anointed leader* (*christou hegoumenou*).
74 Excerpt not found in Ex, Lv, Nm, or Dt.
75 *Prosvetitel'*, 1: 80-81.
76 *Prosvetitel'*, 1: 81.
77 *Prosvetitel'*, 1: 81-82.
78 Is 11:1-3, adapted.
79 *Prosvetitel'*, 1: 82.
80 *Prosvetitel'*, 1: 82-83.
81 *Prosvetitel'*, 1: 84; cf. John Dam, 1.7: 176; *VMCh* Dec., 112.
82 *LXX*: *of the Lord* (*tou kuriou*); Hb: indeclined *YHWH*.
83 Cf. here and for the following argument, John Dam. 1.7: 177; *VMCh* December: 111-112, where Iosif converts John's positive statement into a rhetorical question.
84 *Prosvetitel'*, 1: 84-85.
85 In the Hebrew, Greek, and Slavic *his spirit* can be either a second subject or the direct object.
86 As in *LXX*: *adonai YHWH* in the original.
87 Ten times in Isaiah, the last being 58:1.
88 Four times in Isaiah, the last two being 61:1, 63:14.
89 In the direct object *ruah kodsho* in the initial clause in the grammatically more fluid Hebrew, the adjective *holy* appears as the attribute of *YHWH*/*adonai* (from Is. 63:7), not of *spirit*, so the subject of the second

clause is just *it = spirit*. *LXX*, however, has this as *to pneuma to hagion autou* (*His holy spirit*).
90 *Prosvetitel'*, 1: 85-87.
91 *Prosvetitel'*, 1: 87-88.
92 *Life and Works of Saint Grigentios*, 1.7: 176-177; *VMCh* December: 111-112.
93 *Prosvetitel'*, 1: 88.
94 *Prosvetitel'*, 1: 89
95 *Prosvetitel'*, 1: 90.
96 Or did Iosif mean to write *spirit*?
97 *Prosvetitel'*, 1:103.
98 On Iosif's abilities, see, *MRIV*, 21-49; *NSAW*, 49; Alekseev, *Sochineniia Iosifa Volotskogo v kontekste polemiki 1480-1540-kh gg* (St. Petersburg: Rossiiskaia natsional'naia biblioteka, 2010), 14-64.
99 Note also David Goldfrank, "Nil's and Iosif's Rhetoric of *Starchestvo*," in *Essays in Russian Monasticism*, edited by Goldfrank = *Russian History*, 39, vol. 1-2 (2012): 42-76; *NSAW*, 49.
100 *Prosvetitel'*, 1-2: 55-119, 7: 254-332, 11.1: 405-435, 12: 465-474; AfED, 325-360; also David Goldfrank, "Adversus Haereticos Novgorodensos: Iosif Volotskii's Rhetorical Syllogisms," in *Dubitando: Studies in History and Culture in Honor of Donald Ostrowski*, edited by Brian J. Boeck, Russell E. Martin, and Daniel Rowland (Bloomington, IN: Slavica), 254-274.
101 *Prosvetitel'*, 11.4: 463-464; see also *Stepennaia kniga tsarskogo rodosloviia po drevneishim spiskam*, edited by G. D. Lenhoff and N. N. Pokrovskii, 2 vols. (Moscow: "Iazyki slavianskikh kul'tur": 2007-2008), 2: 268 (Chapter 20, Step 15).
102 *AfED*, 483-484 = *Prosvetitel'*, 48 ("Account").
103 *Peter the Venerable against the Inveterate Obduracy of the Jew*, translated by Irven M. Resnich (Washington, DC: Catholic University of America Press, 2013): the seeming kinship of Peter and Iosif merits a separate study.
104 *MRIV*, 62-63, *NSAW*, 70-71.
105 On Iosif's hostility to humor, *PIV*, 150-151; *MRIV*, 313-314.
106 *Prosvetitel'*, 16: 539-561; also 41 ("Account") = *AfED*, 472.

7   The *Debate with Iosif* (*Prenie s Iosifom*) as a Fictive Disputation

Donald Ostrowski

21 – Pskov-Pecherskii (Caves) Monastery (in 2002). From there the presumed author of the *Prenie s Iosifom*, Artemii, had earlier (mid-1530s-1540s) ventured to Neuhausen (Vastseliina piiskopillinus in Estonia) with the hope of disputing a Roman Catholic.

The disputation is a phenomenon commonly mentioned in Christian and Islamic medieval sources. In some cases, we find accounts of the disputations themselves in regard to who said what and in what sequence. We have records of disputations at the Byzantine court in the first half of the twelfth century, and of one at the Mongol court in Qaraqorum in 1254. Yet, it is generally accepted that there were no disputations in Orthodox Slavic lands before the seventeenth century. We do have one curious sixteenth-century Muscovite text that appears to be a disputation between Iosif, hegumen of the Volokolamsk Monastery, and the monk Vassian, who was from the Patrikeev boyar family. But this work—*The Debate with Iosif Volotskii* (*Prenie s Iosifom Volotskim*)—was probably a literary composition—a fictive disputation at best—and not the record of a face-to-face discussion between the two protagonists.

Since the disputation was such a widespread and well-known phenomenon, one may well ask the reasons for this absence in Slavia Orthodoxa in general and in the Rus' lands in particular. My working hypothesis is that the medieval form of the disputation was primarily an Islamic revival of an ancient Greek form of debate. Islamic intellectual/cultural influence, by means of Jewish intermediaries, penetrated medieval Christian Europe.[1] It also penetrated to Byzantium and to the Mongol court but was blocked from entering Slavic Orthodox lands by Churchmen who perceived disputation as being contrary to the cosmology of the Eastern Church. Nor did secular leaders in Slavia Orthodoxa have any interest in Islamic philosophy or theology. Even if there had been little or no opposition on the part of Churchmen and some interest on the part of the civil authorities, there were few Jewish intermediaries who could have introduced it. Finally, even if the Slavic Orthodox Churchmen and secular authorities had wanted to have a disputation, they may have had, at least until the seventeenth century, few sufficiently skilled in dialectic to act as champions or the Scriptural resources for these champions to draw on. Of those few individuals, from what we can surmise from their extant writings, Iosif and Vassian perhaps could have engaged effectively in disputation had they known the rules.

In order to place the absence of disputation in Slavia Orthodoxa in context, I have undertaken here a brief survey of disputation in non-Slavic Orthodox lands. Discussion of the comparative aspects of disputation is hindered by the absence of any general survey of the subject of disputation east and west. While a short article such as this one by itself cannot adequately fill the gap, it can begin the process of doing so. I return to the *Debate with Iosif* towards the end of this essay.

I

Disputations were well known in the ancient Mediterranean world. Aristotle in the *Topics* makes some general remarks concerning the proceedings of a philosophical dispute.[2] The historian of ancient Greek philosophy Robin Smith, based on his reading of Aristotle, has described "gymnastic dialectic" as an "argumentative sport" in ancient Athens. Smith begins his description by pointing out what has been said before by others, that "[d]ialectical argument differs from demonstrative reasoning in that it is intrinsically a kind of exchange between participants acting in some way as opponents."[3] We see this practice, among other places, in Plato's dialogues. But Smith goes further to describe "structured contests, with rules and judges" in which

> one participant took the "Socratic" role and asked questions, while the other responded to them. The answerer chose, or was assigned, a thesis to defend; the questioner's goal was to refute the thesis. In order to do this, the questioner would try to get the answerer to accept premises from which such a refutation followed. However, the questioner could only ask questions which could be answered by a "yes" or "no"; questions like "What is the largest city in Lacedaemonia?" were not allowed.[4]

Apparently losing a disputation had such a demoralizing effect on young men that Plato in the *Republic* (7: 537–539) has Socrates prohibiting anyone younger than 30 years old from participating.[5] On the basis of these argument contests, Smith defined dialectic as *"argument directed at another person which proceeds by asking questions."*[6] Thus, we can propose that the intent of dialectic is, within a structured thought process, to force an opponent to abandon a premise he holds or to get him to accept a premise he did not accept previously.

During late antiquity, the rules of the debate changed, but the framework of a structure of questions and answers remained. In the mid-third century, Origen was involved in a number of disputations both with Jews and heterodox Christians, including

Candidus, Bassus, and Ambrose, all three of whom were followers of the second-century Gnostic teacher Valentinus. Origen also disputed christological matters with the Arabian bishops Beryllus and Heracleidus.[7] Both Ambrose and Heracleidus are recorded as having converted to Origen's views as the result of being bested by him in their respective disputations. Around 150 years later, Augustine, bishop of Hippo, was involved in disputations with Manichæans (Fortunatus in 392 and Felix in 404), and Pelagians. He also wrote a refutation of the arguments of the Manichæan bishop Faustus in 397–398.[8] In 527, by the command of the emperors Justin and Justinian, Paul the Persian (a Nestorian Christian) debated Photinus (a Manichæan).[9] In 645, the abbot of Chrysopolis (Scutari) Maximus ("the Confessor") debated with Pyrrhus, a former Patriarch of Constantinople and a Monothelite.[10] These were the last debates of late antiquity.

We have accounts of fictive disputations between Muslims and Syrian Christians from the seventh through the tenth centuries. A West Syrian MS from 874 purports to be the record of a disputation between Patriarch Yohannan (John) and an emir of 'Mhaggrāyē. Some scholars have placed that disputation in the 640s. Barbara Roggema has questioned that date for the disputation on the basis of external criticism—too early for a discussion of the inheritance issue. Yet, as she acknowledged, "[m]ost of the issues that appear in Muslim-Christian debates of the eighth and ninth centuries are lacking."[11] Crone and Cook proposed that the last question, on inheritance, was added later.[12] Sydney Griffith calls all these "disputations" apologetics for Christianity, though not attacking Islam.[13] A possible explanation for these apologetics in disputation format is their representing actual disputations that were limited by the Muslim rule makers to discussion of the principles of Christianity, not those of Islam. Christian rule makers made a similar limitation on Jews in their debates in the late Middle Ages.

Public disputations between theologians of differing views were often held at the courts of Islamic rulers. The Medievalist Friedrich Heer credited the Almoha princes, who succeeded the Almoravids in the middle of the twelfth century in Andalusia, with sparking a revival of learning and culture. The methods of theological and political disputations, based on the debates of the Islamic schools of law, were formulated by the ninth century and, according to Heer, came to fruition in the Almoha courts of the twelfth century.[14]

The discussions by Islamic commentators on the rules of the debate were based on Aristotle's advice that he provides in the *Topics*.[15] The Arab Aristotelian al-Fārābī (870–950) discusses two types of disputation:

Type I
1. The questioner obtains the thesis from the respondent through asking a question.
2. Once this has been posited, the questioner should obtain premises that will be useful in refuting the respondent in questioning him.
3. The questioner asks each premise separately.
4. When he has obtained sufficient premises, he announces to the respondent that he has refuted him and presents his syllogism.
5. If the questioner is successful, then an *elenchus* [refutation] has occurred.
6. The respondent is allowed to question the form of the syllogism, but since he has granted each premise, he is not allowed to renege on his previous answers, unless the questioner has distorted one of his previous answers, and used this distortion as the basis of his conclusion. In this case, the respondent must inform the questioner that he has falsified his response and that his *elenchus* is, therefore, not valid.[16]

Elsewhere in the same manuscript, al-Fārābī adds this corollary:

6a. In bringing an objection to the form of the questioner's syllogism, the respondent brings a syllogism that is called *'inad*. *'Inad* is the preserve of the respondent, just as *tabkit* (*elenchus*) is that of the questioner. In the first part of the debate, the respondent preserves the thesis. Only after the questioner has brought his proof is he allowed to defend it.[17]

Although al-Fārābī favors this type of disputation, he does present a second type:

Type II
1. The questioner obtains the thesis from the respondent through asking a question.
2. The questioner may obtain premises contrary to the thesis by asking questions.
3. The questioner presents a syllogism refuting the thesis in which premises not consented to by the respondent are used. He does so when he supposes that the respondent would grant them.
4. In this case, the respondent must consider both the content and form of the *elenchus*.
5. If he disagrees with any of the premises, he informs the questioner by making a statement, not by posing a question.
6. If the respondent objects to the form of the syllogism, he proceeds as in Type I.6.
7. If the respondent successfully refutes the *elenchus*, he has accomplished opposition (*'inad*).[18]

Although the discussion by Abu 'Ali al-Husain ibn Sina (Avicenna) (980–1037) of the format of disputation follows that of al-Fārābī, he differs over whether the discussion begins with the question to the respondent: "this question is superfluous, even if it is indispensable. It is preparatory to what is needed as the object of a disputation, in the same way that setting up a target is not part of the act of throwing something, but rather a necessary preliminary [step] to something's being thrown in its direction."[19] In Ibn Sina's description, the initiative as well as the advantage is always with the questioner. For example, whenever the respondent produces evidence in support of his thesis, the questioner is not obligated to take it into account.

Naṣī al-Dīn Ṭūsī distinguishes between two methods of disputations, which he refers to as that of the Ancients and that of the Moderns. The method of the Ancients is al-Fārābī's Type 1. In the method of the Moderns, the only question the questioner asks concerns the opinion of the respondent. The questioner then attempts to provide a proof refuting that opinion. During the presentation of the proof, the respondent may speak up only when he disagrees with any of the premises stated by the questioner. After the questioner is finished, then the respondent is allowed to dispute the proof.[20] Ibn Sina favored the Type 1 disputation method and criticized the other: "they bring a syllogistic argument with the conclusion, as if it were self-evident and as if there were no consent needed [from the respondent]."[21]

Public disputations were popular also in the Muslim *Taifas* (Chieftancies) of Andalusia in the eleventh century.[22] It is probably from there that they entered medieval Europe. Between the seventh and the end of the eleventh centuries, however, we have no record of any disputation in Christian Europe. In 1096, Gilbert Crispin (d. 1117), proctor of Westminster Abbey, described a courteous disputation he had with a Jew whose name he does not give but who he says was educated at Mainz. In the account, the Jew is the questioner and Gilbert is the respondent.[23] Disputations became common in Christian Europe in the twelfth century. Peter Abelard (1079–1142), according to his own declaration, defeated his teacher William of Champeaux at the University of Paris sometime in the early 1100s, and was famous for his disputation ability.[24] Abelard had hoped to debate Bernard of Clairvaux at Sens in 1140. Instead, he found that Bernard had arranged in advance for his (Abelard's) episcopal condemnation, for Bernard felt he was not up to the task of debating Abelard.[25] When Abelard arrived at the cathedral of St. Stephen, he had the sense he was facing an interrogation, appealed to the Pope, and fled the cathedral. In the end, Abelard's views were condemned, and he died soon after.

In 1204, at Carcassonne, Cathars and Catholics debated openly, according to Heer, for the last time. A jury made up of twenty-six individuals, representing each side equally monitored the proceedings.[26] Successors to the intellectual and secular courts of the Islamic chieftains of Andalusia could be found in the twelfth and thirteenth centuries in Frederick II, the Hohenstaufen Emperor, and the "philosopher kings" of Spain and Portugal. At these courts, disputations occurred between theologians and scholars of Christianity, Islam, and Judaism.[27]

In the universities of the thirteenth and fourteenth centuries, according to Medievalist Lynn Thorndike, sharply circumscribed scholastic debates were frequent.[28] Candidates for degrees were expected to demonstrate their academic abilities by giving lectures and participating in disputations.[29] Students of the Medical Faculty in Paris, according to a document dated to 1270–1274, were required to respond to "a question in the classes of two masters, understanding thereby a formal disputation and not a lecture, or at least once in a general disputation."[30]

We find two forms of disputation in the thirteenth century both of which consisted of the following stages: question, answer, thesis, agreement, refutation, argument, suggested proof, and final resolution. The *disputatio legitima* (also called the ordinary, public, solemn, or magisterial disputation) was the preferred method of teaching in thirteenth- and fourteenth-century Christian European universities.[31] In this method, a master placed a question (such as whether the act of willing presupposes the act of understanding) to a designated student (*respondens*). In replying, the student also had to deal with further questions from the master and from others. The master would then make an informal determination. A more solemn form of the ordinary disputation was connected with the inception or licensing of a master in arts.[32] The other method was the *disputatio de quodlibet* (or free question disputation) and allowed the audience to decide the winner.[33] It was held two times a year—during Lent and at Advent. Anyone present could ask a question, and the respondents, who were trying to sustain a thesis, could change during the course of the disputation. Because of the open nature of the proceedings the dispute was often held in two sessions—the *disputatio* and the *determinatio*. During the second session, a master presided alone and attempted to pull together the various threads of the previous session.[34] In both cases, the master pointed out a question raised by a text, then proceeded to try to answer it (a method called *quaestio*). Masters would also pose questions for students to dispute with each other as part of their instruction. On holidays, masters were known to have a public disputation with each other on controversial issues of the day. Thorndike tells us that in the sixteenth century, however, universities began to abandon the disputation.[35]

In his *Metalogicon*, John of Salisbury (ca. 1115–1180) provides an extended commentary on the art of disputation. Basing his views mainly on Aristotle's *Topics*, John tells us that the discussion is between two persons— "a questioner and an answerer, to whom it is limited, since each is the other's judge."[36] John also warns about disputing like a certain Cornificius (a pseudonym) who was "verbose rather than eloquent" and whose speech would multiply negative particles to such an extent that one had to have the "prudent foresight to bring a bag of beans and peas to disputations" to keep count of whether he was using an equal number of negatives, which would equate to a positive, or an odd number of negatives, which would equate to a negative.[37]

The twentieth-century scholar Ignacio Angelelli points out that the early eighteenth-century work of Johann Friedrich Heine, *Methodus disputandi hodierna ex variis autoribus collecta* (Helmstedt, 1710), makes a distinction between two types of disputation—the argument method and the question method.[38] Heine dealt mainly with the argument method, but the question method, which, according to Angelelli, corresponds to the *ars obligatoria*, a form of medieval disputation, can be found elucidated in the fifteenth-century works of Paulus Venetus (Paul of Venice), the *Logica magna* and the *Logica parva*.[39] As one moves more to the present day, such distinctions tended to be increasingly ignored.

In sources from the Middle Ages in Europe we find mentions of a number of Jewish-Christian disputations (Paris in 1208, Trier in 1223, and by Pope Gregory IX in 1232) as well as extant records of three disputations between Christian authorities and leaders of Jewish communities: the Paris Disputation of 1240 called by Louis IX and presided over by Queen Mother Blanche of Castile, the Barcelonia Disputation of 1263 convened and presided over by James I of Aragon, and the Tortosa Disputation of 1413–1414 presided over by Pope Benedict XIII. The Paris Disputation of 1240 appears to have been more an interrogation than a debate. At issue was the Talmud for having "blasphemies against the Christian religion." The Barcelona Disputation did at least take the form of a debate. James I granted the Jewish representative, Moses ben Naḥman (Naḥmanides) (1194–1270), a guarantee of safety to speak freely, even if what he said might be considered blasphemies against the

Christian religion. Nonetheless, as Hyam Maccoby who translated these texts pointed out, ben Naḥman was not allowed a reciprocal questioning of Christian beliefs, as the Christian representative, Pablo Christiani, who had converted from Judaism, was allowed of Jewish beliefs. This procedure was in keeping, however, with the formal rules of a disputation, which strictly limited how the respondent could answer.[40] According to Maccoby, although the threat of violence hung in the air in Barcelona, prompting ben Naḥman to request ending the disputation early, no recorded violence occurred. Actual violence did break out in connection with the Tortosa Disputation 150 years later. The conduct of the debate, especially in comparison with the Barcelona disputation, may have reflected the Jews' deteriorating position in Spain or the unusual willingness of James I to abide by his guarantee and withstand cries for punishment of the Jews for blasphemy. The Dominican Vincent Ferrer incited anti-Jewish hostility in towns, from which rabbis had been summoned to Tortosa, so that Christian thugs could harass the now "leaderless" people of the communities to convert.[41]

We also have accounts of four disputations between Christians and Jews at Narbonne in the thirteenth century, although one or more of these may have been merely a literary work.[42] Descriptions of all four of these are contained in one manuscript: Me'ir ben Simeon's *Milḥemeth Miṣwah* (*Obligatory War*). On fols. 1–17a is the description of a disputation between ben Simeon and "a priest." On fols. 17a–37b is a disputation between ben Simeon and Guillaume de la Brue, who was Archbishop of Narbonne between 1245 and 1257. On fols. 83a–129b is a disputation between "a learned Christian and a learned Jew." On fols. 214b–228b is the record of a disputation between ben Simeon and an anonymous archbishop, who later became a cardinal. According to Stein, ben Simeon repeatedly questions the compatibility of Christian doctrines with true monotheism, asserts the economic importance of money-lending, and provides rationalist critiques of New Testament passages.[43]

In his *Journey to the Eastern Parts of the World*, William of Rubruck describes a disputation in 1254 at the court of the Mongol Qaghan Möngke in Qaraqorum between Nestorian Christians, Muslims, and Buddhists. Möngke required the participants in the disputation to write down their positions first before the oral part of the confrontation. William refused to join in claiming: "But our Scriptures tell us, the servant of God should not dispute, but should show mildness to all; so I am ready, without disputation or contention, to give reason for the faith and hope of the Christians, to the best of my ability."[44] Since disputations were already common practice in Europe at the time, one can only surmise that William was reluctant to take part in a disputation in which Christian prelates or rulers were not the judges and did not control the proceedings. William's reluctance, however, did not extend to acting as an adviser to the Nestorians in helping them prepare for the disputation.

On the day of the disputation, Möngke sent three judges—a Christian, a Muslim, and a Buddhist—to oversee the proceedings. According to Friar William, at the crucial moment the Nestorians pushed him forward to represent them against the Buddhist champion.[45] The format of the disputation was a question-and-answer one, in which both sides could ask questions that did not require yes-or-no answers. They did, however, require some answer on the part of the respondent as the judges intervened to assure it. The recipient of any particular question could not remain silent.[46] Among the issues of contention William tells us were the omnipotence of God, whether there is one God or many gods, and the nature of evil and from where it comes. At the end, the Nestorians sought to dispute with the Muslims, but the latter declined the challenge. In William's account of it, they said, "We concede that your religion is true, and that everything is true that is in the Gospel: so we do not want to argue any point with you" and that they prayed to God that they be allowed "to die as Christians die."[47] One can only imagine what they most likely really said.

The Muslims at the court in Qaraqorum may well have been the ones to carry the notion and principles of disputation to the Mongol court. Likewise, George Makdisi has argued that the scholastic method in Europe did not originate with the "*sic-et-non*" method attributed to Abelard. Instead, according to Makdisi, not only did the *sic-et-non* method antedate Abelard in Europe, but it also was well known in Islamic lands as *al-khilāf* (or *al-ikhtilāf*) before then. Makdisi sees the diputations between the various schools of Muslim religious law as the "natural habitat" of this method.[48] According to

Makdisi, the *al-khilāf* method was adopted to disputation (*munāẓara*) in education, such that one established oneself as the "top man" in one's field through besting others in public debate.[49]

We have evidence of disputations in Constantinople like those in Islamic courts, but between clerics representing the Eastern and Western Churches. A disputation occurred in 1112 between Grossolanus, the former Archbishop of Milan, and seven Byzantine theologians. It was held in the presence of Emperor Alexius I and Patriarch Sergius II. The most prominent issues were use of azyme (unleavened bread), the *filioque*, and papal primacy.[50] In 1136, a disputation in two sessions was held at the cathedrals of Hagia Sophia and St. Eirene between Archbishop Nicetas and Bishop Anselm of Havelberg, an envoy of the Holy Roman Emperor Lothair.[51] The Emperor John Comnenus presided over the proceedings, and among the audience were three prominent Italian translators of the time: James of Venice, Burgundio the Pisan, and Moses of Bergamo.[52] Issues concerning the merits of Greek patristics, the filioque, and papal primacy were the ones prominently discussed. We have a miniature from Acre in 1290 depicting a disputation between Catholics and Oriental Christians.[53] In 1486, Giovanni Pico della Mirandola (1463–1494) published 900 theses and challenged any scholar to a disputation on any of them for which he would pay that person's travel expenses.[54] Pope Innocent VIII stopped the disputation before it could take place in order to have the theological validity of the theses examined.

In the northern Rus' principalities, we do not have evidence of any formal disputations being held; on the contrary, we have evidence of rejection of them. According to the Novgorodian Chronicle, Vasilii, the bishop of Novgorod, along with the *posadnik* Fedor and the *tysiatskii* Avram, refused a disputation when, in 1347 or 1348, Magnus, the King of Sweden, wanted to convene a council for a debate between Catholic and Orthodox theologians:

> If you want to find out whose faith is better, ours or yours, go to Tsar'grad [Constantinople] to the Patriarch, for we received the Orthodox faith from the Greeks, but with you we will not dispute about the faith.[55]

Two centuries later, the attending prelates of the Moscow Church Council of 1554 refused to dispute with the German residents of Novyi Gorodok over the relative merits of Protestantism and Orthodoxy. In the view of the Council members, Orthodoxy was indubitably superior, so nothing needed disputing.[56]

In point of fact, we have no record of any disputation having occurred in the Slavia Orthodoxa before the seventeenth century. It is not as though the Orthodox Slavic Churchmen had no knowledge of the phenomenon of disputation. A number of European Christian disputations with Jews had been copied in Slavonic in Rus' monasteries.[57] Under the year 1323, the Nikon Chronicle reported a disputation between a Christian merchant and Muslims:

> In the land of the Bulgars ... there was martyred a certain Christian from Jerusalem, a merchant who had great wealth and much learning in philosophy, whose name was Feodor. He debated with them about the faith. They, the accursed ones, could not stand their defeat, so they killed him because of his Orthodox Christian faith on April 21st.[58]

In the *Life of Constantine*, which was being copied in East Slavic redactions from the late fifteenth century on, a fictional, two-part mini-disputation occurs between Constantine and John, the iconoclastic Patriarch of Constantinople. In the first part of the exchange, John asks, "None of you is worthy of being my footstool, so why should I wish to dispute with you?" After Constantine tells him not to be so arrogant, John argues that it is inappropriate to argue with an old man such as himself: "It is not fitting to seek flowers in the fall nor to drive an old man to war...." Constantine then gets John to admit that the soul is stronger in old age and that he is not being driven to physical but to spiritual combat (where presumably the older soul has the advantage).[59] In the second part of the exchange, the dispute itself, John asks a series of four questions concerning why Constantine does obeisance to icons. The author of the *Life* has Constantine defeat his opponents with his answers, but one finds the logic somewhat less compelling than in the first part. I present this exchange in full because it provides an example of what was available to Rus' Churchmen in the sixteenth century in regard to the form of a disputation:

> The old man [John]... said: "Tell me, young man, why bow we not to a broken cross nor kiss it, while you are not ashamed to do obeisance to an icon though it be depicted only in bust-form?"
>
> The Philosopher [Constantine] answered: "The cross has four parts, but if one of its parts is missing it no longer has its image. However, an icon of the face alone is an image and likeness of the one depicted. For whoever sees it, perceives neither a lion's face nor a lynx's but an image of the original."
>
> Then the old man said: "Why bow we to a cross without an inscription when there are also other crosses? However, if an icon is not inscribed with the name of its image, why do you not do obeisance to it?"
>
> The Philosopher answered: "Each cross has the same image as the cross of Christ, but not all icons have one and the same image."
>
> The old man said: "When God spoke to Moses He said: 'Thou shalt not make any likeness.' Why then make you one and bow to it?"
>
> And to this the Philosopher replied: "Had He said: 'Make not any kind of likeness,' you would be correct. But He said: 'Not any,' that is, any unworthy."
>
> Unable to answer, the old man fell silent and was shamed.[60]

What this rendition lacks in content, it makes up for in form.

So, why the reluctance of Rus' Churchmen to debate the fine points of the faith even when they would be in charge of the proceedings? Although we do have evidence of disputations at the court in Constantinople, even in the Byzantine Church we find an unwillingness to engage in religious disputation. In the 1580s, the Patriarch of Constantinople Jeremiah II refused either in person or by letter to dispute with the Tübingen theologians. Jeremiah ends his third reply with these words: "write no longer concerning dogmas; but if you do [write], write only for friendship's sake."[61] It would seem clear that Jeremiah is not embarrassed by potential friendly relations with the Lutherans. Nor does he seem ignorant and unable to engage in disputation. One need only look at his replies to see his command of the patristic literature. Instead, if one understands the Patriarch as acting within the Eastern Church tradition, then one can more easily understand his reluctance to engage in idle disputation. Jeremiah makes that clear in the same "Epilogue" where he writes:

> Therefore, we request that from henceforth you do not cause us more grief, nor write to us on the same subject if you should wish to treat these luminaries and theologians of the Church in a different manner. You honor and exalt them in words, but you reject them in deeds. For you try to prove our weapons which are their holy and divine discourse as unsuitable. And it is with these documents that we should have to write and contradict you. Thus, as for you, please release us from these cares.[62]

If we take his words at face value, then Jeremiah is pained by the contentiousness of the Lutherans over theological matters. When the Lutheran theologians persist in their efforts to dispute with Jeremiah a fourth time, he politely tells them that he has read their rejoinder, that he has not had time to write his reply, and that he will do so sometime soon. He seems, however, to have had some difficulty in finding the time for there is no subsequent letter, not because he and Eastern Church theologians could not engage in disputation, but because they would not. It was pointless from their point of view to split theological hairs.

One problem with the holding of a disputation by Church authorities was finding a champion who not only knew the fine points of the dogma but also was skilled at debating.[63] In Muscovy, not many could meet these criteria. In 1489, for example, the Archbishop of Novgorod Gennadii inquired of the former archbishop of Rostov Ioasaf if the major regional monasteries possessed certain books that the heretics were reading. These included such Old Testament books as Genesis, Proverbs, I and II Kings, and Joshua.[64] Since there was no complete version of the Bible in Rus' lands before 1499, Rus' Churchmen obtained their information about the Bible from lectionaries and a few separate books, such as psalters and gospels. Indeed, it may have been in part a response to the problems involved in dealing with the reading matter of the possible heretics that Gennadii ordered the compilation of his famous Bible.

Ostensibly, some of the monks of the Kirillo-Belozersk Monastery in the mid to late fifteenth century could have developed the skills. They had available to them some of the necessary dialectical literature.[65] Although we have no evidence that either Iosif Volotskii or Vassian Patrikeev was familiar with the structure of disputations, both of them would have been formidable opponents in a disputation.

Another problem with holding disputations is that guarantees of safety must be extended to both sides, as George the Bearded, Duke of Leipzig, extended to Andreas Carlstadt and his entourage (among whom were Martin Luther and Philip Melancthon) in 1519 to come to Leipzig to debate John Eck of Ingolstadt. To the objections of the local bishop, Duke George responded:

> Disputations have been allowed from ancient times, even concerning the Holy Trinity. What good is a soldier if he is not allowed to fight, a sheep dog if he may not bark, and a theologian if he may not debate? Better spend money to support old women who can knit than theologians who cannot discuss.[66]

In 1415, Jan Hus traveled to the Council of Constance with such a guarantee with the idea of engaging in a disputation over the ideas he had acquired from John Wycliffe. Not only was Hus not allowed to engage in a debate but also his guarantee of safety was withdrawn and he was burned at the stake as a heretic. The churchmen at the Council justified their withdrawing of the guarantee on the basis that agreements with heretics have no legitimate standing. When Luther went to Worms in 1520 ostensibly to dispute with theologians of the Church, he too had a guarantee of safety. He also was not allowed to debate, but his patron, Frederick of Saxony, prevented his being captured by forces of the Holy Roman Emperor Charles V by having his own armed men kidnap Luther and whisking him off to a hiding place. In the Rus' principalities, that guarantee would have been provided by civil or ecclesiastical authority, neither of whom was likely to do so. In 1263, James I of Aragon guaranteed the safety of the Jewish respondant ben Naḥman. Although James abided by the guarantee, ben Naḥman subsequently published in response to Christiani's published version his own version of the disputation. James had not issued any protection of ben Naḥman beyond the disputation itself, so, as a result, he was arrested and sentenced to exile. Even if one had a guarantee from the civil authority, a participant in a disputation could not be assured of his safety.

The written genre of debate was popular in late Medieval Roman Christendom. Usually these took the form of metaphorical discussions, according to Haskins, such as "between Soul and Body, Sheep and Wool, Rose and Violet, Ganymede and Helen... Wine and Water, the poor clerk and the rich, the well fed priest and the begging barefoot student of logic..." as well as between the Heart and the Eye. Haskins asserted that this form of literary composition was "reënforced by the disputatious habits of the scholastic age."[67] In sixteenth-century Rus' lands, we find a number of examples of this type of dialogue, including *Prenie zemli i moria (Debate of Land and Sea)*; *Spor dushi s telom (Argument of the Soul with the Body)*; and *Prenie zhivota so smert'iu (Debate of Life with Death)*. All three appear to have been translations made from works written outside Russia. The *Prenie zhivota s smert'iu* seems to be a translation from a German work published in the late fifteenth century.[68] And the *Spor dushi s telom* may be from an earlier Polish or Czech composition.[69] V. N. Peretts proposed in 1917 that *Prenie zemli i moria* derived from ancient Greece as transmitted through Byzantium.[70] These allegorical dialogues, however, usually did not involve the application of any of the principles of disputation.

II

As for the *Debate with Iosif*, it falls into the category of imagined disputation rather than allegorical dialogue.[71] We do not have evidence of any such a debate having taken place between Iosif Volotskii and Vassian Patrikeev in person. Instead, the extant text is in part a pastiche of passages from writings attributed to Vassian and Iosif,[72] and in part has no correspondence with any known writings of the two protagonists. The *Debate with Iosif* consists of 12 exchanges (numbered 4 through 15) between "Iosif" and "Vasian" and an opening fragment that is presumably the end of Vassian's reply no. 3. That fragment discusses wisdom about one's self. The other exchanges discuss heretics (nos. 4–9), miracle workers (nos. 10, 13, and 15); owning of villages by monasteries and churches (nos. 11–12); and church decoration (no. 14).

Traditional historiography has accepted the *Debate* as a more or less authentic work compiled by Vassian in response to accusations made by Iosif.[73] Both Andrei Pliguzov and I have proposed that the former hegumen of the Trinity-St. Sergius Monastery Artemii composed the *Debate* at some time between 1554 and 1556 when he was in exile at the Solovki Monastery.[74] Although parts of the debate are taken verbatim from works of Vassian Patrikeev, other parts attributed to "Vasian" in the *Debate* have characteristic phrases closer to known writings of Artemii.[75] In addition, the four issues discussed in the *Debate*—attitude toward heretics; mocking all the miracle workers and their miracles; advising the grand prince to take away villages from the monasteries; and railing against icons and church adornment—are issues that are more closely connected with Artemii than with Vassian. Finally, Artemii wrote letters in a question-and-answer format with several passages headed *v"pros"* (въпросъ) and *otvet"* (отвѣтъ).[76] The *Debate* can, thus, be seen as an apologetic for the views of Vassian and Artemii. Among the disputes surveyed in this essay it may be closest to the Christian Syrian apologetics of the eighth through tenth centuries that recount fictive disputations with Muslims. It is doubtful, however, that Artemii was aware of the Syriac texts to use as antecedents or inspiration, since we have no Slavonic translations of them and we have no evidence that Artemii knew Syriac or even about this dispute.

In the *Debate*, "Iosif" initiates each exchange with a statement. Then "Vasian" provides a reply. Indeed, Vassian's responses nos. 4 through 7 begin with the word *otvet"* (although none of Iosif's statements are preceded by *v"pros"*). In a disputation, the initiator would be the one asking the questions, but in the *Debate* "Vasian" is the one asking questions, although these, to be sure, are intended as rhetorical, such as "Why, Iosif, do you write so much about this as though losing your mind?" and "Why do you, Iosif, not want to allow repentance for sinners?" Although the procedure in the *Debate* of question and answer does not conform to formal disputation rules, it does indicate a sense on the part of the author of an intellectual contest in which one protagonist tries to defeat the other protagonist through getting him to admit to an unsupportable proposition. In each case, however, "Vasian" rejects the proposition of "Iosif", thus creating "opposition" (or what the Arabic writers called *'inad*) before any syllogism can be applied.

Finally, one notes the appeal to the Bible and writings of the Church Fathers in the replies of "Vasian" that are typical of Medieval and Reformation disputants. We do not know where Artemii might have picked up his notion of disputation. The best guess is that he obtained it through distant echoes from the Reformation going on in Europe at the time.

Parts of the dialogue of "Iosif" seem to derive from parts of his *Prosvetitel'*. Statements 4 and 5 by "Iosif" have similar wording to chapter 13 of *Prosvetitel'*. Statement 6 may be a possible allusion to a similar idea expressed in chapter 13 of *Prosvetitel'* while statements 7 and 8 by "Iosif" may be possible allusions to ideas expressed in chapters 15 and 16 of *Prosvetitel'*.[77] The rest of the statements of "Iosif" (9–15) have no correlation with any of the extant works attributed to Iosif of Volokolamsk. The author of the *Prenie*, insofar as they cribbed from *Prosvetitel'*, misrepresented Iosif's views. Iosif clearly makes a distinction between, on the one hand, people who hold heretical views but are not proselytizing, and, on the other, people who hold heretical views and are proselytizing. The former should be instructed but not punished; the latter should be punished because they are doing harm. The author of the *Prenie* elides that distinction into Iosif's believing all heretics should be punished. In addition, Iosif makes a distinction between heretics who repent without threat of force and those who repent only under threat of force. Iosif allows forgiveness of the former but not the latter. The author of the *Prenie* again suppresses that distinction into Iosif's wanting to punish all heretics who repent. In Discourse 16, Iosif seems to be taking as a given that "God wishes to save all people,"[78] but in the *Prenie* no. 7, Iosif seems to be questioning Vassian's belief in that regard: "Exposition on what Vasian speaks and writes about the merciful God as though he wants to save everyone and lose no one. This he writes in order to make life easy for heretics and apostates, so that heretics, without fearing, will entice and lead Orthodox people into Judaism." That last phrase about leading the Orthodox into Judaism is similar to *Prosvetitel'*, Discourse 15.[79]

The internal references in Vassian's parts in the *Debate* to other discourses, to the "preface", and to a chapter (глава) can be seen in the following table:

Table 1: Internal References in *The Debate with Iosif*

"Reply"	Theme	Reference to	Source used
fragment	wisdom about one's self	-	*Collection of a Certain Elder*
4	heretics	in the 2nd discourse	*Discourse concerning Heretics*
5	heretics	in the 2nd discourse	*Discourse concerning Heretics*
6	heretics	-	*Discourse concerning Heretics*
7	heretics	in the 2nd discourse	
8	heretics	in the 2nd discourse	
9	heretics	in the 2nd discourse	
10	miracle workers	in the preface	*Collection of a Certain Elder*
11	villages	in the 3rd discourse	
12	villages	in the 11th discourse	
13	miracle workers	in the 10th discourse	
14	decoration of churches	-	
15	miracle workers	in the preface	*Collection of a Certain Elder*

The wording in nos. 4 and 5, in which the phrase "in the 2nd discourse" appears, corresponds to the extant *Discourse on Heretics* (*Slovo otvetno*), but the wording in nos. 8 and 9, which also has the phrase "in the 2nd discourse," does not correspond to that

Discourse. Thus, one cannot identify the *Discourse on Heretics* as the definitive source that is mentioned as "the 2nd discourse." The wording in nos. 10 and 15, in which the phrase "in the preface" appears, corresponds to the extant *Collection of a Certain Elder* (*Sobranie nekoego startsa*). Insofar as we can identify the "preface" with the *Collection of a Certain Elder*, then we can posit that the fragment that opens our extant *Debate* derives from the "preface" and not from a fragmentary no. 3. No sources for nos. 7, 8, 9, 11, 12, 13, and 14 for "Vasian" have been found. Nor has the reference to "the 3rd discourse" (in no. 11) been identified. The references to "the 11th discourse" (no. 12) and "the 10th discourse" (no. 13) seem to refer recursively to previous points in *The Debate with Iosif*. I hypothesize that the extant *Debate* represents a work in progress and not a portion of a larger completed work.[80] Perhaps Artemii fled Solovki before he could finish it.

22 – The imagined disputation between the Aristotelian Ibd Rushd (Averroes, 1126-98) and the Neoplatonist Porphyry (234-301) in c. 1350 Manfredus de Monte Imperiali's medical *Liber de herbis et plantis* (Book of Herbs and Plants) captures the essence of this essay's claim that some combination of medieval Islamic and Roman Catholic development of the classical Greek dispute underlay what is a fabricated dispute between Iosif and Vassian.

Although the *Debate with Iosif* is probably not the record of a genuine disputation, as a fictive disputation it does preserve the form of a genuine one. Nonetheless, far more in-depth research needs to be done on the phenomenon of the disputation in Afro-Eurasia in order to place it within its historical context. I have hypothesized in this article that the ancient Greek form of disputation was revived in Muslim lands and carried by Jewish intermediaries to Europe. Yet, I am fully aware of how insufficient my testing of that hypothesis has been. It is clear to me that more work is needed on disputation in general as well as its relationship to Slavic Orthodox lands in particular.

Abbreviations

AAE: *Akty, sobrannye v bibliotekakh i arkhivakh Rossiiskoi imperii Arkheograficheskoi ekspeditsiei imperatorskoi Akademii nauk.* 4 vols. St. Petersburg, 1836.

AfED: *Antifeodal'nye ereticheskie dvizheniia na Rusi XIV–nachala XVI veka.* Edited by N. A. Kazakova and Ia. S. Lur'e. Moscow and Leningrad: Akademiia nauk SSSR, 1955.

PG: *Patrologiae cursus completus. Series graeca.* 161 vols. in 166. Edited by Jacques-Paul Migne. Paris: J.-P. Migne, 1857–1866.

PL: *Patrologiae cursus completus. Series latina*, 221 vols. Edited by Jacques-Paul Migne. Paris: J.-P. Migne, 1844–1864.

PSRL: *Polnoe sobranie russkikh letopisei.* 43 vols. St. Petersburg/ Petrograd/Leningrad and Moscow: Arkheograficheskaia komissiia, Nauka, and Arkheograficheskii tsentr, 1841–2005.

Notes

1   For a different view, that "[t]he medieval dialogue is a direct outgrowth of its classical form" and that Plato's philosopy, Aristotle's logic, and Cicero's rhetoric "in combination with biblical examples of dialogue and a classical tradition of public disputation, were absorbed into early medieval culture via the works of Augustine and Boethius," see Alex J. Novikoff, *The Medieval Culture of Disputation: Pedagogy, Practice, and Performance* (Philadelphia: University of Pennsylvania Press, 2013), 33.

2   Aristotle, *Topics*, book 8, parts 5–12, Internet Classics Archive http://classics.mit.edu/Aristotle/topics.html (last accessed 18.I.2016).
3   Robin Smith, "Logic," in *The Cambridge Companion to Aristotle*, edited by Jonathan Barnes (Cambridge, UK: Cambridge University Press, 1995), 58.
4   Smith, "Logic," 59; Paul Mouraux, "La Joute dialectique d'après le huitième livre des *Topiques*," in *Aristotle on Dialectic: The Topics. Third Symposium Aristotelicum*, edited by G. E. L. Owen (Oxford: Clarendon Press, 1968), 277.
5   Gilbert Ryle, "Dialectic in the Academy," in *Aristotle on Dialectic*, 71. Richard Lim added that "as no truth was held sacred in dialectical disputations, these youths also ran the risk of becoming demoralized and disoriented by their own relentless, iconoclastic debunking of hitherto unquestioned social norms" and "as a consequence of such exercises, cease to respect their elders and the social values treasured by their society." Richard Lim, *Public Disputation, Power, and Social Order in Late Antiquity* (Berkeley: University of California Press, 1995), 35–36.
6   Smith, "Logic," 60 (italics in original).
7   *Entretien d'Origène avec Héraclide*, edited by Jean Scherer (Paris: Editions du Cerf), 1960; Reinhold Merkelbach, "Textkritische Bemerkungen zur 'Debatte des origenes mit Herakleidas,'" *Zeitschrift für Papyrologie und Epigraphik* 3 (1968): 192-196.
8   Lim, *Public Disputation*, 92–98.
9   Samuel N. C Lieu, *Manichaeism in the Later Roman Empire and Medieval China: A Historical Survey* (Manchester: Manchester University Press, 1985), 172–173.
10 PG 91: 287–354. In 638, the Emperor Heraclius (610–641) had proposed a definition of Christ's nature that sought common ground between the Chalcedonian (Orthodox) view and the Monophysite view concerning the nature of Christ. His Monothelite definition, which proposed a single divine energy and single will for Christ, was rejected by both sides. See Ryan M. Strickler's contribution to this volume.
11 Barbara Rogemma, "The Debate between Patriarch John and an Emir of the Mhaggrāyē: A Reconsideration of the Earliest Christian-Muslim Debate," in *Christians and Muslims in Dialogue in the Islamic Orient of the Middle Ages*, edited by Martin Tamcke (Beirut: Orient-Institute/Würzburg: Ergon Verlag, 2007), 39.
12 Patricia Crone, and Michael Cook, *Hagarism: The Making of the Islamic World* (Cambridge, UK Cambridge University Press, 1977), 168n20.
13 Sydney H. Griffiths, "Disputes with Muslims in Syriac Christian Texts: From Patriarch John (d. 648) to Bar Hebraeus (d. 1286)," in

Religionsgespräche im Mittelalter = Wolfenbütteler Mittelalter-Studien, 4, edited by B. Lewis and F. Niewöhner.. (Wiesbaden: Harrassowitz, 1992), 273.
14 Friedrich Heer, *Mittelalter* (Zurich: Kindler, 1961), 390.
15 I derived most of the following information on disputation rules of Arabic writers from Larry Benjamin Miller, "Islamic Disputation Theory: A Study of the Development of Dialectic in Islam from the Tenth through Fourteenth Centuries," (Ph.D. dissertation, Princeton University, 1984).
16 Miller, "Islamic Disputation Theory," 78–79 (citing Al-Fārābī, "Kitāb al-Jadal," Bratislava, ms. 231 TE 41, folia 188b ff. [typescript of M. Galston]).
17 Miller, "Islamic Disputation Theory," 79 (citing Al-Fārābī, "Kitāb al-Jadal," fol. 213b ff.).
18 Miller, "Islamic Disputation Theory," 79 (citing Al-Fārābī, "Kitāb al-Jadal," fol. 188b ff.).
19 Miller, "Islamic Disputation Theory," 80 (citing Ibn Sina, *Kitāb al-Jadal*, edited by F. al-Ahwānī, in *Al-Shifā': al-Manṭiq*, vol. 6 [Cairo: Organisme Generale des Imprimeries Gouvermentales, 1965], 30).
20 Miller, "Islamic Disputation Theory," 81–82 (citing, Naṣīr al-Dīn Ṭūsī, *Asās al-iqtibās*, edited by M. Riṣavī [Tehren: Intishārāt-i Dānishgāh-i Tihrān, 1947], 449).
21 Miller, "Islamic Disputation Theory," 82 (citing Ibn Sina, *Al-Safsaṭa*, edited by F. al-Ahwānī, in *Al-Shifā': al Manṭiq*, ed. I. Madkour, vol. 7 [Cairo: General Egyptian Book Organization, 1958], 75, lines 8–10).
22 Heer, *Mittelalter*, 389.
23 *The Works of Gilbert Crispin, Abbot of Westminster*, edited by Anne Sapir Abulafia and G. R. Evans (London: British Academy/Oxford University Press), 1986, 1–61; English summary and partial translation: Gilbert Crispin, "Disputation of a Jew with a Christian about the Christian Faith (before 1096)," in *The Jews of Angevin England: Documents and Records*, edited by Joseph Jacobs (London/New York: G. Putnam's Sons, 1893; rpt. New York: Gordon, 1977), 7–12.
24 Abelard, Peter, *Historia calamitatum* (*Epistola* 1), PL 178: 115–116.
25 For a discussion of this point, see Leif Crane, *Peter Abelard: Philosophy and Christianity in the Middle Ages*, translated by Frederick and Christine Crowley (London: George Allen and Unwin, 1970), 136–138; Heer, *Mittelalter*, 186, 189.
26 Heer, *Mittelalter*, 350–351.
27 Heer, *Mittelalter*, 389.
28 Hastings Rashdall, *The Universities of Europe in the Middle Ages*, new ed., 3 vols. (Oxford: Oxford University Press, 1936), 1: (*Salerno–Bologna–Paris*), 450–496.

29 Lynn Thorndike, *History of Medieval Europe*, 3rd ed. (Boston: Houghton Mifflin, 1956), 437.
30 *Chartularium Universitatis parisiensis*, 4 vols., edited by Heirich Denifle and Emile Chatelain (Paris: Delalain, 1889–1897; rpt. Brussels: Cultures et Civilizations, 1964), 1: 516 ("Capitulum eorum ad quae tenentur cursum incipere volentes," no. 452 [1270–1274]); cf. Lynn Thorndike, *University Records and Life in the Middle Ages* (New York: W. W. Norton, 1975), 81.
31 By 1200, there were three *studia generale* in Europe: Bologna, Oxford, and Paris. Salerno also had an institution of higher learning at the time, but it specialized in medicine. In 1209, during a strike at Oxford University, some masters left to found a university in Cambridge. And during a strike at Paris during 1229–1231, the civic leader of Toulouse enticed some unemployed masters there to found a university. Joseph H. Lynch, *The Medieval Church: A Brief History* (London: Longman, 1992), 253–254.
32 Gordon Leff, *Paris and Oxford Universities in the Thirteenth and Fourteenth Centuries: An Institutional and Intellectual History* (New York: John Wiley, 1968), 167–169.
33 Heer, *Mittelalter*, 441–442. According to Heer, the *disputatio de quodlibet* was preferred by Thomas Aquinas.
34 Leff, *Paris and Oxford Universities*, 171–173.
35 Thorndike, *History of Medieval Europe*, 684.
36 *The Metalogicon of John of Salisbury: A Twelfth-Century Defense of the Verbal and Logical Arts of the Trivium*, translated by Daniel D. McGarry (Berkeley: University of California Press, 1962), 190–191.
37 *Metalogicon*, 13–15.
38 Ignacio Angelelli, "The Techniques of Disputation in the History of Logic." *Journal of Philosophy* 67 (October 22, 1970): 801. Cf. Johann Friedrich Heine, *Methodus disputandi die hodierna ex variis autoribus collecta* (Helmstedt: 1710).
39 Angelelli, "Techniques of Disputation," 802–803. Cf. *Pauli Veneti Logica magna*, edited by Norman Kretzmann (Oxford: British Academy/ Oxford University Press: 1978).
40 For a dramatization of the disputation, see the film *The Disputation: A Theological Debate between Christians and Jews* (1986), directed by Geoffrey Sax, written by Hyam Maccoby (Princeton: Films for the Humanities, 1991).
41 *Judaism on Trial: Jewish-Christian Disputations in the Middle Ages*, edited and translated by Hyam Maccoby (Rutherford, NJ: Fairleigh Dickinson University Press / London: Associated University Presses, 1982, 84.

42 Siegfried Stein, *Jewish-Christian Disputations in Thirteenth-Century Narbonne* (London: H. K. Lewis, 1969).
43 Stein, *Jewish-Christian Disputations*, 9–10. In this last matter, Stein calls ben Simeon "almost a forerunner of David Friedrich Strauss" (ibid., 10), but points out that he does not apply the same method of criticism as Strauss does to the Old Testament.
44 *The Journey of William of Rubruck to the Eastern Parts of the World, 1253–55* (Surry: Hakluyt Society, 2010), 228.
45 Rubruck, *Journey*, 230–231.
46 Rubruck, *Journey*, 231–235.
47 Rubruck, *Journey*, 234.
48 George Makdisi, "The Scholastic Method in Medieval Education: An Inquiry into Its Origins in Law and Theology, *Speculum* 49, no. 4 (1974): 648.
49 Makdisi, "Scholastic Method," 650n45. On *manāzara*, see Josef van Ess, "Disputationspraxis in der islamischen Theologie. Eine vorläufige Skizze." *Revue des études islamiques* 44 (1976): 37–38.
50 Joan M Hussey, *The Orthodox Church in the Byzantine Empire* (Oxford: Clarendon Press, 1986), 179–180; Jean Darouzès, "Documents byzantins du XIIe siécle sur la primauté romaine," *Revue des études byzantines* 23 (1965): 42–59.
51 Francis Dvornik, *Byzantium and the Roman Primacy* (New York: Fordham University Press, 1966/1979), 145–146; Hussey, *Orthodox Church*, 180–182. Darouzès, "Documents byzantins," 59–65.
52 Anselm of Havelberg, *Dialogi*, 2.1, PL 188: 1163.
53 Bibliotheque Nationale, Paris, ms. Fr 2628, fol. 323; cf. Riley-Smith, *Atlas*, 105.
54 Giovanni Pico della Mirandola, *Conclusiones philosophicae, cabalasticae et theologicae* (Rome: 1486); but see his *Disputationes adversus astrologiam divinatricem*, 2 vols. (Florence: Vallecchi, 1946).
55 *Novgorodskaia pervaia letopis', starshego i mladshego izvodov*, edited by A. N. Nasonov (Moscow-Leningrad: Akademiia nauk SSSR, 1950; rpt. PSRL 3, 2000), 359.
56 *AAE* 1: 251–252.
57 See Alexander Pereswetoff-Morath, *A Grin without a Cat: 'Adversus Judaeos' Texts in the Literature of Medieval Russia 988–1504*, 2 vols. (Lund: Department of East and Central European Studies, Lund University, 2002), 2: 113–198.
58 *PSRL* 10: 188–189.
59 *The* Vita *of Constantine and the* Vita *of Methodius*, translated by Marvin Kantor and Richard S. White = Michigan Slavic Materials, no. 13 (Ann Arbor: University of Michigan, 1976), 10–13.

60 *The* Vita *of Constantine*, 12–13.
61 George Mastrantonis, *Augsburg and Constantinople: The Correspondence between the Tübingen Theologians and Patriarch Jeremiah II of Constantinople on the Augsburg Confession* (Brookline, MA: Holy Cross Orthodox Press, 1982), 306 ("The Third Answer of Patriarch Jeremiah [II] of Constantinople to Tübingen in the year 1581").
62 Ibid.
63 James F. Loughlin, "Religious Discussions," in *Catholic Encyclopedia* http://www.newadvent.org/cathen/05034a.htm (last accessed 18 January 2016), makes this same point in regard to why the present-day Catholic Church rarely approves of disputation as a "method of ventilating revealed truth"—that is: "A champion of orthodoxy, possessed of all the qualifications essential to a public debater, is not easily to be found."
64 *AfED*, 320.
65 On the seven liberal arts in general and dialectic in particular at Kirillo-Belozersk, see Robert Romanchuk, *Byzantine Hermeneutics and Pedagogy in the Russian North: Monks and Masters at the Kirillo-Belozerskii Monastery 1397–1501* (Toronto: University of Toronto Press, 2007), 58–68, 140–146.
66 Roland Bainton, *Here I Stand: A Life of Martin Luther* (Nashville: Abingdon, 1976), 108.
67 Charles Homer Haskins, *The Renaissance of the 12th Century* (Cambridge, MA: Harvard University Press, 1927), 188–189.
68 R. P. Dmitrieva, *Povesti o spore zhizni i smerti* (Leningrad: Nauka, 1964), 11.
69 Roman Jakobson, *Spor duše s tělem. O nebezpečném času smrti* (Prague: Ladislav Kuncíř, 1927); and Lenart, Mirosław Lenart, *Spór duszy z ciałem i inne wierszowane spory w literaturze staropolskiej na tle tradycji średniowiecznej* (Opole: Wydawnictwo Uniwersytetu Opolskiego, 2002).
70 V. N. Peretts, "Svedeniia ob antichnom mire v drevnei Rusi XI–XIV vv," *Germes: nauchno-populiarnyi vestnik antichnogo mira* 21, nos. 13–14 (1917): 207. He speculated that the ultimate source of it was the no-longer-extant ancient Greek play *Earth and Sea* (Γᾶ καί Θάλασσα) by Epicharmus of Kos (ca. 540–ca. 450). Cf. M. P. Alekseev, "'Prenie zemli i moria' v drevnerusskoi pis'mennosti," in *Problemy obshchestvenno-politicheskoi istorii Rossii i slavianskikh stran. Sbornik statei k 70-letiiu Akademika M. N. Tikhomirova*, edited by M. V. Nechkina et al. (Moscow: Vostochnaia literatura, 1963), 33.
71 Three editions of the *Debate* are available: by A. Pavlov in 1863, by Kazakova in 1960, and by me in 1977. A. S. Pavlov, "Polemicheskie

sochineniia inoka-kniazia Vassiana Patrikeeva (XVI st.)." *Pravoslavnyi sobesednik*, October 1863: 200–210, used the ms. Rossiiskaia natsional'naia biblioteka (RNB), Solovetskoe sobranie, no. 941/831, folia 424–428v, as his copy text, but inserted the heading from the ms. RNB, Solovetskoe sobranie, no. 985/875, folio 57. N. A. Kazakova, *Vassian Patrikeev i ego sochineniia* (Moscow and Leningrad: Akademiia nauk SSSR, 1960), 275–281, used the ms. Gosudarstvenyi istoricheskii muzei (GIM), Sinodal'noe sobranie, no. 738, folia 97–102v, as her copy text and provided variants from the three Solovki manuscript copies. Kazakova's publication, but without the variants, can also be found with notes in *A Historical Russian Reader: A Selection of Texts from the Eleventh to the Sixteenth Centuries*, edited by John Fennell and Dmitrii Obolensky (Oxford: Clarendon Press, 1969), 120–125, 196–198. In my dissertation, A 'Fontological' Investigation of the 1503 Church Council" (Ph.D. dissertation, Pennsylvania State University, 1977), 492–516, I used the (1560s) RNB, Solovetskoe no. 941/831 version as my copy text and reported variant readings from the (1580s) RNB, Solovetskoe 963/853, (1650s) RNB, Solovetskoe no. 985/875, folia 57–64, and (1660s) and GIM, Sinodal'noe versions. A fifth manuscript copy from ca. 1600 exists, but has not yet been integrated into any edition: ms. Novosibirsk Publichnaia biblioteka, sobranie Tikhomirova no. 373, folia 416v–421v.

72 In 1937, Nicolas Zernov published a similar pastishe that he composed of extracts from the writings attributed to Iosif and Vassian: *Moscow the Third Rome* (New York: Macmillan, 1937, 40.

73 For a survey, see Ostrowski, A 'Fontological' Investigation," 186–193.

74 Ostrowski, "A 'Fontological' Investigation," 232–239; cf. idem, "Church Polemics and Monastic Land Acquisition in Sixteenth-Century Muscovy," *Slavonic and East European Review* 64 (1986): 363; A. I. Pliguzov, "Prenie s Iosifom," in *Issledovaniia po istochnkovedeniiu istorii SSSR dooktiabr'skogo perioda. Sbornik statei*, edited by B. G. Litvak, V. A. Kuchkin, and A. P. Bogdanov (Moscow: Institut istorii SSSR ANSSSR, 1989), 68–73.

75 Ostrowski, "A 'Fontological' Investigation," 219–231, 232–234.

76 "Poslaniia startsa Artemiia," *Russkaia istoricheskaia biblioteka*, 2nd ed. 4, no. 1 (1908): cols. 1241, 1255, 1363–1364, 1413, 1429, 1434–1435.

77 See for no 4. *AfED*, 488; Iosif Volotskii, *Prosvetitel', ili oblichenie eresi zhitovstviushchikh: tvorenie prepodobnogo ottsa nashego Iosifa, igumena volotskago*, 4th ed. (Kazan: Tipo-litografiia Imperatorskogo unversiteta, 1903), 53, 475; for no. 5 = *AfED*, 495; *Prosvetitel'*, 596–598; for no. 6 = *AfED*, 494; *Prosvetitel'*, 593–594; for no. 7 = *Prosvetitel'*, 512–524, 529–540;

for no. 8 = *Prosvetitel'*, 527. David Goldfrank brought to my attention these similarities in wording and possible allusions to *Prosvetitel'*.
78 *Prosvetitel'*, 547.
79 *Prosvetitel'*, 482, 524; cf. *AfED*, 490, var. б-б.
80 Alternatively, Goldfrank suggests that extracts from *Slovo otvetno* are divided among points 2, 4, 5, 6, and 7; and that extracts from *Sobranie nekoego startsa* are divided among the preface, points 3, 10, and 15 (e-mail, 5 December 2014).

8 Deacon Feodor Ivanov as a Follower of Iosif Volotskii

or *The Enlightener* and "The Wolf and Predator ... Nikon"

Kevin M. Kain

23 – Patriarch Nikon in his Resurrection "New Jerusalem" Monastery as he would represent himself, with a copy of the miracle-working Iveron Mother-of-God icon in the background (1660s).

In his illuminating tale "About Iosif of Volokolamsk" the Old Believer Deacon Feodor Ivanov (d. 1682) charged that "[Patriarch] Nikon defamed Saint Iosif of Volokolamsk the miracle-maker, called him a sneak and slandered and disrespected him and did not kneel down before him."[1] As the cornerstone of his seminal "About the Wolf and Predator and One Marked by God Nikon who is Pastor in Sheep's Skin and Forerunner of the Antichrist" (1670s),[2] Feodor's ideas about Iosif had significant and lasting impacts on assessments of Patriarch Nikon beyond the seventeenth century.

"About the Wolf" appeared in two eighteenth-century redactions and continued to be integrated into new Old Believer works about Nikon through the early 20th century.[3] While simply classified as "lies" in the nineteenth century, the Old Believer charges that Nikon disrespected Iosif were uncritically accepted by Soviet scholars.[4] Most recently, the discovery of Nikon's "Spiritual Will" (*"Dukhovnoe zaveshchanie"*) and the determination that the patriarch copied the majority of it from Iosif's Extended Rule (*"Dukhovnaia gramota"*), lead several scholars to revisit the dissenter's accusations with the aim of dismissing them.[5] Yet, although Feodor's allegations against Nikon were perpetuated by Old Believers for centuries and debated by modern scholars, his defense of Iosif, not to mention the sources which shaped it and the rest of his polemic, remains unexplained. What can "About Iosif of Volokolamsk" and the rest of "About the Wolf" tell us about Iosif's influences on Deacon Feodor?

This study offers comparative analysis of Deacon Feodor Ivanov's "About the Wolf" and Iosif Volotskii's *Enlightener*. Instead of considering what the Old Believer polemic reveals about Nikon's actions in regards to the saint, it focuses on Feodor's adoption of the methods Iosif practiced and the ideas he advocated in his *Enlightener*.[6] Seen from this new perspective, the Old Believer's account of Nikon's alleged abuse of Iosif emerges as a sign of Feodor's affinity for Volotskii, as well as a leading charge against the patriarch. Close readings reveal striking parallels between Ivanov's "About the Wolf" and Volotskii's *Enlightener*, demonstrating the latter to be the likely model for key sections of Feodor's work.[7] Thus, the essay will show that, at the very least, Feodor recognized the utility of Volotskii's writings in his attacks on Nikon and employed them heavily.

Feodor recognized the relevance of such teachings as Iosif's against heresy and on monasticism for his own day and upheld them as paradigms of action. The Old Believer forged direct connections between Nikon and the alleged "judaizing heretics" of Iosif's era, casting the patriarch as an enemy of the saint and his ideals. Following the precedents set in the *Enlightener*, the Old Believer embedded Iosif's thoughts concerning the threats that heresy posed to Russian Orthodoxy in his depictions of those, including Tsar Aleksei Mikhailovich, who, he claimed, concealed or ignored the patriarch's transgressions. Rather than simply citing Iosif's writings, Feodor embodied Volotskii's principles in the deeds of individuals, including himself, who exposed Nikon's (supposed) clandestine heresies, rejected them and revealed them to others. Therefore, it appears that Feodor not only borrowed the authority of Iosif's *Enlightener* in his attack on Nikon, but also conceived of his own efforts as emulations of Iosif's self-identified deeds as anti-heretic crusader.

Although Feodor was not a monastic, he followed Iosif in making monks and monasteries a primary focus in "About the Wolf." In fact, most of Feodor's text is devoted to monastic-related themes, including obedience, disciplining, the inviolability of monastic land holdings and the authority of the monastic fathers.[8] Drawing heavily upon Volotskii's staunch defense of the "monastic image," Feodor simultaneously made it the focus of both his glorifications of Iosif and his condemnations of Nikon as a wolf in monk's habit. Heightening the significance of monastics even further, and utilizing eyewitness testimonials made by monks, including Nikon's former disciples, the Old Believer revealed the patriarch's most heinous alleged heresies, namely abusing the Cross and the image of the Mother of God and slandering monastic saints.[9] Given these purposeful borrowings from the *Enlightener*, it appears that Feodor based his conception of monasticism as a divine institution and monastics as the preeminent defenders of the true faith against heresy on the saint's examples.[10] In short, Feodor employed Iosif's *Enlightener* precisely as the saint intended, as a "how to guide" for exposing and condemning perceived Russian heretics.

Iosif's *Enlightener* as a Paradigm for Early Old Believers

Iosif's *Enlightener* is an authoritative polemical-didactic treatise constituting an original compendium of "ancient" Orthodox teachings. The work's three-part structure combines a cautionary, indicting historical narrative with seminal, discursive polemical writings, first defending and elucidating Orthodoxy and then promoting and defending an inquisition. The first section, "The Account of the Recent Heresy of the Novgorod Heretics," relates the history of Rus'/Russian Orthodoxy, from the advent of Kiev's spiritual enlightenment across five centuries, during which "no one saw heretics anywhere" in Russia to the appearance of the "Judaizing" heresy in Novgorod in the 1470.[11] Charting the emergence of this "judaizing" and its spread to Moscow, Iosif identified individual heretics, including Metropolitan Zosima, and cataloged their alleged actions, including iconoclasm, as well as their philosophical positions, such as "if the monastic life were pleasing to God, Christ himself and the divine apostles would be depicted in the monastic habit, but now we see Christ is depicted and the holy apostles in the secular habit, not in the monastic."[12] Raising the events of his day to near Biblical proportions, Iosif likened his opponents to ancient heretics. Connecting Zosima's secret judaizing and ascension to the Moscow Metropolitanate in 6999 with apocalyptic prophecies about the year 7000, he deemed the hierarch "the forerunner of the Antichrist."[13] Finally, Iosif offered historical examples of Orthodox empires which fell after failing to root out and destroy heretics.[14]

In the first eleven regular discourses of the *Enlightener*, Iosif set up his opponents' (alleged) positions as straw men in order to refute them independently and *en mass*. Qualifying his method, Iosif confirmed that "so wrote our holy, divine fathers against the ancient heretics and multiple places made manifest their names and heresies, so that it would be known among the ancients that those doctrines are the invention of the devil."[15] Clearly establishing his purpose, Iosif explained: "I have compiled together from different divine writings, so that the knowledgeable, having read through, will remind themselves, and the ignorant, having read through, will know. And if someone needs something to refute a heretical uttering, then, with the grace of God, he will find it readied without toil in these following discourses."[16] Given Iosif's stated intent and his profound traditionalism, it is not surprising that the early Old Believers adopted his teachings into their own writings against what they perceived as Nikon's heresies.

It is relatively well established that the first generation of Old Believers was familiar with Iosif's literary legacy and incorporated his *Enlightener* in their own polemics against the "Nikonian" Church.[17] We know, for example, that Feodor's "spiritual father," archpriest Avvakum Petrov, recognized the saint as "one of the pillars of 'ancient piety'" and cited him often.[18] Iosif's place in Feodor's most renowned discourses, including *Response of the Orthodox* ("*Otvet Pravoslavnykh*") (1667-9),[19] "Missive from Pustorzersk to Son Maksim and other Relatives and Brothers in Faith" ("*Poslanie iz Pustozerska k synu Maksimu i prochim srodnikam i bratiiam po vere*") (1678/9)[20] and "Concerning Church Dogmas and the Condemnation of Heretics and Apostates" ("*O tserkovnykh dogmatakh i oblichenie na eretikov i otstupnikov*"),[21] are easily detectable because the author directly cited Volotskii's work. This, however, was not the case with the more unique and developed approach Feodor took in "About the Wolf."

Unlike most early Old Believer polemics which attacked the Nikonian reforms of Church books, rites and rituals, Feodor's stated goal in "About the Wolf" was to highlight Nikon's (alleged) heresy "in addition to his corruption of church dogmas."[22] Adhering to Iosif's demand that heretics, including church hierarchs, be exposed, tried and severely punished for their transgressions,[23] Feodor moved beyond what he perceived as the sham official charges and condemnations pronounced against Nikon at his trial in December 1666 to construct a new more inclusive case. On the one hand, Feodor's indictment introduced new charges of Nikon's heresies which he constructed as if emerging "from below" by the patriarch's underlings, not the clerical elite or state officials. On the other hand, the Old Believer reinvigorated charges, including the accusation that by judaizing at his New Jerusalem Monastery Nikon was preparing the way for the Antichrist—charges which were officially discounted during the proceeding against the patriarch. In both cases Feodor traced the precedents Iosif provided in the *Enlightener*.

N. Iu. Bubnov observed that while the first generation of Old Believer writers often integrated historical materials into their polemics, they were especially attracted to episodes from the Russian past that could be interpreted in new ways in order to support their notion that Russia was precariously near the "End of Time" and "Final Judgment."[24] This holds true for Feodor who found the events in "The Account of the Recent Heresy of the Novgorod Heretics," formulated by Iosif in the context of apocalyptic prophecies about the year 7000 (1492), particularly relevant.[25] In "About the Wolf,"

Ivanov created precise parallels between Iosif's Metropolitan Zosima and the "Novgorod Heretics" and Patriarch Nikon and the "Nikonians." The connections between past and present are immediately evident in the title of Feodor's work. Repeating Iosif's charge that Zosima was a "filthy and evilly demonic wolf dressed in pastor's clothes," Feodor decried Nikon as "wolf and predator who is pastor in sheep's skin."[26] Echoing the notion that the metropolitan was "the forerunner of the Antichrist" and "Satan's first-born," the Old Believer likewise deemed the patriarch "the forerunner of the Antichrist."[27] The reprises, discussed below, continue throughout the work as Feodor repeated several of the same charges Iosif brought against Zosima and the "Novgorod Heretics" as "proof" of his accusations against Nikon. Yet, Ivanov did more than borrow content from Volotskii.

24 – 19th-early 20th c. Old Believer depiction of Patriarch Nikon's alleged conversing with the Devil.

"About the Wolf" reflects not only the historical case of the fifteenth-century Russian heretics, but also Volotskii's proven approach to attacking his enemies as judaizers. Feodor suggested Iosif as a paradigm for his method of 'outing' Nikon in his earlier writings. In one salient example, drawn from his "Missive from Pustozersk to Son Maksim and other Relatives and Brothers in Faith," Feodor explained:

> It is clear that, according to the Holy Bible, the heretical oath is illegal and false and, therefore, invalid. There is an entire narrative about this by reverend father Iosif, the hegumen of Volokolamsk and miracle-maker, in his book the *Enlightener* where he wrote about the Novgorod and Moscow heretics living during his day and openly upholding the Jewish heresy, and [that] Metropolitan of Moscow Zosima, as well as many other upper clergy, were secretly holding the Jewish heresy. He [Iosif] was the only one to condemn them and to suffer many attacks by them when the regular authorities were all silent then like dolts.[28]

This context suggests that Feodor aimed to reveal and denounce Nikon and the Nikonians in "About the Wolf," just as he thought Volotskii exposed and condemned Zosima and the "Novgorod Heretics."[29] Moreover, the notion that Iosif "was the only one to condemn them and to suffer many attacks by them when the regular authorities were all silent" not only shows that Feodor admired the saint's unflinching defense of the True Faith, but also strongly implies that he may have also identified the harsh punishments he received for his denunciations of Nikon (including having his tongue cut out) with what he, believed to be the "suffering" Iosif endured, as a result of his fearless outspokenness.[30] Feodor ingrained the exact same Iosif-inspired ideals into the monks who testified to Nikon's alleged heresies.

Desacralization of the Cross and Image of the Holy Virgin: Accusations "From Below"

Feodor began to introduce "evidence that Nikon is the enemy of Christ and forerunner of the Antichrist" with two eyewitness testimonies purporting that the patriarch repeatedly and purposefully desecrated the Cross of Christ and images of the Holy Virgin. Made by monks in Nikon's service, these restate the accusations that Iosif often raised against Zosima and the "Novgorod Heretics."[31] Furthermore, Feodor modeled his representations of how and why his "witnesses" reacted to the hierarch's alleged heresies on Iosif's *Enlightener*.[32]

Feodor's account of monk "Kirik's" experiences with Nikon appears as a textbook appropriation of Iosif's core teachings.

> While this sly snake was on the patriarch's throne, his assistant, Kirik by name, a man of holy life, was taken, against his will from the staff of the Solovetskii Monastery… . Nikon knew Kirik as a person of obedience and kept him at his disposal using force. Kirik once saw the patriarch's velvet boots. He just wanted to see these very expensive shoes, but saw that the Cross of our Lord, Jesus Christ, was sewn on the insole of one and [an image of] the Holy Virgin with Christ on the other. And he was very scared and his face changed and he told Nikon that this was very bad. He stopped eating and drinking that day. The enemy of Christ asked Kirik: "what is the reason why you do not eat or drink?" He insisted he had a very bad illness and responded: "I cannot!"
>
> The monk was ultimately released unharmed. Yet, "when Kirik came to [Solovetskii] Monastery he told his spiritual father, priest and monk Vitally, about this terrible matter; his spiritual father told the brethren."[33]

Feodor's accusations that Nikon wore a cross and an image of the Virgin in his footwear are clearly based upon the charges that Iosif raised against Zosima and the "Novgorod Heretics." The idea that Nikon concealed his sacrileges in "expensive shoes" simultaneously replicated Metropolitan Zosima's furtive actions and linked the hierarchs' images as wolves in pastor's clothes.[34] The specification that the patriarch had the cross in his insole likewise employs Iosif's claims that Zosima "spoke many blasphemies against the Most Pure Virgin, placing divine and life-creating

25 – 19th-early 20th c. Old Believer depiction of Patriarch Nikon's actual destruction of icons. The Old Believers neglected to note that Nikon, who indeed did innovate with Baroque-influenced iconostasis frames, actually opposed some of the same iconographical innovations the Old Believers rejected.

crosses in unclean places and burning icons, calling them idols." Moreover, the charge mirrors the explanation in the *Enlightener* that these Novgorod dissenters "threw icons into unclean and filthy places: some they bit with their teeth like rabid dogs, others they smashed … and said: 'We defile these icons as the Jews insulted Christ.'"[35] Finally, the notion that Nikon repeatedly desecrated the cross by stepping on it followed Volotskii's claim that the "Novgorod Heretics" habitually abused the symbol. In effect, every step the patriarch took he committed acts of heresy or blasphemy.

The record of Kirik's response to Nikon's heresies displays the hallmarks of Iosif's teachings in the *Enlightener*. While formerly known as "obedient," the monk becomes intransigent as soon as he uncovers Nikon as a heretic. The specification that "he stopped eating and drinking that day" traces Volotskii's repeated references to St. John Chrysostom's warnings, including that "John Chrysostom wrote: 'Beloved ones, many times I told you about godless heretics and now I beseech not to join with them, not in eating, nor drinking, nor in friendship, nor in love; he who does this renders himself alien to Christ's Church'."[36] When the monk "told his spiritual father, hieromonk Vitalii, about this terrible matter and his spiritual father told it to the brethren," he obeyed Volotskii's direction. Thus, his testimony reflects Iosif's belief that "in both the monastery and in society at large... Iosif felt one had a duty to inform upon transgressors... anyone knowing of heretics and not reporting then was in fact in communion with them."[37] In sum, Feodor's Kirik represents as an ideal Iosifite monk an opponent of heresy.

Defamation of the Saints: Iosif and the Monastic Fathers

Feodor continued to draw upon Iosif's "Account" and Discourses (*Slovo*) against Russian heretics and on monasticism and to link them with his own day through charges that "Nikon scolded our holy fathers." These include three additional testimonials espoused 'from below' by Nikon's inferiors alleging that the patriarch "slandered" the saints, rejected their miracles and refused to commemorate them on icons and in rituals.[38] The most developed and revealing in terms of Feodor's affinity for Iosif is "About Iosif of Volokolamsk."[39] The accusations against Nikon contained in this section of Feodor's work represent a concisely condensed reprise of the same ones that Iosif raised against the "Novgrod Heretics."[40] In short, Feodor loaded every phase in "About Iosif Volokolamsk" with references to the *Enlightener*. According to "Testimonies:"

> Nikon defamed Saint Iosif Volokolamsk the miracle-maker, called him a sneak and slandered and disrespected him and did not kneel down before him .... They also said that all the names of all saintly Russian miracle-makers were deleted from the list of the recollection service. Previously all these Russian miracle-makers were named during

the Lord's Prayer. And he scolded all the saints and used insulting words and according to this device of the devil he defamed the reverend Iosif. And Nikon said that all of Iosif's followers and his pupils should be defamed and that all of Iosif's activities were done not according to the heavenly and not for the glory of Christ and his church, but for Iosif's seeking of earthy profits, for lands, woods, waters and properties. All of Iosif's followers were searching for their own profit and not, according to the apostolic tradition, for Jesus Christ.[41]

The Old Believer's claim that Nikon "defamed" and "slandered" Iosif mirrors Volotskii's charge that the "Novgorod Heretics ... blasphemed ... Saint Ephrem" and by extension, repudiated all the Church Fathers and displays distinct parallels with Volotskii's own use and defense of Ephrem of Syria's (ca. 306-73) writings on the Last Days in Discourse 10 of the *Enlightener*.[42] Both Ivanov and Volotskii upheld their predecessors' ideas concerning the end of time in order to reveal their respective enemies, namely Metropolitan Zosima and Patriarch Nikon, as the ultimate heretics - the "forerunner[s] of the Antichrist."[43] Moreover, Iosif, who declared that "everything he [Ephrem] wrote is true, and profitable, and salvific for our souls,"[44] also cited the ancient saint's authority as a monastic father in his defense of Russian monasticism in *the Enlightener*, well as throughout his *Rule*.[45] Feodor, as demonstrated both above and in what follows, likewise employed Iosif's teachings on monasticism in much the same way.

Given the context in which it appeared, Feodor's accusation that Nikon "did not kneel down before him [Iosif]" ("*ne poklanialsia emy*") strongly suggested that the patriarch, like Volotskii's "Novgorod Heretics," who "forbade venerating the divine icons," transgressed by rejecting the Orthodox veneration of icons.[46] With the specific implication that Nikon failed to prostrate before Iosif's image, Feodor created undeniable connections between the patriarch's alleged actions and the saint's extensive discourses on that theme.[47] These are epitomized in Discourse 7 of the *Enlightener* wherein Iosif explained:

We honor and venerate these venerable and dear images, and we conceive as if they are living and standing with us out of unsated love. And on account of this we struggle for the imitation of their God-pleasing life, and we always accept their excellent miracles, which, with the grace of God are from their venerable icons, and holy churches, and the healing relics inside them.[48]

Continuing to borrow from Discourse 7, Feodor combined Iosif's condemnations of the abuse of saints by the "Novgorod Heretics" and their alleged corruption of the Eucharistic Rite into the next phrase of his assault against Nikon. His claim that "all the names of all Russian miracle-makers were deleted from the list of the recollection service" attacked the reform of *Proskomidie*, which was mandated by Nikon's revised Church Service Book (*Sluzhebnik*) of 1655 and drastically reduced number of monastic fathers commemorated during Eucharistic preparations, by associating it with the fifteenth-century heretics.[49] This adaptation of Iosif's work is unmistakable given the fact that earlier in his *Response of the Orthodox* Feodor likened the changes to *Proskomidie* introduced in "Nikonian" text with what "the miracle-maker Saint Iosif of Volokolamsk wrote about the new judaizers, the Novgorod and Moscow Heretics, in his *Enlightener*" concerning their alleged defiling of the same ritual.[50]

Close readings show that Feodor based the second half of "About Iosif of Volokolamsk" on Discourse 11 of Iosif's *Enlightener*. The Old Believer's charge that "Nikon said all of Iosif's activities were made not according to the heavenly and not for the glory of Christ and his church, but for Iosif's seeking of earthy profits for lands, woods, waters and properties" and that "all of Iosif's followers were searching for their own profit and not, according to the apostolic tradition, for Jesus Christ" is a masterful play on the saint's own teachings about the "monastic image."[51] It flipped Iosif's claim that the "Novgorod Heretics" "blasphemed the monastic life, saying that monks have abandoned God's commandment and prophetic, evangelistic, and apostolic Scripture, and via auto-syllogistics and auto-didactics and have invented their life and keep human traditions" on its head.[52] With this highly ironic and meaningful twist, Feodor had Nikon accuse Iosif with the same charges he (Volotskii) claimed the "Novgorod Heretics" made against the Russian monastics and Fathers in the fifteenth century. Continuing to stress the importance of Iosif's teachings on the "monastic image of life", Feodor turned the tables again by assaulting Nikon with the very same charges the patriarch (supposedly) made against the saint. In this way, the Old Believer simultaneously identified himself with Iosif and Nikon with the saint's sworn enemies. This striking overlap reconfirms the central place that Iosif's defenses of monasticism held in Feodor's work and provides a smooth transition to the equally damning set of charges he resurrected in the next section of "About the Wolf."

New Jerusalem Monastery: Nikon as Iosif's Antithesis

Immediately after relating "About Iosif of Volokolamsk" Feodor began an attack on Nikon's New Jerusalem Monastery wherein he cast the patriarch as the saint's polar opposite. Counterpoising Iosif's teaching with the patriarch's alleged deeds, the Old Believer introduced new evidence in support of his primary charge that the hierarch was a "wolf and predator" and "forerunner of the Antichrist." In doing so, he gave renewed urgency to the claims, raised in the early 1660s, that Nikon "robbed" property and judaized while creating his monastery by contextualizing them in terms of Iosif's *Enlightener*.

Feodor continued to qualify Nikon's slanders and defamations of Iosif and other monastic saints by revealing the patriarch's own rejection of the "monastic image of life." The Old Believer's Nikon both accepted the argument of the "Novgorod Heretics" that "Christ and the holy apostles are depicted in the secular habit, not in the monastic habit," and rejected the saint's numerous references to true monks' complete withdrawal from world.[53] Instead of obeying the saint, the patriarch copied his enemies who "invented their own way of living and they left the Lord's commandments and ... lived according to teachings of people."[54] However, unlike the "Novgorod Heretics" who only (supposedly) rhetorically challenged the ideals of Russian monasticism, Feodor contends that Nikon actively spurned the "monastic image" by seeking worldly gains and preying upon monasteries to the point of their annihilation. These ideas are epitomized by Feodor's claim:

> Stealing like a wolf, Nikon like a rascal, grabbed villages and real estate from monasteries... as if a prince of the world, increasing his property, number of slaves and servants and granaries.... He insulted many monasteries and destroyed many of these monasteries and offended many local princes and poor people and tormented many common Christian landholders when he created his New Jerusalem.[55]

While Feodor's report on Nikon's habitual attacks on the "monastic image" is clearly based on Iosif's Discourses, the author's efforts to reveal the hierarch's alleged judaizing at the monastery and to identify him as the "forerunner of the Antichrist" require deeper explication. Tracing the genesis of the Old Believer's recollection, that "the Holy Patriarch of Jerusalem [Paisius Ligarides] spoke correctly about Nikon when he said that the Russian patriarch began to create New Jerusalem [Monastery] it was necessary to await the appearance of a new God on earth, in other words, the Antichrist," reconfirms once again the relevance of Iosif's paradigm for Feodor's cause.[56] Paisius Ligarides introduced the specter of Nikon's judaizing in response to questions posed by the boyar Semen Streshnev on August 15, 1662, claiming: "I hear, O Nikon, that thou art writing about that new Messiah whom the Jews expect, and whom they may hope to see come from a new Jerusalem. At a guess, then, there should be with you in thy New Jerusalem some mother of Antichrist?"[57]

Bishop Aleksandr of Viatka adopted and advanced Ligarides' ideas and presented them to Tsar Aleksei Mikhailovich in a bid to convince the tsar formally to judge the patriarch.[58] Writing to the tsar in December of 1662, Aleksandr reiterated that "the priestly Paisius says: 'Oh the vice! Oh the extraordinary news! Builder of New Jerusalem and the lover of new speeches wasn't there a prophesy about your copy of Jerusalem [concerning the coming of the Antichrist]? Oh Nikon! You start your new letter by consenting with the Jews.'"[59] Given that Feodor was a key member of the circle of early Old Believers which gathered around Aleksandr, it is likely that he would have been well informed about these attempts to connect New Jerusalem with charges of Nikon's judaizing as well as with their being officially rebuffed.[60]

Although Nikon was ultimately condemned for "stealing" land for New Jerusalem during his trial in December of 1666, the notions that the patriarch was judaizing at the monastery and preparing the way for the Antichrist there were flatly rejected by a Russian church council earlier the same year.[61] According to Ligarides's resolution, "the people of the Russian nation are very much scandalized, being ignorant, by this name 'New Jerusalem', especially in these last days, upon which the end of the world have come. And in connection with this scandal, there is very much obloquy against the most holy patriarch."[62] The council's blatant dismissal of Nikon's alleged judaizing at New Jerusalem as "ignorance" and the fact that the charge was never included in the official proceedings against the patriarch might well have appeared to Feodor as a cover up on the hierarchy's behalf.[63] Indeed, it would have again reconfirmed the parallels between Feodor's day and Iosif's when, the Old Believer thought, "the regular authorities were all silent … like dolts. Much like today's authorities, they were afraid of the metropolitan's [Zosima's] anathema."[64] This same line of thinking is evident in the Old Believer's subsequent commentary on what he condemned as Tsar Aleksei Mikhailovich's failure to act against the threats posed by Nikon's heresies.

The Orthodox Ruler's Responsibility

David Goldfrank has clarified that in the *Enlightener* Iosif aimed to "remind the Sovereign of his majesty and responsibilities and to warn him that other 'orthodox empires' had fallen due to heresy" and argued that "curbing heretics required secular authority and force."[65] Employing these same features of the saint's authoritative Discourse 16, Feodor chastened Tsar Aleksei Mikhailovich for abandoning the Orthodox ruler's sacred duties to protect the faithful from heretics. Heeding Volotskii's warnings, he surmised that the tsar, like the rulers in Iosif's Discourse 16 who allowed heresy to creep into their realms, put the Russian tsardom in jeopardy of "falling away from the apostolic church and from Orthodox

Christian belief."[66] Harkening back to Volotskii's example of the "Armenian Empire," where "when the heretics started secretly to sow the evil doctrine amongst unthinking people, first did not deceive many, but after a time they deceived many, and then they stared to sow their filthy heretical seed among the noble people, and also the boyars and the princes," the Old Believer asserted that Nikon tried "to capture the tsar by the leg and drag him to perish, and until the tsar knew about the slyness of his enemy, he, the tsar, lived according to the enemy's guidelines ... and tortured all with various evils: that happened because the tsar was accursed by Nikon and his disciples."[67] Finally, emboldened by Volotskii's core belief that heretics "should not only be condemned, but anathematized, and that tsars and princes and judges should jail them and subject them to severe punishment," [68] Feodor made what may have been his most important and daring charge: "The tsar concealed all of Nikon's wrongdoings. And let the Lord judge the tsar, because the tsar did not render justice for the deeds of Nikon the heretic." Thus, he concluded, "there is no good judge on earth among the people now when we have the last days before the end of the ages."[69]

Conclusions

Although not so blatantly obvious in his borrowings from Iosif Volotskii as Patriarch Nikon, Feodor Ivanov was no less thorough in integrating Volotskii's work into his complex attack on the patriarch. The comparative analysis offered in this essay demonstrates that rather than simply citing Iosif's *Enlightener* in his "About the Wolf," Feodor deeply ingrained the saint's teachings into his representations of Nikon and the patriarch's opponents as well as the Russian clerical elite and Tsar Aleksei Mikailovich. Feodor recognized the significance for his own day of Iosif's writings about the "Novgorod Heretics" and employed Volotskii's method of exposing their supposed secret transgressions against God, His Church and its saints against Nikon. In short, the Old Believer's charges against Nikon, the evidence Feodor offered to support them and the way he presented his case can all be traced to Iosif's *Enlightener*. On the one hand, Iosif's "The Account of the Recent Heresy of the Novgorod Heretics," provided distinct historical contexts essential to the conception and advancement of the notion that the patriarch was judaizing heretic. On the other hand, the saint's discourses served as the Old Believer's primer for revealing and condemning Nikon's heresies and for reproving the Russian and tsar for failing to act against the dire threats they posed to Russian Orthodoxy.

Feodor recounted the patriarch's alleged transgressions as well as how and why others reacted or should have reacted to them in terms of Iosif's *Enlightener*. The Old Believer embodied Iosif's accusations against the "Novgorod Heretics" in Nikon, supporting his ultimate charge that Nikon was the "forerunner of the Antichrist" by repeating many of the same accusations Iosif leveled against his enemies in general, and Metropolitan Zosima in particular. Feodor's Nikon reprised his predecessors' abuses of the Cross and icons (Discourse 6) and attacks on the saints and their miracles (Discourse 10), as well as rejected and attacked the saint's conceptions of the "monastic habit" (Discourse 11). Most importantly, Feodor's carefully packed catalog of Nikon's alleged abuses of Volotskii in "About Iosif of Volokolamsk" represents a remarkable and telling synopsis of saint's core teachings. In making Nikon Iosif's enemy, Feodor counted himself among the saint's followers.

Ivanov also presented Nikon's opponents, including himself, as exemplifying Iosif's doctrines. Feodor invested Volotskii's ideals in monastic witnesses who were well-versed in the details of Iosif's *Enlightener* and faithfully adhered to the saint's instructions. The monks both recognized Nikon's heresies as identified in Discourses 6 and 10 and personally rejected them in accordance with the specific proscriptions defined by Iosif in Discourse 13. Moreover, the monastics honored the saint's demands and self-described example by exposing Nikon's crimes "from below" despite the threat of and/or enduring patriarch's "torments." Thus, the author embraced and promoted Volotskii's image of monastics, joined by pious laymen, as the preeminent defenders of the True Faith against heretics.

Feodor conversely portrayed what he perceived as the official failures to act against Nikon's heresies as replays of the historical precedents narrated in Iosif cautionary "Tale." Most likely reacting to the flagrant official dismissal of accusations of Nikon's judaizing on the eve of the patriarch's trial in 1666, Feodor pilloried the hierarchy of his day as just as he thought the saint did in regards to their fifteenth-century counterparts. Recalling Iosif's examples of "Orthodox Empires" felled by heresy in what he believed to be the "End of Days," and upholding the authority of the saint's teaching about the Orthodox rulers' duty to "condemn and severely punish heretics," in Discourses 13 and 16," he dared to charge Aleksei Mikhailovich with failing to provide justice.

While establishing the central place of Iosif's *Enlightener* in Feodor Ivanov's "About the Wolf," the findings presented here raise new questions about the saint's broader impact on the early Old Believers' thought beyond condemnations of the "Nikonian reforms," especially in regards to the dangers of alleged judaizing. In doing so, the essay opens the study of the origins of Old Believer anti-Judaic rhetoric and stereotypes for the first time. It is tempting at this point to speculate that what Georg Michels determined as the early Old Believers' fear that the Russian Church could be taken over by Jews may be tracked directly to Iosif's *Enlightener*.[70] However, the verification of this hypothesis will require further comparative analysis of Volotskii's work and earlier Old Believer polemics, including not only the writings of Bishop Aleksandr of Viatka discussed above, but also the discourses of others such as Spiridon Potemkin. This new line of investigation will help determine whether Feodor was an innovator in adopting Iosif's anti-Judaic discourse, or if he absorbed and advanced a practice developed by earlier Old Believer followers of Volotskii.

Abbreviations

AfED: *Antifeodal'nye ereticheskie dvizheniia na Rusi XIV-nachala XVI veka.* Edited by N. A. Kazakova and Ia. S. Lur'e. Moscow-Leningrad: Izdatel'stvo Akademii nauk SSSR, 1955.

BAN: Biblioteka Akademii nauk.

MIRPVS: *Materialy dlia istorii raskola za pervoe vremia ego sushchestvivaniia*, 9 vols. Edited by N. I. Subbotin. Moscow and St. Petersburg: 1875-1895.

MRIV: *The Monastic Rule of Iosif Volotsky*, rev. ed. Cistercian Studies 36.

Translated and edited by David Goldfrank. Kalamazoo: Cistercian Publications, 2000.
NSAW: *Nil Sorsky: The Authentic Writings.* Cistercian Studies 221. Translated and edited by David Goldfrank. Kalamazoo: Cistercian Publications, 2008.
PIV: *Poslaniia Iosifa Volotskogo.* Edited by Ia. S. Lur'e and A. A. Zimin. Moscow-Leningrad: Izdatel'stvo Akademii nauk SSSR, 1959.

Notes

1   The idea to investigate Feodor Ivanov's connections with Iosif Volotskii emerged in response to questions raised by David Goldfank in his comments on a paper I presented to Annual Meeting of the Southern Conference of Slavic Studies in March 2012. I thank David for that original inspiration, the related discussions and the thoughtful editorial suggestions that shaped this essay. I also gratefully acknowledge Georg Michels for his constructive critique of this project, as well as his enduring support of and many contributions to my efforts to better understand the early Old Believers, especially Feodor Ivanov. Finally, I thank Nikolai Iu. Bubnov who introduced me to the manuscript copy of Feodor's work analyzed here during my research at the Library of the Academy of Science, St. Petersburg (BAN) in 2001 while on a Fulbright-Hays Dissertation Research Abroad Fellowship.
    Feodor Ivanov (d. 1682), deacon of Moscow's Blagoveshchenskii Cathedral and "spiritual son" to Archpriest Avvakum Petrov, was recognized by Subbotin in *MIRPVS*, 6.3: vi, as "undoubtedly one of the most remarkable of the early Old Believer writers," and by Titova, 227, as "one of the most dangerous opponents for the Nikonians." On Ivanov's life and literary activities, see *MIRPVS*, 6.3: v-xxvii; N. Iu. Bubnov, *Staroobriadcheskaia kniga v Rossii vo vtoroi polovine XVII v.* (St. Petersburg: BAN, 1995), 60-68; Georg Michels, *At War with the Church* (Stanford: Stanford University Press, 1999), 90-96; L. V. Titova and A. T. Shashkov, "Feodor Ivanov," in *Slovar' knizhnikov i knizhnosti drevnei Rusi*, 8 vols. in 4, edited by Dmitrii S. Likhachev et al., (St. Petersburg: Dmitri Bulanin, 1987-2012), 4.3: 92-101.
2   The following analysis is based on the version of "*O volke i khishchnike*" from the 1670s *Pustozerskii sbornik*. It is recognized as the earliest version of "About the Wolf" and is attributed to Feodor Ivanov by N. Iu. Bubnov, *Staroobriadcheskaia kniga*, 243-244. The manuscript

was published in L. V. Titova, "Skazanie o patriarkhe Nikone—publitsisticheskii traktat pustozerskikh uznikov," in *Istoriia russkoi dukhovoi kul'tury v rukopisnom nasledii XVI-XX vv.*, edited by E. K. Romodanovskaia (Novosibirsk: "Nauka," Sibirskoe predpriiatie RAN, 1998), 213-237.

3   Eighteenth-century redations of Feodor's text were published in *MIRPVS*, 6.3: 299-302, and V. N. Peretts, *Slukhi i tolki o patriarkhe Nikone v literaturnoi obrabotke piselei XVII-XVIII vv.* (St. Petersburg: Akademiia Nauk, 1900), 164-167. For the impact of the tales about Nikon originating in Feodor's "About the Wolf" on later Old Believer authors and complilers, see Bubnov, *Staroobriadcheskaia kniga*, 243-245; Idem, "Rukopisnoe nasledie pusterzerskikh uznikov (1667-1682 gg.)," in *Knigotorgovoe i bibliotechnoe delo v Rossii v XVII-pervoi polovine XIX v.*, edited by S. V. Paramonova and S. P. Luppov (Leningrad: BAN, 1981), 69-84; Titova, "Skazanie o patriarkhe Nikone," 227-232; Kevin Kain, "A Comparative, Semiological and Iconographical Analysis of the Tales about Patriarch Nikon Inspired by the 'Life of Kornilii'," in *Mir staroobriadchestva*, 6 vols. to date, edited by I. V. Pozdeeva and E., V. Smilianskaia (Iaroslavl: Izdatel'stvo Remder), 6 (2008), 141-168; idem, "Reading between the (Confessional) Lines: The Intersection of Old Believer Book and Russian Print Cultures," in *The Space of the Book in Russia's Social Imagination*, edited by Miranda Remnek (Toronto: University of Toronto Press, 2010), 165-200.

4   See, for example N. I. Subbotin, *Delo patriarkha Nikona* (Moscow: Tipografiia V. Grachev i ko., 1862), 2-7; N. Gibbenet, *Istoricheskoe issledovanie dela patriarkha Nikona*, 2 pts (St. Petersburg: Tipografiia Ministerstva vnutrennikh del, 1882-1884), 1: i-iv. B. A. Rybakov, "Voinstvuiushchie tserkovniki XVI v," *Antireligioznik* 4 (1934): 26-27, explained that "Nikon, according to the words of his contemporaries, 'insulted the saintly father Iosif Volotskii, called him a slanderer and did not bow down to the image of the saint,'" cited by Ia. S. Lur'e in *PIV*, 97, who accepted the same reference; see also David Goldfrank, "Introduction," in *Essays in Russian Monasticism*, edited by Goldfrank = *Russian History* 39.1-2 (2012): 9.

5   Nikon's "Spiritual Will" was published and analyzed by S. K. Sevast'ianova, "Dukhovnoe zaveshchanie patriarkha Nikona," in *Patriarkha Nikon i ego vremia. Sbornik nauchnykh trudov*, edited by E. M. Iukhimenko (Moscow: Gosudarstvennyi istoricheskii muzei, 2004), 226-247. See also G. M. Zelenskaia, "Obitel' predpodobnogo Iosifa Volotskogo i monastyri sviateishego patriarkha Nikona XVII-XXI vv.," in *Predpodobnyi Iosif Volotskii i ego obitel'*, edited by Igumen Sergii (Voronkov), Monakh Panteleimon (Demenenko), G. M.

Zelenskaia (Moscow: Severnyi palomnik, 2008), 69-70; and Goldfrank, "Introduction," 9n32, who "recognized immediately that this text [Nikon's "*Dukhovnoe zaveschanie*"] was mostly a new redaction of the Introduction and *Slovo* [Discourse] 1 of Iosif's Extended Rule." Sevast'ianova, 232-233, and Zelenskaia, 68, refuted Feodor's Iosif-related charges against Nikon.

6   See Goldfrank's "Hagiographic and Historic Portrait," for a thorough and very useful overview of Iosif's times, life and thought, his introductory essay to this volume, and the most recent review of Iosif's life in A. I. Alekseev, *Sochineniia Iosifa Volotskogo v kontekste polemiki 1480-1510-kh gg.* (St. Petersburg: Rossiiskaia natsional'naia biblioteka, 2010), 14-64.

7   I compared Feodor's "About the Wolf" with Paisius Ligarides' *History of the Condemnation of the Patriarch Nikon* (1667) in "Patriarch Nikon's Image in Russian History and Culture" (Ph. D. dissertation, Western Michigan University, 2004), 261-278.

8   Feodor Ivanov, "*O volke i khishchnike i bogootmetnike Nikone dostoverno svidetel'stvo,izhe byst" pastyre vo ovchei kozhi, predotecha antikhristov*," in BAN, Sobranie Druzhinina, No. 746 (790) *Pustozerskii sbornik* (1790s), folia 86v-90v.

9   Feodor, "*O volke i khishchnike*," folia 86v-89.

10 The former is the primary contention set forth in Iosif's "Discourse 11," the latter in the "Account:" *Prosvetitel'*, 45-46, 406-464; also *AfED*, 474.

11 This trope appeared in the attacks on Metropolitans Isidor and his alleged "disciple" Gregory the Bulgarian in the 1450s-1470s during Moscow's rivalry with the Lithuanian supported separate metropolitanate of Kiev. See, for example, *Russkii feodal'nyi arkhiv XIV-pervoi treti XVI veka*, edited by Andrei Pliguzov (Moscow: Iazyki slavianskikh kul'tur, 2008), 159-61 (No. 34: Metropolitan Iona to Archbishop Iona of Novgorod, April-March, 1459).

12 *Prosvetitel'*, 35 ("Account"); *AfED*, 470.

13 Goldfrank explained that, "in his defense of the general principle of Orthodoxy," Iosif upheld "the validity of the Fathers, the Apostles, and the Gospel, given the fact that the '7000th year' (1492) and hence the 'last age' was about to have passed or had arrived without the Second Coming or the World ending as predicted in some prestigious writings:" *MRIV*, 34. The association of judaizing with the coming of the Antichrist is an ancient trope. Goldfrank also pointed out that, in his *Sobornik*, Nil Sorskii "retained from the original Life of Euthymius the characterization of Nestorians as 'Jewish-reasoning' (*zhidovomudreni*) and of the Monophysite Theodosius as 'precursing the Antichrist:'" *NSAW*, 28n105.

14 *Prosvetitel'*, 16: 542-544.
15 *Prosvetitel'*, 47 ("Account") = *AfED*, 475. I thank David Goldfrank for supplying this and subsequent translations from Iosif's *Enlightener*, which are based on his current research and book project.
16 *Prosvetitel'*, 47-48 ("Account") = *AfED*, 475.
17 Serge Zenkovsky, *Russkoe staroobriadchestvo* (Munich: Wilhelm Fink Verlag, 1970), 350-351, 364; Bubnov, *Staroobriadcheskaia Kniga*, 90-91, 348; see also *MRIV*, 47.
18 Sevast'ianova, "Dukhovnoe zaveshchanie Patriarkha Nikona," 232.
19 See, for example, Feodor Ivanov, *Otvet Pravoslavnykh* (Moscow: Staroobriadcheskoe izdatel'stvo "Tretii Rim," 2005), 17, 32.
20 The text is published in *MIRPVS*, 6.3: 192-250; for the references to Iosif, see, for example, 206.
21 The text is published in *MIRPVS*, 6.3: 269-298; for the reference to Iosif, 271.
22 Georg Michels, *At War with the Church*, 4, 32, established that early Old Believer authors "wrote almost exclusively about Nikon's liturgical revisions and their religious implications" and, 90, that "Ivanov's most important contribution was his work with texts critical of the Nikonian revisions."
23 See, for example, *Prosvetitel'*, 46 ("Account"), 13-15: 475-526; *AfED*, 471, 488-498, 501-503.
24 Bubnov, *Staroobriadcheskaia kniga*, 88-92 and *MRIV*, 34.
25 *Prosvetitel'*, 34-35 ("Account") = *AfED*, 470.
26 *Prosvetitel'*, 43 ("Account") = *AfED*, 473; Feodor, "O volke i khishchnike," f. 85v.
27 *Prosvetitel'*, 42 ("Account"), also 15: 519 (concerning Arhimandrite Kassian of Iur'ev Monastery in Novgorod); *AfED*, 425 ("Iosif to Bishop Nifont of Suzdal: also *PIV*, 161), 473; Feodor, "O volke i khishchnike," folia 85v, 88, 90v.
28 *MIRPVS*, 6.3: 206. In "Discourse 12" of the *Enlightener* Iosif wrote "against the heresy of the Novgorod Heretics, who say that if a heretic is a hierarch, and he de-blesses or anathematizes one of the Orthodox, divine judgment follows upon his judgment. Here is the testimony from the Divine Writings, that if a heretic is a hierarch, and he de-blesses or anathematizes one of the Orthodox, divine judgment does not follow upon his judgment:" David Goldfrank, "Adversus Haeriticos Novgorodensos: Iosif Volotskii's Rhetorical Syllogisms," in *Dubitando: Studies in History and Culture in Honor of Donald Ostrowski*, edited by Brian Boek, Russell Martin, and Daniel Rowland (Bloomington, IN: Slavica, 2012), 249-250.
29 See *Prosvetitel'*, 38, 42-46 ("Account") = *AfED*, 471, 473-474.

30 On Feodor's repressions, imprisonments and corporal punishments see Bubnov, *Staroobriadcheskaia kniga,* 63; Titova and Shashkov, "Skazanie o patriarkhe Nikone," 93-94. Referencing Feodor's corporal punishments Avvakum explained that "they cut out his whole tongue, but left a little bit in his mouth... It healed just as it was at the time, but later on it grew again as before... and they cut off his hand across the palm. By the gift of God it all healed, and he spake clearly and cleanly as before:" *Medieval Russia's Epics, Chronicles, and Tales,* rev. ed., edited by Serge Zenkovsky (New York: Meridian, 1974), 445-446.

31 See, for example, *Prosvetitel',* 38, 42-46 ("Account"), 15: 516-517, 522; *AfED,* 471, 473-474.

32 See, for example, *Prosvetitel',* 45-46 ("Account"), 15: 521-522; *AfED,* 474.

33 Feodor, "O volke i khishchnike," folia 85-88: Feodor attributed the second witness account to "a pupil of Nikon's named Andrean" who "lived with Nikon for many years before he became patriarch." Like Kirik, Andrean discovered that Nikon concealed a cross and image of the Holy Virgin in his footwear. However, unlike Kirik, "monk Andrean was very scared and conceived a hatred for this person with the Lord's mark. From this moment, Andrean began to argue with Nikon for any reason. He could not condemn him because he was afraid he would lose his head and his tormentor beat him many times for this arguing and once he was very vicious and himself locked him in irons and poured molten tin on them and ordered him imprisoned in Paleostrovskii Monastery ... . Andrean himself told this to his spiritual father, the priest and monk Feodosii and he also told all about this precursor of the Antichrist Nikon to me."

34 *Prosvetitel',* 43-44 ("Account") = *AfED,* 473), presents Zosima as a "filthy and evilly demonic wolf dressed in pastor's clothes" immediately before charging him with blaspheming Christ and the Holy Virgin and with putting crosses in "unclean places."

35 *Prosvetitel',* 44 ("Account") = *AfED,* 473: In "Discourse 15," Iosif also charged that the heretic Iurka "placed holy icons under his bed and slept on them:" *Prosvetitel',* 521. While not copied by Feodor, later Old Believer authors, apparently building on this same reference, claimed that one of Nikon's monks "uncovered" an upside down cross in Nikon's bed. For analysis of this later tale, see Kain, "Patriarch Nikon's Image," 371-374.

36 *Prosvetitel',* 13: 479-480 = *AfED,* 489: Iosif has Chrysostom continue with: "Even if someone lives the life of the incorporeal beings, if he communicates in friendship or love with heretics, he will be alien to Christ the Master."

37 *MRIV*, 101. This is implicit in Iosif's "Account" and explicit in "Discourses 13-14" of the *Enlightener*: *Prosvetitel'*, 45-46, 485, 503-509; *AfED*, 474, 491-492, 501-503.
38 Feodor, "*O volke i khishchnike*," folia 88v-89v. Accordingly, Feodor wrote, *inter alia*: "Nikon called holy fools 'mad saints' and did not give permission to depict their faces on icons."
39 Feodor, "*O volke i khishchnike*," folia 88v-89v.
40 For example, *Prosvetitel'*, 39 ("Account"); *AfED*, 471.
41 Feodor, "*O volke i khishchnike*," folia 89-89v. This passage repeats the charges that pseudo-Vassian Patrinkeev has Iosif make against Nil and Vassian in *Prenie s Iosifom*. See N. A. Kazakova, *Vassian Patrikeev e ego sochinenii* (Moscow-Leningrad: Izdatel'stvo Akademiia nauk SSSR, 1960), 280; *NSAW*, 29; and also Donald Ostrowski's contribution to this volume.
42 Iosif claimed that "they blasphemed Saint Ephrem's writings, saying that his writings [about the end of time in the year 7000] are false ... and they not only reproached the writings of Saint Ephrem, but they reproached all the divine, patristic writings:" *Prosvetitel'*, 34-35 ("Account"), 383= *AfED*, 470. On Iosif's broader use of Ephrem's writings see *MRIV*, 27, 34; *PIV*, 72.
43 *AfED*, 428; *PIV*, 161.
44 *Prosvetitel'*, 10: 383.
45 *Prosvetitel'*, 11: 450; *MRIV*, 64, 68, 94, 110, 111, 114, 129, 131, 144, 159: Ephrem is cited as a source twice in the section of Iosif's *Rule* that Nikon copied into his "Spiritual Will:" *MRIV*, 64, 68; Sevast'ianova, "Dukhovnoe zaveshchanie Patriarkha Nikona," 238-240.
46 *Prosvetitel'*, 34 ("Account") = *AfED*. 470. The eighteenth-century "Vyg redaction" of "About Iosif Volokolamsk" specified that Nikon "did not bow down before his [Iosif's] image" ("*ne poklanialsia obraztsu ego emu*"). See Peretts, *Slukhi i tolki o patriarkhe Nikone*, 166; Titova, "Skazanie o patriarkhe Nikone," 229-230. However, Feodor's charge could also be an attempt to refute the fact that Nikon actually visited Iosifo-Volokolamsk Monastery in early November 1656 and prayed "before the saints". If this was the case, Feodor would be in keeping with Iosif's teaching concerning the adoration of relics in "Discourse 7." See, for example, *Prosvetitel'*, 274-275; *AfED*, 342. On Nikon's visit to Volokolamsk, see *Pokhod velikago gosudaria sviatieishago Nikona, patriarkha moskovskago, vseia velikiia, malyia i belyia Rossii v 1656 g.*, edited by A. K. Zhiznevskii (Tver': Tip. Gubernskago pravleniia, 1889), 21; Zelenskaia, "Obitel' predpodobnogo Iosifa Volotskogo," 68.
47 See *Prosvetitel'*, 6-7: 219-342, passim = *AfED*, 325-360, passim; cf. Alekseev, *Sochineiia Iosif Volotskogo*, 242-247.

48 *Prosvetitel'*, 6: 275 = *AfED*, 341-342.
49 Of the twelve monastics named according to the previous *Sluzhebnik* of 1646 only Sergii of Radonezh (Trinity-Sergius Monastery) and Varlaam of Khutyn' (Khutynskii Spaso-Preobrazhenskii Varlaamiev Monastery) remained. Those eliminated from the commemoration, were Antonii and Feodosii (Kiev-Pecherskii Monastery) Kirill (Kirillo-Belozerskii Monastery), Nikon (Trinity-Sergius Monastery), Dmitri of Prilutsk (Spaso-Prilutskii Monastery), Nikita of Pereiaslavl (Nikitskii Monastery) and Zosima and Sabbatii (Solovetskii Monastery). See Meyendorff, 138-150, for a point by point comparison of the rite as presented in the 1646 and 1655 editions of the *Sluzhebnik*.
50 Feodor, *Otvet Pravoslavnykh*, 32. Iosif did not write explicitly about the "Moscow Heretics," but used "Novgorod Heretics" for accused dissidents in both cities. The addition of "Moscow Heretics" is apparently Feodor's invention.
51 Feodor, "O volke i khishchnike," f. 89v.
52 *Prosvetitel'*, 51 ("Account"), 11: 405; *AfED*, 476. Iosif conversely explained that "... St. Peter the apostle imparted the monastic life, ... And all who lived the monastic life wore this habit for all the years they were our reverend and God-bearing fathers, living in monasteries and hermitages, and they performed miracles and were worthy of great gifts from God:" *Prosvetitel'* 11: 424, 431-432. Goldfrank clarifies that no other sources collaborate Iosif's claim that the "heretics" assailed Russian monasticism: *MRIV*, 34.
53 *Prosvetitel'*, 35, 51-52 ("Account"), 11: 405, 435; *AfED*, 470, 476.
54 *Prosvetitel'*, 51 ("Account"), 11: 405 = *AfED*, 476.
55 Feodor, "O volke i khishchnike," folia 89v-90.
56 Feodor, "O volke i khishchnike," folio 90. This charge may also be considered as an adoption of Iosif's teaching on the unique nature of the "Church in Jerusalem" in "Discourse 3:" *Prosvetitel'*, 120-138.
57 William Palmer *The Patriarch and the Tsar*, 6 vols. (London: Trubner, 1871–1876), 1: xxviii.
58 Gibbenet, *Istoricheskoe issledovanie*, 2: 18-27.
59 Gibbenet, *Istoricheskoe issledovanie*, 2: 25.
60 On Bishop Aleksandr's impact as a "founder of Old Belief" and Feodor's central place in the bishop's circle, see Michels, *At War with the Church*, 77-96, esp. 90-96.
61 See "Resolution by the Patriarchs of Alexandria and Antioch about the Deposition of Nikon Patriarch of Moscow from the Patriarchal Throne" in Gibbenet, *Istoricheskoe issledovanie*, 2: 1093–1097; *Sobranie gosudarstvennykh gramot i dogovorov, khraniashikhsia v Gosudarstvennoi kollegii inostrannykh del*, 5 vols. (Moscow: Tipografiia Selivanovskago, 1813-1894), 4: 182–186 (No. 53).

62 Subbotin, *Delo*, 216-217; Palmer, *Patriarch and* Tsar, 4: 624.
63 This assessment follows Georg Michels's conclusion that the early Old Believers in Bishop Aleksandr's circle "were appalled by these [church] lords' failure to abide by what were considered basic moral principles. As a result all of Aleksandr's supporters shared one dominant concern that they voiced in their letters, petitions and short treatises: the Russian Orthodox Church had become corrupt and ... was in need of urgent reform; otherwise, the church would be taken over by Catholics or Jews:" *At War with the Church*, 101.
64 *MIRPVS*, 6.3: 206. Nikon was charged with falsely anathematizing his opponents in the 1660s. See, for example, Palmer 1, xxxi, and the comparison to Iosif's implicit and explicit attacks on Metropolitan Zosima in this regard: *Prosvetitel'*, 45-46 ("Account"), 12: 465-474; *AfED*, 430-433; 474; *PIV*, 165-168; Goldfrank, "Adversus Haereticos Novgorodensos," 246-262.
65 *MRIV*, 37, 102.
66 *Prosvetitel'*, 16: 543-544.
67 *Prosvetitel'*, 16: 542-543; Feodor, *"O volke i khishchnike,"* f. 93.
68 See, for example, *Prosvetitel'*, 13:473 = *AfED*, 488.
69 Feodor, *"O volke i khishchnike,"* folio 89. Titova, "Skazanie o patriarkhe Nikone," 227, concludes that the idea that Tsar Aleksei Mikhailovich failed to act against Nikon's heresies was "most important for the author."
70 Michels, *At War with the Church*, 101.

9 "Their Prayer Is Reaching God…"
Old Believers and Icons in 18th-Century Russia

Evgeny Grishin

26 – 18th c. Old Believer (Vyg Community) small copper triptych of the Deesis (The Virgin and John the Baptist interceding before Jesus for souls of the faithful).

Introduction

In 1783, peasant Savva Belykh, a newly converted Old Believer from the South Viatka region in Russia, was arrested and interrogated for his "unorthodox" religious views. During the investigation by the Kukarka district ecclesiastical board, Belykh openly admitted that he did not venerate "newly painted icons" at home, nor anywhere else, and he did not intend to do so anymore, because "he does not know who painted them. He is sure that they are painted by beard shavers (*britousy*),[1] tobacco consumers, and drunkards."[2] Savva's brother Feofil, who was also jailed for his "schismatic" views, repeated the same statement and added that "he does not want to venerate even old painted icons, because they are venerated by pinchers (*shchepotniki*), that is the ones who make the sign of the cross with three fingers; instead, he venerates icons cast from copper, and he intends to continue to do so."[3]

The Belykh brothers belonged to the priestless branch of the dissident religious movement that arose within the Russian Orthodox Church after the controversial liturgical reforms of Nikon, the Patriarch of Moscow (1652-1666). The changes in the liturgical texts were seemingly formal, however, were perceived by some clerics and laity alike as the signs of the imminent Apocalypse. Soon civil and ecclesiastical authorities labeled the opponents of the reforms as "schismatics" and the whole of the movement as the "Schism," while dissenters themselves preferred to use terms Old Believers and Old Belief.[4]

The largest oppositional movement in the millennium-long history of the Russian Orthodox Church, Old Belief did not resemble the European Reformation of the 16th century or earlier heresies in the Roman Catholic Church. The main reason is that Old Believers did not create an alternative to the official Orthodox Church doctrine, even though already in the end of the 17th century they broke up into numerous very diverse groups and sects. For example, the most radical of Old Believers, adherents of its priestless (*bespopovtsy*) branch that abandoned the priesthood, did not reject the sacrament of ordination per se. Rather, they rejected the possibility of the rightful priesthood in the world which they thought was ruled by the Antichrist. Similarly, Old Believers did not abandon the Orthodox tradition of icon veneration.

Why did the brothers invoke icon veneration in defense of their new confessional affiliation then? And why did they venerate some icons and refuse to worship others? Did they simply prefer Old Believer icons to the ones used in the official church? In this paper I thoroughly examine religious imagery and attitudes to it among Old Believers in the South Viatka region in the end of the eighteenth century. I argue that for local religious dissenters the question of which icons to venerate was directly related to the problems of soteriology and identity. On the one hand, icons played a central role in their spiritual life as a way for communication with God. On the other, the adherence or rejection of a specific type of iconic images shaped their identity as members of a community of "true

Christians." In both of these contexts the perception of icons was not just symbolic, as scholars often assume, but even more so material – iconic images were tangible devices of communication to the deity and manifestation of an identity.[5]

Russian Old Believers and Icon-Painting

Just as for other adherents of Russian Orthodoxy, icons and their veneration occupied a significant, if not central, place in religious life of Old Believers. The difference between Old Believers' and official Orthodox icons traditionally was perceived as lying in the sphere of aesthetics. It is well known that in the second half of the 17th century, a new trend in icon-painting spread in the official Russian church's workshops. More and more artisans were inspired by the Baroque style, adopted from Roman Catholic religious painting, and they started to create images in a more natural manner.[6] In this innovation the first Old Believers saw not just new artistic techniques but the sign of the loss of old Orthodoxy in general. They perceived changes as a departure from the principles of the Russian Church that were so clearly expressed in the *Stoglav*, a codex of the mid-16th century Moscow Church Council of the same name, highly respected among Orthodox believers.[7] A famous statement about icon-painting made by archpriest Avvakum, one of the first of the Old Believers' leaders, vividly conveys the attitude of his followers towards the westernization of iconic art. Avvakum described a newly painted icon of the Savior he saw as follows: "painted with a plump face, red lips, curly hair, fat arms and muscles, thick fingers and likewise the legs with thick hips, and altogether make him look like a German, big-bellied and fat, except that no sword is painted at the hip."[8]

In spite of devout adherence to old ways, during the 18th century, Old Believers' communities developed their own icon-painting schools with distinct artistic styles.[9] The priestless Old Believers of Pomor'e, in the North of European Russia, became especially successful at it.[10] They clearly manifested the commitment to the old Russian tradition of icon-painting as constituted in the articles of the *Stoglav* Council of 1551. According to the Council, and Old Believers, who appealed to its decisions, artisans should not rely on their own judgment; instead, they should "paint icons from ancient images, as Greek artists painted and as Andrei Rublev and other famous artists did."[11] Participants of the *Stoglav* also noted the significance of good morals on the part of the icon-painters. Church hierarchs proclaimed in one of the articles:

> it is right for an icon painter to be humble, gentle, reverential, no lover of vain speech or of mockery, not peevish, not envious, not drunken, not a robber, not a murderer. And he should preserve to a high degree spiritual and bodily purity, taking the utmost pains.[12]

Similarly, priestless Old Believers paid serious attention to the morals of icon painters; at the same time, what was even more significant for them, the icon-painter had to belong to their specific *soglasie* (literally "concordance," a term often used by Old Believers for a religious group) with very few exceptions.[13] The same rule concerned the icons cast from copper, that became especially popular among Russian priestless Old Believers, specifically Pomortsy and Fedoseevtsy,[14] in the 18th century. Started in 1720s, the Vyg community of Pomortsy *soglasie* by the end of the century produced and distributed a vast range of copper images and crosses for different types of use: from body crosses to Deesis compositions for iconostases.[15] As leaders of Fedoseevtsy stated in the rules of own church council of 1752, "Cast [from copper] images [could be] acquired from Christians [i.e. from Fedoseevtsy] or from Pomortsy, while from Nikonians copper [images] should not be accepted nor venerated."[16]

Many of 18th-century Viatka Old Believers, including the Belykh brothers and their fellows, belonged to the Fedoseevtsy *soglasie*. It is not surprising, therefore, that they shared a devotion to copper icons and negatively perceived images used in the official Orthodox Church. Due to the nature of the sources, the study of Viatka Old Believers' attitude towards iconic images helps to explain the relations of Old Believers with their icons in more depth. In other words, the analysis of the 18th-century court cases concerning local communities of believers will disclose a more complex understanding of the role of icons in the "lived Old Belief."

Consequently, this article is not about the doctrinal understanding of icons by the Old Belief; instead, it investigates the practice of dealing with iconic images among the people who identified themselves with one of the Old Believer groups.

Viatka Old Believers and their Icons

I began this paper by recounting how the priestless Old Believers, Savva and Feofil Belykh, refused to venerate "newly painted icons" in favor of copper ones because they were concerned that the painters were "pinchers," beard shavers, tobacco consumers (*tabashniki*), and drunkards.[17] The Belykh brothers were not the only Viatka Old Believers who displayed such an attitude towards icons. In 1786 another Old Believer from the same region, the widow Paraskeva Grigor'eva, admitted that she did not want to return to the official Church and to venerate icons "painted on [wooden] boards," because people who attend this church "pray with the pinch," and also "tobacco consumers and beard shavers" are allowed in it.[18] Forty-five Old Believers revealed similar viewpoints after they were arrested and interrogated in the Urzhum district (South Viatka) in 1784. They stated that they would not attend church anymore, nor partake in sacraments, nor use three fingers in the sign of cross; they also refused to venerate "icons of the Savior and the Most Holy Mother of God and other Holy Saints that were in the church and drawn with paints."[19]

Why did these peasant Old Believers reject worshipping icons that were "painted?" And why would they prefer icons "founded from copper?" Apparently, they strictly followed the rules of Fedoseevtsy *soglasie*, introduced to them by the Kazan' merchant Aleksei Kozhevnikov.[20] Even the icons made from copper but probably by an official Orthodox craftsman had to be rejected as these rules suggested. That is why, in 1783 another Viatka Old Believer and friend of Savva Belykh, Kondratii Postnikov, criticized copper icons, which he saw in the house of his acquaintance, the peasant Vasilii Ziablitsev. In regard to Ziablitsev Postnikov said: "The icons are very good, however, they are made with impure hands, and he should not bow before them."[21] Postnikov also criticized crosses worn by believers on their necks as "unclean"

27 – 18th c. Old Believer (Vyg Community) small copper triptych with the Tikhvin Bogomater, the Vernicle (Christ's face "uncreated by hand"), and Sts. Sergii Radonezhskii and Varlaam Khutynskii.

and encouraged to exchange them for good ones.[22] To my mind this not only is evidence that Viatka Old Believers were obedient to their spiritual leaders, but also suggests that they perceived iconic images (alongside other holy artifacts) in a very peculiar way. In other words, local Old Believers were concerned about the physical purity of icons that they interacted with.

Archival case studies reveal not only commentaries about icons, but also their presence in the practice of local Old Believers. By the beginning of the 1790s there were two Old Believers' centers in South Viatka. They included everything necessary for the full religious life of priestless *soglasie*: a chapel used for baptisms, public prayers, and readings of ecclesiastical books; a cemetery; and an almshouse. The physical manifestations of Old Believers' communities, those chapels, cemeteries, and almshouses, incorporated people who served at these facilities: spiritual leaders of the community, overseeing the chapel and directing prayers and rites, alongside conventuals.[23] The last category consisted of mostly old or handicapped people who chose to live in the almshouse in order to save their souls through service at the cemetery and the chapel.

Among other things necessary for ecclesial life, the chapels at both Viatka Old Believers' centers included *iconostases*, that is the wall consisting of icons in special order and of a specific type that separates the altar area from the rest of the building. A chapel in the village called Turek had only a few icons; however their choice demonstrated the traditional preferences of Russian Orthodox believers. There was the Deesis, the central element of any iconostasis that depicted Christ Pantocrator, the Mother of God, and St. John the Baptist, placed within a gold-plated copper frame. In addition, it contained three Marian icons of different types - Our Lady of Kazan, Our Lady of Smolensk, and Our Lady of the Sign.[24] All of these icons were painted "in their [Old Believers'] way," as Damian Petrov, an official Orthodox archpriest, noted in 1797.[25]

The iconostasis in the second Old Believers' chapel situated near the village called Krasnaia Gorka was richer in icons and utensils. The community this chapel served was bigger than the first one: the Turek chapel community included several dozen families from two areas of the Urzhum district,[26] while the chapel in Krasnaia Gorka was a center for hundreds of families from at least eight areas of the Nolinsk district.[27] The composition of the iconostasis in that chapel is very revealing. It included three levels of images: the lowest level was composed of "icons of the Twelve Great Feasts and some other saints;" the second level consisted of "diverse small wooden and copper icons;" the third and the highest level contained "big old church icons of the Christ, the Virgin, the Forerunner, and Apostles, all of them with copper crowns."[28] The official Orthodox priest Daniil Popov made this description in 1798. He visited the chapel with the permission of this community spiritual leader Iosif Beznosikov. In the report about the chapel Daniil Popov characterized its interior as "adorned with the church-like splendor."[29]

The priests' perceptions of iconostases in both of the chapels are significant because they reflect the types of icons Viatka Old Believers were using. First, they utilized wooden "old-painted" icons, i.e. icons painted before the mid-17th-century Schism, or those perceived to be such icons.[30] The words "big old church icons" in Daniil Petrov's description also implied that these icons were not just ancient but also that they were painted specifically for iconostasis and not for private veneration. Previously, they had been part of the iconostasis in another church or chapel.

Second, it is very possible that Viatka Old Believers used wooden icons painted at one of the Old Belief centers, for example, at the Vyg community in the Russian North. I say "possibly" because archpriest Damian Petrov may have judged old painted icons to be "schismatic," for example, because saints on them were depicted with the two-fingered sign of the cross. The third fact about Old Believers' icons is that one of their chapels included images founded in copper alongside icons drawn "in paints" and on "[wooden] boards." Obviously, Viatka Old Believers denied verbally that they venerated non-copper icons, but in practice they did so.

Apparently, the issue was not the material out of which the icons were made, but rather some other characteristics that made them acceptable or unacceptable. I argue that the main concern of Viatka Old Believers was about the physical purity of the iconic objects rather than the material of production. Savva Belykh and his co-believers worried about "pinchers," beard shavers, mother cursers, drunkards and tobacco consumers contacting their icons, because they perceived such contact to be defiling and desacralizing for holy objects.

Pinch and Beard

What specifically did Viatka Old Believers consider so unclean and apparently sinful?

The sign of the cross with two fingers became the most recognized symbol of Old Belief after 1656 when Patriarch Nikon anathematized all opponents of the changes in liturgical books and started their persecution. The Russian state used this parameter to divide its Orthodox subjects into truly "orthodox" and "schismatics:" the ones who used three fingers were considered faithful, while the ones who used two fingers automatically were labeled as "schismatics" and sometimes even "heretics." Old Believers, on their side, used the same tactics, however, in aggrandized form: for them the three fingers configured in the sign of the cross in a manner similar to a pinch, represented the power of the Antichrist and the approaching end of the world, while two fingers signified the true faith surviving in the final epoch.

The significance of the cross with two fingers for the opponents of liturgical reforms became apparent very soon after its condemnation by the church hierarchy. For example, in June, 1662, coachman from Tiumen' Petr Shadra revealed an apocalyptical message from the Mother of God. She was concerned with the new way of performing service in the churches and usage of "non-true" [i.e. with three fingers] sign of the cross and mother curses by Christians. She said that all of it corrupts the "Orthodox Christian faith" and desecrates churches. She also warned of the end of the world if Christians did not repent: "If the new way of service, introduced by heretics, will be performed in churches again, and mother curses will not be abandoned [by Christians], and [they] will start to use the sign of the cross that is not true one, the life will end soon."[31]

The objection to beard shaving had a different origin. Although often linked with Old Believers and their "backwardness," it had roots in the discourse of the traditionally oriented Russian clergy. For medieval Muscovite clerics and their flock, the beard was a symbol of God's creation, while shaving and cutting of a beard was perceived as a "Latin heresy."[32] In the 17th century, especially in its second half, the process of westernization accelerated and became apparent in some men's appearance. Many noblemen and bureaucrats adopted western (most often Polish) dress and started to shave beards as a symbol of their own progressive orientation. As a result, beardlessness became a red flag for conservative clergy who were afraid of Catholic and Protestant threats to Russian Orthodoxy.

One of the adherents of this view and a vehement opponent of beard shaving was Adrian, Patriarch of Moscow in 1690-1700, who accused beard shavers of committing a "grave and ungodly sin."[33] He saw in shaving and cutting of the beard "the corruption of the manly image adorned by God Himself;" the patriarch anathematized the practice as pagan and heretical, and I would add, essentially diabolical.[34] Tsar Peter the Great, whose reign overlapped with Adrian's tenure in the office of Patriarch, turned westernized fashion into state law by imposing in 1705 a severe financial penalty on the service men and city dwellers who refused to shave their beards and mustaches.[35] Being traditionally oriented, Old Believers shared Adrian's uncompromising view and were highly hostile to Peter's cultural transformations. Obviously, Viatka Old Believers did not differ from their cohorts.

During the Imperial period not only Old Believers, but also Russian peasants in general were very resistant to the westernized beardless appearance. As a rule, scholars attribute this resistance to the general inertness of peasant culture, finding little need to explain "peasant conservatism." However, peasants did not reject all changes, so it is worth considering why they clung so tenaciously to wearing beards. I propose that the reason could be found in icons. The fact is that all adult male saints, not to mention God the Father and Christ, were always depicted on icons with beards. By defending the wearing of beards peasants therefore were defending their likeness to God and His saints, and ultimately their Christian identity. I do not mean that peasants consciously tried to look like Jesus or saints; however, I argue that they constantly had images of ideal Christians and God Himself before their eyes, and those images were bearded.[36]

Tobacco

Another motive in Viatka Old Believers' statements, the attack on the consumption of tobacco, had a special place in Old Believers' teaching in general. During the most part of the 17th century tobacco was banned by Muscovite authorities.[37] The basis for the ban originated from practical as well as religious apprehensions. According to German traveler Adam Olearius, who visited Moscow in 1630s, Tsar Mikhail banned tobacco in 1634 for several reasons: tobacco addiction was believed to be one of the causes of idleness and impoverishment of the lower classes of Muscovite society; it proved to be a fire menace to wooden houses; and, last, tobacco smell disturbed icon veneration. In Olearius' own words: "before the ikons, which were supposed to be honored during church services with reverence and pleasant-scented things, the worshippers emitted an evil odor."[38] This observation of a foreign traveler is pertinent for the present study.

According to the "Tale of the Appearance of the Icon of Our Lady of Kazan' in Tobol'sk," covering the visions happened in the city in 1661, Metropolitan Filipp himself acknowledged the disgust of tobacco smoke by the powers of Heaven. While delivering the message from the Mother of God, Metropolitan Filipp angrily stated: "Instead of incense the air is filled with the damned colored smoke [of tobacco]; this stench is stinky and foul not only to God and his saints, but even to people."[39]

In this and a whole series of other popular texts and stories about tobacco widely circulated in the 17th and 18th centuries in Russia,[40] it is treated as a damned, ungodly plant, which possesses desacralizing powers. A particularly good example is a series of miracles associated with the icon of the Savior Not-created-by-human-hands (the Vernicle) that appeared in the village of Krasnyi Bor (Velikii Ustiug uezd) in the mid-17th century. According to the record known in numerous copies, the Mother of God several times appeared to local women in order to warn the community about immoral deeds. She was especially concerned about the use of alcohol, tobacco and mother-curses by church attendees: "drunken people should come to church and they should not drink tobacco nor curse obscenely." The Mother of God promised disastrous natural cataclysms that could destroy crops and churches if believers did not repent.[41] She fulfilled her warnings in a way when in 1641 she struck one lay tobacco consumer right before the church doors, and ten years later - a deacon who smoked.[42] The connection between the prohibition of tobacco use and the attendance in the church building is of special importance here. Obviously, the smell of tobacco coming from its consumers disturbed the icons as sacred objects and the church as a sacred place.

A legend from the same time period that portrayed tobacco as a "weed" planted by the Devil for the "deception of the God's chosen [people]" can explain this connection.[43] The story follows:

> There was a nun named Jezebel who had sinned and gave birth to a daughter. When the girl reached twelve years of age, she became possessed by the Devil, who flared up lewdness in her. She acted upon the Devil's wishes ever since, and lived in carnality for thirty years. God gave her a chance to repent, but she did not. Then God sent His angel and he made the earth divide, and the rift was thirty cubits wide. Then the earth swallowed that wanton woman, with the Devil in her belly and the cesspool of filth in her bosom. And then it rained over her grave, and on the very same spot the dirt spewed a weed.[44]

That weed was tobacco.

Later on, as legend goes, this weed dispersed among people, and God, in order to protect believers, banned them from using tobacco:

> Condemn this loathsome plant, [said angel to one of the Christian bishops], for it had been planted by Satan over the rotten body of a filthy and accursed harlot. God will ban anybody who smells this weed from His heavenly kingdom and condemn him to the eternal torment. Satan wants to fulfill his burning desire to drown the world in corruption... Whoever neglects my admonition and defies the will of God shall be forever the enemy of Our Lord. His name shall be wiped out from the Book of Life, and he shall be cast to Hell, with hands and legs tied, and the Devil will cast him in a pit full of burning brimstone.[45]

In this legend tobacco was not treated as a symbol of Hell but as its emanation in the terrestrial world. By this reason God forbade tobacco consumers to attend churches or touch holy objects. According to the story, the same Christian bishop, again through the angel, was commanded to ban tobacco consumers "from kissing icons, the Holy Cross, or the Bible, forbid them to receive the Holy Communion."[46] He also had to "prohibit them from attending the divine service until they abandon this accursed weed."[47] Tobacco consumers were even deprived from the bishop's blessing because "their putrid lips and filthy hearts are abomination to the Holy Spirit."[48]

Historian Roy Robson made a very precise observation contrasting the smell of tobacco with the smoke of incense, as he wrote, "while the smoke of incense purified icons, homes, and the faithful, tobacco would defile holy things."[49] This logic lay behind the prohibition of tobacco in 1630, as well as the Mother of God's displeasure with laymen and clergy from Tobol'sk and Krasnyi Bor. Viatka Old Believers, obviously, showed the same attitude towards tobacco and its consumers that resulted in the rejection of icons that even supposedly were touched by them.[50]

Mother Curses and Liquor

Besides the "pinch" in the sign of the cross, beard shaving, and the consumption of tobacco Viatka Old Believers named two more sinful actions that were harmful to the holiness of icons. Savva Belykh and other peasant Old Believers were opposed to drunkards in the church, while Savva's friends from the Nolinsk district of the Viatka region, Ivan Smirnov and Karp Mezentsov, in 1782 also mentioned "mother-cursers" (literally Russian *rugateli skvernomaternoi bran'iu* translated as "swearers using filthy mother curse").[51] As have been shown already, according to many visionaries, mother cursing together with the consumption of tobacco and alcohol were of especial dislike by the Mother of God.

For centuries, right until the late Imperial era, mother cursing in Russian popular culture was considered a ritualistic rather than casual practice. Relating mostly to human reproduction, it obscenely invoked fertility and maternity.[52] For that reason, for example, an apocryphal text ascribed to John Chrysostom[53] asserted that cursing insults the Mother of God, the mother of the person who is cursing, and the Mother-Earth. As a result, cursing provokes God's and the Mary's wrath as nothing else does, Chrysostom says. However, the most remarkable part of this apocryphal writing is the prohibition to attend church and kiss holy objects that is imposed on curser: "The same day as the person barked mother curses his mouth will clot with blood because of evil faith and devil stink coming from his mouth, so this person should not enter God's church that day, nor kiss the crucifix or the Gospel, nor to be given the Eucharist."[54] In one of the versions of this apocrypha among other holy objects the mother cursers were also forbidden to kiss icons.[55] Texts as cited above warned against the contact of the infernal and holy, while the wide dissemination of them suggests that the warnings had a wide and obviously receptive audience.

18th-century folk manuscripts link cursing and drinking, and also make very similar linkages to uncleanliness. As one of them, "The Story about St. Basil the Great," claims, the Mother of God herself prohibited the famous saint to consume liquor because "heady spirit keeps off the Holy Spirit as smoke keeps off bees."[56] The Mother of God, according to the manuscript, added that she could not stand these three sins most of all: adultery, heady spirit, and cursing.[57] Condemnations of alcohol and cursing in relation to the Mother of God were widely dispersed among Russian peasants in the 18th and 19th centuries especially in folk poetry.[58] The evidence about at least one hand-written manuscript concerning alcohol consumption can be found among archival documents on the books possessed by Viatka priestless Old Believers under study.[59]

Icons and Soteriology

Thus, Viatka Old Believers perceived icons not just as holy objects but also as tangible rather than metaphorical tools of their spiritual practice. This becomes obvious in some of their investigatory confessions. For example, the mother-in-law of Savva Belykh, widow Avdot'ia Dmitrieva, affirmed in 1782 that she became convinced that Old Belief is the only "Orthodox faith," while the official faith is "new and corrupted, because the church was attended by tobacco consumers and drunkards."[60] Especially important is the remark Avdot'ia made: "praying alongside them" [tobacco consumers and drunkards] is useless.[61] A similar claim is found in the testimony of another Viatka Old Believer widow, Paraskeva Grigor'eva, from 1786. She referred to the same tobacco consumers, beard shavers, and pinch users attending official church, and added: "that is why it is impossible to gain salvation [in the official church], while in the schism it can be gained."[62] In the same year 60-years old Kseniia Oparina also acknowledged that she preferred to be an Old Believer because "it is easier to gain salvation."[63] She perceived the effectiveness of Old Believers' prayer as a main factor for this. Specifically, Kseniia stressed that Old Believers "pray at home in solitude, and their prayer is reaching God; while [official] Orthodox [believers] often come to church drunk and fed, talk and curse in church."[64]

Another priestless Old Believer from South Viatka, Mikhailo Vetoshkin, was even more explicit about the significance of praying. When the local official priest reproached him for negligence towards the church, Vetoshkin answered: "although he does not attend the church, a church is everywhere, even at home; if you would not pray to God anywhere, you could not expect salvation."[65] Obviously, the practice of praying, private or collective, was central for Viatka Old Believers' credo. Icons, therefore, the important tool enabling the prayer to reach God, became the essential device in achieving the ultimate goal of the believer - the salvation of the soul.[66]

Recently Daniel Kaiser, based on the analyses of various descriptions of the possessions of Moscow's 18th-century townspeople, uncovered a similar pattern in the relation of parishioners of the official Orthodox Church to icons.[67] The findings of Kaiser are not surprising on first sight: the most popular icons among Moscow citizens were the ones depicting the Virgin Mary and various saints, mostly St. Nicholas, while icons of Jesus Christ and his life and death were not so prevalent.[68] However, conclusions drawn from this data are remarkable: "the men and women of 18th-century Moscow saw in their icons a potent lever, by which to access supernatural power." In other words, as Kaiser concludes:

> their choice of icons - concentrating veneration upon icons of the Mother of God and upon icons of saints reputed to perform miracles - points to a worldview that gave short shrift to Christian theology of the incarnation and heavenly redemption, and instead focused attention upon - and generously expanded - Christianity's embrace of miracle in their very terrestrial lives.[69]

Although Viatka Old Believers were more concerned about the salvation of their souls rather than about the accomplishment of specific tasks, as Moscow official Orthodox townsfolk were, both of these cases reveal the same pattern: they used icons as a tangible communication device, central to the religious practice. Such aspects of the religiosity of common people, who do not normally leave diaries or other narrative sources about their own spiritual life, are extremely hard to study.

Conclusion

The case of the eighteenth century Viatka Old Believers shows that their relations with iconic images could not be defined in terms of aesthetics, although I do not deny the presence of the sense of beauty possessed by those people. My point is that their case reveals the presence of a material dimension in these relations. For Viatka's peasant Old Believers the "pinch," beardlessness, tobacco, alcohol, and mother curses were not symbols (as semioticians or cultural historians would suggest) but rather physical objects belonging to the Devil's world, and desacralizing as such. On the other side, icons were not just representations of the holy, "window to the Kingdom," but rather a materialization of it, part of the Kingdom. And as such, they could be desecrated. In this regard, Viatka Old Believers were more material than theological in their relations with icons.

The study of the artifacts of religious beliefs can add to our understanding of confessionalization, the process of which the content and periodization is still debated among historians of Russia.[70] Evidently, in the contact with material objects and through their use, Viatka Old Believers established their own identity and created a community of the followers of "Orthodox faith." The words "Orthodox faith" were not just the learned tenet for people under study, but the very practical, even material claim. They were the ones who venerated the only real, pure, "working" icons, which meant that only their prayers could reach God and His saints. Only their souls therefore would be saved in the afterlife. As a result, iconic images served as a tool for confessional demarcation between official Orthodox and Old Believers.

28 – Cross Cover of the small Deesis triptych.

Abbreviations

ChOIDR: *Chteniia v Imperatorskom obshchestve istorii i drevnostei rossiiskikh pri Moskovskom universitete*. 264 vols. to date. Moscow: Universitetskaia tipografiia, Sinodal'naia tipographiia, 1846-1918
GAKO: *Gosudarstvennyi arkhiv Kirovskoi oblasti*.
PSZ: *Polnoe sobranie zakonov Rossiiskoi imperii. Pervoe sobranie (1649-1825)*. St. Petersburg: Tipografiia II Otdeleniia Sobstvennoi Ego Imperatorskago Velichestva Kantseliarii, 1830.
SKKDR: *Slovar' knizhnikov i knizhnosti Drevnei Rusi*. 8 vols. to date. Edited by D. S. Likhachev, et. al. Leningrad, St. Petersburg: Nauka, Dmitrii Bulanin, 1987-2012.
TODRL: *Trudy Otdela drevnerusskoi literatury*. 61 vols. to date. Moscow, Leningrad, St. Petersburg: Izdatel'stvo Akademii nauk SSSR, Nauka, Dmitrii Bulanin, 1934-2010.

Archival Sources

GAKO, Fond 237 (*Viatskaia dukhovnaia konsistoriia*), opis' 74, No. 830 (*The investigation of "schismatics" Feofil and Savva Belykh, 1782-1783*).
GAKO, F. 242 (*Nolinskoe dukhovnoe pravlenie*), op. 1, No. 248 (*The report of the priest Daniil Popovykh on the illegal "schismatic" cemetery and chapel in the Nolinsk district, 1798*).
GAKO, F. 583 (*Viatskoe namestnicheskoe pravlenie*), op. 1a, No. 859 (*The investigation of "schismatics" Emel'ian Chulkin, Filimon Vetoshkin and Ivan Mironov, 1781-1783*).
GAKO, F. 583, op. 2, No. 1246 (*The investigation of the case of Kukarskaia sloboda peasants' conversion to the "Schism," 1782-1783*).
GAKO, F. 583, op. 3, No. 174 (*The investigation of the case of the "Schism's" dissemination by Feofil and Savva Belykh, 1783-1784*).
GAKO, F. 583, op. 4, No. 61 (*The investigation of the case of blasphemy by "schismatic" Kondratei Postnikov, 1784-1788*).
GAKO, F. 583, op. 4, No. 563 (*The investigation of the arrested "schismatics" of Fedoseevtsy sect, 1784*).
GAKO, F. 583, op. 6, No. 1086 (*The investigation of the case of widow Paraskov'ia Mironova's conversion to the "Schism," 1786-1787*).
GAKO, F. 583, op. 6, No. 1290 (*The investigation of Kseniia Oparina's re-conversion to the "Schism," 1786-1787*).
GAKO, F. 583, op. 10, No. 485 (*The investigation of the case of the "Schism's" dissemination by Epimakh Cherezov, 1790-1792*).
GAKO, F. 583, op. 10, No. 751 (*The investigation of "schismatics" Ivan Mironov, Kondratei Postnikov and Epimakh Cherezov, 1790-1791*).

GAKO, F. 583, op. 11, No. 238 (*The investigation of the petitions of "schismatics" from Glazov, Malmyzh, and Nolinsk districts, 1791-1793*).
GAKO, F. 583, op. 17, No. 1042 (*The investigation of the petition of Old Believers from Urzhum district regarding the utensils confiscated from their chapel by the archpriest Damian Petrov, 1797-1801*).
GAKO, F. 583, op. 17, No. 1111 (*The investigation of the petition of Old Believers from Urzhum district regarding the organization of a separate cemetery, 1797-1800*).
GAKO, F. 583, op. 18, No. 888 (*The investigation of the Old Believers' cemetery and chapel in Nolinsk district, 1798-1799*).
GAKO, F. 583, op. 18, No. 1244 (*The investigation of the case of the burial of deceased official Orthodox parishioners at the Old Believers' cemetery in Nolinsk district, 1798-1801*).
GAKO, F. 583, op. 19, No. 385 (*The investigation of the cases of the resistance among some official Orthodox believers from Nolinsk district to baptize newly born children and perform funeral services at the parish church, 1799-1814*).
Spencer Research Library, MS C38, John Chrysostom, *Extracts from the works, in Russian, with some other works* (end of the 18th century).

Notes

1 The word *britousy* Belykh used literally means "mustache-shavers" not "beard-shavers." However, in this context the term obviously refers to beard-shaving. About the word see: V. I. Dal', *Tolkovyi slovar' zhivogo velikorusskogo iazyka*, 4 vols. (Moscow: Izdatel'stvo "Russkii iazyk," 1989-1991) 1: 128. Dal' also quotes an Old Believer proverb in which context the word *britous* used and which completely repeats Belykh's concerns. It suggests a much wider than just Viatka region dispersion of the ideas expressed by local Old Believers.
2 GAKO, F. 583, opis' 3, No. 174, folio 2v.
3 Ibid., ff. 1-1v.
4 The overview of the mid-17th-century schism and the subsequent development of the Old Belief in Russia can be found in: Robert O. Crummey, *The Old Believers and the World of Antichrist: The Vyg Community and the Russian State, 1694-1855* (Madison, University of Wisconsin Press, 1970); Serge Zenkovsky, "The Russian Church Schism: Its Background and Repercussions," *Russian Review*, 16.4 (October 1957): 37-58.; Georg Michels, *At War with the Church: Religious Dissent in Seventeenth-Century Russia* (Stanford: Stanford University Press, 1999); Paul Meyendorff, *Russia, Ritual, and Reform: The Liturgical Reforms of Nikon in the 17th Century* (Crestwood, NY: St. Vladimir's

Seminary Press, 1991).
5   I employ the "material culture approach practiced by the whole range of scholars in different disciplines. Developed in the 1980s and 1990s under the influence of anthropology, archeology, and art history, material culture is a part of a wider phenomenon called the "material turn" in humanities and social sciences. Scholars of material culture propose to "read texts as objects" and not the other way around. In other words, they understand the "material turn" as an "attempt to understand objects not as substitutes for words, but as the nonverbal articulation" of all kinds of phenomena of social and physical realities. Thus, religion in this view is not just the sum of tenets of belief, but a "social discourse of material forms, sensations, texts, and human behaviors;" see: "Introduction," in *The Visual Culture of American Religions*, edited by David Morgan and Sally M. Promey (Berkeley: University of California Press, 2001), 16. See also: Birgit Meyer, et al., "The origin and mission of Material Religion," *Religion* 40 (2010): 207-211, and publications of newly started journal *Material Religion: The Journal of Objects, Art and Belief.*
6   On the debates on the iconic aesthetics in the second half of the seventeenth century see Iu. N. Dmitriev,"Teoriia iskusstva i vzgliady na iskusstvo v pis'mennosti drevnei Rusi," *TODRL* 9 (1953): 97-116; Oleg Tarasov, *Icon and Devotion: Sacred Spaces in Imperial Russia*, (London, UK: Reaktion Books, 2002), 134-142.
7   Tarasov, *Icon and Devotion*, 119-133.
8   Cited by N. Andreev, "Nikon and Avvakum on Icon-Painting," *Revue des études slaves*, 38 (1961): 43. On the views of Avvakum and other 17th and 18th-century Old Believers on icons see A. N. Robinson, "Ideologiia i vneshnost' (Vzgliady Avvakuma na izobrazitel'noe iskusstvo)," *TODRL* 22 (1966): 353-381, esp. 371-373.
9   On the Old Believers' icon-painting see: T. E. Grebeniuk, "Vetkovskaia ikona," in *Staroobriadchestvo v Rossii (XVII-XX vv.): Sbornik nauchnykh trudov*. 4 vols. to date, edited by E. M. Iukhimenko (Moscow: Iazyki slavianskoi kul'tury, 1994-2010), 3: 274-90; I. L. Buseva-Davydova, "Staroobriadcheskaia ikonopis' i ee granitsy: materialy k diskussii," in *Staroobriadchestvo v Rossii (XVII-XX vv.): Sbornik nauchnykh trudov*. 4 vols. to date, edited by E. M. Iukhimenko (Moscow: Iazyki slavianskoi kul'tury, 1994-2010), 4: 496-519.
10 V. G. Druzhinin, "K istorii, krest'ianskogo iskusstva XVIII-XIX vekov v Olonetskoi gubernii (Khudozhestvennoe nasledie Vygoretskoi Pomorskoi obiteli)," *Izvestiia Akademii nauk SSSR*, Seriia 6, no. 15-17 (1926): 1481-1482.
11 *Stoglav*, 128. In one of the most famous and complete 18th-century

Old Believers' accounts of their views, known as "Pomorskie otvety" (1723), its creators referred to Stoglav Council as one of the authorities in regard of icon-painting. They specifically quoted the passage cited above: *Pomorskie otvety*, 351.
12 Cited by Tarasov, *Icon and Devotion*, 173-174.
13 "Ustav Pol'skii," in Livanov, F. V., *Raskol'niki i ostrozhniki. Ocherki i rasskazy*. 4 vols. (St. Petersburg: Tipografiia M. Khana, 1868-1873), 3: 44; "Preniia ili bor'ba za ustav "Pol'skii" (1809)," in *Sbornik dlia istorii staroobriadchestva*, 2 vols., edited by Nikolai Popov (Moscow: Universitetskaia tipografiia, 1864-1866), 2: 28.
14 About Pomortsy and Fedoseevtsy and their spiritual centers in Pomor'e and Moscow see: Crummey, *Old Believers*; Irina Paert, *Old Believers: Religious Dissent and Gender in Russia, 1760-1850* (Manchester, UK/New York: Manchester University Press, 2003).
15 V. G. Druzhinin, "K istorii," 1483-1488; idem., "Vvedenie (Iz korrektury knigi V.G. Druzhinina 'O pomorskom lit'e')," in *Russkoe mednoe lit'e: Sbornik statei*, 2 vols., edited by S. V. Gnutova (Moscow: Sol Sistem, 1993), 2: 106-120; I. Ia. Zotova, "'Na pamiat' potomstvu': Mednolitoi obraz v staroobriadcheskom molitvennom obikhode," in *Staroobriadchestvo v Rossii (XVII-XX veka)*, 4: 622-636.
16 "Ustav Pol'skii."
17 GAKO, F. 583, op. 3, No. 174, f. 2v. The word *tabashnik* in 18th-century Russian referred to a person who either consumed tobacco often or sold it: *Slovar' Akademii Rossiiskoi*, 6 Parts (St. Petersburg: Imperatorskaia Akademiia nauk, 1789-1794) 6: 2.
18 GAKO, F. 583, op. 6, No. 1086, f. 1v.
19 Ibid., F. 583, op. 4, No. 563, f. 4.
20 About Aleksei Kozhevnikov and his activities on the territory of South Viatka see: I. F. Farmakovskii, "O pervonachal'nom poiavlenii raskola v Viatskoi Eparkhii," in *Viatskie eparkhial'nye vedomosti* 6 (1868), chast' neofitsial'naia, 99-101; I. V. Pochinskaia, "Iz istorii staroobriadchestva Viatskogo kraia. Fedoseevtsy (vtoraia polovina XVIII - nachala XX veka)," in *Ocherki istorii staroobriadchestva Urala i sopredel'nykh territorii*, edited by I. V. Pochinskaia (Ekaterinburg: Izdatel'stvo Ural'skogo gosudarstvennogo universiteta, 2000), 46; GAKO, F. 237, op. 74, No. 830, ff. 2v.-3; Ibid., F. 583, op. 10, No. 485, ff. 1-1v.; and others.
21 Ibid., F. 583, op. 4, No. 61, f. 1v.
22 Ibid.
23 The Viatka Old Believers' case perfectly demonstrates what constitutes the material world of the religion: "religion is inseparable from a matrix or network of components that consist of people, divine beings or forces, institutions, things, places, and communities:" Meyer et al., "The origin and mission of Material Religion," 209.

24 The Mother of God is overwhelmingly the most popular personage in the Russian Orthodoxy. On Mary and Marian icons in Russian pre-Revolutionary church see: Vera Shevzov, *Russian Orthodoxy on the Eve of Revolution* (New York: Oxford University Press, 2004), ch. 6 ("The Message of Mary").
25 GAKO, F. 583, op. 17, No. 1042, f. 4.
26 The petition for the organization of the Old Believer cemetery near Turek village signed heads of fifty-four families: Ibid., F. 583, op. 17, No. 1111, ff. 2-3.
27 The scope of Krasnaia gorka center can be understood if to collate the areas of residence of its visitors and conventuals (Ibid., F. 583, op. 18, No. 888, ff. 11-11v.; Ibid., F. 583, op. 18, No. 1244; and Ibid., F. 583, op. 19, No. 385) and the lists of the Old Believers of Fedoseevtsy orientation living in these areas (Ibid., F. 583, op. 11, No. 238, ff. 20-48v.)
28 By crown here meant an adornment covering the halo of the icon: Ibid., F. 242, op. 1, No. 248, ff. 3-3v.
29 Ibid., f. 3.
30 About the practice of imitations of old-painted icons in 19th century Russia see Tarasov, *Icon and Devotion*, 326-344.
31 E. K. Romodanovskaia, *Sibir' i literatura. XVII vek* (Novosibirsk: Nauka, 2002), 328.
32 *Stoglav* (St. Petersburg: Tipografiia Imperatorskoi Akademii nauk, 1863, 124. The example of the negative perception of beard shaving and its connection to the "Latin heresy" see also in the 13th-century Byzantine "Prenie Panagiota s Azamitom" published in 1644 in Russia in the compilation of polemical works called "Kirillova kniga." *Kirillova kniga* (Moscow: Pechatnyi dvor, 1644), f. 235.
33 "Poslanie patriarkha Adriana," in *Raskol'nich'i dela XVIII stoletiia. Izvlecheniia iz del Preobrazhenskogo prikaza i tainykh rozysknykh del Kantseliarii*, 2 vols., edited by G. V. Esipov (St. Petersburg: Tipografiia Tovarishchestva "Obshchestvennaia pol'za," 1861-1863), 268.
34 Ibid., 70.
35 *PSZ*, t. 4, no. 2015 (January 16, 1705), 282. See also: Ibid., t. 7, no. 3944 (April 6, 1722), 642.
36 See also about the meaning of beards on the icons: Tarasov, *Icon and Devotion*, 92-93. See also 18th-beginning of 19th-century Old Believers' proverbs regarding the beard and its relation to God-like image: I. Snegirev, *Russkie v svoikh poslovitsakh: Razsuzhdeniia i izsledovaniia o ruskikh poslovitsakh i pogovorkakh*, 4 vols. in 2 (Moscow: Universitetskaia tipografiia, 1831-1834) 1.2: 48.
37 Matthew Romaniello, "Muscovy's Extraordinary Ban on Tobacco," in *Tobacco in Russian History and Culture from the Seventeenth Century to*

       the Present, edited by M. Romaniello and Tricia Starks, (New York: Routledge, 2009), 9-25.
38 *The Travels of Olearius in Seventeenth-Century Russia,* translated and edited by Samuel H. Baron (Stanford: Stanford University Press, 1967), 146. See also the account of the 17th-century English traveler who most likely copied Olearius' report on tobacco: "Besides (which was the particular disgust of the Patriarch) they presented themselves before their Images with so reeking and smoaky a breath, that, perhaps he was afraid, they would poison their Saints, with the stink of their Tobacco:" Guy Miege, *A Relation of Three Embassies from His Sacred Majestie Charles II to the Great Duke of Muscovie, the King of Sweden, and the King of Denmark: Performed by the Right Noble the Earl of Carlisle in the Years 1663 and 1664* (London: Printed for John Starkey at the Miter in Fleetstreet near Temple-Barr, 1669), 46.
39 Romodanovskaia, "Skazanie," 51. In 17th-century Siberia the word "shar'" was used for Chinese tobacco: Erika Monahan, "Regulating Virtue and Vice: Controlling Commodities in Early Modern Siberia," in *Tobacco in Russian History and Culture,* 67.
40 T. F. Volkova and N. V. Ponyrko, "Povesti o tabake," in *SKKDR,* 3.3: 44-47; V. P. Adrianova-Peretts, "Staroobriadcheskaia literatura XVIII veka," in *Istoriia russkoi literatury,* 10 vols. in 13, edited by Institut literatury/Institut russkoi literatury (Pushkinskii Dom) (Moscow: Izdatel'stvo Akademii nauk SSSR, 1941-1954), 4.2: 95.
41 Cited by Paul Bushkovitch, *Religion and Society in Russia: the Sixteenth and Seventeenth Centuries* (New York: Oxford University Press, 1992), 116; about the copies of the story, A. S. Orlov, "Narodnyia predaniia o sviatyniakh russkago severa," in *ChOIDR,* 1 (1913), 47-55.
42 Bushkovitch, *Religion and Society* in Russia, 116.
43 "Legenda o proiskhozhdenii tabaka," in *Pamiatniki starinnoi russkoi literatury,* 4 vols in 2, edited by N. I. Kostomarov and A. N. Pypin (St. Petersburg: Tipografiia P. A. Kulisha, 1860-1862), 2: 427; about the text see also Volkova and Ponyrko, "Povesti o tabake."
44 Translation cited by Roy R. Robson, "Old Believers in Imperial Russia: A Legend on the Appearance of Tobacco," in *The Human Tradition in Modern Russia,* edited by William B. Husband, (Wilmington, DE: SR Books, 2000), 22.
45 Ibid., 25.
46 Ibid., 28.
47 Ibid.
48 Ibid.
49 Ibid.
50 See also Old Believer's proverbs regarding tobacco from the 18th and 19th centuries in: Snegirev, 1.2: 50; Dal', *Poslovitsy,* 14-15.

51 GAKO, F. 583, op. 2, No. 1246, f. 1
52 B. A. Uspenskii, "Religiozno-mifologicheskii aspekt russkoi ekspressivnoi frazeologii: semantika russkogo mata v istoricheskom osveshchenii," in *Semiotics and the History of Culture: In Honor of Jurij Lotman*, UCLA Slavic Studies 17, edited by Morris Halle et al., (Columbus, OH: Slavica Publishers, Inc., 1988), 197-232.
53 Ibid., 212. This document is known in an 18th century source: A. Rodosskii, *Opisanie 432-kh rukopisei, prinadlezhashchikh S.-Peterburgskoi dukhovnoi akademii i sostavliaiushchikh ee pervoe po vremeni sobranie* (St. Petersburg: Tipografiia A.O. Bashkova, 1893),, 393; about this text in different versions: Bulanin, 535-539.
54 Rodosskii, *Opisanie*, 425.
55 Spencer Research Library, MS C38, ff. 247-247v. See also other example of the condemnation of the mother curses in the 17th-century Tobol'sk: Romodanovskaia, "Skazanie," 51.
56 Cited by A. A. Panchenko, *Khristovshchina i skopchestvo: Foklor i traditsionnaia kul'tura russkikh misticheskikh sekt* (Moscow: OGI, 2004), 132.
57 Ibid.
58 Ibid., 132-134. It is noteworthy that Fedoseevtsy Old Believers did not condemn alcohol consumption per se, at least the inhabitants of the communities on Polish lands, see, for example, article 13 in the so called "Polish rule" (Ustav Pol'skii) (1752), 45. The prohibition of *kirmashy* (taverns) attendance (article 7-9) is rather dealing with the condemnation of profane activities during ecclesiastical feasts and the prohibition of the contacts with infidels. Likewise, article 18 prohibits festive singing, dancing, playing on musical instruments, etc.: Ibid., 44-45. See also about similar prohibitions in *khlysty* sect: Panchenko, *Khristovshchina i skopchestvo*, 139-140.
59 GAKO, F. 583, op. 1a, No. 859, ff. 23v.-24.
60 Ibid., F. 237, op. 74, No. 830, f. 4v.
61 Ibid.
62 Ibid., F. 583, op. 6, No. 1086, f. 1v.
63 Ibid., F. 583, op. 6, No. 1290, f. 1v.
64 Ibid., f. 2.
65 Ibid, F. 583, op. 10, No. 751, ff. 13-13v.; see also: Ibid., F. 583, op. 4, No. 61, f. 1v.
66 Viktor Zhivov, "Handling Sin in Eighteenth-Century Russia," in *Representing Private Lives of the Enlightenment*, edited by Andrew Kahn (Oxford: Voltaire Foundation, 2010), 147, characterizes such type of salvation, i.e. "attained through the instrumentality of holy men, wonder-working icons, sacred wells and so on," as "illicit."

According to Zhivov, it was a manifestation of the traditional Russian religiosity that was not subdued by the state and church in spite of their continuous urge to do so during second half of the 17th and 18th centuries.

67 Daniel H. Kaiser, "Icons and Private Devotion among Eighteenth-Century Moscow Townsfolk," *Journal of Social History* 45.1 (2011): 125-147.

68 Ibid., 128-131.

69 Ibid., 141. Similar relations with religious material objects demonstrated twentieth century Catholic peasants from Hispanic New Mexico: Thomas J. Steele, *Santos and Saints: The Religious Folk Art of Hispanic New Mexico* (Santa Fe, NM: Ancient City Press, 1994), 103-114.

70 Robert Crummey dates the beginning of confessionalization in Russia to the second half of the seventeenth century: "Ecclesiastical Elites and Popular Belief and Practice in Seventeenth-Century Russia," in *Religion and the Early Modern State*, edited by James D. Tracy and Marguerite Ragnow Cambridge, UK: Cambridge University Press, 2004), 52-79; on the other hand, Alexandr Lavrov connects it to "the reform of piety" undertook by Peter the Great in the first quarter of the eighteenth century: *Koldovstvo i religiia v Rossii. 1700-1740 gg.* (Moscow: Drevlekhranilishce, 2000), 60-73. On the notion of confessionalization see: Thomas A. Brady, Jr. "Confessionalization: The Career of a Concept," in *Confessionalization in Europe, 1550-1700. Essays in Honor and Memory of Bodo Nischan*, edited by John M. Headley, Hans J. Hillerbrand and Anthony J. Papalas (Aldershot: Ashgate, 2004), 1-20; Susan R. Boettcher, "Confessionalization: Reformation, Religion, Absolutism, and Modernity," *History Compass* 2 (2004): 1-10.

Part III

Orthodoxy and Modernity

Orthodoxy and Modernity: Introduction

Valeria Z. Nollan

Moving out of the religiously intense, if more constrained world of Iosif and the first generations of Old Believers, we come to more familiar modern territory. We would like to imagine that if the extraordinary figure of Iosif Volotskii were to come back to life, now compelled to adapt to our multi-confessional societies, he would cast a sharply critical eye upon the vicissitudes experienced by major world religious movements in our times. Steadfast in his defense of durable traditions, canons, and laws, and committed to his activism as an Orthodox Christian pastor, he would also throw himself passionately and competently into the fray of explication of what he considered "right-believing" and what he deemed heretical. He would mourn the large-scale persecution by the Bolsheviks and new Soviet government of Russian Orthodox hierarchs and monastics in the 1920s, and of the general population—maybe some non-Orthodox, too—during the horrors of the 1930s and World War II. And he undoubtedly would admire the heroism of the Orthodox Christians who preserved their faith in the "catacomb" church's underground networks and cells throughout Soviet Russia and Georgia. He would keenly follow the trials and tribulations faced by the Russian bishops who found themselves in exile from their beleaguered native land, but who received material comfort and spiritual guidance in Sremski Karlovci, Serbia. He would maintain a genuine vested interest in the preservation by the newly-formed Karlovci Synod of Bishops (ROCA/ROCOR[2]) of pre-1917 Russian Orthodox traditions, dogmatic theology, canon laws, and *praxis* throughout the apocalyptic twentieth century. He would form precise opinions on the series of meetings between representatives of the ROCOR Synod of Bishops and the Moscow Patriarchate (MP) that culminated in the historic Act of Intercommunion of 2007. And surely he would rejoice at the reunification of the estranged jurisdictions of the Russian Orthodox faith, the healing of decades of brokenness of the faith whose beliefs and laws he himself had tirelessly championed in his own inimitable way.

The five essays of the Orthodoxy and Modernity section of this book engage competing and conflicting religious understandings that arose within the context of the profound challenges stemming from the developments within Roman Catholicism and Protestantism, which threatened to marginalize the traditions of the ancient Orthodox faith in Russia, Greece, and elsewhere. Singularly, each of the five essays elaborates a moment in time, whether more broadly conceived historically or writ large symbolically, which represents a variation on the theme of the ancient patristic faith's reflection or refraction in the multi-ethnic and multilayered mirror of modernity.

The first two of the group—Randall A. Poole's "The Defense of Dignity in 19th-Century Russian Thought" and Lucien J. Frary's "Russian Policy and the Change of Dynasty in Greece (1862-1864)"—provide some historical framework for the socio-political and religious events under consideration. A well-published specialist in modern Russian thought, Poole elegantly captures the salient intellectual and religious-philosophical currents sweeping Russia in the 19th century, currents profoundly influenced by Hegel and especially Kant and focusing on the dignity, morality, and inner freedom of the individual who finds him- or herself in inner confrontation with the State. Reminding readers of Russia's tradition of enlightened absolutism that perhaps reached its zenith during Catherine II's rule (1762-96) and continued into the following century, Poole successfully undertakes a summary of 19th- and early-20th-century Russian idealist philosophy in dialogue with Orthodoxy and questions of humanist thought. From Slavophiles Ivan Kireevskii and Alexei Khomiakov, to Westernizers Vissarion Belinsky, Alexander Herzen, and Boris Chicherin, and finally to the special place occupied by the speculative religious philosophy of Vladimir Soloviev, Poole situates the individuals and movements in which they participated within the issues of

Orthodoxy, human dignity, and the quest for integral knowledge. It was precisely Orthodox Christianity's insistence on the absolute value of the human being that grafted onto "the idealism of Russian liberalism" a defense of human rights—as Orthodox mysticism and the Incarnation sanctified the material world, so the sanctified material world elevated and preserved the dignity and rights of the "enfleshed" human being.

The second essay by 'Eastern Question' specialist Lucien J. Frary, "Russian Policy and the Change of Dynasty in Greece (1862-1864)," concentrates similarly on the 19th century but shifts to politics and international relations and directs its ethnic focus to Greece during the decades from c. 1830, when Greek independence was won from the Ottoman Turks, to the Greek Revolution in 1862. Based upon hitherto underutilized papers from the Imperial Russian foreign ministry archive, Frary shows that in both of these events, Russian policy was one of the decisive factors in the outcome. The essay traces the struggles between secular nationalism and the more traditional Orthodox ecumenism in the dynastic considerations that would determine what constituted Hellenism in the future. Indeed, modern Greek identity evolved in a synthesis between these two powerful forces of nationalism and the ancient patristic faith defended by Greece for so many centuries. While Poole's essay demonstrates how intellectuals and theologians could comprise a haven and bulwark against the interference of an autocratic state, Frary's elucidates how considerations of ethnicity and religious affiliation, though at times in conflict when more than one state was involved, could determine the direction that a country's identity would take.

If Poole's essay elucidates the first generations of secular Russian thinkers promoting a European-influenced Orthodox theology consistent with modern notions of the individual, and Frary's describes Russia's modernizing state employing its great power influence to bolster Orthodoxy within newly independent Greece, Christopher D. L. Johnson's contribution takes us into the mental world of a learned 19th century Western Christian, who viewed Orthodoxy with a combination of trope-filled condescension towards seeming backwardness and admiration for the alleged authenticity of ancient roots. The title of Johnson's

"Eastern Christianity as 'Survival' and 'Oriental Other' in the *Lectures* of Arthur Penrhyn Stanley" goes to the heart of this outlook, consistent with the 'Orientalist' vogue of the time toward the non-West. Just as Edward Said's 'Orientalist' European wished to appropriate the useful 'Ancient' from contemporary Egypt to strengthen Europe, so the immensely popular and respected Stanley hoped to employ this "caricature" (Johnson's term) of an "immutable" and "mystical" Eastern Christianity "as a corrective for the West." Paradoxically, but maybe not unexpected in the light of the West's immense overall influence at the time, Johnson sees some of these same characteristics appearing as positives in Orthodox anti-Western polemics.

But some of these characteristics appear as well among modern Orthodox thinkers without the slightest hostility toward the West. In the penultimate essay, "How the Philokalic Tradition Came to Modern (Literary) America," a genuine tour de force, Church historian and religion and theology scholar Fr. John McGuckin elaborates how, from the Hellenistic world of Late Antiquity through the Byzantine Empire and up to contemporary America, Eastern Christianity's depth and mystical profundity have informed some of the ways in which various cultures conceptualize their connection with the Divine. Ranging from the centuries that produced the *Philokalia* to the various incarnations and intertextuality of this foundational "love of goodness" collection, such as St. Paisii Velichkovskii's Russian *Dobrotoliubie*, McGuckin's discussion argues forcefully that within the context of a Christian world outlook, Orthodoxy's counterpart to such South Asian spiritual strains as the non-dualisitic Advaita Vedanta can provide the fulfilling endpoint for an individual's search for stability. His examination of the contents and representative articulators of the Philokalic texts includes the topics of noetic consciousness as the "evolutionary goal (telos) of our species" and the "Prayer of the Heart" (Jesus Prayer), which evolved as central to monastic and secular prayer. The religio-philosophical discussion culminates and is personalized in contemporary America, in New York, in the guise of J. D. Salinger's literary characters Franny and Zooey (short story and novella published as the book *Franny and Zooey*, 1961). Promoting with rich illustrations the notion that the full weight and authenticity of the Eastern Christian tradition possess the transformational power to heal lost souls, McGuckin assembles the central concepts of his essay—Christian humility, brotherly love, patience, and compassion—as fresh and relevant to the struggles of today's individuals.

The final essay by Russian Orthodoxy specialist Valeria Nollan utilizes the historical and religio-philosophical material of the previous four indicating the commonalities among the great Christian traditions to affirm the abiding connections between the Russian Orthodox Church (Moscow Patriarchate) and Roman Catholic Church as logical extensions of the longstanding cultural relations between Russia and Italy. These relations, we must remember, were already quite significant in Iosif's lifetime and even influenced his monastery's architecture, as mentioned in the introductory chapter to this volume—even while he vigorously opposed the "Latin" (i.e., Roman Catholic) doctrine of the procession of the Holy Spirit from the Father *and the Son* (*filioque*). Accordingly, Nollan's discussion foregrounds in particular several features of the two cultures as essential for the stability of these connections: an ancient faith tradition, as set forth in the first section of this book, of a single church that breathes with "two lungs" (term of Pope John Paul II); a preference for a spiritualized beauty over practicality or utilitarianism; and the recognition of a sanctified material world justified by the Incarnation of Christ. These major features common to Russia and Italy are elaborated and problematized in the difficulties—of politics, aesthetics, and protocol—of establishing the first freestanding Russian Orthodox Church in Rome in the history of Christian Italy. Because of the combination of faith, determination, love, and feeling for ecclesiastical beauty, the project was brought to fruition in 2009. This final essay brings the collection inspired and informed by Iosif Volotskii to a close.

Notes

1 The two names of the church jurisdiction are used synonymously. The Russian Orthodox Church Abroad (ROCA) is the original name: the

stone plaque on the red brick building of the Synod of Bishops at 75 E. 93rd St. in New York, NY bears this name. The name was changed after World War II to the Russian Orthodox Church Outside of Russia (ROCOR).

10   The Defense of Human Dignity in Nineteenth-Century Russian Thought

Randall A. Poole

29 – Aleksandr Radishchev (1749-1802), unknown Artist.

30 – Ivan Kramskoi 1905 painting of Vladimir Soloviev (1853-1900).

I

Nineteenth-century Russia presents a striking paradox: it was the most absolutist regime in Europe and yet its intellectual history, from Alexander Radishchev at the very beginning of the period to Vladimir Soloviev at its end, produced a powerful and multifaceted defense of human dignity.[1] This paradox is not hard to explain: Russia's oppressive political and social reality gave the defense of human values greater urgency than farther west in Europe, where such values were more secure and better realized in practice. Moreover, the monolithic state order of the Russian autocracy necessitated that this defense take place mostly in the realm of ideas. The result is the very rich tradition of Russian humanist thought.

The origins of this paradox are closely related to those of the Russian intelligentsia.[2] Under Catherine the Great (reigned 1762-1796) and Alexander I (reigned 1801-1825), Russia's small educated public generally shared the autocracy's ideology of enlightened absolutism. Educated, civic-minded Russians, usually members of the nobility, were encouraged to believe that they could work with the regime toward the goal of social progress. This shared Enlightenment framework started to break down in the second half of Alexander I's reign and it ended altogether under the despotic rule of Nicholas I (reigned 1825-1855) in the second quarter of the nineteenth century. Nicholas's firm reassertion of autocracy, after the abortive Decembrist rebellion of 1825 that tried to prevent his accession to the throne, frustrated the ambitions of progressive Russians to influence public policy and to shape their country's future. They were prevented from forming the type of civil society that might have been able, over the long run, to transform Russia into a liberal democratic polity. Some critics of the regime became so alienated that they formed an intelligentsia, from which a full-fledged revolutionary movement emerged by the 1860s. Other critics were more liberal and some, like the Slavophiles, were even conservative. Whether these liberal and conservative intellectuals also belonged to an intelligentsia in some broader sense is not an issue that I wish to pursue here. But Russian thinkers of all stripes forcefully advanced and defended their ideas against the autocracy and against each other. They wrote brilliant works of literature, social criticism, and philosophy, systematically defending the human values that were so flagrantly violated by both the autocracy and the revolutionary movement.

One current of Russian humanist thought was liberalism.[3] Over the course of the century, it took on the broad meaning of a social philosophy of human dignity and of human rights. To be sure, not all Russian humanists were liberals; some, like the Slavophiles, Alexander Herzen, and Leo Tolstoy, rejected the defining liberal criterion of the rule of law (conceived as the necessary enforcement of human rights). Other Russian humanists were impatient with liberalism as "small deeds"—practical social, educational, and cultural work (*kul'turnichestvo*) among the Russian people—and as something to be developed in theory until the day came when it could more fully be put into practice. Russian liberalism did achieve a very high level of theoretical development, rivaling anything in European social thought. Nineteenth-century Russia's two greatest philosophers, Boris Chicherin and Vladimir Soloviev, were also its greatest liberal theorists. This was not a coincidence: in Russia, philosophy did not have the luxury of being "purely philosophical," in the sense of being concerned primarily with method. Where human dignity was under constant assault from autocrats and revolutionaries, philosophy, too, or rather philosophy especially, had to take up its defense.

II

By its very nature, human dignity is a global concept. Histories of the idea can be traced in all of the world's major religious and philosophical traditions, from Confucianism and Hinduism to the Abrahamic religions.[4] A seminal western formulation of the idea is Giovanni Pico della Mirandola's splendid oration, *De hominis dignitate* (1486), often regarded as the manifesto of the Italian Renaissance. In it Pico recounts how God made man a "creature of indeterminate nature" and said to him:

> The nature of all other beings is limited and constrained within the bounds of laws prescribed by Us. Thou, constrained by no limits, in accordance with thine own free will, in whose hand We have placed thee, shalt ordain for thyself the limits of thy nature. . . . We have made thee neither of heaven nor of earth, neither mortal nor immortal, so that with freedom of choice and with honor, as though the maker and molder of thyself, thou mayest fashion thyself in whatever shape thou shalt prefer. Thou shalt have the power to degenerate into the lower forms of life, which are brutish. Thou shalt have the power, out of thy soul's judgment, to be reborn into the higher forms, which are divine.[5]

Pico believed that the wondrous capacity for self-determination and perfectibility was the source of human dignity. Almost exactly three centuries after his oration, an even more influential statement of human dignity appeared, Immanuel Kant's *Groundwork of the Metaphysics of Morals* (1785), a work that, despite its brevity, is "one of greatest and most influential achievements in the history of philosophy."[6] In it Kant locates human dignity in autonomy of the will or in self-determination, very much as Pico had done. Kant's conception of human dignity had a powerful effect on Russian humanist thought, so it might be useful to review his argument at the outset.

The main idea of the *Groundwork* is the autonomy of the will, or self-determination by the moral law. Kant says that autonomy is the *"supreme principle of morality"*; without it there can be no true morality or self-determination, only externally determined or coerced behavior (G 89/4:440).[7] His next link is dignity: in a key formulation he writes that autonomy is "the ground of the dignity of human nature and of every rational nature" (G 85/4:436). In other words, morality, "and humanity insofar as it is capable of morality, is that which alone has dignity" (G 84/4:435). Kant's whole argument is analytic through-and-through: the distinctive human capacity is autonomy or self-determination, i.e., free fulfillment of the moral law given by pure reason. This capacity (morality) is the ground of dignity and of personhood itself, which amount to the same thing. Kant also uses the term "practical reason" to designate the capacity of reason to determine the will by its own ideals, the moral law first of all. So, in the end, autonomy, self-determination, practical reason, morality, dignity, and personhood turn out to be closely related concepts which explicate each other. The striking analytic character of Kant's practical philosophy is the basis of its truth, if you accept the metaphysical premises of autonomy (pure reason and free will). By the end of the nineteenth century, Russia's idealist philosophers did accept them. They embraced Kant's conception of autonomy, dignity, and personhood as their own.

Like Pico, Kant related human dignity to perfectibility, another idea that is analytically derived from the core concept of autonomy. Kantian perfectibility is simply infinite self-determination. He stressed that the moral law must always remain an ideal, for self-determination is possible only by an ideal. Once an ideal is positively or externally given, it is no longer an ideal but a fact.

With that, self-determination closes down and becomes external determination; autonomy becomes heteronomy. This has the interesting implication that dignity and personhood itself seem to depend on what might be called "ideal self-determination." Kant defines perfect virtue or holiness as the complete conformity of the will with the moral law, but he holds that this is a state that human beings can never achieve, not even in the afterlife. We are capable only of *"endless progress"* or of infinite perfectibility toward holiness. Such infinite progress is the premise of Kant's postulate of immortality: the soul itself must be "endless" in order to pursue "endless progress" (PrR 238/5:122). The moral law always remains as an ideal, it always drives progress toward it, and therefore it always enables the "ideal self-determination" that is a condition of human dignity and personhood.

III

The relevance of the Piconian-Kantian conception of human dignity to nineteenth-century Russian thought is obvious from the very beginning of the period. Alexander Radishchev (1749-1802) was one of the most important thinkers of the Russian Enlightenment. He is best known for his *Journey from St. Petersburg to Moscow*, published in 1790. It is a searing attack on serfdom and autocracy as gross violations of the rule of law, which principle Radishchev eloquently defended as the basis of his liberal social philosophy. Catherine the Great had him condemned to death for his views but commuted the sentence to ten years of Siberian exile. While in exile he wrote an essay entitled *On Man, His Mortality and Immortality*. Apparently published posthumously in 1809, the treatise was the first major theoretical work of Russian philosophy. In its first pages Radishchev echoes Pico. He states that man's distinguishing quality is that "he can perfect himself, and he can also become depraved. The limit in either direction is still unknown. But what animal can accomplish so much, for good or for evil, as man?"[8] Radishchev adduces various arguments on behalf of the soul's mortality and immortality, concluding in favor of immortality. One of his arguments is very similar to Kant's, though he may have drawn it from other Enlightenment sources. In Radishchev's account, the soul strives toward endless self-perfection. This process is infinite, it continues after death, and it entails immortality.[9] Perfectibility through inner self-determination, together with the possible metaphysical implications of this distinctively human capacity, would prove to be an enduring theme in Russian philosophical thought.

As early as the 1780s, Russians recognized Kant as an outstanding philosopher. In 1794 there was a proposal to elect him to the Russian Academy of Sciences. In the first decade of the nineteenth century he was the subject of academic lectures and of articles. The *Groundwork of the Metaphysics of Morals* was translated in 1803 and a manuscript translation of the *Critique of Pure Reason* was in circulation by 1820.[10] By then, however, Kant's influence, though it would return in full force later in the century, was already beginning to be displaced by that of his idealist successors as the Enlightenment waned in Russia. Schelling was the first to capture the Russian imagination, in the 1820s, followed by Hegel in the 1830s.[11] The Russian reception of Schelling and German romanticism, on the one hand, and of Hegelianism, on the other, formed the two philosophical poles of the famous Slavophile-Westernizer controversy, which took shape in the 1840s.[12] Slavophilism was the most important romantic movement in Russia. It maintained that the country should return to its allegedly native principles of Christian love, faith, and community, which were said to be embodied in the Russian Orthodox church and in the peasant commune. The Westernizers advanced their ideas within the philosophical framework of Hegelianism, in direct opposition to Slavophile conservative romanticism. They were united by a general belief that Russia should develop along western, European lines.

I would argue that the Slavophiles and Westernizers advanced their respective social philosophies, philosophies of history, and conceptions of national identity out of a more fundamental concern, shared by both sides, over how best to promote human dignity and personhood. The Slavophiles wanted to protect the integrity, spiritual unity, and inner wholeness of the human person against what they considered to be the destructive, atomizing forces of western rationalism and individualism. The Westernizers wanted to defend precisely what the Slavophiles opposed, the rational autonomy of the person (in the more general and not necessarily Kantian sense of autonomy). Their ideal was the autonomous individual who realizes him or herself through conscious action in history. But in their defense of human dignity, the two sides were perhaps not as far apart as has been assumed.

IV

To see this, let us take a closer look, first, at the Slavophile conception. The leading Slavophile philosopher was Ivan Kireevskii (1806-1856). Recently he has been called the "most powerful philosophical mind of his generation."[13] He laid out the Slavophile theory of integral personhood (*tsel'naia lichnost'*) most comprehensively in his late essay "On the Necessity and Possibility of New Principles in Philosophy" (1856), and also in the related and essential "Fragments" published a year later by Aleksei Khomiakov (1804-1860).[14] The main theme of the 1856 essay is the compatibility of faith and reason. Kireevskii argues that faith should be the ground of reason, or more precisely that it should ground reason in divine being. This is his landmark concept of "believing reason," which integrates and achieves the

31 – Ivan Kireevskii (1806-1856).

wholeness of mind, spirit and soul necessary to appreciate the full truth of reality. The faith that grounds reason in divine being, the faith that makes it an integral, "believing reason," can only come from within. This is the condition of dignity, a point he emphasizes. True faith cannot come from external authority, the Catholic Church being his prime counterexample. Significantly he remarks that the Reformation "restored to human beings their dignity and also won for them the right to be reasoning beings" (240). But Protestantism and the rationalist philosophy that followed it, culminating in Hegelianism, erred in seeking to ground reason in itself, rather than in divine being as revealed through inner faith. The true path was indicated by the Greek church fathers, whose works Kireevskii had studied and translated during his visits to the Optina Monastery near his country estate.[15]

Greek patristic theology, interestingly enough, was one of the sources of the Renaissance idea of human dignity.[16] Kireevskii highlights this important historical connection: "The eyes of many Europeans were opened by the writings of the Holy Fathers that were brought from Greece after its fall" (253). In his view this was a missed opportunity for the West to return to the universal church. Instead there followed further division with the Reformation and Counter-Reformation. Protestantism achieved individual freedom, but at the cost of unity; Catholicism continued along its historical path of unity without individual freedom. By contrast, the Orthodox church, as Kireevskii imagined it, respects freedom of conscience while preserving unity in its understanding of faith as the inner revelation of one divine truth. Faith, or inner consciousness of the divine, does not constrain "the free development of the natural laws of reason" (260). Reason grounded in faith and freely developing from it is, as we have seen, Kireevskii's concept of believing reason. Rooted in the ancient teachings of the Greek church fathers, it forms the main "new principle" in philosophy suggested in the title of his essay. This new principle or something like it was also recognized by Schelling, whom Kireevskii calls "one of those beings who are born not once in centuries but once in millennia" (271).[17]

Believing reason is the basis of Kireevskii's theory of the integral human person. In one of his most famous passages (from one of the "fragments"), he writes that faith:

embraces the entire wholeness of the human being.... Therefore, believing thought is best characterized by its attempt to gather all the separate parts of the soul into one force, to search out that inner heart of being where reason and will, feeling and conscience, the beautiful and the true, the wonderful and the desired, the just and the merciful, and all the capacity of mind converge into one living unity, and in this way the essential human personality is restored in its primordial indivisibility [285].

In another fragment, he affirms personhood and human dignity, declaring that "only a reasoning and free personality is what is essential in the world. It alone has a distinctive significance. Everything else has only a relative significance" (284). Rationalism is not adequate to the essential, because it operates at the level of the relative and abstract; it separates the subject and object of knowledge from each other and so prevents "integral knowledge." Believing reason, by contrast, is capable of bringing them together in an immediate, concrete intuition. It is true to reality in its ontological or noumenal essence, whereas rationalism grasps only phenomena. It is a kind of inner revelation or immediate apprehension that penetrates to the heart of reality, ultimately to God, thus grounding the human person in divine being.[18] These ideas would have great influence on Russian religious philosophy later in the nineteenth century.[19]

V

The defense of human dignity was also a major theme among the Westernizers, though they took a different—Hegelian—philosophical approach to it. Hegelianism had a profound impact on Russian thought. Initially, in the second half of the 1830s, it was largely interpreted as a philosophy of "reconciliation with reality," a type of intellectual compensation for the near absence of public life in Russia under Nicholas I. Riasanovsky called it a "strange chapter" in Russian intellectual history, one based on a reading of Hegel's famous thesis, "What is real is rational, what is rational is real."[20] Reality was rational because it was a necessary aspect of the self-realization of the absolute; therefore the only logical course was to be reconciled with it, no matter how oppressive it seemed. This conservative historicist approach soon gave way, however, to a Left-Hegelian "philosophy of action," which resulted in the affirmation of individual freedom, responsibility, and dignity. The emphasis shifted from the self-realization of the absolute in history, which implied the individual's reconciliation before historical necessity, to the self-realization of the individual through active participation in history. By this stage (the early 1840s) Hegelianism self-consciously formed the philosophical framework of the Westernizers in their struggle against Slavophile conservative romanticism.[21]

The most visible figure among the Westernizers, indeed one of the founding members of the Russian intelligentsia, was the famous literary critic Vissarion Belinskii (1811-1848). He experienced a period of "reconciliation with reality," replete with accolades to the "most rational necessity" of the Russian tsar,[22] but soon rejected it for active participation in history. He took up the defense of the free, autonomous individual, which he now insisted ought not to be reduced to being a mere instrument of absolute spirit realizing itself in history. In March 1841 he wrote, "The fate of the subject, the individual, the person is of more importance to me than the fate of the whole world."[23] In these words Belinskii vindicates, in Walicki's formulation, "the particular (the real, living individual) against the tyranny of the universal (the Absolute, Reason, and the Spirit)." His affirmation of the autonomous individual against totalizing philosophical systems (such as Hegelian absolute idealism) came at the cost, however, of a certain tendency toward materialism, Ludwig Feuerbach's ideas in particular.[24]

Alexander Herzen (1812-1870), the founder of "Russian socialism" and among the most famous Russian thinkers, never experienced a period of "reconciliation with reality," but he did undertake a serious study of Hegel's philosophy.[25] The result was two long cycles of essays, *Dilettantism in Science* (1843) and *Letters on the Study of Nature* (1845-1846), the best products of Russian Left Hegelianism. In "Buddhism in Science," the most important essay from the first cycle, Herzen argues that the person or self comes into its own through concrete, active participation in history, not "Buddhist" withdrawal in abstract, universalizing thought (Hegel's "panlogism"). The self must master and appropriate the universal (or universal ideals), in the process personalizing the universal and universalizing itself (as Herzen's thought might be formulated). It must realize the universal in the particular, bringing it down to earth and raising the earth up to it. This process is history, and in it the self realizes its own autonomy, rationality, and dignity. That is the basic meaning of Herzen's dictum, "Action is the personality itself" — free, rational, and conscious action in history. It is a positive reconciliation, an Aristotelian "live unity of theory and practice." In some of his most famous words, Herzen wrote: "It is only in rational, morally free, and passionately energetic action that man arrives at the actuality of his personality and immortalizes himself in the phenomenal world. In such action man is eternal in the transient, infinite in the finite."[26]

In *Letters on the Study of Nature*, Herzen remains occupied with the theme of how the autonomous person realizes itself through reconciling the particular and universal, but he turns more to the epistemological foundations of his theory. Thus, he begins with basic methodological problems involved in the study of nature, outlining two ways of looking at the world. First are empirical methodologies and natural sciences, which concern themselves with particulars and with factual data. Second are speculative philosophical approaches such as idealism, which deal with universals. But neither empiricism nor idealism is sufficient on its own, and each tends to lead naturally to the other. True knowledge of the world requires a synthesis of both approaches.[27] "This synthesis," Walicki writes, "would benefit not only science but also — even chiefly — the development of the human personality." This is so because empiricism, by itself, fragments the human personality and threatens it with disintegration, while idealism (metaphysics) crushes it under the weight of the universal.[28] A sounder, more stable, and more holistic approach to the person rests on a synthesis of empiricist and idealist principles, or on a type of "integral knowledge" of the world (to borrow the Slavophile term, though in their epistemologies and theories of the person Herzen and Kireevskii are quite different thinkers).

In 1847 Herzen left Russia. During the first several years of his lifelong emigration, he developed an alternative vision of the future of Russia. His conception, known as "Russian socialism," combined elements from Petr Chaadaev, the Slavophiles, and the Westernizers: the "privilege of backwardness" in a country without the burdens of the past and thus freer to create its own future, the communalism of the Russian people, and the personality principle of the westernized elites. Herzen based his hopes for Russian socialism on a voluntaristic philosophy of history directed against teleological systems of historical necessity. He laid out his new philosophy of history, which repudiated important tenets of his earlier Hegelianism, in *From the Other Shore* (1850). His defense of individual liberty and critique of ideologies that threaten such liberty are well known, in part because they were championed by Sir Isaiah Berlin.[29] According to Herzen, history is a "whirlwind of chance," an open field of contingency and possibility within which human beings are free to realize their moral uniqueness and autonomy. He insisted that the individual ought never to be sacrificed to intellectual abstractions such as historical progress or the happiness of future generations. The defense of pluralism, the intrinsic value and dignity of the individual, and open-ended development were all important themes, but he neglected the vital importance of law in the defense of human dignity, liberty, and rights.[30]

VI

The Westernizers formed a broad camp spanning a range of political views from radical to liberal. The anarchist Mikhail Bakunin (1814-1876) was a radical if ever there were one; he can hardly be ranked among the great defenders of human dignity.[31] Belinskii and Herzen occupied an intermediate position. The main liberal Westernizers were Timofei Granovskii (1813-1855), Konstantin Kavelin (1818-1885), and Boris Chicherin (1828-1904). All three were Moscow University historians who, following Hegel, believed that the goal of the historical process, in Russia as in Europe, was the emancipation of the individual through the rationalization of social relations and law. Kavelin and Chicherin defended the rise of the centralized Muscovite state in this process. They founded the "state school" of Russian historiography, which held that the state was the main agent of progress in Russian history.

Kavelin's 1847 essay, "A Survey of Juridical Life in Old Russia," is one of the defining statements of Russian Westernism.[32] It is also an eloquent defense of human dignity and of personhood as the guiding principles of progressive historical development.[33] Kavelin attributed these principles to the advent of Christianity, which revealed to human beings an inner spiritual world, infinitely more precious than the external, material world. Christianity challenged humanity to express and develop its spiritual potential, and this "had to change completely the nature of history." With the Christian challenge to spiritual self-realization, "human *personhood* had to acquire a great, holy significance that previously it did not have." Thus arose, Kavelin writes, the idea of human dignity, the idea of the infinite and absolute value of the human person. This "completely new view of man" freed him from slavery to nature and to external circumstances: "man went from being determined to being determining," in his apt formulation. Kavelin's conclusion to this seminal passage is that the principles of "absolute human and personal dignity" (*beskonechnoe, bezuslovnoe dostoinstvo cheloveka i chelovecheskoi lichnosti*) and of humanity's "fullest possible moral and intellectual development" have, since their introduction by Christianity, become the "slogans of all modern history." In fact, he writes, "there is one goal for all peoples of the modern Christian world: unconditional recognition of human and personal dignity [*dostoinstvo cheloveka, litsa*] and man's all-round development. But all go toward this goal by various, infinitely diverse paths, like nature itself and the historical conditions of peoples."[34]

Chicherin studied with Kavelin and followed his teacher in making human dignity the foundation of his mature social and legal philosophy, though that would come mainly later, in the last two decades of the century. Thus Chicherin, Russia's greatest Hegelian philosopher, was the living link between the 1840s and the neo-idealist revival at the end of the century.

VII

Meanwhile, a new period in Russian intellectual history began with Alexander II's succession to the throne in 1855. The intelligentsia turned toward radicalism as the hopes of the Great Reforms turned to frustration and disappointment. Thinkers such as Nikolai Chernyshevskii (1828-1889), Nikolai Dobroliubov (1836-1861), and Dmitrii Pisarev (1840-1868) advanced various combinations of materialism, scientism, utilitarianism, and "rational egoism." Their outlook, frequently referred to as "nihilism," was notoriously embodied by Bazarov, the hero of Ivan Turgenev's novel *Fathers and Children*.[35] Though the worldview of the radical intelligentsia was charged with humanist pathos, its philosophical flaws prevented it from dealing successfully with the problem of human dignity. Its materialism and reductive positivism denied both free will and the ideals by which the will can alone be self-determining.[36] If one follows the Kantian concept of personhood as consisting in ideal self-determination, then the radicals undermined personhood at its very foundations. As Pisarev put it, "I see in life only a process, and I eliminate purpose and ideal."[37]

Positivism formed the general climate of progressive public opinion in Russia down to the twentieth century. In its most reductive forms, it took a naturalistic view of the world, asserting that the only reality, or at least the only one that we can know, is the empirical world of positively-given sense data. Yet the dominance of positivism was never complete. Pisarev, in the words quoted above, was responding to Petr Lavrov (1823-1900), who was an important theorist of Russian populism, the main revolutionary movement of the 1870s. In his influential essay cycle *Historical Letters* (1868-1869), Lavrov argued that progress was not a necessary historical law unfolding of its own accord but rather a moral task to be accomplished by "critically thinking individuals" inspired by ideals such as justice and human dignity.[38]

By the 1880s, a new wave of idealism broke upon the Russian philosophical scene and increasingly dominated it until the Bolshevik Revolution. It mounted a powerful revolt against positivism.[39] The first salvos were major ones: Boris Chicherin's *Science and Religion* (1879) and Vladimir Soloviev's *Critique of Abstract Principles* (1880). The late-century idealist revival is generally referred to as Russian neo-idealism to distinguish it from the idealism of the second quarter of the century, which, as we have seen, owed more to Kant's successors than to Kant himself. Russian neo-idealism raised the defense of human dignity to new levels. A prominent role in these developments was played by the Moscow Psychological Society, founded in 1885. Its name is somewhat misleading: though it did conduct and publish psychological research, its greater significance in Russian intellectual history is as the first and main center of the growth of Russian philosophy in this period. A key factor in the society's success was its journal *Questions of Philosophy and Psychology* (1889-1918), Russia's first regular, specialized journal in philosophy. In 1902 the society published *Problems of Idealism*, a large collective work that advanced a powerful critique of positivism and an innovative idealist defense of the main principles of liberalism.[40] By then the society had become the theory center of Russian liberalism. Chicherin and Soloviev, as Russia's greatest idealist philosophers and liberal theorists, were its most distinguished members.[41] They and their followers in the society, for all the differences among them, shared the same essential conception of liberalism: its first principle was human dignity—the ground, in turn, of human rights, whose enforcement defined the ultimate purpose and justification of the rule of law.

VIII

Chicherin is best known as Russia's greatest Hegelian philosopher.[42] He always considered himself a Hegelian, remarking in 1900 that he regarded Hegel as "the last word of idealist philosophy."[43] But beginning in the 1870s he adopted a liberal, Kantian interpretation of Hegel, so much so that Evgenii Trubetskoi, who knew him well, thought that his defense of the intrinsic value of personhood marked the "sharpest difference between Hegel's panlogism and Chicherin's individualistic worldview."[44] Chicherin's restoration of the Kantian principle of human dignity makes him the father of Russian neo-idealism. The key to his mature philosophy is his conception of human nature: he held that human beings are persons because they are endowed with reason and will, neither of which can be wholly explained by the positive or empirical sciences.[45] This alone makes man a "metaphysical being," in his phrase.[46] The metaphysical nature of personhood (reason and will) is the ground of human dignity, an argument Chicherin pursues at length and that is central to his conception of idealism.

32 – 1905, portrait by Leonid Pasternak of the veteran liberal scholar and zemstvo leader Boris Chicherin (1828-1904)

He defines reason as consciousness of the absolute, or of the absolute principle. It is "consciousness of pure law," of necessity and universality, in both knowledge (theoretical reason) and action (practical reason).[47] The practical form of consciousness of the absolute is the moral law, "which was revealed in all its profundity by the father of modern metaphysics, Kant."[48] Chicherin was strongly influenced by the *Groundwork of the Metaphysics of Morals*.[49] The Russian philosopher adopted its main principle as his own: the "supreme dignity" of the human person is a matter of self-determination according to the moral law, as he put it in his masterpiece, *Philosophy of Right*, published in 1900.[50] Like Kant, he considered practical reason to be the ground of personhood: "Freedom of the will constitutes . . . the basic definition of man as a rational being. Precisely because of this is he recognized as a person [*litso*] and are rights ascribed to him."[51] In a significant passage, he summarizes the nature and properties of personhood, emphasizing its intrinsic dignity:

> The source of this supreme dignity of the human being and of all the demands flowing from it consists in the fact that he carries in himself consciousness of the Absolute, that is, this source lies precisely in the metaphysical nature of the subject, which raises it above the whole physical world and makes it a being having value in itself and demanding respect. In religious language this is expressed in the saying that we are created in the image and likeness of God.[52]

The "image and likeness" of God was a powerful metaphor for human dignity for other Russian neo-idealists as well, Vladimir Soloviev in particular, as we will see.

Chicherin called idealism the true philosophy of freedom and named Kant its founder. "There is not and cannot be any other foundation of inner freedom and morality," he wrote.[53] Note this categorical endorsement of Kant by someone who considered himself to be a Hegelian philosopher. Not all Russian idealists followed Chicherin in his Kantian conception of idealism, but many did, including Soloviev. They also considered idealism to be the true philosophy of progress, of the ever closer approximation of imperfect, finite reality to the perfect, infinite ideal, or of what Kant called "perfectibility."[54]

Chicherin held that human dignity, as the first principle of liberalism, was the absolute value underlying society, law, and the state.[55] He recognized that human beings are social by nature and that their higher potential as persons cannot be realized apart from society.[56] The existence of society requires that the external liberty of people be mutually delimited as right (*pravo*) under coercive juridical law (*zakon*). In his definition, "right is a person's external freedom, as determined by a universal law (*obshchii zakon*)." In another formulation, "Society consists of people, and for all of them it is extremely important that the areas left to the freedom of each be precisely delimited and protected by law, and this is the task of right."[57]

Chicherin's conception of right is essentially "negative liberty," in the sense made famous by Isaiah Berlin. Very much unlike Berlin, however, Chicherin stresses that right is metaphysical in origin:

For external liberty becomes a right, that is, a demand, only because it is a manifestation of a person's inner, absolute freedom. . . . This is also the basis of respect for a person, the source of any right. . . . Right is an ideal demand in the name of an ideal principle. Human beings are recognized as free only on account of their metaphysical essence; they have rights and demand respect only on account of their suprasensible nature.[58]

Freedom is the one source, both of right (external liberty) and morality (inner liberty as self-determination). The essential difference between them consists in the respective relationship of law to freedom in each sphere. The law that determines right, or the law of right (*zakon prava*), is juridical, purely external, and backed by coercive power. The moral law (*nravstvennyi zakon*) is directed only toward conscience and must be freely fulfilled. It can never be coerced by virtue of the nature of morality as inner freedom.[59] Coerced fulfillment of the moral law, according to Chicherin, destroys the possibility of true morality and self-determination, and thus radically undermines the very foundations of human dignity and personhood.

Chicherin insisted that morality not be subject to juridical law or any coercion. But he did not think the reverse followed, that right and law are based only on coercion and that morality is to be excluded from their sphere. Rather, morality demands respect for right and the juridical order, since they are basic requirements of the existence of society, "without which the realization of moral principles would remain an empty phantom."[60] As he often affirms, "Morality demands respect for right, because it demands respect for human personhood and the law defending it."[61] When juridical law is observed not from fear of external punishment but out of consciousness of duty, then, he argues, it is not coerced but observed by free moral conviction.[62]

This is an important qualification to his view that the threat of coercion is the distinctive criterion of the juridical law that upholds right.[63] From it a series of questions arise, to wit: Which factor is more important, coercion or moral consciousness; does the balance shift with historical development; and, perhaps most important, doesn't the rule of law, in the higher sense of the limitation of arbitrary state power, ultimately rest on civil society, i.e., a citizenry with a well-developed legal consciousness? The tension in Chicherin's thought between coercion and morality in the observance of law proved to be a very creative one in the future development of Russian liberal theory. In general, the tendency was to deemphasize coercion in favor of consciousness.[64]

Chicherin's definition of right, and the distinction he draws between right and morality, are Kant's. In *Property and State* the Russian philosopher wrote of his German predecessor, "the true foundations of morality and right were revealed by him." Kant understood freedom as the one source of both in its dual manifestation: "in the inner sphere, where it is subject to the moral law, and in the external sphere, where it is governed by the law of right [*zakon prava*]."[65] In *Philosophy of Right* Chicherin says that the distinction between morality and right was "fully explained" by Kant.[66] In his essay on Kant in *History of Political Theory* he cites Kant's famous definitions in *The Metaphysics of Morals* that right is the coexistence of everyone's freedom in accordance with a universal law and that it authorizes the use of coercion (MM 387-388/6:230-231).[67]

Chicherin's indications that morality demands respect for right and the juridical order took him directly to the problem of natural law and justice, terms that signified virtually the same concept for him.[68] He prefers "justice," which he defines in terms of core (metaphysical) human equality.[69] "True justice," he writes, "consists in the recognition for all of equal human dignity and freedom."[70] The minimal requirement is equality before the law or equality of rights. In the chapter of *Philosophy of Right* devoted to the topic of personal rights, Chicherin contrasts the French Revolution's declaration of a whole series of natural and inalienable rights to Kant's view that there is only one innate right, freedom, from which all the others derive.[71] He accepts Kant's position, but asks in what sense can freedom be considered an innate right. Not in the sense, he says, of some "state of nature" apart from any civil order. "Authentic human freedom is not the freedom on an animal," he declares, "but civil freedom, subordinated to universal law. Only on account of this subordination does freedom become a right."[72]

Chicherin's social conception of human rights follows directly from his (and Kant's) definition of right as external liberty under law. He preferred to speak not of natural rights but of *pravosposobnost'*— the natural human capacity or potential to bear rights,[73] a potential that can be realized only in society, which is its whole justification. The realization of this potential is the (long and violent) historical process by which "natural man" is transformed into a citizen, "disciplined and respecting the right of others."[74]

The Kantian principles of liberalism form what Chicherin calls "individualism," or respect for the absolute value and dignity of the human person. Individualism is the "source and foundation" of any sound social theory but does not in itself complete such a theory. To complete it, Chicherin turned to Hegel, whose "great contribution" was to have outlined, in his "objective ethics," a rational social order in which people could find their higher unity and pursue the true realization of their freedom and dignity.[75] Space prevents me from pursuing the details here, but from the beginning of his account in *Philosophy of Right*, Chicherin interprets Hegel in a Kantian, liberal direction to safeguard the sanctity of the human person, maintaining that the higher social order of Hegel's objective ethics "achieves its true significance only when it is based on the rights and claims of the individual person."[76] He emphasized in particular the autonomy of civil society relative to the state: "For human personhood, for its freedom and rights, this recognition of the autonomy of civil society could not be more important."[77] He thought that the rule of law ultimately rested on a strong civil society suffused with a consciousness of human dignity, civil rights, and justice.

IX

Vladimir Soloviev (1853-1900), Russia's greatest religious philosopher, is usually portrayed as a rather different type of thinker than Chicherin, both in substance and style. Walicki presents them as representatives of the "old" and "new" Russian liberalism.[78] There is much truth in this contrast. But the similarities between the two philosophers are at least as significant as the differences.

Soloviev embedded his defense of human dignity within his

philosophy of Godmanhood (*bogochelovechestvo*, also translated theanthropy, divine humanity, or the humanity of God). In his *Lectures on Godmanhood* (delivered in 1878), his doctoral thesis *Critique of Abstract Principles* (defended and published in 1880), and in other works, he stipulates that human beings combine in themselves three principles: the absolute or divine principle, the material principle, and (between them) the distinctively human principle, which is rational autonomy or the capacity for self-determination.[79] The middle, human principle of autonomy is derived entirely from Kant.[80] Godmanhood combines the divine and human principles. It is the free human realization of the divine idea in ourselves and in the world. It is the realization of humanity's divine potential: deification or, to use the patristic term, *theosis*. It is, in short, the human project of building the kingdom of God. Soloviev always maintained that Godmanhood cannot be achieved without human autonomy: "The divine content must be appropriated by a human being *from within himself*, consciously and freely," through the fullest development of human rationality.[81]

The Russian philosopher Semën Frank wrote that the concept of Godmanhood extends the Chalcedonian dogma of Christ the God-man's two natures to all of existence.[82] It extends it, at any rate, to all human persons. I would argue that the concept is a distinctively Kantian interpretation of Chalcedon that emphasizes the autonomy of the human principle relative to the divine. In every human person, the divine element (the "image of God" in us) must be freely recognized and embraced by the human element (that is, by reason and will). Our task is to bring our nature into ever closer "likeness" or conformity with God. Christ achieved this perfect conformity, and he did so through an act of the rational human will.[83] As Oliver Smith puts it, "The humanity of Christ is 'spiritualized' or divinized not despite his humanity but because of it."[84] We are to follow Jesus' example and teaching: "Be perfect even as your Father in heaven is perfect" (Matthew 5:48, one of Soloviev's favorite verses). This is the true, divine-human path to the kingdom of God: divine in that God is the ideal of perfection, human in that the task of perfectibility is ours. Soloviev followed Kant in thinking that the kingdom of God could come only through the kingdom of ends, Kant's famous ideal of a moral order whose members respect each other as persons or ends-in-themselves.[85]

The autonomy and perfectibility by which our intrinsic potential divinity alone can be realized form the ground of human dignity. The divine principle in itself is not the source of human dignity; it must be coupled with the distinctively human principle of self-determination. For this connection Soloviev was deeply indebted to Kant, whose conception of autonomy and dignity he called the "essence of morality."[86] The Russian philosopher insisted that the realization of our divine potential be internally rather than externally determined (autonomously rather than heteronomously, in Kant's terms). Otherwise human dignity would be deprived of its basis. Salvation apart from self-determination would violate human dignity or at any rate be accomplished past it.

Soloviev's most powerful and systematic defense of human dignity is *Justification of the Good* (1897), widely regarded as the most important Russian work of moral philosophy. The very concept of the "justification of the good" is human perfectibility or progress toward Godmanhood. It is Soloviev's version of Kant's theology of moral perfectibility—Kant's notion, as we have seen, of "endless progress" toward holiness and of the postulates therefrom of immortality and of the existence of God. Soloviev preferred to speak of the divine principle or divine image in us rather than merely of Kant's moral law, but the "image" of God functions as the ideal just like Kant's moral law, while the human "likeness" to God describes our capacity for self-determination and infinite perfectibility according to the image or ideal.[87] In one passage he calls the image of God the power of representation (of absolute perfection) and the likeness of God the power of striving (to achieve it). This "double infinity" belongs to everyone. "It is in this that the absolute significance, dignity, and worth of human personhood consist, and this is the basis of its inalienable rights."[88] In another passage, perhaps the most capacious in *Justification of the Good*, he wrote: "The absolute value of man is based, as we know, upon the *possibility* inherent in his reason and his will of infinitely approaching perfection or, according to the patristic expression, the possibility of becoming divine (*theosis*)."[89]

Soloviev consistently held that human perfectibility (again, progress toward Godmanhood) is realized in society and develops in history. His social philosophy was first presented in comprehensive form in his doctoral dissertation, *Critique of Abstract Principles*. There he emphasizes an essentially negative or classically liberal understanding of law that generally follows Kant (without acknowledgement).[90] Like Chicherin, he subscribed to a social conception of human rights based on Kant's definition of right as external liberty under law. In his account, freedom is the innate or natural property of the person, but in the state of nature its external manifestation is simply a matter of individual power. Freedom becomes a right only in society, when it is recognized by others.[91] The recognition of each other's freedom, which necessarily involves its mutual and equal delimitation, is what makes freedom into a right. According to Soloviev, I can assert my freedom as a right in relation to others only if I respect their freedom as a right, or, "in other words, if I recognize the equality of all in this respect." On this basis he arrives at the following basic definition: "*Right is freedom conditioned by equality.*" This definition combines the individualistic principle of freedom with the societal principle of equality, so that right can also be defined as "*the synthesis of freedom and equality.*"[92] He agreed with Kant and Chicherin that law, to be effective, must be backed by force.[93]

Soloviev also embraced the idea of natural law, which he thought ought to guide the actual, historical development of positive law as its rational essence and normative ideal. The goal is an ever more lawful and just society, and the ever fuller realization of human potential. In his words, "Freedom, as the foundation of all *human* existence, and equality, as the necessary form of all *societal* existence, in combination form *human society* as a *lawful order.*"[94] Law is an essential but not the highest principle of Soloviev's social philosophy. It deals with the means by which people pursue their ends, not the ends themselves (which ends Soloviev defined as the pursuit of moral perfection in the free unity of spiritual love). He directly followed Kant in defining his social ideal as the ethical (and not merely juridical) community of the "kingdom of ends," which both philosophers thought of as the church. Soloviev called it "free theocracy."[95]

X

The philosophical legacies of Chicherin and Soloviev inspired and informed *Problems of Idealism*, published by the Moscow Psychological Society in 1902. The volume's impressive exposition of the philosophical foundations of liberalism strategically coincided—as its organizers intended—with the first stages of the Russian Liberation Movement that would culminate in the Revolution of 1905. The project was planned by Peter Struve, who had just completed his evolution from Marxism to idealism, and by Pavel Novgorodtsev, a legal philosopher at Moscow University. The defense of human rights was integral to their conception of liberalism, as it was to Chicherin's and Soloviev's.[96] This was so, I would suggest, because their conceptions were self-consciously idealist, specifically Kantian, and firmly grounded in the principle of human dignity. The idealism of Russian liberalism distinguishes it from other contemporary European liberalisms, which were generally positivistic in their philosophical outlook.[97] If there was a relative paucity of appeals to human rights in nineteenth-century European liberalism as a whole, as some historians today claim, then this philosophical difference might help to explain it.[98]

Earlier in this chapter I noted that in the circumstances of autocratic Russia, liberalism was something to be developed mainly in theory until the day when it could be put more fully into practice. That day seemed to have arrived in 1905, when civil society, inspired to take up the defense of human dignity and human rights, was just strong enough to force Nicholas II to concede a constitution. But Nicholas continued to think of himself as an autocrat and to do everything possible to impede Russia's further liberal development. Under the enormous strains of the Great War, the old regime collapsed in February 1917. In October of that year, the Bolsheviks, heirs of the radical intelligentsia and of the old revolutionary movement, took power and proceeded to impose their own autocracy on Russia. In 1922 Lenin exiled almost hundred leading members of the country's humanistic intelligentsia.[99] He understood well enough that its defense of human dignity was inimical to the Bolshevik vision of Russia's future. Like the nihilists before him, he rejected the very notion of the ideal. The most obvious example of this goes to the heart of Leninism: in 1902 he pronounced the workers incapable of developing their own true consciousness, which, as a result, would have to be externally imposed on them. For Lenin everything was a matter of external determination by the party, not of individual self-determination. Thus he undermined human dignity at its very foundations. For this reason Nikolai Berdiaev wrote, "Lenin did not believe in man."[100]

Abbreviations

HRP: *A History of Russian Philosophy, 1830–1930: Faith, Reason, and the Defense of Human Dignity.* Edited by G. M. Hamburg and Randall A. Poole. Cambridge: Cambridge University Press, 2010.

HRT: *A History of Russian Thought.* Edited by William Leatherbarrow and Derek Offord. Cambridge, UK: Cambridge University Press, 2010.

RP: *Russian Philosophy.* Edited by James M. Edie, James P. Scanlan, Mary-Barbara Zeldin, and George L. Kline. 3 vols. Chicago: Quadrangle Books, 1965; Knoxville: University of Tennessee Press, 1976.

Notes

1 This chapter is based on a public lecture delivered at Rhodes College (February 2014), St. Mary's University of Minnesota (April 2013), the College of St. Scholastica (January 2013), and the University of Toronto (February 2012). The development of a distinctive Russian tradition of philosophical humanism focused on the defense of human dignity is the main theme of *A History of Russian Philosophy, 1830–1930: Faith, Reason, and the Defense of Human Dignity*, edited by G. M. Hamburg and Randall A. Poole (Cambridge, UK: Cambridge University Press, 2010).

2 On the origins and nature of the Russian intelligentsia, see Isaiah Berlin, *Russian Thinkers,* edited by Henry Hardy and Aileen Kelly, rev. 2nd ed. (London: Penguin, 2008); G. M. Hamburg "Russian

Intelligentsias," in *HRT*, 44–69; *The Russian Intelligentsia*, edited by Richard Pipes (New York: Columbia University Press, 1961); Philip Pomper, *The Russian Revolutionary Intelligentsia* (New York: Crowell, 1970); Marc Raeff, *Origins of the Russian Intelligentsia: The Eighteenth-Century Nobility* (San Diego: Harcourt Brace Jovanovich, 1966); and Nicholas V. Riasanovsky, *A Parting of Ways: Government and the Educated Public in Russia, 1801–1855* (Oxford: Oxford University Press, 1976).

3   Randall A. Poole, "Nineteenth-Century Russian Liberalism: Ideals and Realities," review essay, *Kritika: Explorations in Russian and Eurasian History* 16, no. 1 (Winter 2015): 157-181.

4   *Human Rights: Comments and Interpretations*, edited by Jacques Maritain (New York: Columbia University Press, 1949). This volume collects the main papers of UNESCO's inquiry into the philosophical and religious foundations of human rights, conducted in 1947 at the request of the UN Commission on Human Rights to help inform its work on the Universal Declaration of Human Rights. In his introduction to the symposium, Maritain wrote that "faith in freedom and democracy is founded on the faith in the inherent dignity of men and women." He notes that while the history of declarations of human rights is relatively recent, beginning with the English Bill of Rights (1689), the history of the idea of "the dignity and brotherhood of man" is very long. See *The Human Rights Reader: Major Political Essays, Speeches, and Documents from Ancient Times to the Present*, edited by Micheline R. Ishay, 2nd ed. (New York and London: Routledge, 2007), Maritain quotations at 3. See also Ishay, *The History of Human Rights: From Ancient Times to the Globalization Era* (Berkeley: University of California Press, 2004); Paul Gordon Lauren, *The Evolution of International Human Rights: Visions Seen*, 3rd ed. (Philadelphia: University of Pennsylvania Press, 2011); and Peter N. Stearns, *Human Rights in World History* (New York and London: Routledge, 2012).

5   Giovanni Pico della Mirandola, "Oration on the Dignity of Man," translated by E. L. Forbes, in *The Renaissance Philosophy of Man*, edited by Ernst Cassirer et al. (Chicago: University of Chicago Press, 1948), 223–227.

6   Allen W. Wood, *Kant's Ethical Thought* (Cambridge, UK: Cambridge University Press, 1999), 12.

7   References to Kant are to *The Cambridge Edition of the Works of Immanuel Kant*, in this case to the volume *Practical Philosophy*, translated and edited by Mary J. Gregor, introduction by Allen Wood (Cambridge, UK: Cambridge University Press, 1996). This volume contains, among Kant's works that I have used here, *Groundwork of the Metaphysics of*

Morals (G), *Critique of Practical Reason* (PrR), and *The Metaphysics of Morals* (MM). The first page reference is to the Cambridge edition, the second to the standard German edition of Kant's works, *Kants gesammelte Schriften* (as indicated in the margins of the Cambridge edition). Kant writes that "neither fear nor inclination but simply respect for the [moral] law is that incentive which can give actions a moral worth" (G 88/4:440).

8   The treatise is translated in part by Frank Y. Gladney and George L. Kline in *RP* 1: 77–100, here 78.

9   Alexander Radishchev, "On Man, His Mortality and Immortality," in *RP* 1: 99–100. See also Andrzej Walicki, *History of Russian Thought from the Enlightenment to Marxism*, translated by Hilda Andrews-Rusiecka (Stanford: Stanford University Press, 1979), 50–52.

10 Z. A. Kamenskii, "Kant v Rossii (konets XVIII—pervaia chetvert' XIX v.)," in *Filosofiia Kanta i sovremennost'*, edited by Teodor Il'ich Oizerman (Moscow: Mysl', 1974), 289–328; Thomas Nemeth, "Kant in Russia: The Initial Phase," in *Studies in Soviet Thought* 36, nos. 1–2 (1988): 79–110; and Nemeth, "Kant in Russia: The Initial Phase (Continued)," in *Studies in Soviet Thought* 40, no. 4 (1990): 293–338.

11 Alexandre Koyré, *La philosophie et le problème national en Russie au début du XIX-e siècle* (Paris, 1929); Koyré, *Études sur l'histoire de la pensée philosophique en Russie* (Paris, 1950); D. I. Chizhevskii, *Gegel v Rossii* (Paris: "Dom Knigi" and "Sovremennye Zapiski," 1939). For a perceptive recent study of the Russian reception of Schelling and Hegel, see Patrick Lally Michelson, "Slavophile Religious Thought and the Dilemma of Russian Modernity, 1830–1860," *Modern Intellectual History* 7, no. 2 (2010): 239–267.

12 Andrzej Walicki, *The Slavophile Controversy: History of a Conservative Utopia in Nineteenth-Century Russian Thought*, translated by Hilda Andrews-Rusiecka (Oxford: Oxford University Press, 1975/Notre Dame: University of Notre Dame Press, 1989).

13 Sergey Horujy, "Slavophiles, Westernizers, and the Birth of Russian Philosophical Humanism," in *HRP*, 49.

14 Both the essay and the fragments can be found in *On Spiritual Unity: A Slavophile Reader*, translated and edited by Robert Bird and Boris Jakim (Hudson, NY: Lindisfarne Books, 1998), 234-291. Subsequent citations made parenthetically in the text.

15 See Abbott Gleason, *European and Muscovite: Ivan Kireevsky and the Origins of Slavophilism* (Cambridge, MA: Harvard University Press, 1972), 236-257.

16 Werner Jaeger emphasizes the Greek influence: "From the Renaissance the line leads straight back to the Christian humanism of the [Greek]

fathers of the fourth century A.D. and to their idea of man's dignity. . . . With the Greeks who emigrated after the fall of Constantinople (1453) there came to Italy the whole literary tradition of the Byzantine East, and the works of the Greek fathers were its choicest part." See Jaeger, *Early Christianity and Greek Paideia* (Cambridge, MA: Harvard University Press, 1961), 100-101. See also Paul Oskar Kristellar, *Renaissance Thought and Its Sources*, edited by Michael Mooney (New York: Columbia University Press, 1979); and Charles Trinkaus, *In Our Image and Likeness: Humanity and Divinity in Italian Humanist Thought*, 2 vols. (Chicago: University of Chicago Press, 1970/Notre Dame: University of Notre Dame Press, 1995).

17 Walicki has emphasized Kireevsky's debt to European romanticism, especially the later Schelling's philosophy of revelation (*Philosophie der Offenbarung*)—in opposition to Hegel, in whom both Schelling and the Slavophiles saw the culmination of European rationalism. Walicki, *Slavophile Controversy*, 121-178.

18 Walicki, *Slavophile Controversy*, 155-156. Another fragment contains the following words: "Justice, morality, the spirit of the people, human dignity, and the sanctity of lawfulness can all be felt only along with an awareness of the eternal religious relations of humanity" (291). The "sanctity of lawfulness" is an interesting "non-Slavophile" expression in this context.

19 Vladimir Soloviev, for example, was much indebted to them, as even the titles of some of his earlier philosophical works betray: *The Philosophical Principles of Integral Knowledge* (1877) and *Critique of Abstract Principles* (1880). The first has recently been translated: Vladimir Solovyov, *The Philosophical Principles of Integral Knowledge*, translated by Valeria Z. Nollan (Grand Rapids, MI and Cambridge, UK: William B. Eerdmans, 2008).

20 Riasanovsky, *Parting of Ways*, 211-212.

21 Walicki, *History of Russian Thought*, ch. 7, "The Russian Hegelians—From 'Reconciliation with Reality' to 'Philosophy of Action.'"

22 The quoted phrase is from Belinskii's 1839 review of Zhukovskii's poem "The Anniversary of Borodino." The review is quoted at length in Riasanovsky, *Parting of Ways*, 213–215.

23 Vissarion Belinskii, "Letters to V. P. Botkin," translated by Philip Rahv, in *RP* 1: 304. His 1847 letter to Nikolai Gogol was also much celebrated. The letter was in response to Gogol's *Selected Passages from Correspondence with Friends*, in which the Russian novelist, theretofore regarded as a keen critic of Russian state and society, humbly and piously accepted the Orthodox Church and the whole tsarist system, including serfdom. Belinskii penned a scathing denunciation that

could also be read as directed against the Slavophiles. He chided Gogol for failing "to observe that Russia sees her salvation not in mysticism or asceticism or pietism, but in the advances of civilization, enlightenment, and humanity. She needs not sermons . . . or prayers . . . but the awakening in the people of a sense of their human dignit, lost in the mud and filth for so many centuries; she needs rights and laws which conform not to the teachings of the Church but to common sense and justice." Vissarion Belinskii, "Letter to Gogol," translated by James P. Scanlan, in *RP* 1: 313.

24 Walicki, *History of Russian Thought*, 126.
25 Martin Malia, *Alexander Herzen and the Birth of Russian Socialism, 1812-1855* (Cambridge, MA: Harvard University Press, 1961), esp. ch. 10 on his Hegelianism.
26 Herzen, "Buddhism in Science," in *RP* 1: 332, 334. See also Walicki, *History of Russian Thought*, 129–131, and Horujy, "Slavophiles, Westernizers," 40-42. The classic exposition of Herzen's Hegelian defense of the autonomy and dignity of the human person is Gustav Shpet, *Filosofskoe mirovozzrenie Gertsena* (Petrograd: Kolos, 1921).
27 Alexander Herzen, "Letters on the Study of Nature," in *RP* 1: 338–343.
28 Walicki, *History of Russian Thought*, 131-134, quotation at 132.
29 Isaiah Berlin, *Russian Thinkers*. See also Aileen M. Kelly, *Toward Another Shore: Russian Thinkers between Necessity and Chance* (New Haven: Yale University Press, 1998) and Kelly, *Views from the Other Shore: Essays on Herzen, Chekhov, and Bakhtin* (New Haven: Yale University Press, 1999).
30 Herzen, *From the Other Shore and the Russian People and Socialism*, translated by Moura Budberg and Richard Wollheim, with an introduction by Isaiah Berlin (London: Weidenfeld and Nicolson, 1956); Derek Offord, "Alexander Herzen," in *HRP*, 52–68; and Walicki, *History of Russian Thought*, ch. 10, "The Origins of 'Russian Socialism.'"
31 Aileen M. Kelly, *Mikhail Bakunin: A Study in the Psychology and Politics of Utopianism* (New Haven: Yale University Press, 1987).
32 For summary and analysis see Derek Offord, *Portraits of Early Russian Liberals: A Study of the Thought of T. N. Granovsky, V. P. Botkin, P. V. Annenkov, A. V. Druzhinin and K. D. Kavelin* (Cambridge, UK: Cambridge University Press, 1985, 2009), 178-186.
33 Bogdan Kistiakovskii called him "the first thinker to substantiate the theory of personality [or personhood] in Russian literature." See B. A. Kistiakovskii, "The 'Russian Sociological School' and the Category of Possibility in the Solution of Social-Ethical Problems," in *Problems of Idealism: Essays in Russian Social Philosophy*, translated and edited by Randall A. Poole (New Haven: Yale University Press, 2003), 325-355, here 335.

34 K. D. Kavelin, "Vzgliad na iuridicheskii byt drevnei Rossii," in Kavelin, *Nash umstvennyi stroi: Stat'i po filosofii russkoi istorii i kul'tury*, edited by V. K. Kantor and O. E. Maiorova (Moscow: Pravda, 1989), 19-20.
35 Richard Pearce, "Nihilism," in *HRT*, 116–140.
36 Victoria S. Frede, "Materialism and the Radical Intelligentsia: The 1860s," in *HRP*, 69-89; and Walicki, *History of Russian Thought*, ch. 11, "Nikolai Chernyshevsky and the 'Enlighteners' of the Sixties."
37 Dmitrii Pisarev, "Nineteenth-Century Scholasticism," in *RP* 2: 77.
38 Peter Lavrov, *Historical Letters*, edited and translated by James P. Scanlan (Berkeley and Los Angeles: University of California Press, 1967); Thomas Nemeth, "Russian Ethical Humanism: From Populism to Neo-Idealism," in *HRP*, 90–107; and Walicki, *History of Russian Thought*, ch. 12, "Populist Ideologies."
39 For the broader European revolt against positivism, see H. Stuart Hughes, *Consciousness and Society: The Reorientation of European Social Thought*, revised ed. (New York: Vintage Books, 1977).
40 Cited in note 33 above.
41 For an authoritative account of Chicherin and Soloviev as liberal philosophers, see Andrzej Walicki, *Legal Philosophies of Russian Liberalism* (Oxford: Oxford University Press, 1987), chs. 2 and 3.
42 The preeminent scholars of Chicherin are Andrzej Walicki and Gary Hamburg, whose works on him are invaluable: Walicki, *Legal Philosophies of Russian Liberalism*; G. M. Hamburg, *Boris Chicherin and Early Russian Liberalism, 1828–1866* (Stanford: Stanford University Press, 1992); Hamburg, "Boris Chicherin and Human Dignity in History," in *HRP*, 111–130; and *Liberty, Equality, and the Market: Essays by B. N. Chicherin*, edited and translated by G. M. Hamburg (New Haven: Yale University Press, 1998).
43 Boris Chicherin, *Filosofiia prava* (Moscow, 1900), 24. The book was serialized in *Voprosy filosofii i psikhologii*, 1898-1899.
44 E. N. Trubetskoi, "Uchenie B. N. Chicherina o sushchnosti i smysle prava," in *Voprosy filosofii i psikhologii* 16: 5, kn. 80 (1905): 353-381, here 367.
45 Chicherin, *Filosofiia prava*, 26-28, 54.
46 Chicherin, *Filosofiia prava*, 7.
47 Chicherin, *Nauka i religiia*, 2nd ed. (Moscow, 1901), 113.
48 Chicherin, *Liberty, Equality, and the Market*, 359; the quotation is from the key first chapter (cited below as "Liberty") of his *Sobstvennost' i gosudarstvo*, 2 vols. (Moscow: 1882-1883).
49 Chicherin's essay on Kant in his *Istoriia politicheskikh uchenii*, 5 vols. (Moscow: 1869-1902), vol. 3: 324-374 (cited below as "Kant"), contains

a good exposition of the *Groundwork* with citations to the German text (330-336). Hamburg, "Boris Chicherin and Human Dignity in History," *HRP*, 124, refers to Chicherin's "remarkably sympathetic" account here of the *Groundwork* (and of the *Critique of Practical Reason*). In a chapter of *Philosophy of Right* entitled "The Moral Law and Freedom," Chicherin presents the main conclusions of the *Groundwork* as his own (*Filosofiia prava*, 170-177).

50 Chicherin, *Filosofiia prava*, 176. He also writes, "The whole moral dignity of man is based on the free fulfillment of the [moral] law" (31).
51 Chicherin, *Filosofiia prava*, 53.
52 Chicherin, *Filosofiia prava*, 55.
53 Chicherin, "Kant," 339-340.
54 In one of Chicherin's formulations, "Humanity's whole development proceeds from ideal aspirations. Reason, in the name of as of yet unrealized goals, reworks what is [*sushchestvuiushchee*]. As soon as we renounce idealism, we will also have to renounce progress, and with it freedom, which serves as its instrument." Chicherin, *Nauka i religiia*, 129 (note).
55 Chicherin, *Filosofiia prava*, 53 (also see 65-66). Hamburg presents a careful explication of *Philosophy of Right* in his "Boris Chicherin and Human Dignity in History," *HRP*, 119-128.
56 Chicherin, *Nauka i religiia*, 123; "Liberty," 353-354.
57 Chicherin, *Filosofiia prava*, 84, 86; also see "Liberty," 363-364.
58 Chicherin, *Nauka i religiia*, 124-125.
59 Chicherin, *Filosofiia prava*, 88-89; "Liberty," 365.
60 Chicherin, *Filosofiia prava*, 90.
61 Chicherin, *Filosofiia prava*, 188.
62 Chicherin, *Filosofiia prava*, 172.
63 According to E. N. Trubetskoi, Chicherin, "like the majority of contemporary jurists, sees in coercion the essential characteristic of law [*pravo*]." He thinks this is mistaken. See Trubetskoi, "Uchenie B. N. Chicherina," 362.
64 Leon Petrazycki's psychological theory of law, though it was broadly positivist rather than idealist, was also an important factor in this development. See Walicki, *Legal Philosophies of Russian Liberalism*, chapter 4.
65 Chicherin, *Sobstvennost' i gosudarstvo*, vol. 1: 41.
66 Chicherin, *Filosofiia prava*, 175.
67 Chicherin, "Kant," 345-346, 348. For good overviews of Kant's concept of right, see Wolfgang Kersting, "Politics, Freedom, and Order: Kant's Political Philosophy," in *The Cambridge Companion to Kant*, edited by Paul Guyer (Cambridge, UK: Cambridge University Press, 1992), 344-

348; and Paul Guyer, "Kantian Foundations for Liberalism," in Guyer, *Kant on Freedom, Law, and Happiness* (Cambridge, UK: Cambridge University Press, 2000), 239-243.

68 He uses the term "natural law" to distinguish between positive or statutory law and the higher norms to which it should be subject. Natural law is not enacted, "and therefore is not coercive law, but a system of universal juridical norms issuing from human reason that ought to serve as a measure and guide for positive legislation." Chicherin, *Filosofiia prava*, 94.

69 Chicherin, *Filosofiia prava*, 95-96. Also see the last chapter, "Equality," of the first book of *Sobstvennost' i gosudarstvo*, 1: 238-269. It is translated in Hamburg, *Liberty, Equality, and the Market*, 380-405.

70 Chicherin, *Filosofiia prava*, 99.

71 Chicherin, *Filosofiia prava*, 105; also see "Kant," 349. Chicherin's derivation of equality and basic personal rights from innate freedom closely follows Kant's formulation in *The Metaphysics of Morals* (MM 393-394/6:237-238).

72 Chicherin, *Filosofiia prava*, 106.

73 For examples, see "Hegel" and "Equality" in *Liberty, Equality, and the Market*, 299, 386. See also Walicki, *Legal Philosophies of Russian Liberalism*, 138.

74 Chicherin, *Filosofiia prava*, 106.

75 Chicherin, *Filosofiia prava*, 228.

76 Chicherin, *Filosofiia prava*, 228. The nature of Chicherin's Hegelianism changed over the course of his career, from "conservative liberalism" to "classical liberalism," with 1866 being a watershed. That year saw both the publication of Chicherin's *O narodnom predstavitel'stve* (*On Popular Representation*) and the shift in Russia's political climate toward the autocratic retrenchment that characterized the remaining decades of the old regime and that gave rise in turn to the revolutionary movement. In this climate, Hamburg argues, "Chicherin sought ways to secure the sphere of individual liberty against infringements by both state and society as a whole." Hamburg, *Boris Chicherin and Early Russian Liberalism*, 342. The results were clear by 1882, when Chicherin published *Property and State*, with its classic liberal emphasis on individual rights and civil law. As Walicki characterizes the change, "the new element in Chicherin's political views was his growing realization that political authority as such must be qualified and restricted, and that therefore he could no longer support the Hegelian doctrine of the unlimited sovereignty of the state." Walicki, *Legal Philosophies of Russian Liberalism*, 137. For more on this intellectual evolution, see Walicki, *Legal Philosophies of Russian Liberalism*, 132-139,

155-164; Hamburg, "An Eccentric Vision: The Political Philosophy of B. N. Chicherin," constituting the introduction to *Liberty, Equality, and the Market*, 1-65, esp. 53-65; and Hamburg, "Boris Chicherin and Human Dignity in History."
77 Chicherin, *Filosofiia prava*, 259.
78 In his *Legal Philosophies of Russian Liberalism*, the chapter on Chicherin is subtitled "the 'Old Liberal' Philosophy of Law" and the chapter on Soloviev is subtitled "Religious Philosophy and the Emergence of the 'New Liberalism.'"
79 For further development see my chapter, "Vladimir Solov'ëv's Philosophical Anthropology: Autonomy, Dignity, and Perfectibility," in *HRP*, 131-149.
80 In *Critique of Abstract Principles*, Soloviev closely paraphrases and directly translates large parts of the *Groundwork of the Metaphysic of Morals*. See *Kritika otvlechënnykh nachal*, in *Sobranie sochinenii Vladimira Sergeevicha Solov'eva*, 2nd ed., edited by S. M. Soloviev and E. L. Radlov, 10 vols. (St. Petersburg, 1911-1914), 2: 44-62. In addition to these two chapters, he devotes three more, plus an appendix, to Kant's ethics and conception of rational autonomy, drawing also on (paraphrasing and quoting at length) the *Critique of Pure Reason* and the *Critique of Practical Reason*. See *Sobranie sochinenii*, 2: 62-72, 89-116, 371-397.
81 Soloviev, "Istoricheskie dela filosofii" (1880), in *Sobranie sochinenii*, 2: 410.
82 S. L. Frank, "Introduction," in *A Solovyov Anthology*, edited by S. L. Frank, translated by Natalie Duddington (London: SCM Press, 1950), 15-16.
83 Soloviev, "The Great Dispute and Christian Politics" in *A Solovyov Anthology*, 77.
84 Oliver Smith, *Vladimir Soloviev and the Spiritualization of Matter* (Boston: Academic Studies Press, 2011), 119.
85 For further development, see my essay, "Kant and the Kingdom of Ends in Russian Religious Thought (Vladimir Solov'ev)," in *Thinking Orthodox in Modern Russia: Culture, History, Context*, edited by Patrick Lally Michelson and Judith Deutsch Kornblatt (Madison: University of Wisconsin Press, 2014), 215-234.
86 Soloviev, *Kritika otvlechënnykh nachal*, in *Sobranie sochinenii*, 2: 44.
87 Vladimir Solovyov, *The Justification of the Good: An Essay on Moral Philosophy*, translated by Natalie A. Duddington, edited and annotated by Boris Jakim (Grand Rapids, Mich.: William B. Eerdmans Publishing Company, 2005), 145. At points I have modified the Duddington translation in accordance with the Russian text: *Opravdanie dobra: nravstvennaia filosofiia*, in *Sobranie sochinenii*, 8: 3-516.

88 Solovyov, *The Justification of the Good*, 176 (translation modified); see also at 152.
89 Solovyov, *The Justification of the Good*, 296.
90 Soloviev, *Kritika otvlechënnykh nachal*, 152-155.
91 Soloviev, *Kritika otvlechënnykh nachal*, 152-153.
92 Soloviev, *Kritika otvlechënnykh nachal*, 153.
93 Soloviev, *Kritika otvlechënnykh nachal*, 136.
94 Soloviev, *Kritika otvlechënnykh nachal*, 155. Despite certain changes in his legal philosophy in *Justification of the Good*, Soloviev remained convinced of the basic principles of law that he set forth in *Critique of Abstract Principles*. He reprinted its two main chapters on law, together with two sections from *Justification of the Good*, in *Law and Morality: Essays in Applied Ethics* (1897), which serves as a good overall statement of his philosophy of law. It is translated in *Politics, Law, and Morality: Essays by V. S. Soloviev*, edited and translated by Vladimir Wozniuk (New Haven: Yale University Press, 2000), 131-212. For astute analyses of Soloviev's social and legal philosophy, see Walicki, *Legal Philosophies of Russian Liberalism*, 165-212, and Paul Valliere, "Vladimir Soloviev (1853-1900)," in *The Teachings of Modern Christianity on Law, Politics, and Human Nature*, edited by John Witte Jr. and Frank S. Alexander, 2 vols. (New York: Columbia University Press, 2006), 1: 533-575.
95 For details, see Poole, "Kant and the Kingdom of Ends," 223-228.
96 In 1901, as he was planning *Problems of Idealism*, Struve published one of his most remarkable essays (and dedicated it to Soloviev), "What is True Nationalism?" For him, any true nationalism must rest on true liberalism, which demands "recognition of the inalienable rights of the person." P. Borisov [Struve], "V chem zhe istinnyi natsionalizm?" in *Voprosy filosofii i psikhologii* 12: 4, kn. 59 (1901): 493-528 (quoted phrase at 512); reprinted in his collection of articles, *Na raznye temy* (St. Petersburg, 1902), 526-555. For analysis see Richard Pipes, *Struve: Liberal on the Left, 1870-1905* (Cambridge, MA: Harvard University Press, 1970), 300-307.
97 John Stuart Mill is a good example. There were positivistic currents of Russian liberalism, too, represented most notably by Pavel Miliukov.
98 To quote one of these historians: Human rights, after their initial formulation in the Atlantic revolutions of the late eighteenth century, "almost disappeared from political and legal discourse in the nineteenth century." Human rights "in their specific contemporary connotations are a relatively recent invention." Stefan-Ludwig Hoffman, "Introduction: Genealogies of Human Rights," in *Human Rights in the Twentieth Century*, edited by Stefan-Ludwig Hoffman

(Cambridge, UK: Cambridge University Press, 2011), 1, 3. See also Samuel Moyn, *The Last Utopia: Human Rights in History* (Cambridge, MA: Harvard University Press, 2010).
99 Stuart Finkel, *On the Ideological Front: The Russian Intelligentsia and the Making of the Soviet Public Sphere* (New Haven: Yale University Press, 2007); and Lesley Chamberlain, *Lenin's Private War: The Voyage of the Philosophy Steamer and the Exile of the Intelligentsia* (New York: St. Martin's Press, 2006).
100 Nicolas Berdyaev, *The Origin of Russian Communism*, translated by R. M. French (Ann Arbor: University of Michigan Press, 1960), 127.

11 Russian Foreign Policy and the Change of Dynasty in Greece (1862-1864)

Lucien J. Frary

33 – King Othon (Otto) of Greece (1815–1875, r. 1838-1862) riding with his consort Amalia of Oldenberg (1818-1875), 1853.

Introduction

The relationship between the ecumenicity of the Christian religion and the autonomy of the modern nation state operated as a central point of contention among clerics, politicians, and worldly intellectuals once the Greek state became independent in about 1830. A brief review of three phases of scholarship concerning this problem helps clarify the crystallization of modern Greek identity. The first wave began with the field-setting oeuvre of Konstantinos Paparrigopoulos, who, in his major synthesis published in the

1870s, argued that the Greeks of antiquity were the ancestors of those of modern times. According to his interpretation, Byzantium served as an intermediary link connecting the glorious classical past with the less eminent modern Greek reality.[1] Central to Paparrigopoulos' understanding of the Byzantine Empire was the ideological underpinning of the universal Church as both the chief element legitimizing the state as well as the core of what it meant to be a civilized Greek or Hellene. During the five centuries of Ottoman rule following the conquest of Constantinople in 1453, Orthodoxy remained the fundamental factor differentiating the Greek people from their Muslim overlords. Religious antagonism thus served as the defining factor leading to the outbreak of the Greek Revolution in 1821. Thanks to Paparrigopoulos' influence, Orthodoxy figured prominently in subsequent historical interpretations of Greek self-consciousness.

Starting in the mid-twentieth century, a second phase of scholarship, led by the literary specialists Nikolaos Politis and Konstantinos Dimaras, began to challenge Paparrigopoulos's views by highlighting the modern, ethnic roots of national identity and the effect of Greek merchants and intellectuals trained in the West during the era of the Enlightenment on nationhood formation.[2] In particular, Dimaras and his school shed new light on the secular roots of the movement for Greek independence. The impact of the French Revolution began to displace the prominent role of religion in a perspective that underscored the role of intellectuals, such as Rigas Velestinlis and Adamantios Korais, in the movement for secession from the sultan.[3]

More recently, a third wave of scholarship began to subject the work of Dimaras to critical questioning. Spearheaded by a sophisticated series of articles and books by Paschalis Kitromilides, religion was reinstated into debate about the formation of Greek national identity.[4] Influenced, in part, by the groundbreaking work by Elie Kedourie and Benedict Anderson, Kitromilides stresses the incongruence between secular nationalism and Orthodox ecumenism, arguing that the two concepts clashed in Greece as the forces of modernity took root. Thus, the first decades of the independent Greek kingdom, according to Kitromilides, were characterized by the friction between religion and secular nationalism.

The present essay builds upon this body of scholarship and argues that modern Greek identity, originally based on the Ottoman Orthodox religious community, developed into a synthesis of modern nationalism and traditional religious beliefs during the complex process of state-building that took place during the first decades of independence. It focuses on the Greek Revolution of 1862, which led to the downfall of the King Othon, a Bavarian Catholic, and his replacement with King George from Denmark, a convert to Orthodoxy, to illuminate the symbiosis between religion and secular nationalism. Based upon Russian archives, the essay highlights the religious factor behind the rebellion and demonstrates that King Othon was unable, as a Catholic, to unite the Greek people. Childless and professing an 'alien religion,' after thirty years of absolutist rule King Othon lost the loyalty of his subjects. However, by the second half of the nineteenth century, a primary desire of the Greek people was for territorial expansion. The consequence was a weakening of religious forces (and therefore Russian influence) on social and political life and a secularization of society.[5] The essay thus reveals the syncretic nature of Greek national identity: a hybrid of traditional religious and modern secular forces.

Manuscripts and archives from the Russian embassy and consulates in Greece and the eastern Mediterranean broaden our perspective on the history of Eastern Orthodoxy. Largely untapped sources from the embassy in Athens and consular posts such as Syros, Corfu, and Patras present abundant firsthand testimony on the 1862 Greek upheaval, the problems inherent in Greek society, and the rivalries among European powers in the fledgling kingdom.[6] The testimonies of Russian officials provide valuable snapshots of Greek society of the times. Official dispatches and personal letters, pamphlets and newspaper clippings, and other materials in Russian Foreign Ministry archives provide multi-faceted reflections on a diverse range of social and religious issues. By relating anecdotes and travel impressions, personal encounters and interviews, the copious correspondence of Russian ambassadors and consuls cast fitful beams of light upon conditions within the Greece and provides historians with a treasure-trove for the study of the Eastern Orthodoxy in general.

Church and Sovereign in Independent Greece

After a brutal and bloody ten-year war between Muslims and Christians in the Peloponnese, the central mainland, and the Aegean Archipelago, the Greek Christians at last won their independence in about 1830. Although the struggle for secession from the Ottoman sultan began independently, the European great powers played a key role in putting an end to this "war of extermination" by demanding that Greece should enjoy self-government within narrowly confined borders.[7] The so-called protecting powers (Russia, France, and Great Britain) continued to intervene in the new state's construction well after its formation.

At various constitutional assemblies during the revolutionary years the Greeks themselves considered the type of government that would take shape. At this point the concepts of constitution, nation, and sovereignty first entered the vocabulary of the masses and challenged traditional beliefs in religion, monarchy, and family allegiance.[8] Constitutions created during the War for Independence articulated the notion of natural rights. A turning point in the development of Greek identity appears in the provisional constitution ratified by the National Assembly at Epidaurus in 1822. Article 2 specified that "All indigenous inhabitants of the Land of Greece (Hellas) believing in Christ are Hellenes and are entitled to an equal enjoyment of every right."[9] At an early stage, two cultural orientations, both the secular category and the Orthodox religious one, were central to self-awareness.

In terms of state building, another transition point occurred in the spring of 1827, when, during the Third National Assembly in Troezen, the Greek leadership declared a republic and offered Ioannis Kapodistrias (the former co-foreign minister of Tsar Alexander I) the presidency of the new state. According to the Troezen constitution, religion remained a powerful element of identity: it defined Greeks as all those born in the country or from Ottoman-occupied lands, who, "believe in Christ" and wish to fight with the insurgents or live in Greece.[10] At the Fifth Greek Constitutional Congress, which met at Napoli de Romanie in 1832, the second article of the Constitution declared Eastern Orthodoxy the official religion of state. The third clause stipulated that citizens constituted all indigenous Greeks who professed Christianity. Article 6 on executive power stated that the sovereign "must profess the dominant religion of the state...before being proclaimed the sovereign he must swear an oath before the Senate that he will maintain the dominant religion of the country."[11] The Greeks themselves, however, were not destined to play the determining role in the choice of their monarch.

The safest way to prevent the further disintegration of the Ottoman state, according to the protecting powers, was to establish a monarchy in Greece with clearly defined borders. Before the final decisions were made, the Greeks established a provisional government. President Kapodistrias, after visiting with the leadership of the major European states, arrived at his new post in January 1828.[12] Aware that his position was only temporary, he urged the powers to find a suitable sovereign in a timely fashion.

Orthodoxy is a constant theme in Kapodistrias's writings during his four-year presidency. His professional papers and personal letters in Russian archives are crowded with statements about God, Providence, oracles, and miracles. Remarkably, he maintained an extensive correspondence about religious issues with St. Petersburg. Foreign Minister Karl V. Nesselrode praised the president for a clairvoyant attitude about "the essential need to institute close, positive relations between the Greek clergy and the Patriarchal See."[13] The president exchanged a number of letters with Patriarch Agathangelos I (1826-30) as soon as he took power in September 1817.[14] Regarding the future Greek monarch, Kapodistrias warned that "if he possesses another religion," other than Orthodoxy, "the Greeks will always consider him to be a foreigner and they will not submit to his authority."[15]

> If the prince will swear his oath in a chapel, then the Greeks who are around him will accompany him. The archbishops, the priests and the mass of the people are sincerely religious. In order to avoid a scandal, the prince should dispense with the duties of his own religion and take on those of Orthodoxy. Otherwise the people will believe that he has no religion and the nation will think that their leader has abandoned them. I won't design to describe for you the baleful consequences of such a state of affairs.[16]

Yet the task of finding a suitable sovereign was not simple. The European cabinets considered dozens of candidates for the position in a process that generated a huge correspondence. Prince Leopold of Saxe-Coburg was the initial favorite. Leopold exchanged scores of letters with Kapodistrias that covered the whole range of governmental responsibilities. Yet Kapodistrias continued to protest that the protecting powers were ignoring the importance of religion. In April of 1830, he wrote to Nesselrode that, "the Greek Orthodox religion has been declared by the Greek government the religion of state. The protocols of London [establishing the independent Greek state] remain silent in this respect. An establishment of a perfect equality among the diverse religions will not carry the epithet of Christianity" among the Greeks. St. Petersburg also insisted that Leopold embrace the religion of the country if he were to be considered legitimate.[17] The issue became moot when Leopold withdrew his nomination.

In February 1832, the Allied Powers offered the Greek throne to Prince Otto (Othon in Greek) a seventeen year-old Catholic of the Bavarian Wittelsbach dynasty and the son of philhellene King Ludwig. Greece in turn became a monarchy under the vague guarantee of the three powers. Of a possible constitution, there was not a word, although the Greek ministers maintained their offices. When Prince Othon arrived in January 1833, expectations were running high.[18]

34 – King Othon.

Russia and the Question of King Othon's Succession

The Eastern Question in the middle decades of the nineteenth century constituted a multifaceted source of international conflict that involved matters of commerce, diplomacy, religion, culture and more.[19] Russia's military defeat in the Crimean War (1853-56) did little to dispel the antagonism common among the European powers. Russian entanglement in Near Eastern affairs stemmed from a variety of forces: the shared border with the sultan, the economy of southern Russia, and the traditional policy of defending Orthodoxy.

In 1832, Russia sent a special mission to persuade King Ludwig of Bavaria of the need for his son convert to Orthodoxy. Persistent appeals failed to alter Othon's views, yet Russia never slackened its efforts. Unlike Catherine II of Russia, who emphasized her devotion to Orthodoxy, Othon abstained from conversion. Indeed, Othon worshiped at Catholic masses in the royal palace. He did not appear in Orthodox churches, even during holidays. He made no pilgrimages to religious shrines and showed little deference to the religious elite. In sum, the king refused to consider the crown well worth a liturgy.

The fortunes of Greece were never as low as the years following the Crimean War. By the late 1850s, Othon began to face sterner opposition among a new generation of politicians. His quasi-constitutional domestic policy that worked in the past became chronically unstable. A free press began to openly criticize the throne.[20] Public protests and clandestine organizations multiplied.

Had Othon and Amalia had an heir the days of the Bavarian dynasty may not have been numbered. Yet they remained childless, and the question of succession was much debated.[21] Article 40 of the Constitution of 1844 stipulated that the king must embrace the faith of the Eastern Orthodox Church and raise his children in the same dogma. This provision raised the question about the primacy between international agreements and the king's promise to his people. Othon and his family hoped, in vain, that the Greeks would eventually compromise. The English lawyer Nassau W. Senior, who visited Greece at the time, attested to the negative public attitude towards Othon's Catholicism. "Our sovereign cannot be Turkish; he

35 – Aleksandr Ozerov (1817-1900), Russian "Minister" in Athens (1857-1861). Aas chargé d'affaires in Constantinople, 1852-1853, he had played a significant role in the run-up the Crimean War, in which religious disputes and Russia's prestige as protector of Orthodox interests abroad were a major contributing factor.

must, therefore, be Greek," Senior noted during an interview with a government official. "He may not be so in the first generation. A German and a Catholic may be put there; but his children must speak Greek and belong to the Greek Church...What care we for this Bavarian dynasty?"[22]

Without offspring, Othon's younger brothers Luitpold and Adalbert were to receive the crown in order of primogeniture. Both refused to renounce Catholicism.[23] Nevertheless, a joint treaty between Great Britain, Bavaria, France, Greece, and Russia in November 1852 endorsed Article 40.[24] Unprepared to accept the constitutional condition the king chose to ignore it. To reconcile public opinion, Luitpold made plans to visit Athens in 1862.

Russian Enbvoy Extraordinary and Minister Plenipotentiary in Athens Aleksandr Petrovich Ozerov attributed the government's domestic difficulties to the issues of religion and succession. In December 1861, he urged Othon to decide the crucial question of an heir, arguing that the internal situation in the country had become precarious.[25]

Russia and the Greek Revolution of 1862

By 1861, the king had recognized that his situation was becoming increasingly precarious.[26] The material situation in the country was in serious decline, and political factions and agitations were the norm. Ozerov's reports are dominated with by the labyrinth of intrigues, and camarillas common to Greek politics.

In July, King Othon left Athens for Karlsbad where he sought counsel from relatives about the succession. Queen Amalia governed Greece as regent. In a bizarre episode in September, a student named Aristide Dosios attempted to assassinate her while on a promenade in the capital. Dosios was arrested and imprisoned for life. He refused to repent, claiming that the country was governed by tyrants.[27] Alarmed, Othon hastened his return.

The assassination attempt, the issue of succession, a ministerial crisis, crop failures, the death of a famous bishop, and other troubles amplified public turmoil. In February 1862, the garrison of Nafplion and several smaller fortresses revolted and dug in at the fortresses of Palamedis and Itch-Kalé.[28] The officers at Nafplion formed a provisional government and declared an end to Othon's rule. Their first proclamation announced their program: strict observance of the constitution, an end to the current system of government, and the convocation of a National Assembly.[29] The rebels issued a statement to the great powers, thanking them for support, assuring them of their loyalty to the constitution, and denouncing the regime as arbitrary and intolerable. "A constitution, which means the division of the executive, legislative and judiciary branches, has disappeared. The system of centralization has destroyed liberty, justice and equality. The government uses special laws illegally, and its partisans ignore the national question, support fraudulent elections and are guilty of a thousand other faults."[30] Meanwhile, unrelated disturbances broke out on Santorini, Catholics and Orthodox fought in the streets on Syros, and rumors of revolt in Epirus and Thessaly circulated.[31]

The government in Athens responded by sending all available troops to Nafplion. Dozens of arrests of prominent military and senatorial families followed, and the universities and high schools were closed. The new Russian resident Count Andrei Dmitrievich

Bludov (who replaced Ozerov in February) reported that the Greek Holy Synod issued a circular calling on the clergy and the faithful to support and obey the monarchy.[32] When loyal troops killed twenty insurgents in Nafplion the British and French representatives stood by. In contrast, Bludov expressed "the gracious benevolence and sympathetic interest of Russia for the throne and all those people attached to the crown."[33] "Frankly and seriously," Bludov wrote to Aleksei Borisovich Lobanov-Rostovskii, Russian minister in Constantinople, "I think that for the moment, the trouble is purely local and accidental. It is an abscess produced by bad vapors (excuse the play on words) of the ambitious and intransigent, but it's not yet the lesion preceding the plague."[34]

Franz Antonovich Sandrini, the Russian vice-consul in Patras, complained of the decline of commercial activity due to the disturbances. According to his reports, the local branch of the National Bank suspended all accounts and loans, threatening a great number of businesses. Arrests of prominent lawyers and government officials followed, as did the closure of all schools.[35] Months of Sandrini's reports detail the actions of brigands and rebel chiefs in the Morea, Akarnania, and the Gulf of Corinth. He asserted that Garibaldi was forming an expeditionary force of 4,000 for Greece.[36]

The national holiday in March transpired without incident. The Ministry of Justice published a circular granting amnesty to those soldiers who revolted or deserted. A five-day armistice ended the bloodshed, yet the public remained restive. In April royal troops entered Nafplion as hundreds of insurgents escaped onboard French and British ships bound for Smyrna.[37]

Meanwhile, Bludov observed that since his arrival in Athens everyone was preoccupied with the resurrection of the Byzantine Empire. Among the various factions, the "Philorthodox [pro-Russian party] consider the Greek Church as the great edifice ordained to liberate all the Christian nations of the Orient. The leaders believe themselves destined to be the civilizers, and therefore the masters of the future of their coreligionists. The impatient ones among them demand a new sovereign taken from one of the great powers."[38] Bludov admitted to receiving Russophiles at his home, where he advised them to be patient and desist from disturbances.

As the various factions regrouped, the country sank deeper into crisis. Bludov remarked that a principle cause of the general hostility to the Bavarian dynasty was its refusal to accept Article 40 of the constitution. He complained that if the next sovereign were not Orthodox, then the country would have to submit to two generations of rulers imposed contrary to domestic law, popular will, and international stipulations. In the event that the future sovereign were not Orthodox, Bludov's "humble but profound conviction" was that Russia should renounce such an arrangement.[39]

Unrest broke out again in the first week of October 1862 when the military chiefs in the old Venetian fortress of Vonitsa gave the signal for a general uprising. Sandrini sent warning of this revolt to Bludov and applied for a Russian ship of war for protection.[40] Sandrini displayed excellent intelligence of the affair; he indicated the course that the revolt actually followed. The insurrection, led by General Theodoros Grivas, gained the support of the landed notable Venizelos Rouphos in Patras. The garrison of the city revolted along with the police, as the government lost control of the city. Sandrini described the conditions:

> The city of Patras presents something sinister at the moment…all the boutiques are hermeneutically sealed, and the patrols wear tricolor ribbons while traveling up and down the avenues. One continually hears gunshots in the air. In short, nearly the whole population is in arms and news of the call for a Provisional Government is acclaimed with cries of 'Long Live the Nation! Long Live Liberty! Down with Tyranny!'[41]

Days later, the people and garrison in Athens openly denounced the Bavarian dynasty.[42] Part of the impetus for the insurrection came from the failed putsch at Nafplion, the result of which did not placate the wishes of Greek captains. Another crisis in the government, this time over the organization of the military and the National Guard, roused the rivalry of Greek soldiers, both regular and irregular. Calls for territorial expansion and menacing rumors of the movement of Ottoman troops stimulated passions among the people. Bands of Muslim-Albanian brigands and a proliferation of secret missions abroad fired the flames of national emotion.

Assured that the danger was groundless, Othon and Amalia embarked on a tour of the countryside. According to the Russian newspaper *Syn otechestva* (*Son of the Fatherland*) the king, "who rarely leaves the palace," was responding to the widespread disorder by visiting the provinces.[43] In a move to regain popularity, Othon led military exercises and made calls for unity in the Peloponnesus. On 10 October, the king and queen made an appearance in the Piraeus on the frigate *Amelia*. A huge crowd assembled in Athens began shouting, "Long live the nation! Long live the country!"[44] Shots were fired and regular soldiers joined in the popular uprising. A new Provisional Government led by the Hydriote politician Dimitrios Voulgaris abolished "the royal rule of Othon and the regency of Amalia by unanimous decision of the Greek nation." The Greek Holy Synod responded by announcing its loyalty to the Provisional Government. The new government convoked a National Assembly to organize the country to elect a new sovereign.[45] Russian readers learned of the turn of events and the text of the Provisional Government's first decree appeared in its entirety in *Syn otechestva*.[46]

Othon tried to return to Athens, but was unable to disembark at the Piraeus. Bludov, following his official instructions, attempted to convince the king that he had better leave the country. A group of artillery and infantrymen gathered outside Bludov's window seeking Russian support. He replied that, "I am following the instructions of the spring, which ordered me to do all I could to make sure of the personal health of his majesty's family."[47] Despite the fact that Russia traditionally opposed democratic revolutions, its verdict in this case accorded with the Greek people. "If I were to characterize the catastrophe in one phrase," wrote Bludov, "I would say that the Bavarian dynasty was overthrown by a conspiracy of the entire country."[48] Despite objections raised by the queen, Othon eventually accepted the *fait accompli*.

The public response to the turn of events was jubilant. On Syros, the Russian Vice Consul Eberhard reported that the whole population, with the clergy in the lead, marched to Othon Square in almost unanimous support of the revolt. There they participated in a mass, in which they prayed for all those who had fallen for the country. "The population is delirious with joy," wrote Eberhard.[49] In Patras, Sandrini reported that the people, elated, were preoccupied over the questions of the succession and the extension of frontiers.⁵⁰ *Syn otechestva* reported of the rapture and delight of the people [*narod*] when informed that they had been "saved from the yoke of the [king's] oppression. It is difficult to believe how much dissatisfaction is felt among all classes of society [*obshchestvo*], and especially the lowest class, against the dynasty."⁵¹

The minister of police held King Othon at Kalamata and the *Amelia* returned to the Piraeus. Othon responded with a brief communication claiming his love for the country and resolution to avoid bloodshed.⁵² He and his queen soon departed Kalamata on the British steamer *Scylla*, never to set foot in Greece again. "Slow, pedantic, and childless, gossips had at different times claimed that he was impotent and mentally backward."⁵³ When he died five years later in Bavaria, he continued to maintain his claims to the throne. Most accounts agree that he genuinely loved his adopted country and people, but he underestimated the new generation of leaders and the discontent caused by a king who professed an alien religion and failed to produce an heir.

The storm that swept away the Bavarian dynasty reached the major capitals of Europe. St. Petersburg opposed the dethroning of the Bavarian king. The Russian position was not altogether gloomy, however. Othon's overthrow could lead to a new Orthodox king. At first Bludov's reaction was restrained. He wrote, rather curiously, that, "Russia has no self-interest in the question that is the order of the day. Russia only wishes that the wellbeing of Greece be assured and that the Orthodox faith protect the dethroned Catholic prince. Russia is indifferent to the result of schemes and intrigues fomented by the partisans of Britain."⁵⁴ Attention now turned towards finding a new king, as the country plunged into confusion.

Chancellor Aleksandr Mikhalovich Gorchakov viewed the events in Greece as another contest with Great Britain for mastery of the Near East. Frustrated with the conduct of Othon, he conceded the right of the people to control their own destiny. Disdainful of the principles of popular right and republican notions, Gorchakov favored a strong monarchy led by a sovereign with connections to Russia. The diplomatic negotiations between Russia and Great Britain that followed centered on international treaty obligations and the rights of the Bavarian crown. In conversations with the British

Foreign Secretary Lord Russell, Gorchakov refused to consider the throne vacant unless Bavaria abandoned its rights. "But if a Bavarian prince was brought forward, fulfilling all the conditions of the existing treaties, and especially the stipulations regarding religion, then the Russian Government would offer that Prince to the Greek nation, without peremptorily pressing or imposing him."[55] In other words, the Russian chancellor defended traditional Russian interests: placing an Orthodox king on the throne, sanctioned by the principle of legitimacy and the inviolability of treaties. At the same time, Gorchakov shunned from defending the national will with respect to religion. A staunch defender of autocracy and an implacable opponent of popular sovereignty, Gorchakov invoked Article 40 of the Greek Constitution of 1844, which stipulated that the Greek king share the religion of his subjects. "Article 40 must be strictly maintained" wrote Gorchakov, for it "will be the most powerful link between the sovereign and the people." In a telegram to Athens, he emphasized the need to dispel any hopes for expansion of the frontiers.[56]

In short, the great powers recognized the right of the Greeks to dethrone their king and claim another. Nevertheless, clutching to the right of intervention, they set about considering who would become the next sovereign. According to the Protocol of London Greek Conference of 1830, the protecting powers ruled out considering any candidate "connected with" the three royal families. Gorchakov objected, for it "would exclude all the princes of Europe, who are all connected; at this rate the Greeks would never get a King. You would drive them into a Republic."[57] The problem from the point of view of Britain was that very few candidates fulfilled the qualification.

One candidate was Prince Nicholas of Leuchtenberg-Romanovskii, a nephew of the tsar, a Russian subject by birth and an Orthodox Christian. As chance would have it, he was the son of a Bavarian prince and had a Bavarian title. This naturally aroused the suspicion that Russia was grooming him as a candidate for the Greek throne. Although he did enjoy some popularity, Gorchakov ruled out the possibility of the Duke of Leuchtenberg from the onset. He wrote spirited objections to both Bludov and the Greek government in response to accusations claiming that Russia desired special dynastic connections.[58] Nevertheless, according to Sandrini thousands of people turned out on the streets of Patras shouting "Long Live Co-Religionist Russia! Long live the Prince of Leuchtenberg! The Nation doesn't want a non-Orthodox Prince!"[59] When the Russian warship *Osliaba* anchored in the port of Syros early in 1863, a crowd formed demanding that the new king be Orthodox from birth.[60] In response to numerous petitions, Bludov responded "with general phrases" that Russia had no favorite, other than "the well-being of the country and of the Orthodox rite."[61]

In this case, Lord Russell, the British foreign secretary, prevailed, yet Gorchakov had also won a considerable point. The British and many of the Greek themselves favored Prince Alfred, the second son of Queen Victoria. Alfred's first visit to Greece in 1859 made a large impression on the people.[62] Hugely popular, 'Alfredakis', as the Greeks called him, gained their affection from his assumed support of their irredentist campaign. Bludov wrote that, "Anglomania reigns supreme. The people dream of Prince Alfred, the immediate appendage of the Ionian Islands and grand hopes for the future."[63] He complained bitterly of the Provisional Government's decision to arrest prominent supporters of the "Orthodox party," who opposed revolutionary action, such as the Senator Anastasios Christides and Ioannis Philimon, a prominent historian and the editor of the pro-Russian newspaper *Aion (The Century).*[64]

In a plebiscite held in December 1862, Alfred received 230,016 votes out of 241,202.[65] Prince Gagarin, in Athens on special mission, protested to the Provisional Government against the partisans of England, who chanted the Te Deum, staged evening illuminated processions and gathered in groups outside the British minister's home. Similar demonstrations occurred in Patras.[66]

Why had Greece suddenly become so Anglophile? The reasons were diverse. Greek colonies abroad supported Alfred's candidacy, prominent merchants donated large sums to promote him, and a growing middle class was sympathetic to Britain. Significantly, closer ties with Britain promised enosis with the Ionian Islands, at the time a British protectorate. More subjectively, Ozerov attributed Alfred's popularity to the character of the Greek people, who were "poetic, sophistic and easily tempted by café discussions."[67] At any rate, as a member of the British royal house Alfred was ineligible to ascend the Greek throne. Thus by conceding the Duke of Leuchtenberg, Gorchakov ensured that no member of the British royal house could be considered.[68] The election of Prince Alfred, though invalid, was not without importance. It was a manifestation of Greek Anglophilia. Russian influence seemed to have been eclipsed.

Othon was overthrown, yet the type of government was never in question. The protecting powers set about finding another monarch. The task was not easy, and each power wanted its own candidate to prevail. Gorchakov desired an Orthodox king. He repeatedly pointed to the Treaty of 1852, which ratified Article 40 of the Greek Constitution. Granting that the religious question was a Greek concern, he affirmed that the previous treaty was based on the conviction that the religion of the people should be the sovereign's religion. "We desire that the sovereign profess or embrace the Orthodox faith," wrote Gorchakov, "the symbol of liberation and the indissoluble link between Greece and Russia."[69]

When the Greek kingdom was first formed the Greek people merely ratified the decisions of the protecting powers. The insurrection of 1862, which laid down the principle of popular sovereignty, made it impossible to maintain this precedent. Yet the Greek National Assembly appealed to the protecting powers for guidance and the search continued. At last, the choice fell on Prince Christian William Ferdinand Adolphus George of Holstein-Sinderborg-Glücksburg, the second son of the King of Denmark.[70]

Enthusiasm in Athens and the provinces knew no bounds, as a period of uncertainty ended. Like his predecessor, George was a minor at the time of his accession in March 1863.[71] George was different from his successor, however, because the Greek National Assembly elected him unanimously. A decree of the Assembly named him the "constitutional King of the Hellenes," under the title King George I. Article 2 of the proclamation decree stipulated that his heirs must profess the Eastern Orthodox faith.[72] According to the same decree, Greece was "a monarchical, independent, and constitutional state." Thus, the principle of national sovereignty was preserved. The Treaty of 1832 that placed Othon on the throne was declared invalid.

The insurrection of 1862 marked an important stage in the development of national self-determination. As Sandrini wrote in 1862, "today no one recognizes any exclusive parties, neither French, nor English, nor Russian nor Bavarian. The Hellenic element forms the true general opinion."[73] The revolt also marked an important phase in the secularization of the Greek people. No longer willing to consider their sovereign legitimate under the grace of God, they now insisted on the will of the people.

Politically savvy, King George soon demonstrated his willingness to abide by the Constitution of 1864 and respect the legislative assembly. Unlike his predecessor, he pledged faithful observance of the laws and the constitution. Destined to remain on the throne for fifty years, King George's blend of liberal ideas and reverence for the church brought stability to the kingdom. He attended Orthodox liturgy in the main cathedrals and was on good terms with the church leadership.[74] In 1867, he married Ol'ga Konstantinova Romanova, the granddaughter of Nicholas I. Also popular, she engaged in charity works, including building schools and founding hospitals such as the Evangelismos in Athens, while advocating modern translations of the Bible.[75] The royal couple raised their eight children according to the Eastern Orthodox tradition.

The unification of the Ionian Islands with Greece in May 1864 increased George's popular esteem.[76] Russian Consul Eberhard wrote from the Island of Syros that news of the union of the islands produced an enthusiasm bordering on delirium. St. Petersburg made no objections to Britain abandoning the protectorate, as long as the reunion took on a monarchical form.[77] According to Bacheracht, the Russian representative on Corfu, the Ionian people were happy with King George, and eagerly awaited the complete assimilation of the Ionians and the kingdom. When the union became official, a crowd of pro-Russian supporters greeted the Russian imperial frigate *Oleg* in the harbor of Corfu. A "huge mass of people" welcomed King George in the Cathedral of St. Spiridon, where local clergy performed a liturgy in Russian.[78]

Conclusion

The events of 1862-64 are an important landmark in Greek society as well as in Russia's relationship with the Balkan Orthodox peoples. They illustrate the duality of Greek national consciousness and the increasing modernization of Greek society. They also show how St. Petersburg modified its policy towards Greece during the eventful period between the upheavals of 1848, the Crimean War, and Italian efforts at unification. By 1862, Russia's attitude towards the Greek kingdom became less sympathetic as its policy twisted and turned between the Orthodox Slavs and Orthodox Greeks. Since the beginning of the kingdom's foundation, Russian diplomacy aimed at promoting a strong monarchy and flourishing economy. Paramount in the policy of St. Petersburg was the insistence that the Greek king share the religion of his subjects and that the borders remain unchanged. Russia favored conservative elements in Greek society, and supported the institution of the Greek Church after its reconciliation with the Ecumenical Patriarchate in 1850. However, in the years following the change of dynasty, St. Petersburg, influenced by public opinion and desiring of a post-Crimean era victory, began to formulate a new course in favor of Slavic independence. Russian reading society responded with Panslavism, a movement in conflict with Panhellenism. Violent disputes among between Greek and Bulgarian partisans ensued. As the Slavic independence movement gained momentum, Athens began to play an auxiliary role in Russian policy formulation.[79]

The correspondence between the Russian Ministry of Foreign Affairs and the embassy in Athens contains an interesting document demonstrating Russia's pro-Slavic orientation at this time. Prince Gorchakov, in his opening instructions to Bludov (upon his appointment to Greece in 1861) commented directly on the nature of Russian policy towards Balkan Orthodoxy. Previously, Russia's attitude had been in favor of ecumenism. By 1861, however, Russia began to support the morseling of the Mother Church into autocephalous national Churches, by showing active support for the Slavic people when they came in conflict with the Greek hierarchy. Whereas Russia was far from abandoning Greece altogether, from the mid-1860s onwards one group was clearly favored over the other. "The lines of affection and sympathy," wrote Gorchakov, "founded on a common faith and solidarity of traditional interests unites Russia and the people of Greece." While proclaiming the necessity to remain faithful to the Protocol of London and the Greek Constitution, Gorchakov brought a more delicate subject to Bludov's attention: "the repercussions in Greece over the religious difference between the Ecumenical Patriarchate in Constantinople and the Bulgarian nation." Underscoring the traditional rights that Russia accorded all Ottoman Christians, Gorchakov wrote that, "among the races which for centuries have been protected under its aegis, our natural sympathies have always agreed with the Bulgarians." The Russian foreign minister instructed Bludov to take special measures in the future to ensure the livelihood of Bulgarian Christians (an emphasis absent in decades of instructions to the Russian ambassador to Greece).[80]

Testimony of individuals who, due to their occupation, follow closely the events in a particular period and area, and report systematically on actions and personalities, are sources of great historical value. This is particularly the case if the people in question are gifted with critical minds, prodigious powers of concentration, and the ability to form accurate observations. Russian ambassadors, consuls, and agents in Greek territory provided reports of this kind. One aspect of their testimony concerns Russian policy towards the change of dynasty in Greece. Overall, they demonstrate that Russian support for Orthodoxy in the Balkans remained a strong, perhaps paramount, element shaping foreign policy in the post-Crimean decade.

Abbreviations

AVPRI: Arkhiv vneshnoi politiki Rossisskoi imperii.
BFSP: *British Foreign and State Papers.*
OV: *Odesskii vestnik.*
SO: *Syn otechestva*

Notes

1 K. Paparrigopoulos, *Istoria tou ellinikou ethnous*, 6 vols. 5th ed. (Athens: Eleftherodakis, 1925). See also, K. Dimaras, *Konstantinos*

Paparrigopoulos: i epochi tou — i zoi tou — to ergo tou (Athens: Morphotiko Idryma Ethnikis Trapezis, 1986); idem, "*Istoria tou ellinikou ethnous*: vivliographiko semeioma," *Eranistis* 7 (1969): 193-202.

2 See, for example, N. Politis, *Laographika symmeikta*, 3 vols. (Athens: Paraskeva Leoine, 1920); and idem, *Eklogai apo ta tragoudia tou ellinikou laou* (Athens: Estia, 1925); K. Th. Dimaras, *Neoellinikos Diaphotismos*, 3rd ed. (Athens: Ermis, 1983); idem, *Istoria tis neoellinikis logotechnias*. 8th ed. (Athens: Ikaros, 2000).

3 See also, Stephen G. Xydis, "Modern Greek Nationalism," in *East European Nationalism*, edited by Peter Sugar (Seattle: University of Washington Press, 1969), 207-258; and Leften Stavrianos, *The Balkans since 1453* (New York: Holt, Rinehart, Winston, 1958), 269-282.

4 See Paschalis Kitromilides, *Enlightenment and Revolution: The Making of Modern Greece* (Cambridge, MA: Harvard University Press, 2013); idem, *The Enlightenment as Social Criticism. Iosipos Moisiodax and Greek Culture in the Eighteenth Century* (Princeton, NJ: Princeton University Press, 1992); and idem, *An Orthodox Commonwealth: Symbolic Legacies and Cultural Encounters in Southeastern Europe* (Ashgate: Variorum, 2007).

5 See, V. A. Makrides, "Secularization and the Greek Orthodox Church in the Reign of King George I," in *Greek Society in the Making, 1863-1913. Realities, Symbols and Visions*, edited by Philip Carabott (Aldershot: Variorum, 1997), 179-196.

6 All the documents in this essay come from the Arkhiv Vneshnei Politiki Rossiskoi Imperii (Archive of Foreign Policy of Imperial Russia, hereafter AVPRI), specifically collections 133 (Kantseliariia MID), 159 (Formuliarnye spiski), 165/2 (Afiny-missiia), 180 (Posol'stvo v Konstantinopole). For each source, I cite the exact archival reference, including collection (f. = *fond*), index (op. = *opis*), file (d. = *delo*), and page (l.= *liniia*). The document's place of composition and date (the Julian calendar used by Russia followed twelve days behind the Gregorian calendar in the nineteenth century), is followed by the archival reference.

7 On the Greek Revolution as a religious "war of extermination," see Davide Rodogno, *Against Massacre: Humanitarian Interventions in the Ottoman Empire 1815-1914* (Princeton, NJ: Princeton University Press, 2001), 63-90; Gary J. Bass, *Freedom's Battle: the Origins of Humanitarian Intervention* (New York: Alfred A. Knopf, 2008), 51-136; and Justin McCarthy, *Death and Exile: the Ethnic Cleansing of Ottoman Muslims, 1821-1922* (Princeton, NJ: Darwin Press, 1984), 9-13.

8 See Nicholas Kaltchas, *Introduction to the Constitutional History of Modern Greece* (New York: Columbia University Press, 1941); and Anna Couderc, "Religion et identité nationale en Grèce pendant

la révolution d'indépendance (1821-1832): Le creuset ottoman et l'influence occidentale," in *La Perception de l'Héritage Ottoman dans les Balkans*, edited by Sylvie Gangloff (Paris: l'Harmattan, 2005), 21-41.
9   On the translation of the article, see Loukia Droulia, "Towards Modern Greek Consciousness," *The Historical Review/La Revue Historique* 1 (2004): 51-52. See also, Elli Skopetea, *To "Protypo Vasileio" kai i Megali Idea: opseis tou ethnikou provlimatos stin Hellada, 1830-1880* (Athens: Ekdoseis Polytypo, 1988), 35-38; Nikos Rotzokos, "The Nation as a Political Subject: Comments on the Greek National Movement," in *The Greek Revolution of 1821: A European Event*, edited by Petros Pizanias (Istanbul: The Isis Press, 2011), 151-70.
10 See Douglas Dakin, *British and American Philhellenes during the War of Greek Independence, 1821-1833* (Thessaloniki: IMXA, 1955), 145-48.
11 Greek Constitution, 5th National Convention, Napoli de Romanie, March 1832, AVPRI, f. 180, op. 517/1, d. 2627, ll. 170-81. See also, Kaltchas, *Introduction*, 88-89.
12 C. M. Woodhouse, *Capodistria. The Founder of Greek Independence* (London: Oxford University Press, 1973), 330-350.
13 Nesselrode to Kapodistrias, St. Petersburg, 28.02.1830, AVPRI, f. 180, op. 517/1, d. 2621, ll. 29-32.
14 Kapodistrias to Agathangelos I, the Patriarch of Constantinople, Nafplion, September 1830, AVPRI, f. 180, op. 517/1, d. 2627, ll. 92-93. See also, Manouil Gedeon, *Patriarchikoi Pinakes*, 2nd ed. edited by N. L. Phoropoulos (Athens: Syllogos pros Diadosin Ophilimon Biblion, 1996), 607.
15 Kapodistrias to Nesselrode, Nafplion, 6/18.03.1830, AVPRI, f. 180, op. 517/1, d. 2621, l. 35.
16 Kapodistrias to Nesselrode, Nafplion, 6/18.03.1830, AVPRI, f. 180, op. 517/1, d. 2621, l. 36.
17 Kapodistrias to Nesselrode, Nafplion, 9/21.04.1830, AVPRI, f. 133, op. 469, d. 93 (1830), ll. 63-64.
18 The standard biography of King Othon is L. Bower and G. Bolitho, *Otho I, King of Greece* (London: Selwyn & Blount, 1939). On the first years of the Greek kingdom, see Lucien J. Frary, *Russia and the Making of Modern Greek Identity, 1821-1844* (Oxford: Oxford University Press, 2015).
19 See the various essays in *Russian-Ottoman Borderlands: The Eastern Question Reconsidered*, edited by Lucien J. Frary and Mara Kozelsky (Madison: University of Wisconsin Press, 2014).
20 In Athens, still a town of only 20,000, there were no less than 22 newspapers and 4 periodicals. See A. S. Skandamis, "O ellinikos typos kata tin periodon tou Othonos," *Deltion tis Istorikis kai Ethnologikis Etaireias tis Ellados* 19 (1967-1970): 251-304.

21 On this topic, see E. Poulakou-Rebelakou, et al., "The Lack of a Child, the Loss of a Throne: The Infertility of the First Royal Couple of Greece (1833-1862)," *Journal of the Royal College of Physicians of Edinburgh* 41 (2011): 73-77.
22 Nassau W. Senior, *A Journal Kept in Turkey and Greece in the Autumn of 1857 and the Beginning of 1858* (London: Longman, Brown, Green, Longmans, and Roberts, 1859), 358-359.
23 See also, E. Driault and M. Lhéritier, *Histoire diplomatique de la Grèce de 1821 à nos jours*, 5 vols. (Paris: P.U.F., 1925-26), 2: 366-367; Kaltchas, *Introduction*, 108.
24 *BFSP*, XLI, (1852), 36-38; Kaltchas, *Introduction*, 108, 122.
25 Ozerov to Nesselrode, Athes, 5 January 1862, AVPRI, f. 133, op. 469, d. 1 (1862), ll. 8-9. On the career of Ozerov, see "Ozerov, Aleksandr Petrovich (1835-99)," AVPRI, f. 159, op. 464, d. 2465.
26 E. Prevelakis, *British Policy towards the Change of Dynasty in Greece, 1862-63* (Athens, n.p.: 1953), 47-72; Barbara Jelavich, "Russia, Bavaria and the Greek Revolution of 1862-1863," *Balkan Studies* 2 (1961): 125-50. A. S. Skandamis, *Selides politikes istorias kai kritikis (I triakontaetia tis vasileias tou Othonos, 1832-1862)* (Athens: n.p., 1961), 757-838, covers the military aspects of the rebellion. *Ta en Elladi politika gegonota tou 1862 kai ta en to "Parnasso" kataloipa tou D. Voulgari*, edited by Marias Mantouvalou (Athens: Philogikos Syllogos Parnassos, 1971), contains a valuable collection of documents.
27 Driault and Lhéritier, *Histoire diplomatique*, 2: 471.
28 Ozerov to Lobanov-Rostovskii, Athens, 2 February 1862, AVPRI, f. 180, op. 517/2, d. 1173, ll. 12-13; Ozerov to Gorchakov, Athens, 3 February 1862, AVPRI, f. 133, op. 469, d. 1 (1862), ll. 33-38; Driault and Lhéritier, *Histoire diplomatique*, 2: 473. *OV*, no. 20 (22 February 1862) reported on the mutiny.
29 Ozerov to Gorchakov, Athens, 3 February 1862, AVPRI, f. 133, op. 469, d. 1 (1862), ll. 33-38; Driault and Lhéritier, *Histoire diplomatique*, 2: 474; Prevelakis, *British Policy*, 25-26.
30 Bludov to Gorchakov, Athens, 17 February 1862, AVPRI, f. 133, op. 469, d. 1 (1862), ll. 65-68; *OV*, no 24 (3 March 1862).
31 Ozerov to Gorchakov, Athens, 3 February 1862, AVPRI, f. 133, op. 469, d. 1 (1862), ll. 33-38; Eberhard to Bludov, Syros, 7 February 1862, *ibid*, ll. 52-54.
32 Bludov to Gorchakov, Athens, 17 February 1862, AVPRI, f. 133, op. 469, d. 1 (1862), ll. 55-57. Bludov's career is outlined in "Bludov, Andrei Dmitrievich (1847-63)," AVPRI, f. 159, op. 464, d. 371.
33 Bludov to Gorchakov, Athens, 10 February 1862, AVPRI, f. 133, op. 469, d. 1 (1862), ll. 43.

34 Bludov to Lobanov-Rostovskii, Athens, 27 February 1862, AVPRI, f. 180, op. 517/2, d. 1173, l. 23.
35 Sandrini to Bludov, Patras, 12 February 1862, AVPRI, f. 165/2, op. 507, d. 830 (1862), ll. 9-10; Sandrini to Bludov, Patras, 17 February 1862, *ibid*, l. 16. For Sandrini's service record, see "Sandrini, Frants Antonovich," AVPRI, f. 159, op. 464, d. 2964.
36 Sandrini to Bludov, Patras, 1 August 1862, AVPRI, f. 165/2, op. 507, d. 830 (1862), l. 113; Prevelakis, *British Policy*, 28-29. On the enthusiasm for Garibaldi, see Franco Venturi, "L'immagine di Garibaldi in Russia, all'epoca della liberazione dei servi," *Rassegna storica toscana* 6.4 (1960): 307-324.
37 Sandrini to Bludov, Patras, 26 March 1862, AVPRI, f. 165/2, op. 507, d. 830 (1862), l. 61; Bludov to Gorchakov, Athens, 14 April 1862, AVPRI, f. 133, op. 469, d. 1 (1862), l. 121.
38 Bludov to Gorchakov, Athens, 21 April 1862, AVPRI, f. 133, op. 469, d. 1 (1862), l. 129.
39 Bludov to Gorchakov, Athens, 18 August 1862, AVPRI, f. 133, op. 469, d. 1 (1862), l. 185; Bludov to Gorchakov, Athens, 18 August 1862, AVPRI, f. 133, op. 469, d. 1 (1862), l. 186.
40 Sandrini to Bludov, Patras, 8 October 1862, AVPRI, f. 165/2, op. 507, d. 830 (1862), ll. 127-28; Sandrini to Bludov, Patras, 11 October 1862, *ibid*, l. 137; Bludov to Gorchakov, Athens, 13 October 1862, AVPRI, f. 133, op. 469, d. 1 (1862), ll. 200-03; Driault and Lhéritier, *Histoire diplomatique*, 2: 480.
41 Sandrini to Bludov, Patras, 10 October 1862, AVPRI, f. 165/2, op. 507, d. 830 (1862), ll. 134-135.
42 Detailed reports of the revolts that followed in Akarnania, Missolonghi and Corinth appeared in *Moskovskie vedomosti*, no. 225 (16 October 1862), no. 226 (17 October 1862), no. 230 (21 October 1862), no. 231 (24 October 1862), no. 234 (27 October 1862), no. 258 (25 November 1862), no. 264 (2 December 1862).
43 *SO*, no. 238 (4 October 1862).
44 *SO*, no. 246 (13 October 1862), no. 257 (26 October 1862); Driault and Lhéritier, *Histoire diplomatique*, 2: 487.
45 Bludov to Gorchakov, Athens, 13 October 1862, AVPRI, f. 133, op. 469, d. 1 (1862), ll. 200-203. See also, Proclamation of the Provisional Government, Athens, 11 October 1862, in *BFSP*, LVIII (1868), 1017-18.
46 *SO*, no. 248 (19 October 1862), no. 257 (26 October 1862).
47 Bludov to Gorchakov, Athens, 13 October 1862, AVPRI, f. 133, op. 469, d. 1 (1862), l. 210.
48 Bludov to Gorchakov, Athens, 20 October 1862, AVPRI, f. 133, op. 469, d. 1 (1862), l. 219.

49 Eberhard to Bludov, Syros, 16 October 1862, AVPRI, f. 133, op. 469, d. 1 (1862), ll. 224-226.
50 Sandrini to Bludov, Patras, 16 October 1862, AVPRI, f. 133, op. 469, d. 1 (1862), ll. 226-227.
51 *SO*, no. 259 (29 October 1862).
52 T. Evangelides, *Istoria tou Othonos, Vasileos tis Ellados (1832-1862)* (Athens: A. G. Galanos, 1893), 795, 819; Prevelakis, *British Policy*, 53-54.
53 Campbell and Sherrard, *Modern Greece*, 95.
54 Bludov to Gorchakov, Athens, 20 October 1862, AVPRI. F. 133, op. 469, d. 1 (1862), l. 221. Gorchakov commented in the margin, "très juste".
55 Napier to Russell, St. Petersburg, 19 November 1862 (n.s.), 7 December 1862 (n.s.), in *BFSP*, LVIII (1868), 1063, 1099.
56 Gorchakov to Bludov, St. Petersburg, 9 November 1862, AVPRI, f. 133, op. 469, d. 1 (1862), l. 502; Gorchakov to Bludov, St. Petersburg, 23 October 1862, *ibid*, l. 385; Gorchakov to Bludov, St. Petersburg, 19 November 1862, *ibid*, l. 409; Prevelakis, *British Policy*, 36.
57 Napier to Russell, St. Petersburg, 14 November 1862 (n.s.), in *BFSP*, LVIII (1868), 1054.
58 Gorchakov to Bludov, St. Petersburg, 18 November 1862, AVPRI, f. 133, op. 469, d. 1 (1862), l. 404.
59 Sandrini to Bludov, Patras, 18 November 1862, AVPRI, f. 165/2, op. 507, d. 830 (1862), l. 171.
60 Eberhard to Bludov, Syros, 15 January 1863, AVPRI, f. 133, op. 439, d. 5 (1863), l. 85.
61 Bludov to Gorchakov, Athens, 5 January 1863, AVPRI, f. 133, op. 469, d. 5 (1863), l. 21.
62 Douglas Dakin, *The Unification of Greece, 1770-1973* (London: Ernest Benn, 1972), 88; D. Michalopoulos, *Vie politique en Grèce pendant les années 1862-1869* (Athens: National and Kapodistrian University, 1981), 73.
63 Bludov to Gorchakov, Athens, 10 November 1862, AVPRI, f. 133, op. 469, d. 1 (1862), l. 243.
64 Bludov to Gorchakov, Athens, 24 November 1862, AVPRI, f. 133, op. 469, d. 1 (1862), ll. 281-285.
65 Bludov to Gorchakov, Athens, 26 January 1863, AVPRI, f. 133, op. 459, d. 5 (1863), l. 92; Prevelakis, *British Policy*, 117; Richard Clogg, *A Short History of Modern Greece* (Cambridge: Cambridge University Press, 1979), 82; Michalopoulos, *Vie politique en Grèce*, 96. Additional results of the plebiscite include the Duke of Leuchtenberg 2400, an Orthodox 1917, and the Emperor of Russia 1841.
66 Gagarin to Gorchakov, Athens, 23 January 1863, AVPRI, f. 133, op. 469, d. 5 (1863), l. 506; Sandrini to Bludov, Patras 18 November 1862,

AVPRI, f. 165/2, op. 507, d. 830 (1862), ll. 168-70. For Russian protests against pro-British demonstrations, see Bludov to Gorchakov, Athens, 29 November 1862, AVPRI, f. 133, op. 469, d. 1 (1862), ll. 273-274.
67 Ozerov to Goncharov, Athens, 6 January 1861, AVPRI, f. 133, op. 429, d. 1 (1862), l. 9.
68 Prevelakis, *British Policy*, 73-104 details the contest between Alfred and Leuchtenberg.
69 Gorchakov to Bludov, St. Petersburg, 29 December 1862, AVPRI, f. 133, op. 469, d. 1 (1862), l. 447. See also, Napier to Russell, St. Petersburg, 22 November 1862 (n.s.), in *BFSP*, LVIII (1868), 1076-1077.
70 Prevelakis, *British Policy*, 133-169. For assessments of political life in the early years of the new dynasty, see Michalopoulos, *Vie politique en Grèce*; Domna Dontas, *Greece and the Great Powers, 1863-1875* (Thessaloniki: IMXA, 1966), 1-62; Driault and Lhéritier, *Histoire diplomatique*, 3: 1-179; Walter Christmas, *The Life of King George of Greece* (New York: McBride, Nast & Company, 1914), 11-187.
71 Gorchakov to Bludov, St. Petersburg, 21 March 1863, AVPRI, f. 133, op. 469, d. 5 (1863), l. 540.
72 Decree of the National Assembly, 18 March 1863; Bludov to Gorchakov, Athens, 23 March 1863, AVPRI, f. 133, op. 469, d. 5 (1863), ll. 225-231; in *BFSP*, LIV (1863), 39-40; Prevelakis, *British Policy*, 157; George Finlay, *A History of Greece*, 7 vols. (Oxford: Oxford University Press, 1877) 7: 292; Kaltchas, *Introduction*, 130. On the issue of the king's title, see Prevelakis, *British Policy*, 167-168.
73 Sandrini to Bludov, Patras, 3 May 1862, AVPRI, f. 165/2, op. 507, d. 830 (1862), l. 69.
74 Bludov to Gorchakov, Athens, 19 October 1863, AVPRI, f. 133, op. 469, d. 5 (1863), l. 412.
75 See Queen Olga's personal archive in the Gosudarstvennyi Arkhiv Rossiiskoi Federatsii (GARF), f. 601. O. V. Sokolovskaia draws on these materials in *Grecheskaia koroleva Ol'ga Konstantinovna – Pod molotom sud'by* (Moscow: Institut slavianovedeniia RAN, 2011); idem, *Rossia na Krite. Iz istorii pervoi mirotvorcheskoi operatsii XX veka* (Moscow: Indrik, 2006); and idem, "Epistoliarnoe nasledie korolevy Ellinov Ol'gi Konstantinovny Romanovoi kak istoricheskii istochnik," in *Gretsiia: natsional'naia ideia, obshchestvo, gosudarstvo, XVII-XX vv*, edited by T. V. Nikitina (Moscow: Put', 2001), 177-192.
76 Gagarin to Gorchakov, Athens, 16 May 1864, AVPRI, f. 133, op. 469, d. 3 (1864), l. 81. See also, C. C. Eldridge, "The Myth of Mid-Victorian 'Separatism': The Cession of the Bay Islands and the Ionian Islands in the Early 1860s," *Victorian Studies* 12.3 (1969): 331-346; H. Temperley, "Documents Illustrating the Cession of the Ionian Islands to Greece,

1848-1870," *Journal of Modern History* 9.1 (1937): 49-65; Thomas W. Gallant, *Experiencing Dominion: Culture, Identity, and Power in the British Mediterranean* (Notre Dame: University of Notre Dame Press, 2002), 12-14; and Finlay, *History of Greece*, 7: 311-314.

77 Eberhard to Bludov, Syros, 29 September 1863, AVPRI, f. 133, op. 469, d. 5 (1863), l. 393; "Pièces relatives à l'annexation des Iles Ionniens à la Grèce," AVPRI, f. 180, op. 517/2, d. 3503 (1864); Gorchakov to Bludov, St. Petersburg, 19 December 1862, AVPRI, f. 133, op. 469, d. 1 (1862), l. 520.

78 Bacheracht to Bludov, Corfu, 19 October 1864, AVPRI, f. 165/2, op. 507, d. 860 (1864), ll. 37-38; Gagarin to Gorchakov, Corfou, 1 June 1864, AVPRI, f. 133, op. 469, d. 3 (1864), ll. 87-88.

79 For the context of this process, see Dietrich Geyer, *Russian Imperialism: The Interaction of Domestic and Foreign Policy, 1860-1914*, trans. Gregory Freeze (New Haven: Yale University Press, 1987); Lora Gerd, *Konstantinopol'skii Patriarkhat i Rossiia 1901/1914* (Moscow: Indrik, 2012); idem, *Konstantinopol i Peterburg: tserkovnaia politika Rossii na pravoslavnom Vostoke, 1878-1898* (Moscow: Indrik 2006); and Ada Dialla, *I Rosia apenanti sta Valkania: Ideologia kai politiki sto devtero miso tou 19ou aiona* (Athens: Ekdoseis Alexandreia, 2009).

80 Gorchakov to Bludov, St. Petersburg, 27 October 1861, AVPRI, f. 133, op. 469, d. 5 (1863), ll. 618-620.

12   Eastern Christianity as 'Survival' and 'Oriental Other' in the *Lectures* of Arthur Penrhyn Stanley

Christopher D.L. Johnson

36 – Rev. Arthur Penhryn Stanley (1815-1881), 1872 *Vanity Fair* caricature.

Since at least the time of Herodotus, authors have made a generalized cultural distinction between East and West that often goes beyond simple geography.[1] Historians throughout the centuries have followed suit by taking this distinction for granted and attributing a basic nature or essence to these opposing spheres. Historians such as Edward Gibbon,[2] Adolf von Harnack,[3] and Arthur Penrhyn Stanley (1815-1881) have influenced successive centuries of scholarship on 'non-Western'[4] forms of Christianity by imposing this bi-polar schema on Christianity despite the fact that Christianity originally emerged in a geographical area that was neither 'Western' nor 'Eastern', but a culturally hybrid 'melting pot', and despite the fact that Christianity has remained global throughout its history. Throughout the centuries, the imagined borders of these spheres have been repeatedly redefined depending on the context and rhetorical or political need of the moment. For instance, while ancient Greece is typically considered central to the concept and self-identity of the 'West', 19th century English and American authors often relegated modern Greece to the West's periphery, at best. Many times their accounts contrasted the 'orientalized' Christianity in modern Greece, which was seen as defiled by influences from the religion of ruling Ottoman Turks, with the country's idealized ancient past and what they saw as a more progressive, enlightened Christianity in the West. In previous centuries there had been much interest in a hidden kingdom of Christians in the 'Far East' that would unite with the West against common enemies, as witnessed in the legends of Prester John.[5] Yet, often when existing communities of Christians were encountered in countries such as India and Ethiopia, they were found lacking by European Christian standards. Often this disappointment was explained by the Eastern Christian relation to or association with more 'thorough' (i.e. non-Christian) Orientals.[6] This was compounded by a disappointment at the fortunes of Eastern Christians under Ottoman Turkish leadership.

While the Orient has most often been associated with non-Christian religions, the presence of non-Western forms of Christianity complicated the neat conceptual duality of Orient and Occident for many authors, serving as a *tertium quid* that challenged the assumption of their mutual exclusivity. The legacy of Edward Said has made it obvious that any depiction of the 'Other' often says more about the views and motives of the one doing the depicting than the one depicted, and that such distinctions can have profound and lasting effects.[7] Therefore, analyzing accounts that use Orientalist rhetoric sheds light on the agendas and legacies of their authors and helps to explain how certain discourses have come to be taken for granted as given truths in scholarship and popular opinion. The following remarks will consider one such account, Arthur Penrhyn Stanley's *Lectures on the History of the Eastern Church*, in the context

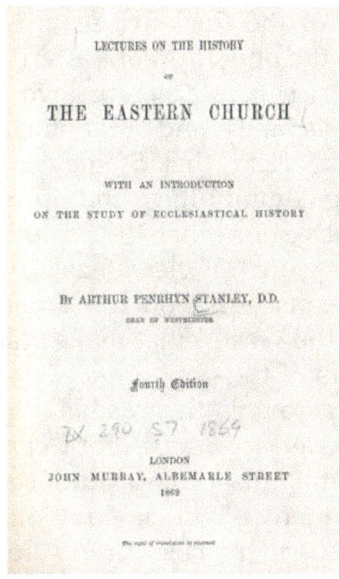

37 – Title Page (orig., 1861).

of Orientalism.[8] In this text, Stanley, who was Dean of Westminster and an Oxford Professor of Church History, offers an especially rich 19th century Orientalist description of Eastern Christianity that is driven by a number of complex motives and agendas.[9] Stanley's account, while unavoidably linked to contemporary colonial and Orientalist projects and rhetoric, shows less concern for Western intervention in Eastern Christian affairs than other contemporary sources.[10] Though occasionally expressing a desire to impose external reform or conversion on these communities, Stanley more often focuses on the implications of studying Eastern Christianity for Western Christian dialogue, identity, and unity. Here, the Eastern churches are valued mainly for their rhetorical usefulness to the West as an instructive 'survival'[11] from the past and a conceptual 'Other', rather than as a tool for any overtly political ends.

Stanley's *Lectures*, the first of which was given in 1857, were based on his historical research on Christianity and his trips to the Middle East and Russia, and were originally published together in 1861. The twelve lectures begin with a fairly comprehensive survey of the various Eastern Christian churches, followed by six lectures on the Council of Nicaea, the Emperor Constantine, and Athanasius of Alexandria. Four of the final five lectures deal with Russian Orthodoxy (which is the only form of Eastern Christianity that has its own lectures), with a separate lecture devoted to the relationship between Eastern Christianity and 'Mahometanism'. The subjects of the chapters make clear that Stanley is more interested in history than in living communities, and, in many ways, Stanley's account is representative of similar 19th century accounts of Eastern Christianity. In other words, it views Eastern Christians and their religion through the discourse on the Orient as fundamentally distinct from that of the West. What make Stanley's account stand out from many others of the period are his scholarly background and his ambivalent sympathy towards his subject.

Lectures on the History of the Eastern Church is one of the few books of its era that attempts a compendious survey of all forms of Eastern Christianity, many of which would have been more or less unknown to Stanley's readers. His *Lectures* are also unique in being a combination of scholarship in ecclesiastical history and his direct observation of Eastern Christians. Many other sources of the era lack either knowledge of the history of Eastern Christian churches or firsthand knowledge of their contemporary representatives. Stanley's account shows an encyclopedic scope of knowledge and even occasional sympathy towards Eastern Christianity, but just as often it reveals the prevailing attitude of disparagement or dismissiveness towards anything deemed 'Oriental'. The sympathy Stanley sometimes exhibits is most often related to a purpose that he believes the Eastern Churches can provide for Western Christians. He sees them as having an instructive role based on the fundamental otherness that he ascribes to them. They provide contrast and help Western Christians to see their own similarities and progressiveness in the face of the East's backwards otherness. 'Oriental Christianity' is stuck in the past like a fly in amber and can show Western Christians their own past and the distance they have traversed. Thus, for Stanley Eastern Christianity is a 'survival' that "carries us back to the earliest scenes and times of the Christian religion"[12] in order to help create "materials for a new epoch" in the West.[13]

Despite being considered a survival from an earlier age, this form of Christianity is not viewed as a pure or authentic form, but rather one that has been degraded by its Oriental environment "whether from character, or climate, or contagion."[14] This is clear from Stanley's use of Orientalist rhetoric to link Eastern Christianity to common tropes about the Orient, which enables him to use it as a constructive foil for Western Christianity. For him, "The Eastern Church was, like the East, stationary and immutable; the Western, like the West, progressive and flexible" and this "singular immobility [...] is in great part to be traced to its Eastern origin."[15] To make this conceptual connection to the constructed Orient he makes frequent use of well-worn phrases such as "repose of the East," "Oriental seclusion," and "grown-up children."[16] In addition, Stanley liberally uses stock characterizations of the Orient as stationary and backwards, barbarous and degraded, savage, speculative, immutable, mystical, dark and mysterious, dry, bare, and thirsty, and stagnant.[17] Regarding the past of Eastern Christianity, Stanley claims it is so stationary that "properly speaking, the Eastern Church has no history."[18] This statement, which borrows the theme of 'timelessness' common to many works in the Orientalist tradition, ignores centuries of complex theological, political, and historical developments for the sake of maintaining a caricature of Eastern Christianity as conceptually and not simply geographically 'Oriental'. In other words, Stanley insists that there has been no development in Eastern Christianity as there has been in the West, which explains for him the reason for widespread Western ignorance concerning the Eastern Churches. So slight has its historical influence been that Stanley rhetorically asks why one would even bother studying Eastern Christianity at all, if it is "a field which the course of civilization seems to have left behind."[19] Stanley may have had more knowledge about the history and practice of Eastern Christianity than most Anglicans at the time, but clearly his commitment to classifying the faith as essentially Oriental warps his presentation of the subject beyond recognition, revealing his knowledge of it as ultimately superficial and betraying his overall antipathy to the Eastern Church.

Stanley also has thoughts regarding the future of Eastern Christianity and is not completely pessimistic. Though he states that the future of Christianity as a whole lies in the West and that Eastern Christianity was just a "temporary halting place," Stanley does see "a future also for the Church of the East," and is concerned for the "re-awakening of the Churches of the East."[20] Just what this means is not fully spelled out at this point, but it is indicated later as a Western-driven process of reform.[21] Many of Stanley's contemporaries have clear colonial and interventionist aims, and, while these are not obvious as the primary motivations for him, he does on occasion suggest such an agenda. For instance, he quotes with approval a work by English military engineer William Cornwallis Harris that describes Ethiopian Orthodoxy as "the remains of the wreck of Christianity, which, although stranded on a rocky shore,

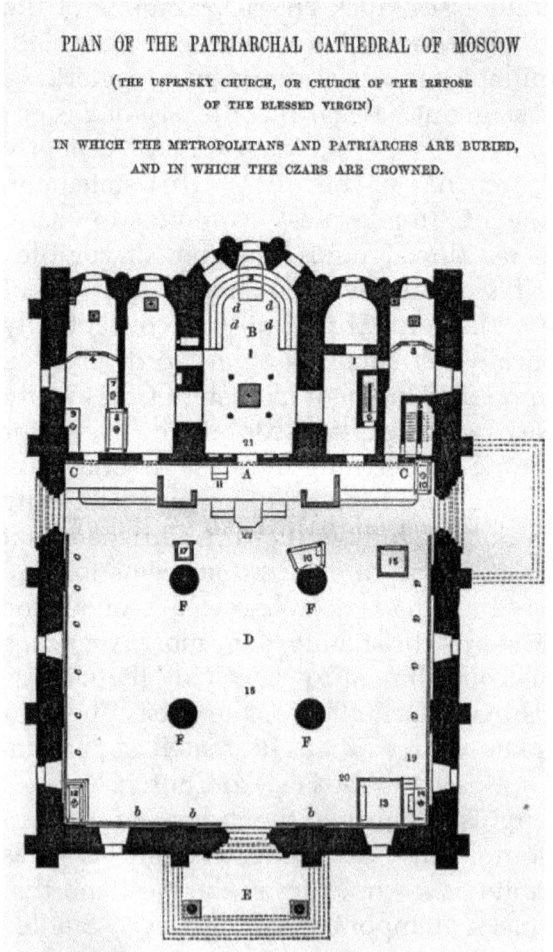

38 – Floor Diagram Moscow's Uspenskii Sobor (Dormition Cathedral) at the end of the 1869 edition of Stanley's *Lectures on the History of the Eastern Church*.

and buffeted by the storms of ages, is not yet wholly overwhelmed [...] European civilization might be applied."[22] Stanley later claims, "although he [the Oriental Christian] may become a European, yet we can by no possibility become Asiatics."[23] Moreover, in the case of Russian Orthodoxy, Stanley says that, while "A Russian [...] is an Asiatic but with the sensibility and intelligence of a European [...] a barbarian, but with the speech and communications of civilization," this "superficial coating of civilized life" helps to bring the inner barbarian "into contact with us, whom else we should never catch at all."[24] Stanley does not have much hope of reaching other Eastern Christians, such as Armenians, Syrians, or Ethiopians, but "the Oriental [...] in the Russian Church is within our touch."[25] Here is a clear indication that Stanley hopes to see the Westernization of Eastern Christianity and its 'purification' from Oriental influences. Despite these statements, his most central concern seems to be in using Eastern Christianity as a corrective for the West. Thus, what exactly are the purposes that Stanley says Eastern Christianity can serve to prevent it from remaining, in Harris's image above, an unsalvageable wreck? Primarily he sees it as serving as a survival from Western Christianity's past and as its opposite that can act as a contrast for the purpose of Western Christian unity.

Stanley assumes the concept of survivals, which are, in this case, forms of early Christianity that have supposedly survived unchanged for centuries, frozen in time. These are not just historical curiosities for the Victorian scholar, but provide a direct glimpse of an earlier phase of religious evolution. Stanley's own answer to his rhetorical question about why these churches without histories are worth studying is that they "[carry] us back to the earliest scenes and times of the Christian religion."[26] By doing so, they show Western Christians how far they have evolved from their origins. In Stanley's words: "The proper distances, the lights and shades of the foreground which we ourselves occupy, of the prospect which we ourselves overlook, cannot be rightly represented without bearing in mind the enormous, dark, perhaps unintelligible, masses which form the background that closes the retrospect of our view."[27] Even though Stanley acknowledges that Eastern Christianity may appear as a dead trunk to his reader, he claims it is also the "aged tree, beneath whose shade the rest of Christendom has sprung up" and has been saved from controversies and change by its "sluggish barbarism and stagnation" and "Oriental seclusion."[28] Often, it appears that Stanley's preconceptions about the inherent nature of the Orient trump his wide, yet apparently superficial knowledge of the history of Eastern Christianity.[29] It is obvious from a brief look at many of Stanley's *Lectures* that he recognizes there have been more than a few controversies in Eastern Christian history, but he is precluded from acknowledging this because it is at odds with the stereotype he adopts of the Orient as unchanging and passive. What Stanley describes as static and, thus, backwards would be described from an Eastern Christian perspective as faithful to tradition and the early church, while what he views as progress would be likely seen from that perspective as a deviation from handed-down rule of faith and worship.

Additionally, since Westerners are ignorant of and indifferent to Eastern Christianity, Eastern Christian churches provide a helpful point of comparison in debates between Western Christians, who have no stake in these churches, which "awaken no feelings except those which are purely historical."[30] Eastern Christianity is "unknown and therefore fresh to us,"[31] but its usefulness goes beyond this. Stanley claims "the West can only be understood after having seen the East. A green field, a rushing stream, a mountain clothed with verdure from head to foot, will, I believe, always assume a new interest in the eyes of one who has come from the dry, bare, thirsty, East."[32] Oriental Christianity shows various stripes of Western Christians what they have in common by confronting them with their Oriental opposite.[33] Though the Eastern traditions have lessons to teach Protestants and Catholics due to their different historical trajectories, ultimately their best lesson is their Oriental strangeness which highlights the "consanguinity and likeness"[34] of Western Christian churches to help them overcome more minor differences. As "a Church which is Protestant and Catholic at once," it can serve as a tool for Western Christian unity by "[cutting] across the grain of our most cherished prejudices."[35] By saying Eastern Christians are "Protestant and Catholic at once," Stanley does not mean having the best of both worlds, but a "two edged disappointment"[36] that has the qualities of each side that the other bemoans. When either form of Western Christianity encounters its

Oriental opposite, "That figure which seemed so imposing when it was the only one which met our view, changes all its proportions, when we see that it is overtopped by a vaster, loftier, darker figure behind."[37]

As this discussion has shown, while Stanley often makes use of Orientalist tropes, his approach towards Eastern Christianity is unusually sympathetic for his time. Yet this is only when compared to the much more derisive statements common to his era. His ambivalence is partly explained by the fact that, despite being inherently 'Other' as Oriental, Eastern Christianity is useful for his own agenda. If Christianity is primarily associated with the idea of a progressive West that is the antithesis of everything the passive, silent Orient is said to be, the idea of Oriental Christianity is by definition a paradox in itself. As Oriental, it is considered to be inevitably exotic, passive, otherworldly, gaudy, backwards, etc., yet it is also a form of Christianity, "however corrupted and degraded a form,"[38] and so it is also regarded as somewhat familiar, recognizable, and deserving of sympathy. It is tainted by the Orient in some sense, but also distinct from it. This mixture of presumably unmixable elements, Orient and Occident, creates a kind of cognitive dissonance for Stanley. He claims that Eastern Christianity stands "on the confines of the East and West, drawn eastward by its habits, by its lineage, by its local position; drawn westward by the inevitable, onward, westward progress of Christianity and of civilization."[39] In other words, it is caught between two polarized conceptual extremes and eventually will need to resolve this tension by evolving towards a Western ideal or else fading into further Oriental obscurity.

This essay has highlighted passages in Stanley's *Lectures on the History of the Eastern Church* that indicate several perspectives on Eastern Christianity, all drawing from standard Orientalist rhetoric and cultural caricatures. A colonialist Western missionary perspective is apparent in some passages, which describe a mandate to reach and convert Eastern Christianity to rid it of its Oriental nature through Westernization. Other parts of his *Lectures* focus on the historical and comparative usefulness of Eastern Christianity to the West. Eastern Christian communities are survivals frozen in time from the early stages of Christianity which the West has surpassed but which also remind Westerners of their own progressiveness and superiority. These Oriental communities, beliefs, and practices also spotlight the similarity, or even "consanguinity,"[40] of various Western Christian confessions by acting as a stark contrast that relativizes any minor differences in the West for the sake of its religious unity. The notion of Eastern Christianity as 'Oriental Other' ultimately seems to be the driving image in Stanley's *Lectures* rather than the secondary notion of Eastern Christianity as root or origin. Though he agrees a 'survival' can be instructive, he sees it as primarily characterized by its backwardness, which is in opposition to Western progress. Stanley does show a desire for more Western missionary intervention and seems to occasionally reveal imperialist ambitions, yet his Orientalist depictions of Eastern Christianity serve more as a foil for Western Christianity than as a justification for intervention or missionary work. Stanley stands out from other thinkers of the time for his historical knowledge, his firsthand experience with Eastern Christian communities, and, most of all, his occasionally sympathetic perspective based on the role that he sees Eastern Christianity playing in the needs of Western Christians at the time.

Despite the positive role Eastern Christianity occasionally plays in Stanley's *Lectures*, there is an unavoidable paternalism and sense of superiority that the *Lectures* share with most Victorian accounts.[41] Though it is an improvement upon the complete disdain that was more common for the time, Stanley's view of the Eastern Churches as restorative and unifying for the West is still bound to the same conceptual opposition of 'us' and 'them', which ultimately only serves the purposes of the former.[42] Therefore, an analysis of Stanley's *Lectures* both challenges the reduction of all Orientalist rhetoric to purely colonialist aims by showing the complex motivations behind his characterization of the Christian Orient, and shows that, despite his relative progressiveness, his account still bears the marks of all-too-common racist generalizations of the East, a sense of Western cultural and religious superiority, and a tendency towards interventionism. As a historian, Stanley is doubtless aware of the violence and injustice committed throughout the history of Western Christianity, but this does not inspire any self-reflection on why he still insists on a civilizational distinction that assumes the East is fundamentally backwards and barbaric while the West is progressive and enlightened. For Stanley and most others of his era, this is simply a matter of cultural essences and involves a fundamental conceptual difference between East and West that trumps the evidence of history or experience.

Like Gibbons and Harnack before him, thinkers such as Stanley have contributed to a discourse with a persistent legacy. Many of the same stereotypes persist in contemporary accounts, although in attenuated form. These contemporary descriptions are also typically based on the ideological needs and agendas of the authors and their own cultural projects, which often relate to the exercise of religious authority and claims of difference and superiority.[43] Not only does analyzing 19th century sources such as Stanley's show how writers of this period tried to reconcile what was seen as an oxymoronic conceptual contradiction of a Christianity that was also considered Oriental, but the presence of Orientalist rhetoric in these accounts also helps to explain current descriptions of Eastern Christianity as changeless, primarily mystical, opposed to the West and rationality, etc. Ironically, this is a tendency that is found in both Western anti-Orthodox polemics and Orthodox anti-Western polemics.[44] The present argument is not that Eastern Christianity lacks many of the characteristics that are traditionally attributed to it, but that the selective emphasis of these characteristics to the exclusion of others likely owes a debt to earlier Orientalist writings that insist on conceptually distinguishing the Orient from the Occident.

While one can find many less sympathetic and more imperialistic descriptions of Eastern Christianity, this analysis has shown that even a theologically liberal scholar such as Stanley, who was relatively knowledgeable about Eastern Christianity, could not escape from imposing the inherited conceptual distinction of Orient and Occident and putting it to use for his own theological agendas. If that was the case in the 19th century, it is equally the case today when Eastern forms of Christianity are often still defined negatively in opposition to a Western standard. However, disenchantment with the rationalism and progressivism that pervade Stanley's *Lectures* culminated in the middle of the twentieth century with the 'turn east' in which many of the terms once used to negatively characterize the Orient took on positive connotations. Terms like 'ancient' and 'mystical' were transformed from accusations into compliments. Yet, many of the generalizations still commonly thought of as uniquely Eastern Christian are likely derived from this Orientalist legacy with its ethnocentric bias and colonialist overtones. This very fact should give pause to those who casually distinguish the generic characteristics of Eastern and Western Christianity as if there were clear-cut, natural distinctions between these two faith traditions, rather than recognizing the distinction as being the result of a centuries-old discourse used for various political and religious ends.

Notes

1 J. J. Clark, *Oriental Enlightenment: The Encounter Between Asian and Western Thought* (London: Routledge, 1997), 4; Larry Wolff, *Inventing Eastern Europe: The Map of Civilization on the Mind of the Enlightenment* (Stanford: Stanford University Press, 1994), 287-278; and *Heaven on Earth: Art and the Church in Byzantium*, edited by Linda Safran (University Park, PA: Penn State University Press. 1997), 12.
2 Averil Cameron, "The Use and Abuse of Byzantium," in *Changing Cultures in Early Byzantium*, edited by Averil Cameron, (Surrey, UK: Ashgate Variorum, 1996), 6.
3 Paul L. Gavrilyuk, "Harnack's Hellenized Christianity or Florovsky's 'Sacred Hellenism': Questioning Two Metanarratives of Early Christian Engagement with Late Antique Culture," *St. Vladimir's Theological Quarterly* 54, no. 3-4 (2010): 323-344.
4 In the context of this chapter, 'Eastern Christianity' refers not to basic theological differences that began to distinguish Christianity in the Western and Eastern Roman Empire in the mid-first millennium, but to the idea of an 'Oriental' Christianity that is the opposite or counterpart to an enlightened, progressive, and evolved Western Christianity. For an extensive description of the general characteristics of this constructed Orient, see Edward W. Said, *Orientalism* (New York: Vintage Books, 1994 [1978]).
5 Francis M. Rogers, *The Quest for Eastern Christians: Travels and Rumor in the Age of Discovery* (Minneapolis: University of Minnesota Press, 1962).
6 The phrase "in the shadow of the Orient" was originally penned in

1909 by Arthur D. Howden Smith in reference to Bulgaria. See Maria N. Todorova, *Imagining the Balkans* (Oxford: Oxford University Press, 1997), 15. This phrase can also be applied to attitudes about Eastern Christianity more generally that consider it to be tainted by the Orient in some sense but also distinct from it. Beyond Todorova's excellent account of balkanism, this phenomenon has been further explored in relation to the Balkans, Eastern Europe, and Russia by a number of authors. On balkanism, see Milica Bakic-Hayden & Robert M. Hayden, "Orientalist Variations on the Theme 'Balkans': Symbolic Geography in Recent Yugoslav Cultural Politics," *Slavic Review* 51, no. 1 (1992): 1-15; Milica Bakic-Hayden, "Nesting Orientalisms: The Case of Former Yugoslavia," *Slavic Review* 54, no. 4 (1995): 917-931; K. E. Fleming, "Orientalism, the Balkans, and Balkan Historiography," *The American Historical Review* 105, no. 4 (2000): 1218-1233; and Vesna Goldsworthy, *Inventing Ruritania: The Imperialism of the Imagination* (New Haven, CT: Yale University Press, 1998). On Orientalism in relation to Eastern Europe and Russia, see Sally Henderson, "The Elephant in the Room: Orientalism and Russian Studies," *Slovo* 19, no. 2 (2007): 125-135; Matthew L. Miller, "American Philanthropy among Russians: The Work of the YMCA, 1900-1940, Volume I" (PhD dissertation, University of Minnesota, 2006), 146-203, recently published as *The American YMCA and Russian Culture: The Preservation and Expansion of Orthodox Christianity, 1900–1940* (Lanham, MD: Lexington Books, 2013), 59-86; and Larry Wolff, *Inventing Eastern Europe* (Stanford: Stanford University Press, 1994).

7   Said, *Orientalism*, 197.
8   Several recent studies of Eastern Christianity have explored, critiqued, or made mention of the legacy of Orientalism and constructions of 'East' and 'West' in relation to Orthodoxy: George Demacopoulos and Aristotle Papanikolaou, *Orthodox Constructions of the West* (New York: Fordham University Press, 2013); Veronica della Dora, *Imagining Mount Athos: Visions of a Holy Place from Homer to World War II* (Charlottesville, VA: University of Virginia Press, 2011), 142; Chris Hann and Herman Goltz, "Introduction: The Other Christianity?" in *Eastern Christians in Anthropological Perspective*, edited by Chris Hann and Herman Goltz (Berkeley, CA: University of California Press, 2010), 1-32; Christopher D. L. Johnson, *The Globalization of Hesychasm and the Jesus Prayer: Contesting Contemplation* (New York: Continuum, 2010), 137-143; Christopher D. L. Johnson, "'He Has Made the Dry Bones Live': Orientalism's Attempted Resuscitation of Eastern Christianity," *Journal of the American Academy of Religion* 82, no. 3 (2014): 811-840; John A. McGuckin, "Orthodoxy and Western Christianity: The

Original European Culture War?" in *Orthodoxy and Western Culture: A Collection of Essays Honoring Jaroslav Pelikan on His Eightieth Birthday*, edited by Valerie R. Hotchkiss and Patrick Henry (Crestwood, NY: Saint Vladimir's Seminary Press, 2005), 85-107; idem, *The Orthodox Church: An Introduction to its History, Doctrine, and Spiritual Culture* (Hoboken, NJ: Wiley-Blackwell, 2008), 1-4; James R. Payton, Jr. *A Light from the Christian East: An Introduction to the Orthodox Tradition* (Downers Grove, IL: IVP Academic, 2007), 47; Victor Roudometof, *Globalization and Orthodox Christianity: The Transformations of a Religious Tradition* (New York: Routledge, 2014) 2-4, 19-20; William van den Bercken, *Holy Russia and Christian Europe: East and West in the Religious Ideology of Russia* (London: SCM Press, 1999), 1-6; and Paul Valliere, "Introduction to the Modern Orthodox Tradition," in *The Teachings of Modern Orthodox Christianity on Law, Politics, and Human Nature*, edited by John Witte, Jr. and Frank S. Alexander (New York: Columbia University Press, 2007), 1-32.

9   Several works have been published about Dean Stanley's life and correspondence: Albert Victor Baillie & Hector Bolitho, *A Victorian Dean: A Memoir of Arthur Stanley, Dean of Westminster* (London: Chatto & Windus, 1930); Rowland E. Prothero, *The Life and Correspondence of Arthur Penrhyn Stanley* (New York: C. Scribner's Sons, 1893); John Witheridge, *Excellent Dr. Stanley: The Life of Dean Stanley of Westminster* (Wilby, UK: Michael Russell Publishing, Ltd., 2013).

10 For a further exploration of Orientalist rhetoric in 19th century British and American accounts of Eastern Christianity, see Johnson. "He Has Made the Dry Bones Live."

11 Stanley's lectures predate Tylor's use of the concept of survivals in relation to cultural and religious evolution. See Edward B. Tylor, *Primitive Culture* (New York: J. P. Putnam's Sons, 1920 [1871]). Hogden traces the concept, not to Darwin, but Tylor's primary geological influence, Charles Lyell, and more generally to similar ideas of cultural development circulating earlier in the century and even before. See Margaret T. Hodgen, "The Doctrine of Survivals: The History of an Idea," *American Anthropologist* 33, no. 3 (1931): 307-324. For a more recent analysis of survivals, see Laavanyan Ratnapalan, "E.B. Tylor and the Problem of Primitive Culture," *History and Anthropology* 19, no. 2 (2008): 131-142.

12 Arthur P. Stanley, *Lectures on the History of the Eastern Church* (London, UK: J. M. Dent & Co., 1907 [1861], 56.

13 Stanley, *Lectures*, 48.

14 Stanley, *Lectures*, 75

15 Stanley, *Lectures*, 75-76.

16 Stanley, *Lectures*, 56, 75, 294.
17 Stanley, *Lectures*, 55, 57, 62, 71, 75, 79, 89, 91, 92
18 Stanley, *Lectures*, 55.
19 Stanley, *Lectures*, 55.
20 Stanley, *Lectures*, 17, 91.
21 Stanley, *Lectures*, 93, 278.
22 Stanley, *Lectures*, 64.
23 Stanley, *Lectures*, 93.
24 Stanley, *Lectures*, 278.
25 Stanley, *Lectures*, 278.
26 Stanley, *Lectures*, 56.
27 Stanley, *Lectures*, 56.
28 Stanley, *Lectures*, 92, 75.
29 Stanley's relatively favorable view of Eastern Christianity can be compared to more typical 19th century accounts found in Matthew L. Miller's dissertation and recent monograph (2006, 2013: see above, note 6). Miller quotes a number of disparaging assessments by Western missionaries. For them, because of the "gorgeous display, semi-barbaric pomp, and endless changes of sacerdotal dress, crossings, genuflections," [...] "there is little room for intellectual worship" in those "nominal Christians" of "the degenerate churches of the East" who are "superficially Christianised" (2006, 154-155, 160, 159). They view the Eastern Church as a fossil, "an antediluvian petrifaction," and, "like other branches of paganized Christianity, she offers a stone to those who are hungering for the Bread of Life" (2006, 167, 159). Yet, Miller also distinguishes between the harshly negative accounts of Baptists and Congregationalists, whose worship is focused primarily on sermons, and the more sympathetic tone of Episcopalians and Anglicans with more liturgical worship (2006, 160, 162-163). Stanley clearly fits into the second category. Miller makes several other relevant observations, such as emphasizing the link between how Orthodox Christian immigrants are viewed by their new communities and how their religious traditions are viewed (2006, 163), as well as the link between various Protestant denominations' perspectives on Roman Catholicism and Islam and their assessments of Eastern Christianity (2006, 153-154). See Johnson, "He Has Made the Dry Bones Live," for a more detailed discussion of descriptions of Eastern Christianity that are much less charitable than Stanley's, many of which are almost identical to the above statements recounted by Miller.
30 Stanley, *Lectures*, 87.
31 Stanley, *Lectures*, 88.
32 Stanley, *Lectures*, 91.

33 Stanley, *Lectures*, 91.
34 Stanley, *Lectures*, 91.
35 Stanley, *Lectures*, 88.
36 Stanley, *Lectures*, 88.
37 Stanley, *Lectures*, 89.
38 Stanley, *Lectures*, 65.
39 Stanley, *Lectures*, 93.
40 Stanley, *Lectures*, 91.
41 The positive uses Stanley finds for Eastern Christianity do not correspond to any inherently positive qualities. Instead, he finds its "barbarism" and "degradation" (57) lamentable, yet instructive to the West.
42 Said, *Orientalism*, 115.
43 For one example of such an agenda, see Miller on the use of Eastern Christians as intermediaries in the conversion on Ottoman Muslims, an idea that also had powerful political implications ("American Philanthropy among the Russians", 153-154).
44 This internalization of Orientalist rhetoric can be seen historically in Pan-Slavic and Pan-Orthodox descriptions of Eastern Christianity recently analyzed in Roland D. Clark, "Nationalism and Orthodoxy: Nichifor Crainic and the Political Culture of the Extreme Right in 1930s Romania," *Nationalities Papers: The Journal of Nationalism and Ethnicity* 40, no. 1 (2012): 107-126; and Denis Vovchenko, "Modernizing Orthodoxy: Russian and the Christian East," *Journal of the History of Ideas* 73, no. 2 (2012): 295-317. Such a phenomenon is also relevant to contemporary accounts of conversions to Orthodoxy seen in Amy Slagle, *The Eastern Church in the Spiritual Marketplace: American Conversions to Orthodox Christianity* (DeKalb, IL: Northern Illinois University Press, 2011), 17, 34; and D. Oliver Herbel, *Turning to Tradition: Converts and the Making of an American Orthodox Church* (New York: Oxford University Press, 2013), 146.

13 How the Philokalic Tradition Came to Modern (Literary) America

John Anthony McGuckin

39 – J.D. Salinger's Franny contemplating, from Masha Deykeute's 2010 literary blog

Ancient Foundations: What the *Philokalia* was

The word *philokalia* first appeared in Christian literature in the hands of Clement of Alexandria[1], where it means what it literally suggests to first sight: 'the love for what is beautiful' (or good). It was a philosopher's term for seeking the good life, and elevating canons of beauty to entice the development of the mind and soul,[2] replacing the material goods sought after by the baser desires of human nature. In patristic times it was also a word for scholarly research.[3] But the word also bore a different set of resonances which applied from patristic times, and which certainly carried over into the minds of the 18th century compilers of what we know today as a famous collection of ascetical texts. It means in this instance no more and no less than a "Compendium." And while the *Philokalia* that we know today is perhaps the most famous collection of Eastern monastic literature, it certainly was not the first, and has not been the last. A *Philokalia* is more or less, then, a portable 'Library of the Fathers', but since this was compiled by monastics of the post classical ages—it a library swung away from patristic dogmatics towards the Fathers' words on ascetical living, the mastery of the soul's inner peace, and the doctrine of prayer.

The collection of texts follows a broad but generic master-theme: the correlation of the search for inner stability (what we might call the anthropological *aporia*) with the quest for the transcendental vision of God (which we might call the theological *aporia* - productively dynamic perplexity). This was the classic concern of most ancient sophistic *theoria*, Christian or not, from Plato onwards. The ancient Christians have a profound philosophy of prayer, and actually used their experience of spiritual consciousness to advance the ancient world's longstanding religious attempt to correlate anthropology and theology. This deep and distinctive philosophic position grew out of the major epistemological problematic left by Plato's inheritance--and its successive revisionings. The early Christian monastic sophists stood in a long line of psychological taxonomists of the ancient world. The Christian sophists, of course, relied not on the texts of the philosophers' *scholae* (though most of the greater fathers certainly continued reading them), but more on the sacred texts of the Bible, and the growing body of 'patristic' literature known to the monastics as the *Paterika* or the *Niptic* fathers. Engagement with the text, therefore, was always an integral part of the ascetic Christian experience. It was not applicable to all, at all times, but always a part of the mental and spiritual 'struggle' (*ascesis, podvig*) was of the intelligentsia among the monastics, those who would, over the course of the centuries, emerge as the veritable leaders and shapers of the ascetic movement. This same, age-old, juxtaposition of the love of patristic texts and the love of the ascetical life which they reveal can be seen much to the fore in all of the most notable Philokalic revivals of the early modern and contemporary ages: St. Paisii Velichkovskii's dissemination of the Russian *Philokalia*, known as the *Dobrotoliubie*; St. Nikodemos and St. Makarios's collation of the Greek *Philokalia*, the advocacy of the literature in the *Way of the Pilgrim*, and that modern Philokalian, Fr. Dumitru Staniloae, who has made of the Romanian *Philokalia* an even larger collation than any of his more famous predecessors. The combining of the love of the scholarly life with the love of the monastic traditions of prayer has carried on in all of the modern translators of the *Philokalia*--especially that English rendition of the Astir edition by Palmer, Sherrard and Ware,[4] which has given the Philokalic collection perhaps its widest ever exposure in history.

What I refer to as the epistemic *aporia* left behind in the ancient world by Plato and his commentators was critical to the early Christian ascetics. It concerns the nature of the soul's knowledge: namely its own knowledge of the self, and its knowledge of true reality, and thus its potential awareness of Absolute reality. In terms of its knowledge of the self, Plato had already suggested the necessity of a distinction between a higher and a lower soul. Christians, as can be seen in the trajectory from Origen, Didymos the Blind and Evagrios, through St. Maximus Confessor, developed this dyadic epistemology into a triadic division of the soul, and thus also of its epistemic range: a body-soul awareness, a psychic level of awareness, and ultimately a noetic sensibility. In the lower range this concerned existential rootedness and sensibility; in the middle level it concerned theoretical deduction; and in the higher level it concerned spiritual intuition. This important Byzantine contribution to the history of philosophy has been ruined in translation, unfortunately, by the incapacity of English language literature to recognize its seminal innovation in the history of ancient psychology, and its consuming vice of habitually making reductivist synonyms of the different key terms: particularly the fundamental epistemic differentiations of human awareness at the somatic, the psychic, the logical, and the noetic levels. Anglo-

Saxon, frankly, does not have enough sophistication in its semantic vocabulary to chart the finesse of the ancient distinctions in cognitive theory.

Let it suffice to say that what most of the monastic theorists are aiming at is the very specific sense of allowing noetic awareness to emerge in the graced human consciousness after somatic and psychic levels of awareness have been ordered and stilled, so the difficult third and highest level can be coaxed into action. The epistemic point here is that the human organism strains after awareness, rises over great ages of historical and cultural achievement to higher and higher levels of consciousness, refined and refining, until the dawning (noetic) awareness that subjectival personhood is enhypostatized in the divine: namely, finds its ground of being and its co-inherence within the Godhead which originated it, and to which it naturally strives to return. From God we came. To God we go. To put it another way, Spiritual (noetic) consciousness is the evolutionary goal (*telos*) of our species. It is odd, therefore, to have to note that today it is perhaps the most neglected aspect of our intellectual endeavors.

The shorthand for this profound doctrine of prayer (which is at one and the same time a radically new Christian epistemic theory) is the 'Prayer of the Heart'.[5] The Jesus Prayer, which is the focus of many of the later Philokalic writings, is but one instance of the wider tradition of this 'Prayer of the Heart.'[6] Let me point out the connection of the Jesus Prayer to this epistemology: the theory of the Prayer (simple enough for a child, and complex enough never to master in a lifetime) was that the recitation of the words and the physical posture gave a skeletal structure to somatic consciousness. The *theoria* contained in the content of the words (being a summation of the entire Gospel of salvation) gave a matrix for the psychic consciousness; and the progressive stilling of both these levels of *aisthesis* by the repetitive cycles of recitation would allow for the emergence, in its wordless and imageless character, of that elusive dove--the *noetic* consciousness, whereby the human soul might awake in its upper levels of sensibility into the unmediated presence of God.

Eastern Christian Prayer and its Text Traditions: *Paterika* Collections

The *Philokalia* as we know it today from its two 18th century iterations, the Athonite *Philokalia* and the Slavonic *Dobrotoliubie*,[7] is not a new phenomenon. It lies within a tradition that reaches back to the very foundations of Christianity. It is the most renowned of a much larger body of literature known in Orthodoxy as the *Paterika*, or collections of the writings of the fathers. The *Paterika* collections were always a matter of monks collating and editing, building collations of the 'best of' out of existing manuscripts that were circulating on the basis of personal recommendations. It was chiefly a matter of monks individually copying and soliciting manuscripts, for this was all in the age before print. Often the copyists were the monastic librarians. The emergence of the 18th century Philokalias is exactly coterminous with the end of the age of manuscript copying, and the dawn of the age of print. The earliest instances of *Paterika* were popularized in the 4th century as the monastic movement took shape. First at this formative era was the *Apophthegmata Patrum*, the sayings and deeds of the desert Fathers. The genre was very popular in classical Byzantine times. In the 12th century the *Evergetinos* (originating at the large Constantinopolitan monastery of Theotokos Evergetes) amounted to a large multi-volume *Paterikon* that had a massive distribution and subsequently formed generations of Orthodox in the 'tales and deeds of the saints.' From the 10th century onwards there was an explosion of Russian, Romanian, and Serbian *Paterika* collections.

The *Philokalia* and *Dobrotoliubie* are, therefore, the two most famous examples of this ancient genre of *Paterikon*, as it entered printed format. Their story begins, as does so much else concerning the post-Byzantine reshaping of Orthodox experience, on Mount Athos. The modern *Philokalia*, therefore, has two versions: the first was published second (because its editor largely worked in manuscript copying modality), and the second was published first, because it was designed for mass print format. That first 'predecessor' is St. Paisii Velichkovskii's *Dobrotoliubie* and the second is the *Philokalia* of St. Nikodemos the Athonite and St. Makarios of Corinth.

40 – Paisii Velichkovskii (1722-1794), opposite the title page of the first *Dobrotolubie* printing (1793).

Paisii's *Dobrotoliubie*

Saint Paisii Velichkovskii lived from 1722 to 1794. He was a Ukrainian by birth. But the locus of his major life's work, and his spiritual reputation, have established him as one of the greatest 'honorary' Romanian Orthodox saints, because of his base at Neamţ. He is a major Orthodox master of the early modern age who can rank with the great saints of the past.[8] His life, written immediately after his funeral on the last four blank pages of the monastery's Menaion, made its way, by 1847, along with his collation of patristic ascetic texts, to the great centre of Optina Hermitage,[9] where through the 19th century it established Paisii's reputation in Russia. Ordained in 1758 as a young priest monk on Mount Athos after several years as a solitary, St. Paisii established a community focused on the prayer of the heart, with an extensive typikon featuring long hours of the Jesus Prayer. This drew harsh criticism from other Athonites (especially from the archimandrite of the Kavsokalyvia Skete, Abbot Athanasius), for whom this spiritual approach was 'untraditional,' by which they meant that reliance on Byzantine hesychastic writers was seen as odd in the age of Orthodoxy's 'Babylonian Captivity'.[10]

Scouring the libraries on Athos, Paisii tried to make a collation of the ancient *Paterika* on prayer, largely because he thought there no longer survived a tradition of living elders capable of initiating his monastics into the secrets of this form of prayer rising through the degrees of spiritual consciousness. He often complains of the difficulty of finding enough manuscripts to work from, as well as the labor involved in rendering everything into Slavonic out of the Byzantine Greek.

In 1764 Paisii and 64 of his monks set sail for Moldavia and came to the Dragomirna monastery in Bucovina. Here Paisii blended the great monastic rules of Sts. Basil, Theodore the Studite, and Nil Sorskii. In his synthesis great emphasis was placed on spiritual attentiveness (*prosoche*), obedience to the elder, and the fervent prayer of the heart.[11] At Dragomirna his work of translating manuscripts was redoubled. The community at Dragomirna grew to 350 monks and in 1779 settled at Neamţ, where it expanded to 700. It was at Neamţ that Paisii's literary project of the *Dobrotoliubie* entered a new phase of life because of his access to more numerous copyists who were linguistically skilled. Different from all the *Paterika* that had preceded it (which generally stressed the life of prayer and the need for ascetical struggles), the Neamţ collection gave precedence to the concept of the Prayer of the Heart as the chief guide and goal of the monastic life: indeed, it was the apex of a Christian life, whether lived in the world or in the monastery. Having again roused the loud opposition of self-styled Orthodox traditionalists to this preference of the Prayer of the Heart, St. Paisii produced a considered apologia in 1793 addressed to the brethren of the Poiana community.[12] In this final work he again turns to the witness of the fathers and adduces 35 of the ascetical writers to demonstrate that his teaching is at one with the ancient doctrine of the greatest Orthodox spiritual writers.

St. Paisii was anticipated in the actual publication of a *Philokalia* by the Greek saints Makarios and Nikodemos. When he heard of their edition at its appearance in Venice in 1782, he lost no time in making a Slavonic version of a large portion of it: 24 of the original 36 texts, but with added collations from his own sources, too. His editorial choices were guided by a decision to omit the more 'difficult' fathers such as Maximus the Confessor, and even Gregory Palamas. This was sent to press to St. Petersburg in 1793, and also to Iasi. Curiously, the Greek *Philokalia* had very little impact in its first edition. It appeared 'before its time' in the Greek Orthodox world, as it were. It was destined to be Paisii's Slavonic version, the *Dobrotoliubie* that set fire to the Russian Orthodox world and brought about a veritable Philokalic revolution, changing the face of modern Orthodox spirituality.

Paisii died on November 15, 1794, aged seventy-two years. He was buried somewhere in the monastery at Neamț. (It may be his relics which erupted a spring of water on the death of the dictator Ceaucescu in 1997 in the graveyard there). A new and posthumous development of the Starets's mission came about when Neamț monastery established its own printing press and distribution center in 1807.[13] The press issued many Romanian editions of the Fathers in the early 19th century and in 1822 a second edition of the Slavonic *Dobrotoliubie* appeared, amplifying the first with further texts taken from the Greek *Philokalia*. The majority of the original Paisian manuscript translations were never set into print form, but at the beginning of the 19th century they were collated into a vast manuscript codex of 1004 pages.[14]

The Greek *Philokalia*: Sts. Nikodemos and Makarios

To describe this part of the tale we must begin again, for the three great figures of the Philokalic tradition, Nikodemos, Makarios, and Paisii, were all once living close together on Athos, but never seem to have met. After Makarios failed to connect with Paisii and enter his Skete, he decided instead to emulate his hero's work on Athos by diverting funds to direct St. Nikodemos to gather manuscripts for printed dissemination. St. Nikodemos from the outset recognized that this was the age of print. He was an indefatigable writer, and from the time he started to gather materials he had his eyes fixed on the Greek printing houses in Venice, which he hoped would bring out his labors in good, sellable editions.

Now known as St. Nikodemos the Hagiorite, Nicholas Kallivourtsis was born in 1749 on the island of Naxos. He studied at Smyrna and then made his way to Mount Athos in 1775, where he was tonsured as monk Nikodemos in the Dionysiou monastery. He died on Mount Athos on July 14th 1809, aged 60, after a lifetime of scholarly activity as a canon-lawyer,[15] a hymnographer,[16] and translator of numerous spiritual works. He was canonized by the Greek church in 1955. His relics rest at Karyes (his own Skourtaios skete) on Mount Athos. St. Nikodemos was a leading member of the Athonite Kollyvadic movement,[17] a monastic movement that sought a renewal of Orthodoxy's ancient spiritual and liturgical traditions. It was from their immersion in this movement that both he and Makarios of Corinth first understood the need to 'rescue' patristic spiritual theology from the dust under which it had disappeared in early modern Church life.

Makarios Notaras was also one of the leaders of the Kollyvadists on Mount Athos, where he retreated after a short time as the bishop of Corinth.[18] St. Makarios was born into a rich family of the island of Hydra in 1731. He tried as a youth, against the wishes of his father, to enter the Mega Spelaion Monastery in the Peloponnesus, but was forcibly brought back home, where he embarked on a deep and prolonged study of the Church fathers and mystical texts. In 1764, he was appointed as bishop of Corinth by Patriarch Samuel I of Constantinople. Here he began a reformist educational program. The Russo-Turkish War in 1768 caused him to flee with his family for safety, and by the time he was able to resume residence in Corinth, the Phanar had confirmed the appointment of another bishop to his place, giving Makarios license to take up residence anywhere he chose 'without canonical hindrance.' In 1777, aged 46, he first came to the Holy Mountain and made contact with the 28 year-old monk Nikodemos, giving him the paid commission to collate and arrange a good edition of the Patristic texts he himself had assembled from manuscripts lodged at Vatopedi Monastery. Makarios funded his Philokalic project by the philanthropy of the Moldo-Wallachian Voivode John Mavrogordatos; and subsequently in 1783, the year after the *Philokalia* appeared, he persuaded the Greek merchant John Kannas to fund the publication of the multi-volume Paterikon, *Evergetinos*.[19] Makarios retired to Ikaria and Patmos for a while, and after 1790 finally took up residence in a hermitage on the island of Chios. Here he wrote works of encouragement for Greeks to resist the Turkish yoke, and composed a *New Martyrology*. He died there in 1805.

Nikodemos's role in this large set of works was not simply that of a printer's assistant. It was he who arranged all the material chronologically, writing introductions to the whole and to the various books, adding notes in the process. The modern English *Philokalia* has purposefully omitted all this material. Nikodemos added extra source materials, amplifying Makarios's original idea, and carrying it through to completion in the bishop's absence. To this extent, both the bishop and the monk were authentically joint collaborators.

The Greek *Philokalia* gathers the fathers of the hesychastic tradition from the 4th to the 15th centuries. The juxtaposing of the ancient writers (Evagrios Pontike, and Maximus Confessor, for example) is meant to make the intellectual claim that the Byzantine Hesychastic fathers of the tradition of Gregory Palamas and Gregory of Sinai, were in faithful continuity with the patristic writers, and indeed that the earlier monastic writers at their very best were harbingers and 'prophets' of the later hesychastic teachings. The Palamite hesychastic school, of course, had several themes of its own, which were reflective of late medieval conflicts over the issue of the knowledge of God. These arguments came to a head in the time of the Byzantine civil war of the 14th century, and are synopsized in the conflict between Gregory Palamas (defending the Athonite traditions of mystical prayer) and Barlaam of Calabria, a Byzantine theologian who had accused the Athonites of heresy for claiming that they could see God's own uncreated light in the time of prayer.[20] Nikodemos organized all this material on prayer chronologically. It seems obvious to us moderns to do it that way, but in earlier times such matter had usually been arranged alphabetically or topically. His choice was to deliberately launch the large hypothesis that all the valid line and spiritual pedigree of patristic teachings on prayer ran up to and through the Hesychastic fathers, to culminate in the neo-hesychastic tradition of the Prayer of the Heart. This was the tradition to which the Kollyvadic revival belonged. The making of the *Philokalia* was, for Nikodemos and Makarios, as much as it had been for Paisii: a strong defense of their own authenticity as Orthodox monastics, and a brave apologetic against the current *status quo* on the Holy Mountain and elsewhere in the Orthodox corridors of power (such as Russia and Ukraine, for example) where heavily westernized scholastic patterns of thought were in the ascendancy.

There is much within the collection of Philokalic texts, then, that is not simply identifiable as the tradition of the 'Prayer of the Heart.' The Jesus Prayer as such is not often mentioned in the texts. But it is equally true that, issued with a view to its being a library of reference for practitioners of the Jesus Prayer, the entire corpus could be seen to offer a progressive movement from the ancient fathers, through the Byzantine masters, direct to the door of the 18th century Prayer of the Heart revival with its stress on spiritual eldership (*starchestvo*). Such was surely its intent. This has been its effect ever since it was published. Today the *Philokalia* has escaped from the monastery, for good or ill. The context that the Athonite and Paisian monks always had in mind, namely that these texts would direct the spiritual life under the close advisement of a monastic Elder, has now disappeared, but the compensation is the immeasurably greater familiarity that so many people now have with the classics of Orthodox ascetical tradition. Paisii, Makarios, and Nikodemos could hardly have dreamed that their labors, so often against the grain of 18th century Orthodox attitudes, would lead to such a revival --would lead to such riches enjoying their greatest exposure ever in the course of the long ages of history. But soon after the first appearance of the texts, a controversy arose about the wisdom of allowing these delicate traditions of manipulating consciousness to circulate without the supervision of an elder. This question leads us down the road of controversy in two steps to today. The first is the delivery of the 19th century Russian mystical tradition to Paris after the fall of the Tsar; and the second step leads from post 1917 Paris to 1960's America: how the Philokalic tradition came to these shores.

The *Philokalia* in America

Stage 1. Paisii's Russian Emulators

St. Paisii's work was taken up by a powerful school after him. Many of his first disciples became spiritual masters in their own right, taking his teaching back to Russia and the Ukraine after their Elder's death, and thus enabling his readers in the next generation, and especially in the early 19th century, to assume his mission at one remove. This included such great saints as St. Serafim of Sarov (1754-1833), the Optina elders, and (later) Bishop St. Ignatii Brianchaninov (1807-1867) and St. Feofan the Recluse (1815–1894).

St. Feofan (Govorov) was a learned Russian monk who had spent time at the Kiev Mohyla Academy and at Jerusalem before becoming the rector of St. Petersburg Theological Academy. He was consecrated as bishop of Tambov in 1859, and then transferred to Vladimir, but in 1866 he abruptly renounced public office in the Church and was allowed by the Holy Synod to become a recluse at Vichenskii monastery. After 1872 he devoted himself more and more to strict seclusion, seeing no one but the hegumen and his confessor, but acting as a guide to many who sought his counsel in writing. He used his state episcopal pension to help many of the poor, and also built a small hermitage chapel where he celebrated the liturgy daily. His chief form of ascesis became the translation of patristic texts. In the course of his labors, between 1876 and 1890, he made a new translation in the Russian language of the four-volume Slavonic *Dobrotoliubie*. It was a translation to which he added many extra texts, making it a vastly amplified form of Paisii's work. It was issued in print in five volumes between 1877 and 1905. Feofan was closely aware of St. Nikodemos' works. Feofan restored to the vernacular Russian the *Dobrotoliubie* collation of St. Maximus the Confessor and St. Gregory Palamas, both of whom had been omitted by St Paisii; and he added extracts from the Sinaitic Fathers and St. Isaac of Niniveh, which both Philokalic versions had omitted, expanding the texts from St. Symeon the New Theologian.

The Optina fathers were also important disseminators of the *Dobrotoliubie* tradition. Paisii's reputation among them as a master of the Prayer of the Heart, and as a model hegumen needed no introduction. The image of St. Serafim of Sarov, as practitioner of the Prayer, who so luminously showed its effects in changing the elect disciple into a radiant icon of Christ, was high on their spiritual horizons. The Optina Pustyn' was located at Kaluga south of Moscow, and throughout the 19th century it was the major locus for Slavic Orthodoxy of promoting the Philokalic movement. The mid-19th-century Metropolitan Filaret Drozdov of Moscow (1762-1867)[21] actively encouraged Hegumen Moses's ambitious publishing program there, which disseminated Russian translations of patristic works. Until the forced closure of the Pustyn' in 1923 by the Soviets, Optina was a center of living elders (especially notable among them, Sts. Leonid, Makarii, and Amvrosii).[22] Their hesychastic spirituality and particular stress on spiritual eldership attracted numerous leaders of the wider so-called Slavophile movement,[23] as well as writers and intellectuals, such as Turgenev, Gogol, Dostoevsky, and Leontiev. Dostoevsky's *Brothers Karamazov* reflects much of what he had observed in the Optina Elder Ambrose.[24]

This great movement of hesychastic elders that came after St. Paisii passed on the tradition of the Jesus Prayer by also freeing it from the confines of the monastic life, handing it as a precious heritage to a vast range of Orthodox lay devotees. It is a hesychastic tradition that has shown itself capable of dynamic adaptation from the cell of the hermit to the busy life of the layperson, the invocation of the Holy Name being a healing, a stilling, and an enlightenment in a world where the traditional supports of Orthodox life (the village church, the nearby monastery) are today few and far between. The several authors of the narrative that finally became the 'Way of the Pilgrim' had contact with this circle, too. Such texts deliberately tried to put into popular and accessible form these deeply monastic secrets. Although the Optina encouragement of lay disciples, allied with Feofan's Russian vernacular translations, had also encouraged the widening of the availability of the Jesus Prayer among Christian laity, there were still conflicts at play between those who felt such a tradition could not make the transition to the world without strict supervision of an elder and those who wished to use the texts independently as their own guides. Ignatii Brianchaninov and the Optina elders generally disapproved of making the Jesus Prayer public. Starets Amvrosii Grenkov (1812-1892) of Optina was a strong opponent of the 'Way of the Pilgrim,' a textual conflation of the works of Archimandrite Mikhail Kozlov (1826-1884) and Hieromonk Arsenii Troepol'skii (1804-1870). The Pilgrim tradition – more properly the *Rasskaz Strannika – Candid Tale of a Pilgrim to his Spiritual Father*) – has been valued from its first English appearance for its allegedly artless simplicity of being written by an unlettered peasant. But it was nothing of the sort,[25] emerging as it did very consciously from two Russian mystics and clerical litterateurs. The Pilgrim tradition was really arguing two important things:

first that the Jesus Prayer changed the ascetical consciousness; and secondly that the Philokalic texts could substitute for the lack of a useful supply of living elders. Both things greatly alarmed the Optina monks. But even so, by this trajectory (accelerated by the translation of the *Pilgrim* and other Russian writings on prayer into English after the World War I by the Paris exiles, and culminating in the translation into English of the Greek *Philokalia*), the greater Philokalic tradition began its voyage out of the monastic world into the global village. And nowhere is that global village more epitomized than in New York, where we find ourselves, in one interesting act of literary transmission between the Orthodox world of the Philokalic texts and modern America's first reception of them.

Stage 2. The Religiously Plural Village: America's New Awakening

It would be important in this context for a fuller picture to speak of the arrival of the Zen master D. T. Suzuki (1870-1966) in California, and the rapid popularization of an American form of neo-Buddhism in the latter half of the 20th century. This movement rapidly disseminated key texts of the Asian religious tradition in English and was an integral part of the consciousness-raising horizons of the 1960's. It made mysticism acceptable, despite the frowns of the ascendant Christian establishment. But we do not have time for that here, except to mention the significance of the Advaita Vedanta tradition underlying the Asian religious metaphysics of consciousness. This means Non-Dualist consciousness. A terribly clichéd synopsis of it might read as follows: From the 60's onwards, Asian religion taught Americans that interiority was mystical, pacific, even desirably modernist. But when they looked at their Christian structures they found things that were decidedly not that. It is in this wider social context that the works of the novelist J. D. Salinger can be placed in the scene. He was not only a famously popular writer on the wave of the beat generation, but a serious student of Advaita.[26] He was, as is abundantly clear, also a close reader and student of the Philokalic tradition as it had come to his notice from the 'Way of the Pilgrim.' It was Advaita consciousness from this outside observer that brought forward the shy maiden of Orthodoxy as a viable Christian advocate of mystical consciousness-

-and the medium chosen was the apparently simple Russian peasant Pilgrim.

Franny and Zooey is Salinger's Manhattan-based short story about a sister, Franny Glass, and her brother Zooey, both in their early twenties, and hyper-intelligent. They symbolically stand, for the novelist, as a cipher of the Seer in our myopic age–where the seer may not exactly be gifted with clear sight, let alone clairvoyance. The two works first published in the New Yorker in 1955 and 1957 appeared together as a novella in 1961. Franny's story revealed to a very large reading public the existence of the *Way of the Pilgrim*, which became for American Protestants and Catholics alike, a major road into Orthodox spiritual practice: and actually introduced many Orthodox to the traditions of the Jesus prayer for the first time in their living memory.

Franny is having an existentialist crisis in her campus town during the weekend of the Yale game. She has seen through the self-centeredness and superficiality of all life around her, and existence has turned to ashes on her tongue. In Franny's emotional collapse, as recounted in the story, she turns to the constant recitation of the Jesus Prayer. She learned it, Salinger tells us, from the book *The Way of the Pilgrim*, which she clings to desperately in her existential crisis, much to her mother, Bessie's, alarm. Here, Bessie is a cipher of that earth-motherly common sense which classifies religious perception as incipient lunacy. Franny has learned from the raggedy Pilgrim who recited the prayer thousands of times a day, that this may indeed be a passport through a toxic world – and so her mind, in existential overdrive, turns to this deep and slow burn of mental focus in the prayer in order to inoculate herself. But her ploy backfires. The recitation of the prayer threatens to become another phobia for her, and so she is rescued by the precocious Zooey who tries his best to solace her with brotherly love and advice. In the end (after his phone-in masquerade pretending to counsel her in the *persona* of his own elder brother, he has to pass her on to the actual "elder" Buddy (cipher for the starets – the truly wise oracle - "Buddy" here symbolizing the *anam cara* or soul-friend) who by telephone lances the boil of the young woman by exorcising the ghost of their mutual eldest brother Seymour, psychologist and erstwhile spiritual guru of the family, who had committed suicide

41 – J.D. Salinger's Franny's head with a Russian church as the back of the skull, a 2013 book cover redesign by Ambrosia Shapiro.

some years earlier (himself a cipher of the existential pain that causes us to turn from the world in anguish at its ugliness).

The Jesus Prayer which Franny has been clinging to – suggested as the only proper response to existence rightly perceived – namely, that a soul should cry out 'Lord have mercy!' (like to a Bodhisattva's anguished cry of compassion) is first revealed to be a false solution for young Franny, before being suggested to the attentive reader as perhaps the only true solution to the pain of existence that tempts us to despair. Elder Brother (Starets Buddy) reveals to her the resolution in the shifting of the emphasis of the prayer from a cry of pain: 'Lord have mercy': in the sense of - Lord have mercy on us in this unspeakable mess! to a cry of deeper trustfulness, in the sense of: 'Lord have mercy on us who trust in you for help that is sufficient to our needs.' This resolution is given in Salinger by the image which Buddy distils from Seymour's teachings to the family (and I ask to be excused from Salinger's "sexist size-ism" here) that there is always a 'Fat Lady' present in every sophisticated gathering. This lady serves as an important denouement in Salinger's pot, and she is meant (so Buddy tells the reader) as a symbol of that person at the back of the parish hall who asks inappropriately simple questions at every event that aspires to be culturally sophisticated - and the dead Seymour's point (which Buddy recalls to his younger siblings here) is that instead of wishing to silence, or despise that person (their innate response of rejection before the harshness of the real world), it is this voice which is actually that of Christ; and until one is able to make that perception one cannot understand what true wisdom is; because one cannot define and perceive wisdom except through the lens of compassion. "There isn't anyone out there who isn't Seymour's Fat Lady," Buddy concludes for Franny's sake. The point is that we are all the "Fat Lady" at the back with the foolish questions, whom we began by despising. And Christ himself is the holy Fool in our midst; and it is no less than this double insight that rescues Franny. None of us is 'cool', as she wants the world to be. Being uncool is OK: it allows us to have mercy on ourselves and on other people, because we understand that God only relates to us through his compassion. Mercifulness is love. Love is the true fabric of existence. Whether or not her new insight allows her to see that this is the same wisdom which is contained in the Jesus Prayer, and her unbalanced exegesis of it – is another matter we do not learn in Salinger. We suspect however that Franny may be all right now – even if she would be well advised to reassess her relationship with her campus boyfriend Lane Coutell.[27]

Being a curious philosophic student of Advaita Vedanta, Salinger slyly inserts this as Zooey goes into his room before phoning Franny in the pretense of his brother– for he preps himself by rehearsing all the philosophical wisdoms of the ages that he and Buddy have written out aphoristically and posted on the back of his bedroom door. Our novelist also quite clearly recognizes, at a time very few professional theologians had, that the Byzantine tradition of the prayer of the heart, as he found it in the *Pilgrim*, was clearly akin to this tradition of Advaita insight, but that this Philokalic path (unlike all other inroads to it) was truly an occidental experience, at the core of ancient Christianity, not an alien importation. This is quite remarkable, for Salinger wrote at a time when few commentators, if any, had recognized that this is the epistemic heart of Plato's *aporia* about the knowledge of the soul, something that greatly concerned the Byzantine writers Evagrios and St. Maximus the Confessor.

Epilogue

What have we done with the Philokalic tradition after it came to America? Well, we have not even started to unravel all its implications it. When we can more fully exegete the critically important relationship between this great prayer and the Byzantine epistemic theory that lies behind it, we may start to perceive its more profound mysteries. In the meantime, we need to take to heart the American symbol of Franny, and be wary of using the endless cycles of the 'Lord Have Mercys' to make us even more neurotic than we presently are. The latest twist in the mutations of the Jesus Prayer in modernity is the growing practice, one advocated by several leading advocates of the Jesus Prayer such as the Romanian Archbishop Dr. Serafim Joanta, and the priests of the monastery of Starets Sophrony in Essex, of practicing the Jesus prayer in common. In such a case the leader of the recitation must set a tonality of deepening peace and slowness. In such a case, too, the form of words has to be changed slightly, omitting "me a sinner," in favor of 'have mercy on us' (since one cannot attribute sin to anyone other than the self); and certain clarification has to be made that the processes of breathing and heart-rate associated with the combination of the individually-voiced prayer of each person have to be carefully detached from that of the public leader's.[28] The Jesus Prayer is designed for a singular alteration of the individual consciousness and must, sooner or later, even in a public recitation, descend into a deeply personal rhythm. In regard to this aspect, when Christians begin to explore the actualities of the differing levels of consciousness of the soul, it is wise to remember the strong sense of the Optina hermits that this process needs an experienced guide—even while admiring the courage of many great devotees of the prayer, who insisted that it ought to have wide and public dissemination. Salinger gave us a cheeky wink in his novella that here was a Christian *Pranayama*. Truth be told, there is something here even greater still.

Abbreviations

OMPP: *Orthodox Monasticism Past and Present.* Edited by J. A. McGuckin. Theotokos Press. New York. 2014/Piscatawy: Gorgoas Press, 2015.
PG: *Patrologia Cursus Completus, Series Graeca.* 161 vols. Edited by Jacques-Paul Migne. Paris: Imprimerie Catholique, 1857-1866.

Notes

1   St. Clement of Alexandria, *Paedagogus.* 3.7, PG 8: 607-612.
2   St. Gregory the Theologian uses the verb *philokaleo* in the sense of 'what one is really enthusiastic about: Gregory of Nazianzus, *Epistle* 33, PG 37: 73A.
3   St. Epihanios of Salamis, *Panarion* 16.1.3, in Epihanius *(Ancoratus et Panarion),* 3 vols. + index vol, Griechische christliche Schriften der ersten drei Jahrhunderte 27, 31, 35, and subsequent revised editions, edited by Karl Holl, Jürgen Dummer, et al. (Leipzig: Hinrichs'/Berlin: Akademie, De Gruyter, 1915-2006), 1: 210; trans. by F. Williams: *The Panarion of Epiphanios of Salamis* ["Against All Heresies"], 2 vols., Nag Hammadi and Manichaean Studies 35-36, rev. ed., 63, 79 (Leiden: Brill, 1987-1984, 2009-2013), 1: 39; a form of the word *philokalia* is found in a dozen places in the *Panarion*: see the Index vol., 197. Cyril of Scythopolis (Kirillos von Skythopolis), "Bios tou hosiou patros hēmōn Saba" 66, in *Kirillos von Skythopolis*, Texte und Untersuchungen zur Geschichte altchristlichen Literatur 49, no. 2, edited by Eduard Schwartz, 167; trans. by R. M. Price: *Life of St. Saba* 66, in idem., *Lives of the Palestinian Monks,* Cistercian Studies 114 (Kalamazoo, 1991), 177. St. Neilos, *Epistle* 3.25, PG 79: 381-384.
4   *The Philokalia: The Complete Text, Compiled by St. Nikodimos of the Holy Mountain and St. Makarios of Corinth*, 4 vols., translated and edited by G.E.H. Palmer, Philip Sherrard, and Kallistos Ware (London: Faber and Faber, 1979-1995).
5   Further see J. A. McGuckin. "The Prayer of the Heart in Patristic and Early Byzantine Tradition," in *Prayer and Spirituality in the Early Church*, 5 Vols., edited by P. Allen, W. Mayer, L. Cross, et al. (Queensland: Australian Catholic University. Centre for Early Christian Studies, 1998-2009), 2: 69-108.
6   I have discussed this further in my study, *Standing in God's Holy Fire: The Byzantine Tradition* (London: Darton, Longman, and Todd, 2001). See also idem, "The Shaping of the Soul's Perceptions in the Byzantine Ascetic Elias Ekdikos," *St. Vladimir's Theological Quarterly* 55, no. 3

(2011): 343-363; idem, "The Eros of Divine Beauty in St. Maximus the Confessor *(c. 580-662),*" in *The Concept of Beauty in Patristic and Byzantine Theology,* edited by J. A, McGuckin (New York: Theotokos Press, 2012), 170-191.

7   'Dobrotoliubie' is a Slavonic calque of *Philokalia.* St. Paisii Velichovskii called his edition of 1793 this, echoing the *Philokalia* of Sts. Nikodemos and Makarios, which had been prepared on Athos and had recently appeared in print at Venice. But Paisii's work was not wholly dependent on that of the Athonites.

8   I have treated of his life and times more extensively elsewhere: J. A. McGuckin. "The Life and Mission of St. Paisius Velichovsky: 1722-1794. An Early Modern Master of the Orthodox Spiritual Life," *Spiritus* 9, no. 2 (2009): 157-173.

9   1847, 1890, 1892. The printed biography of Paisii by Platon from 1836 is found in A. E. Tachiaos, *The Revival of Byzantine Mysticism among Slavs and Romanians in the 18th century* (Thessalonica: Aristoteleion Panespistēmon, 1986), 153-255, following his publication of Paisii's autobiography (3-91) and Metrophanes's [Mitrofan's] biography of Paisii (95-150). Platon's version was also issued in English by the St. Herman of Alaska Brotherhood from Platina California (under the mistaken impression that it was the Biography of Metrophanes), under the title: *Blessed Paisius Velichkovsky: The Man behind the Philokalia: The Life and Ascetic Labos of Our Father, Elder Paisius, Archimandrite of the Holy Moldavian Monasteries of Niamets and Sekoul, Optina Version by Schema-Monk Metrophanes,* translated by Seraphim Rose, 2nd edition (Platina, CA: Saint Hermann of Alaska Brotherhood, 1994).

10 A term signifying the long early modern period where scholastic modes of thought from Kiev and Poland had heavily reorganized Orthodox dogmatics, displacing biblical and patristic modes of theology.

11 The rule of Paisii is discussed in Archbp. Serafim Joanta. *Romania: Its Hesychastic Tradition and Culture* (Wildwood, CA: St. Xenia Scete, 1992), 128-157, esp. 140; and Rev. Sergii Chetverikov, *Starets Paisii Velichkovskii: His Life, Teachings, and Influence on Orthodox Monasticism,* trans., Visily Lickwar and Alexander Lisenko (Belmont, MA: Nordland, 1980), 110-117.

12 "To the Adversaries and Detractors of the Spiritual Prayer that is the Jesus Prayer." Text in: I. Smolitsch, *Moines de la sainte Russie* (Tours: Mame, 1967), 98-104.

13 Cf. Joanta, *Romania: Its Hesychastic Tradition and Culture,* 150.

14 Is now lodged as ms. no. 1455 in the Library of the Romanian Academy.

15 He assembled the influential collation of Greek canon law known as

the *Pedalion* or Rudder, adding much commentary of his own; see St. Nikodemos Hagiorites, *Pedalion: The Rudder of the Orthodox Catholic Church*, trans. D. Cummings (Chicago: The Orthodox Christian Education Society, 1953; rpt. New York: Luna, 1983).

16 He composed 50 liturgical hymns.

17 The title Kollyvadists was an ironic slight against them from their opponents. They had advocated a return to stricter more authentic standards of Orthodox theology, liturgy, and spirituality. Opponents tried to fasten on one aspect only, so as to caricature them – their claim that the Kollyva (boiled wheat) memorials for the dead ought to take place only on Saturdays. Among the leading Kollyvadists apart from Nikodemos, was Makarios of Corinth his collaborator in the Philokalia project, and Athanasios of Paros.

18 See his biography by C. Cavarnos. *St Makarios of Corinth*, Modern Orthodox Saints, vol. 2 (Belmont, MA: Institute for Byzantine and Modern Greek Studies, 1993); also S. G. Papadopoulos, *Hagios Makarios Korinthou: Ho Genarchēs tou Philokalismou* (Athens: Akritas, 2000).

19 It is clear, therefore, that the modern edition of the *Evergetinos* was designed from the beginning as the companion study to the *Philokalia*. The *Evergetinos* has now finally had a fine English translation in four volumes prepared by Archbishop Chrysostomos and Monk Patapios (Etna, CA: Center for Traditionalist Orthodox Studies. 2008). To date the English translation of the Greek *Philokalia* remains incomplete.

20 If they could see it with their material eyes, he argued, it could not be the (immaterial) uncreated light. The apparently abstruse point masked a much wider set of related ideas: was it possible to know God directly in this life. Out of the argument came Palamas's distinction of the Essence and energies of God. While God was Unknowable and Unapproachable in his essence, he was discernible and close to his Church through his (Uncreated) Energies. In touching these energies of God, however, Palamas argued that we touched the authentic and Unapproachable God, wholly and immediately.

21 This important and scholarly figure served as Metropolitan of Moscow, 1821-1867.

22 Further see: Vladimir Soloukhin's collection *Pis'ma iz Russkogo muzeia, Chernye doski, Vremia sobirat' kamni* (Moscow Moldaia gvardiia, 1990, translated by Valeria Nollan: *A Time to Gather Stones: Essays by Vladimir Soloukhin* (Evanston, IL: Northwestern University Press, 1993), in which the author's long third title essay traces the history of Optina.

23 Its leaders were Kireevskii and Aksakov, and most notable religious thinkers included Khomiakov, Soloviev and Berdiaev.

24 For interesting related discussions see: Tea Jankovic. "Purifying

the Heart in Order to See: Praxis and Perception in Dostoevsky's *The Brothers Karamazov*," in *OMPP*, 505-512, and Rico Monge, The Centrality of St. Isaac the Syrian's Ascetical Theology in Dostoevsky's *The Brothers Karamazov*," in *OMPP*, 499-504.

25 The complex literary history of the *Rasskaz Strannika* is discussed more extensively in my article: "Eastern Orthodox Prayer: The Rasskaz Strannika," in *Contemplative Literature: A Comparative Sourcebook*, edited by L. J. Komjathy (Albany: State University of New York Press, 2015), 359-406.

26 See further: Elizabeth N. Kurian "'Salinger and the Hindu View of Life," *Indian Journal of American Studies*, 17, no. 1-2 (Winter-Summer, 1987): 37-44.

27 Since Salinger's death it has emerged that he had been developing, extensively over many years, further narratives based around the Glass family.

28 One cannot observe classical respiratory technique on the in-breath and out-breath when one is publicly vocalizing the prayer in this way.

14 The Russian Orthodox Church in Italy Today
A Kaleidoscope Clarifying Itself

Valeria Z. Nollan

> . . . it often felt as if I were watching the country's story through a kaleidoscope, as every few weeks the lens was twisted and the colours split into new and disconcertingly different arrangements.[1]

42 – St. Catherine's Russian Orthodox Church in Rome, overlooking the Vatican and St. Peter's Basilica.

The discussion below treats the historic developments in the relations between the Russian Orthodox Church and Roman Catholic Church that have occurred in Moscow and Rome in recent years, and which represent the logical culmination of a process that has been evolving since the late nineteenth century. My comments are informed by relevant religio-philosophical master concepts of Vladimir Soloviev (1853-1900), whose importance for Russian Orthodoxy goes without saying; less well-known is the enduring, even visible presence of Soloviev's writings in Rome in Roman Catholic settings.[2] Representing the contemporary iterations, respectively, of the branches of the Christian church of the Eastern and Western Roman Empires, Russian Orthodoxy and Roman Catholicism evolved under differing historical and theological circumstances. Russian Orthodoxy, unlike Roman Catholicism, did not define itself according to such major upheavals as the Renaissance and Reformation in Western Europe; instead, it developed along quieter paths characterized less by monumental change than by its particular interactions with the policies of the Russian tsars.

The 19th and 20th centuries witnessed the continuation of differing evolutionary paths for Russian Orthodoxy and Roman Catholicism. By the early 20th century, Russian Orthodoxy had produced a body of theological and religio-philosophical writing known as the 'Neopatristic school', which drew its strength and clarity from theological-classical sources. In 2007 the historic unification of the two major jurisdictions of Russian Orthodoxy took place, the first step towards repairing the atrocities committed against the Orthodox Church under Communist rule. These same two centuries in Roman Catholicism witnessed the major events of the First Vatican Council (1869-1870), which codified after several centuries of practice the doctrine of papal infallibility (1870); and of the controversial Second Vatican Council known as 'Vatican II' (1962-1965), which did not produce major theological changes, but set into motion a series of minor, though important changes in the *praxis* of the Church.[3] It would seem that by the dawn of the 21st century some kind of *rapprochement*, if not actual unity of the two largest ancient branches of Christianity would suggest itself to those deeply involved in the life of these two faith traditions.

Paul Valliere writes about what Alexander Schmemann called a "Russian school of modern Orthodox theology, "Neopatristic thinkers are theological classicists, like Roman Catholic Neo-Thomists and Protestant Neo-Orthodox theologians."[4] This statement suggests that, with respect to the evolution of the Russian Orthodox and Roman Catholics, there exist similarities between the two churches in their engagement of theology against the background of historical developments and contexts; and that, because of the practice of articulating theology in connection with history, such similarities would act in a positive way to enable the Orthodox and Catholics to produce a dialogue with each other. However, as Valliere points out:

> . . . there is an important difference in the role classicism has played in modern Orthodoxy as compared with western communions. In modern Roman Catholicism and Protestantism classicists have usually had plenty of critics to contend with, whereas in Orthodox theology the Neopatristic school has had the field more or less to itself for decades. So commanding is the Neopatristic school that even the theological dialogue between Orthodoxy and the western churches since the middle of the twentieth century has been a dialogue between various western theologies on the one hand and Neopatristic Orthodoxy on the other.[5]

Soloviev, who died in 1900, did not live to see the Bolshevik Revolution of 1917 and ensuing break-up of the Russian Orthodox Church in the 1920s. His grand philosophical project of creating, through the re-integration of the three main branches of Christianity—Orthodoxy, Catholicism, and Protestantism—and rich infusion of elements of Judaism, a universal church was not realized. To the contrary, the destruction carried out by the Soviet regime of the Russian Orthodox Church as a fully-developed ecclesial body made Soloviev's project even more unrealizable. However, significant repair of at least the Russian Orthodox branch of the Christian church came about by the signing of the Act of Canonical Communion between the Moscow Patriarchate and the Russian Orthodox Church Outside of Russia (ROCOR) on May 17, 2007—an event of enormous significance both for Russian religious history and for world Orthodoxy. Ever since this unification of Russian Orthodoxy, which sutured the damage caused by seventy years of systematic oppression of the church under the Soviet dictatorship, the question of possible dialogue, if not a narrowing of the chasm, between the ancient Christian churches of the East and West has hung heavily in the air. I take up this question by considering the state of the contemporary Russian Orthodox Church in Italy (particularly in Rome) under the leadership of Patriarch Kirill of Moscow and All Russia, whose tenure began with his enthronement in 2009 and continues into the present time. Noteworthy for Russian Orthodoxy in Italy is the historic event of the establishment in 2009 of the Russian Orthodox Church of St. Catherine of Alexandria the Great Martyr (Chiesa Ortodossa Russa di S. Caterina di Alessandria Grande Martire)--the first Russian church ever to be built in Rome. This event has occurred within a larger religious context and broader patterns of pilgrimage to Italy by Russians; my acquaintance with it draws from my research and interviews in Rome during the summers of 2008, 2010, and 2012.

At first mention, the topic of the Russian Orthodox faithful in Italy raises the question of why Russians might be drawn to Italy, particularly in contemporary times that are witnessing in the Russian Federation a resurrection and revival of Orthodoxy, its ministry, and its institutions. After all, "[t]he Russian state and generous donors have helped [the Russian Orthodox Church, Moscow Patriarchate] restore or build 25,000 churches in Russia and over 60 countries in the last 25 years."[6] It is helpful in this regard to recall that in the sixth century of the first millenium much of Italy was a part of the Eastern Roman Empire, with its capital of Constantinople, and that in this historico-religious context medieval Rus' received the faith tradition whose sensibilities define its culture. Rus' acquired Orthodoxy from Greece through Byzantium, and similarly Byzantine Orthodox sensibilities established themselves in the southern part of Italy. Through these influences the Russian cultural and spiritual connections with Italy extend back over one thousand years. In addition to these religious and political connections, there exist strong aesthetic similarities between the cultures of the two countries: The quest to create beauty of a spiritual nature, often at the expense of practicality, has remained a defining feature of both

Italy and Russia.⁷ This form of beauty is not of a surface kind: it grows out of the deep mysticism that permeates both countries. It is a beauty with a moral and spiritual content, as Soloviev observes, proceeding from Fyodor Dostoevsky's maxim (associated with Prince Myshkin of *The Idiot* [1869]) that beauty will save the world. Dostoevsky had in mind, as Nikolai Berdiaev clarifies in his *The Russian Idea*, "the transfiguration of the world and the coming of the Kingdom of God, and this is the eschatological hope."⁸

In Soloviev's essay "The Universal Meaning of Art" (1890) he affirms the following concerning beauty and morality (in Vladimir Wozniuk's translation): in an artistic embodiment of the spiritual world "ethical activity is transformed into aesthetic activity; for material objective reality can be introduced into moral order only through its illumination, its inspiration, i.e., only in the form of beauty. Thus, beauty is necessary for the fulfillment of the good in the material world, for only by it is the evil darkness of this world illuminated and subdued."⁹ For Soloviev beauty can not only raise inspiration, embody goodness, and create through its material form an access to the spiritual world—it can also subdue evil. For both the Italians and the Russians this type of spiritual content underlies the creation of works of beauty--its intent is to connect heaven and earth, and as such Soloviev viewed it as having the potential to unify humankind. Such generalizations about the aesthetic category of beauty in two countries risk drawing on national stereotypes, but precedents exist in the works of many notable Russian writers and philosophers, for example, Berdiaev and Dmitrii Likhachev (1906-1999), not to mention those of Dostoevsky and Soloviev himself.¹⁰ Moreover, Soloviev's assessments of culture never emerged as simplistic: They were profoundly informed by his pilgrimages and research trips to foreign countries, as well as by his voluminous correspondence with some of the most significant religious and intellectual figures of his time, such as Croatian Roman Catholic Bishop Josip Juraj Strossmeyer (1815-1905).

The Russian nobility has its own tradition of making pilgrimages to Italy, especially to Bari and Rome.¹¹ Originally a Greek city that was captured by the Normans in 1071, Bari evolved into a city in the Kingdom of Naples and held this status for almost eight centuries; in 1860 it became part of the Italian kingdom.

Since the twelfth century the city has been called «Бар-Град» or even «Николай-Град» by Russians, for it possesses the relics of St. Nicholas of Myra, or Nicholas the Wonderworker, one of the most venerated saints in Russia (and indeed in all of Christendom). His relics were translated to Bari in the eleventh century: in October of 1089 Pope Urban II placed the relics of Nicholas into a new silver reliquary, which was installed under the altar in the Basilica di San Nicola. Peter the Great's son Aleksei and Nicholas II as heir-apparent made pilgrimages to Bari. In fact, the latter tsar is associated with the establishment of the Basilica. It was initiated by the Venerable Martyr Elizaveta Fyodorovna in a letter in 1911 to her brother Nicholas II. Through the efforts of both of these people the Basilica was established, and it has been a functioning cathedral since May of 1913. It is thus not surprising that, after Jerusalem, Constantinople, and Rome, Bari remains an especially sacred place for Russians.

Tsar Nicholas II is also associated with the efforts to found a Russian Orthodox Church in Rome. A one-hundred-acre piece of property, with a famous Roman urban residence, the Villa Abamelek, on its site, was chosen for the construction of the Church of St. Catherine of Alexandria the Great Martyr. The land on which the villa stands originally belonged to the Russian nobleman of Georgian and Armenian ethnic background Semyon Semyonovich Abamelek-Lázarev. Efforts to establish the church were halted by the Bolshevik Revolution and Soviet regime, which were more interested in persecuting religion than promoting it. Only after the fall of communism in 1991 could these efforts be renewed, and finally, on May 24, 2009 the church was officially consecrated. It represents the first free-standing Russian Orthodox church in the city's history; there had been (and still exists) a Russian Orthodox church in a palazzo near the Termini train station since the 1930s, but it did not have its own external structure. Initially, when the project to build the church was revived, the Vatican proposed to Patriarch Aleksii II of Russia several possible church buildings that could be redesigned to accommodate Orthodox needs, but the Patriarch felt that a new church should be built. It was built without any funding from the Russian government; rather, in step with Russian tradition, its construction was funded entirely by private and public donations, uniting Russians from the homeland with those abroad in Italy. During the construction period in 2005 the future patriarch Kirill met in Rome with Pope Benedict XVI; their encounter was ceremonial (on the occasion of the Pope's enthronement), but it was also marked by warmth and respect. The church project proceeded according to plan and the necessary protocol.[12]

Both Orthodox clergy and the Russian ambassador to Italy maintain that St. Catherine's church could not have been completed without the active participation and intervention of the Patriarch. When I spoke with Hieromonk Antonii (Sevriuk), priest of the church in Rome on June 24, 2012 immediately after the liturgy, he had just returned from a trip to Moscow—he had met with Patriarch Kirill, and reported to the members of his parish in Rome that the Patriarch was very concerned about their well-being and praying fervently for them.[13] The historic significance of having a free-standing Russian Orthodox church in Rome was clearly on the Patriarch's mind. From the Patriarch he brought back a blessing for the congregation, as well as the affirmation that he had been hearing positive news about the new Russian church in Rome. Fr. Antonii also conveyed to the parish the Patriarch's entreaty that its members love the Orthodox faith and stay strong in it. In the context of the fledgling Russian Orthodox church's existence in the territory of the heart of world Catholicism, such an entreaty becomes even more powerful and poignant.

When one stands at the entrance to St. Catherine's Church, one has the distinct impression that its elevation above the city equals that of St. Peter's Basilica. And this is not only my impression; the online news site *Rome Reports* noted, perhaps in a more idealistic spirit than historical accuracy, on Aug. 19, 2012: "The Russian Orthodox Church and the Catholic Church have shared friendly relations for years ... With this new church, the relations between Moscow and Rome not only include words, but they are now close enough to look up[on] each other." Indeed, it seems as if the two ecclesiastical shrines are gracefully tipping their "hats" to each other. This is architecture making a poetic and theological statement. However, the story of the height of St. Catherine's is more complex and even somewhat amusing: its architect Andrei Obolensky described that, by agreement with the officials of Rome, St. Catherine's could not rise higher than St. Peter's Basilica. The planned elevation of St. Catherine's turned out to be slightly higher than St. Peter's—but if the architect were to eliminate the last section of the church's bell tower, the proportions of the whole structure would have been ruined. His solution: to lower the ground on which the church would be built by the required amount, so that the elevation of the two churches would be approximately the same.[14]

If ecclesiastical architecture can possess philosophical or theological or even political symbolic value, it is possible that one main reason for constructing the Russian Orthodox Church of Great Martyr Catherine of Alexandria very high on a hill involved its architectural interaction with St. Peter's Basilica. To have a church on a hill is typical in Russia—both Vladimir Soloukhin (1924-1997) and Alexander Solzhenitsyn (1918-2008) have written on the tradition of erecting churches in a location visible to the faithful: on a hill and often by a river for practical purposes. But to erect a Russian Orthodox Church at the top of several sets of steps on a high hill directly to the south of St. Peter's Basilica could symbolically suggest a position of what the Orthodox call "humble pride," of equality to the Catholic structure and counterpoint to its dogmatic theology. When one stands outside the Trapeza at the lower level of the Church of St. Catherine (at the concrete railing),[15] one looks directly (neither up nor down) over to St. Peter's. The impression is powerful, and striking. To be sure, the church's location is on one of a series of Positano-like hills, and to be seen at all it must rise over those hills with their apartments built vertically into the landscape. Nevertheless, the ultimate effect is one of vertical equality with St. Peter's.

During the three-hour consecration ceremony of the church, Archbishop Mark Egor'evskii, Vice-Chairman of the Moscow Patriarchate Department for External Church Relations, addressed the congregation. In a later interview he noted, "The Russian church stands near St. Peter's, and this symbolizes the common witness of the Orthodox and Catholic Churches before the challenges of our time, as our Churches through their temples in the Eternal City assert the eternal values of Christianity."[16] Obolensky also affirmed this fact, pointing out that its being so close to the Vatican was unprecedented for a non-Catholic religious structure. "But perhaps because they have the Vatican in their backyard, the Russian Orthodox priests have excellent relationships with their Catholic counterparts."[17] On the parish level a commonly-held view is that of Fr. Vladimir of St. Catherine's: "They come to our liturgies, to our masses in Italian, and they see how we pray. And also we go to them for their liturgies and also pray. And also we have, this city of Rome has a lot of saints' relics, so we also go to pray before these relics and to ask permission from Catholic priests, and they are very friendly to us."[18] Among the Catholic priests who attend the Russian Orthodox liturgy at St. Catherine's are those who are dissatisfied with the reforms of the Second Vatican Council of 1962-1965 and are relieved to be able to experience a more traditional liturgical service.[19] At the very least, there seems to be respect, goodwill, and some curiosity on both sides.

Archbishop Mark Egor'evskii elaborated on the meaning of Rome for the Russian Orthodox faithful in an interview in which he describes the history of the founding of the Church of St. Catherine in Rome.[20] Among other results of the establishment of this church, it fulfills the wish of many Russians around the world to see their own church in Rome; moreover, in a broader cultural way the church connects the Russian Orthodox faithful in the diaspora (in Italy and elsewhere) with their counterparts in the Motherland. On the church's official website one finds a short history of the its coming-into-being:

> The first person who had the idea to build an Orthodox church in Rome, at the end of the XIX century, was Archimandrite Kliment (Vernikovskii).... Moved by patriotic feelings, [he] failed to convince the church authorities to undertake this project. [His vision was spiritual, but also patriotic—he was convinced of the Russian] government's "need to have an Orthodox Church [to honor] the dignity and greatness of the Fatherland in the city of the Holy Apostles Peter and Paul.[21]

The evolution of this project is long, involving the following personages: Tsar Nicholas II, Grand Duchess Elizaveta [sister of the Tsar], Grand Duke Sergei Aleksandrovich, and Mikhail

Nikolaevich, among others. In 1915 a Commission for Construction chaired by Prince S. S. Abamelek-Lazarev purchased, on behalf of the Russian government, a parcel of land along the banks of the Tiber River, near Margareta Bridge. By 1916 the sum of 165,000 rubles had already been gathered, which was quite sufficient for building the church. However, the Bolshevik Revolution of 1917 prevented the realization of the project. Today in the Church of St. Nicholas in Rome the book of tenders for the construction of the church has been preserved, with the signature and stamp of A. I. Nelidov, Russian Ambassador to Italy under Nicholas II. In the early 1990s the question of the need to have a Russian Orthodox Church in Rome was raised again, and the idea received the blessing of Patriarch Aleksii II. In 2001 the Russian commission charged with the construction project identified the specific territory of the Russian Abamelek villa on which the church would be built. On January 14, 2001, Archbishop Innokentii of Korsun, in the presence of Russian Foreign Minister I. S. Ivanov, blessed the foundation stone of the future site of the church. In June 2002, thanks to the efforts of the Russian Embassy in Italy, the building permit was obtained.[22]

The project's culmination came on May 24, 2009, when the Chiesa Ortodossa Russa di S. Caterina di Alessandria Grande Martire was formally consecrated—this was an occasion of great solemnity and joy for the Orthodox faithful. The official website of the Serbian Orthodox Church describes on April 30, 2004 Patriarch Kirill's report on the final preparations for the consecration to the Board of Trustees of the Russian Orthodox Church at a meeting that took place in Danilov Monastery. Moscow Mayor Iurii Luzhkov was present, making a helpful contribution that gives one a sense of the intricate practical details connected with the consecration: Luzhkov "stressed the importance of additional electricity supplies to the building [to those] required for its normal operation. This would speed up the installation of ventilation in the church 'in order to dry everything and put it in order.'"[23]

Soloviev also develops some of these themes in the Third Address (1883) of his *Three Addresses in Memory of Dostoevsky*:

... seeing as in our time also Rome alone remains chaste and steadfast amidst a stream of anti-Christian civilization and from it alone resounds a calming, but cruel word of censure as well to the godless world, we will not ascribe this to some kind of incomprehensible human obstinacy alone, but will also recognize here the clandestine power of God. And if Rome, unshakable in its holy place, and striving moreover to bring to this holy place all humanity, moved forward and changed, fussed about, profoundly fell and arose anew, then it is not for us to judge it for these fussings and falls....[24]

Soloviev remained more forgiving of the Roman Catholic Church's "fussings and falls" than the Russian Orthodox Church and non-Orthodox Christians worldwide could be in the late 20th and early 21st centuries, for various reasons. A headline from Stetson University's website *Russia Religion News*, which monitors and summarizes developments in religion in Russia and its Slavic neighbors, states, "Orthodox less optimistic than Catholics about relations."[25] According to a report on Interfax on May 4, 2004, a Vatican representative acknowledged that the Catholic Church had made mistakes in Russia in openly attempting to convert Orthodox believers to Catholicism, when its official position articulated that Russia did not represent for the Vatican a "missionary field." It also did not help relations when a document was discovered at the level of the Vatican during the last years of the papacy of John Paul II and patriarchate of Aleksii II with plans to expand Catholicism in Russia. The following statement was issued by the Vatican and reported by *Catholic World News* on February 18, 2002: "The Holy See is preparing to transform the apostolic administrations of Russia into regular dioceses--a move that is certain to provoke a very negative reaction from the Russian Orthodox Church."[26] In a less controversial spirit Pope John Paul II made the statement that the Church breathes with two lungs, East and West--but the practical implications of such a thought are questionable if one recalls the long history of the Catholic Church's attempts to absorb Orthodox into itself from the times of the Fourth Crusade's sack of Constantinople of 1204. At the least, Pope John Paul II's comment leaves open the door for mutual respect and cautious cooperation. The Russian Orthodox have built their few churches on Italian soil for two reasons: to provide places of worship for the Orthodox faithful who are located outside of Russia, and to honor Rome's place in Christianity by maintaining a sacred place of witness in the Eternal City.

It may be that Soloviev's grand philosophical and spiritual project of a Universal Church (with all of Christianity reunited) was unsuccessful, but important and major strides have been made by both sides, East and West, to find common ground and start breathing the same air. The following words from a letter written by Patriarch Kirill to Pope Benedict XVI and dated March 1, 2013 support these claims:

> I have warm memories of our meeting when you were elected to the Roman See. During your ministry we received a positive impetus in the relations between our Churches, responding to the modern world as a witness to Christ crucified and risen. I sincerely hope [that] what developed during your active participation, a good trusting relationship between the Orthodox and the Catholics, will continue to grow with your successor.[27]

Both sides, the Orthodox and the Catholics, are in recent times underscoring the common ground between the two confessions, rather than their theological differences.[28] In particular, the Roman Catholic Church has been actively seeking reconciliation with the Orthodox Church since the years of the papacy of John Paul II (1978-2005). The two oldest branches of Christianity share a long tradition: medieval Rus accepted Christianity in 988 (the traditional dating of this event), less than one century before the schism between Eastern and Western Christianity—usually identified as culminating in 1054 (although more serious rifts between the two sides occurred earlier than that date[29]). Thus Russian Orthodoxy coexisted with Roman Catholicism for 1,000 years, and, more broadly, ancient Orthodox Christianity (as the Christian tradition of the Eastern Roman Empire) developed alongside Roman Catholicism since at least the early fourth century.

During the period of spring, 2013 to spring, 2014, however, the common ground carefully laid in interactions between Patriarch Kirill and Pope Benedict XVI was muddied by a series of events, which included the resignation (very likely for reasons of physical frailty) on February 28, 2013 at the age of 86 of the pope, and the Ukrainian uprising on Maidan Square in Kiev. The Moscow Patriarch was faced with developing a relationship with the new Pope Francis, who was inaugurated (he resisted the term "enthroned") on March 19, 2013 and whose positions on major issues could differ substantially from those of his predecessor—who was (and is) still alive.[30] Relations between the two leaders initially proceeded in a cordial and correct manner; however, the prospect for a meeting between them was clouded by the participation in the Kiev uprising by members of the Catholic communities in that city: "On May 28 [2014], Patriarch Kirill spoke of a 'cooling' in relations with the Vatican, stemming from Greek-Ukrainian Catholics' involvement in the protests in Kiev and their political positions, which the patriarch described as 'Russia-phobic.' He has said that the situation in Ukraine casts a 'very sad shadow over the relations with the Holy See.'"[31]

Another complex matter that needs resolution is the relationship and hierarchical positioning (with respect to each other) of the Ecumenical Patriarchate of Constantinople, the Roman Catholic Papacy, and the Orthodox Moscow Patriarchate. With the fall of Constantinople to the Turks in 1453 the assumption arose in the Slavic East that the center and leadership of world Orthodoxy would be transferred to Moscow. The Russian Orthodox Church currently has 165 million of the estimated 250 million Orthodox faithful in the world; by contrast, the local Orthodox church in Constantinople (Istanbul) has approximately only 3,000 members. To be sure, church tradition is powerful, but the enormous discrepancy between the number of members of the Orthodox Church in Russia and that of the Church in Istanbul also emerges as significant. With the fall of communism in the Soviet Union in 1991, the Moscow Patriarchate has relatively quickly re-entered the dynamics of Orthodox Christianity around the world. "The Russian Orthodox Church (ROC), by far the largest church in the Orthodox world and increasingly influential at home and abroad, has long been wary of the closer ties Francis and Bartholomew want to work towards."[32] Finally, the Vatican emphasizes Rome's preeminence among the ancient Christian sees of the first millenium.

But there have also been positive developments even in this climate of instability: On May 31, 2014 Patriarch Kirill sent Pope Francis a warm and encouraging congratulatory message on the occasion of the first anniversary of his papacy, in which he praised the pope for his "care for the suffering and the destitute" and the "duty of brotherly love," and noted the "high level of mutual understanding and the desire of both sides to strengthen the Catholic-Orthodox cooperation in order to uphold Christian spiritual and moral values in the modern world. . . ."[33]

It may be that the bridging of the gap between Russian Orthodoxy and Roman Catholicism will not be effected along dogmatic theological or hierarchical lines, for differences between canonical positions and individual personalities are extremely difficult to overcome. Aleksei Khomiakov (1804-1860), a major articulator of 19th century Slavophilism and the first Russian Orthodox lay theologian, initiated a fresh approach to bringing about a unity between the two churches: ". . . in contrast to the conventional polemics of his day, Khomiakov maintained that the main factors separating the Christian West and East were not essentially doctrinal, but relational, dispositional, and, ultimately, experiential."[34]

Within Khomiakov's latter three factors—the relational, dispositional, and experiential--one can locate an essential commonality in the aesthetic principle permeating the spiritual expressiveness of both churches, the Orthodox and Catholic, and both the Russian and Italian cultures as a whole. What Italy as the older culture and Russia as the more recent one have always shared is a powerful aesthetic sensibility that transcends religion alone: the aesthetic principle seems equally strong in all aspects of the two cultures. Indeed, the Italians and Russians manifest a need for beauty for anthropological as well as spiritual reasons: individuals *require* beauty in order to preserve their humanity. This does not imply a superficial beauty, but beauty understood in moral as well as aesthetic terms: beauty as possessing rich moral content, as being able to drive away evil, as being able to raise inspiration and connecting the individual with the divine—here aesthetics converge with theology in both cultures: all this is justified by the Incarnation.[35] Thus the Roman Catholics and Russian Orthodox are *materialists for spiritual reasons*[36]—beauty must be accessed specifically in material form, rather than as dry philosophical or theological propositions. In both cultures and their spiritual traditions beauty as a creation of God, as a part of God's world, is sacred and embodies in physical form the tenets of the Christian faith.

The feeling for beauty is highly developed in Italy and Russia, the above associations among religion, morality, and beauty being apprehended directly and even apophatically by the people of these countries. In palpable ways that engage the five senses beauty is present in the Christian mystical spirituality and material culture of Roman Catholicism and Russian Orthodoxy. As Dostoevsky affirmed in *The Idiot*, beauty will save the world—but it must be beauty of a particular kind, thick with the content of divinity, morality, and aesthetic harmony. Vladimir Soloukhin (1924-1997), a well-known Russian Orthodox poet and essayist, further affirmed the Dostoevskian and Solovievian meaning-ladenness of beauty, connecting it not only with spirituality, but also with a feeling of harmony in a person's soul, with civilization, and with nature and a serene landscape:

> Landscape is synonymous with beauty, and beauty is a spiritual category. Not by accident has landscape become the subject of art, the subject of painting, literature, and even music. ... contemplating [nature's] beauty arouses in a person's soul the most elevated, pure, and radiant feelings and lofty thoughts . . .[37]

The salvific potential of beauty is ubiquitous in Italian and Russian cultural production. If God created the world and he loves his creation, it follows that the entire world is equally dear to him, that all of its components are sanctified.[38] Two recent films, one Italian and one Russian, exemplify the attention paid in these two cultures to beauty as possessing a regenerative and spiritual power: *The Great Beauty* (2013, dir. Paolo Sorrentino) and *The Russian Ark* (2002, dir. Aleksander Sokurov).[39] *The Great Beauty* chronicles in a visually stunning manner the moral decadence existing in contemporary Rome among the wealthy. Even the hierarchs of the Vatican are not exempt from a casual attitude towards the spiritual life and moral values in general. With the progression of the film the impression of there being no path for redemption compounds itself—until the appearance of a saintly nun (called la Santa—the holy one) who has taken a vow of poverty and whose presence challenges the acquisition of spirituality without struggle. La Santa not only defies what is humanly possible for her age (stated in the film as 104 years), but in a surrealist scene with white flamingo-type birds landing on a terrace joyfully reveals that she knows the Christian names of all of the birds that have landed there. The scene becomes thrilling when la Santa unexpectedly breathes powerful "winds" at the birds, sending the entire flock flying into the heavens. The search for faith and defeat of moral decadence are fulfilled by the discovery of the power of asceticism, and in the joyful seeing of the divine in beautiful material things (animate and inanimate) of the world—which God created and loves. Similarly, the search for Russia's place in European culture is fulfilled in *The Russian Ark* by the realization, growing in the film, that the St. Petersburg Hermitage functions as a metaphor for the stream of Russian history that is once again carrying it ever closer to Europe—through a love of art and culture, and through the moral and aesthetic power of a spiritualized beauty.

In a recent diaconal letter on the Russian Orthodox website ДІАКОНЪ [The Deacon] Archdeacon Stefan (Puchkov) clarifies the sanctifying role of beauty in Orthodoxy:

> ... these days we [the Orthodox] lag behind the Protestants and Catholics in significant ways in the matter of proseletysing about Christ. But let us also remember that the beauty of our cathedrals, the beauty of our choral singing, and the beauty of our services also represent such proseletysing, and our attentiveness to this external beauty must be ongoing, as should be our attentiveness to the "condition of the inner person" and to the beauty of our soul.[40]

If beauty can save the world through an ongoing attentiveness to the inner state of a person, achieved by the spiritual vigilance Elder Zosima in Dostoevsky's *The Brothers Karamazov* (1881) describes as "constantly walking around ourselves," then it can provide a bridge between the two major Christian confessions of Russian Orthodoxy and Roman Catholicism, for those who would wish for such a bridge to be established.[41]

Abbreviation

CS1M: *Creation and Salvation*. 2 vols. Edited by Ernst M. Conradie. Volume 1: *A Mosaic of Selected Classic Christian Theologies*. Berlin: LIT Verlag, 2012.

Notes

1. Tobias Jones, *The Dark Heart of Italy* (London: Faber and Faber, 2004), xii.
2. For example, at the entrance to the Pontificio Istituto Orientale (the world-renowned research library for East-West church relations), a quotation from Soloviev referring to "all-unity in Christianity" hangs in a prominent place on the stuccoed wall. This is not surprising, for Soloviev, who was born into Russian Orthodoxy and remained Orthodox all his life, maintained an admiration for the Roman Catholic Church as an expression of his Christian ecumenism. For a description of the library's mission and holdings, see its official site: http://www.pontificio-orientale.com/gallery-and-multimedia/51.html (last accessed 15 April, 2016).
3. See *Vatican Council II: The Conciliar and Post Conciliar Document*, Vol. 1, edited by Austin Flannery (Grand Rapids: Eerdmans), 1992), for example, 481-482 ("Marriages Between Roman Catholics and Orthodox") and 483-487 ("Directory Concerning Ecumenical Matters: Part One").
4. Paul Valliere, *Modern Russian Theology: Bukharev, Soloviev, Bulgakov* (Edinburgh: T&T Clark, Ltd, 2000), 6.
5. Valliere, *Modern Russian Theology*, 6.
6. Tom Heneghan, "Russian church the absent player at pope-patriarch summit," *Reuters*, May 19, 2014, http://www.reuters.com/article/2014/05/19/us-pope-holyland-russia-idUSKBN0DZ13B20140519 (last accessed 15 April 2016).

7   The president of Italy between 2006-15, Giorgio Napolitano, included "the need to preserve the beauty of Italy" —and here beauty is understood in its spiritual, ethical sense--in the platform of his presidential campaign. I thank Monica Cognolato for pointing out this campaign information to me.
8   Nicholas Berdyaev, *The Russian Idea*, trans. R. M. French (Boston: Beacon Press, 1992), 157.
9   V. S. Soloviev, *The Heart of Reality*, trans. Vladimir Wozniuk (Notre Dame, IN: University of Notre Dame Press, 2003), 69.
10 Berdyaev, *The Russian Idea*; Dmitry Likhachev, *Reflections on Russia*, trans. Christina Sever (Boulder, CO: Westview Press, 1991); Soloviev, *The Heart of Reality*.
11 For a rich analysis of what she terms the "Russia-Rome paradigm," see Judith E. Kalb, *Russia's Rome: Imperial Visions, Messianic Dreams, 1890-1940* (Madison, WI: University of Wisconsin Press, 2010), 26.
12 A detailed history of the idea of establishing a Russian Orthodox cathedral in Rome can be found under the official website of the Moscow Patriarchate: http://stcaterina.com/ (last accessed 15 April, 2016).
13 Personal interview, Rome, July 1, 2012.
14 *Russkii dom na beregakh Tibra. Istoriia sozdaniia pravoslavnogo khrama Sviatoi Velikomuchenitsei Ekateriny v Rime* ("Miasnoi Dom Borodina, 2010"), DVD.
15 This personal experience took place on June 23, 2012.
16 "New Orthodox Church in Rome," n.a., *Interfax*, March 31, 2006, http://www.orthodoxchristianity.net/forum/index.php?topic=8603.0 (last accessed 15 April 2016).
17 *Russkii dom na beregakh Tibra*, DVD.
18 "Russian Orthodox parish in Rome reaches final stages of construction," n.a., *Rome Reports*. April 8, 2009.   http://www.romereports.com/pg140048-russian-orthodox-parish-in-rome-reaches-final-stages-of-construction-en (last accessed 30 March 2016).
19 It is one of history's grand ironies that the traditional language of the Mass, Latin, has been relegated to the past in Catholic parishes, remaining only in those churches designated as "Old [Latin] Rite" churches.
20 *Russkii dom na beregakh Tibra*, DVD.
21 "Russian Orthodox church of St. Catherine the great martyr." Official website of the Moscow Patriarchate: http://stcaterina.com/ (last accessed 15 April, 2016).
22 The information in this paragraph was translated from the Russian and paraphrased by me in order to craft a condensed version of the

longer narrative provided on the Moscow Patriarchate's website: http://stcaterina.com/ (last accessed 15 April 2016).

23 "Consecration of Russian church in Rome scheduled for May 24," Interfax religion, 30 April 2009, Official website of the Serbian Orthodox Church, http://www.spc.rs/eng/consecration_russian_church_rome_scheduled_may_24 (last accessed 15 April, 2016). I attended liturgies at the church in June and July of 2012: there was excellent ventilation. If the church has air-conditioning, it was not operating during those services.

24 Soloviev, *Heart of Reality*, 27. For a more sustained discussion on how Soloviev situates Roman Catholicism within his grand philosophical project of *all-unity* (*vseedinstvo*), see the "Translator's Introduction" to Soloviev's Филосовские начала цельного знания, in Vladimir Solovyov, *The Philosophical Principles of Integral Knowledge*, translated by Valeria Z. Nollan (Grand Rapids, MI: Eerdmans, 2008), 1-18.

25 "Orthodox less optimistic than Catholics about relations: Vatican Representative Acknowledges That Catholics Made Mistakes in Russia." Stetson University: *Russia Religion News*. Interfax. May 6, 2004. http://www2.stetson.edu/~psteeves/relnews/0405a.html (last accessed 30 March 2016).

26 "Catholic / Orthodox Relations: Understanding the New Dioceses in Russia." *Catholic World News*, February 18, 2002, http://www.aidrussia.org/News_Detail.asp?Title=Understanding%20the%20New%20Dioceses%20in%20Russia (last accessed 15 April, 2016).

27 Patriarch Kirill of Russia. "Letter from Patriarch Kirill to Pope Emeritus Benedict XVI," *Catholicism Pure and Simple*, March 4, 2013. http://catholicismpure.wordpress.com/2013/03/04/letter-from-patriarch-kirill-to-pope-emeritus-benedict-xvi/ (last accessed 15 April 2016).

28 These would include, but not be limited to, the *filioque* controversy, the doctrinal attitude towards Mary, Mother of God, the doctrine of the infallibility of the pope, and the calendar (Julian versus Gregorian) issue.

29 See Steven Runciman, *The Eastern Schism: A Study of the Papacy and the Eastern Churches During the XIth and XXIIth Centuries* (Eugene, OR: Wipf & Stock; orig. publ. Oxford Press, 1955), 159-170.

30 See Paul Elie, "The Pope in the Attic," *The Atlantic*, vol. 313, no. 4 (May 2014), 46-54.

31 Kathy Schiffer, "Next Will Pope Francis Meet with Patriarch Kirill?" June 5, 2014, http://www.patheos.com/blogs/kathyschiffer/2014/06/next-will-pope-francis-meet-with-patriarch-kirill/ (last accessed 30 March 2016).

32 Heneghan, "Russian church the absent player at pope-patriarch summit." For a detailed account of the meeting of Ecumenical

Patriarch Bartholomew and Pope Francis in Jerusalem on May 25, 2014, see Stavros H. Papagermanos, "An Apostolic Pilgrimage of Peace, Love, and Truth," *Orthodox Observer*, vol. 79, no. 1296 (June 2014), 1, 9.

33 Heneghan, "Russian church the absent player at pope-patriarch summit."

34 Vera Shevzov, "The Burdens of Tradition: Orthodox Constructions of the West in Russia (Late 19th-Early 20th CC.) in *Orthodox Constructions of the West*, edited by George E. Demacopoulos and Aristotle Papanikolaou (New York: Fordham University Press, 2013), 89. See also the collection of essays *A. S. Khomiakov: Poet, Philosopher, Theologian*, edited by Vladimir Tsurikov (Jordanville: Holy Trinity Seminary Press, 2004.

35 Here Soloviev's religio-philosophical position converges perfectly with that of canonical Orthodoxy. A genuine spiritual beauty can distinguish what is good and true. The Incarnation also justifies the veneration of icons, for the icon in remembering its heavenly prototype in material form (paint and wood) participates in the transfiguration of beauty. See Leonid Ouspensky, *The Theology of the Icon*, 2 vols. (Crestwood, NY: St. Vladimir's Seminary Press, 1992), especially vol. 1.

36 I thank Gary Saul Morson for pointing out this wittily-phrased connection to me.

37 Vladimir Soloukhin, "Civilization and Landscape," in his *A Time to Gather Stones*, trans., Valerie Z. Nollan (Evanston, IL: Northwestern University Press, 1993), 229-230.

38 See Denis Edwards, "Athanasius—The Word of God in Creation and Salvation," in *CS1M*, 37-51, esp. 48-50.

39 *The Great Beauty* (La grande bellezza) won the Academy Award for Best Foreign Language Film of 2013. *The Russian Ark* (*Russki kochveg*) won several international awards in 2002.

40 Archdeacon Stefan (Pushkov), Diaconal Letter, *DIAKON*", n.d. trans. by Valeria Nollan, accessed April 15, 2016. [...мы сейчас значительно уступаем протестантам и католикам в деле проповеди о Христе. Но будем помнить, что и красота храмов наших, красота пения хора, красота службы тоже являются такой проповедью, и забота об этой внешней красоте должна быть нам присуща, как и забота об «устроении внутреннего человека», забота о красоте своей души.]. http://www.deacon.ru/ (last accessed 15 April 2016).

41 The saga continues: On February 12, 2016 an extraordinary meeting took place between Patriarch Kirill and Pope Francis in Havana, Cuba, in order to jointly address the major issue of worldwide persecution of Christians. This was the first meeting of such high-level representatives of the Russian Orthodox and Roman Catholic churches since the Council of Ferrara-Florence (1438-1439).

Contributors

Lucien J. **Frary** is Associate Professor of History at Rider University. He is the author of *Russia and the Making of Modern Greek Identity, 1821-1844* (Oxford University Press, 2015) and co-editor of *Russian-Ottoman Borderlands: The Eastern Question Reconsidered* (University of Wisconsin Press, 2014). His current project is about cosmopolitan aristocrats and Russian foreign policy in the first decades of the nineteenth century.

David **Goldfrank** is Professor of History and Director of Medieval Studies at Georgetown University. Primarily a specialist in pre-modern Russian history, his books include *The Monastic Rule of Iosif Volotsky* (Kalamazoo, 1983; rev. ed., 2000); *The Origins of the Crimean War* (London, 1993); *A History of Russia: People, Legends, Events, Forces* (with Catherine Evtuhov, Lindsey Hughes, Richard Stites, Boston/New York 2003); and *Nil Sorsky – The Authentic Writings* (Kalamazoo, 2008). He is currently working on a monograph on Iosif and a critical translation of his *Prosvetitel'*, as well as preparing for publication the late Andrei Pliguzov's collection of 268 documents, *The Archive of the Metropolitans of Kiev and all Rus'*.

Evgeny **Grishin** is a PhD candidate at the History department of the University of Kansas. His research interests lie in early modern Russian history, material culture, and religious studies. His dissertation project is focused on the Old Believers in Russia in the seventeenth and eighteenth centuries.

Christopher D.L. **Johnson** is currently Assistant Professor of Religious Studies at the University of Wisconsin-Fond du Lac. His dissertation was revised and published as *The Globalization of Hesychasm and the Jesus Prayer: Contesting Contemplation* (Continuum, 2010). His subsequent and current research projects look at contemporary Eastern Orthodox practice, spirituality, and identity.

Kevin M. **Kain** is a Senior Lecturer in Humanistic Studies and History at the University of Wisconsin Green Bay, whose scholarship focuses on Russian Orthodox culture. A recipient of research grants from Fulbright-Hays, the Kennan Institute, Woodrow Wilson Center, and National Endowment for the Humanities, he is co-editor and translator (with Ekaterina Levintova), of *From Peasant to Patriarch: Account of the Birth, Upbringing and Life of His Holiness Nikon Patriarch of All Russia* (Roman and Littlefield 2007) and author of numerous essays on Nikon, Old Believers and Russian monasticism. He is currently working on a major study of Nikon's impact upon Russia.

Rev. Dr. Joshua **Lolla**r, Lecturer in Religious Studies and University of Kansas, and Rector, St. Nicholas Orthodox Church in Lawrence, Kansas, is a scholar of Greek patrisitics, specializing in the thought of St. Maximus the Confessor. His *To See into the Life of Things: The Contemplation of Nature in Maximus the Confessor and his Predecessors* was published by Brepols in 2013.

Edward **Mason** is an advanced PhD candidate at the history department of the University of Kentucky. His research interests lie in fourth century church/state relations, Tetrarchic administrative reforms, and late antique architecture. His dissertation examines the integration of Christianity into the imperial administration under the Constantinian dynasty.

John A **McGuckin** is the Nielsen Professor of Byzantine History at Union Theological Seminary, New York, and Professor in the Religion Department of Columbia University. An Archpriest of the Romanian Orthodox Church, he is the author of many works on Early Christian thought, including studies of St. Cyril of Alexandria (1994, 2004) and of St. Gregory of Nazianzus (2001). Editor as well of the two-volume *Encyclopedia of Eastern Orthodox Christianity* (2011) and author of *The Ascent of Christian Law: Patristic and Byzantine and Byzantine Formulations of a New Civilization* (2012), his next monograph, on the Church of the First Millennium, is scheduled to appear with IVP Academic in 2017.

Valeria Z. **Nollan** is Professor Emerita of Russian Studies at Rhodes College, Adjunct Professor at Trexas Tech, and the immediate past president of the Association for the Study of Eastern Christian History and Culture. Active as a lecturer internationally on topics related to Russian literature and culture, her recent publications include a scholarly translation of Vladimir Solovyov's *The Philosophical Principles of Integral Knowledge* (Eerdmans, 2008) and an article on St. John Maximovich of Shanghai and San Francisco (2015). She is currently finishing a biography of Sergei Rachmaninoff.

Donald **Ostrowski** is Research Advisor in the Social Science and Lecturer in History at the Harvard University Extension School. He is the author of *Muscovy and the Mongols: Cross-Cultural Influences on the Steppe Frontier 1304–1589* (Cambridge University Press, 1998), editor of *The Povest' vremennykh let: An Interlinear Collation and Paradosis*, 3 vols. (Cambridge, MA: Harvard Library of Early Ukrainian Literature, 2003), and co-editor of *Portraits of Old Russia: Imagined Lives of Ordinary People 1300–1725* (M. E. Sharpe, 2011) and the ASEC conference volume *Tapestry* (see the Preface here). He also chairs the Early Slavists Seminars at the Davis Center for Russian and Eurasian Studies at Harvard University. His current main research interest is authorship studies, and he is working on a book manuscript tentatively titled *Interconnections: Russia in World History, 1450–1800*.

Randall A. **Poole** is Professor of History at the College of St. Scholastica in Duluth, Minnesota. He is the translator and editor of *Problems of Idealism: Essays in Russian Social Philosophy* (Yale University Press, 2003); co-editor (with G. M. Hamburg) of *A History of Russian Philosophy, 1830-1930: Faith, Reason, and the Defense of Human Dignity* (Cambridge University Press, 2010); and author of numerous articles and book chapters on Russian intellectual history and philosophy.

Joshua **Powell** is a doctoral candidate in Byzantine history at the University of Kentucky and is the Upper School Director of Veritas Christian Academy, in Lexington, KY.

Jennifer **Spock**, ASEC President at the time of the 2013 Conference, is Professor of History at Eastern Kentucky University and Series Editor of *Eastern Christian Studies*, a sub-series of *Ohio Slavic Papers*. Author of numerous articles on Solovki Monastery and other aspects of late medieval and early modern Russia, she has anchored two and co-edited a third of ASEC's four conference volumes to date.

Prof. Dr. Ludwig **Steindorff**, was born at Hamburg, became a student of history, Slavic philology at Heidelberg and Zagreb, earned his Ph. D. at Heidelberg in 1981 and his Habilitation at Münster in 1990, and has been Professor of East and South East European history at Kiel since 2000. Having special fields of interest are monastic culture in Old Russia and medieval urban history of South Eastern Europe, his publications include the monograph *Memoria in Altrußland. Untersuchungen zu den Formen christlicher Totensorge.* (Stuttgart, 1994); *Das Speisungsbuch von Volokolamsk/Kormovaja kniga Iosifo-Volokolamskogo monastyrja. Eine Quelle zur Sozialgeschichte russischer Klöster im 16. Jahrhundert* (aided by von Rüdiger Koke, Elena Kondraškina, Ulrich Lang und Nadja Pohlmann, Cologne et al., 1998); and his edited *Religion und Integration im Moskauer Russland: Konzepte und Praktiken, Potentiale und Grenzen 14.-17. Jahrhundert* (Wiesbaden, 2010).

Ryan W. **Strickler** is a PhD candidate at Maquarie University, Sidney, Australia. He currently teaches as a part time instructor for Western Michigan University. His research interests lie in the development of literary construction of political and religious authority in the Byzantine Empire, particularly in the wake of the crises of the seventh century. His dissertation examines apocalyptic discourse as a coping mechansim in seventh-century Byzantine literature.

www.ingramcontent.com/pod-product-compliance
Lightning Source LLC
Chambersburg PA
CBHW050328230426

43663CB00010B/1780